MW00783999

Conspiracies and Conspiracy Theories
in the Age of Trump

Daniel C. Hellinger

Conspiracies and Conspiracy Theories in the Age of Trump

Daniel C. Hellinger
International Relations
Webster University
St. Louis, MO, USA

ISBN 978-3-319-98157-4   ISBN 978-3-319-98158-1   (eBook)
https://doi.org/10.1007/978-3-319-98158-1

Library of Congress Control Number: 2018951556

Cover credit: White House Photo/Alamy Stock Photo
Cover design by Henry Petrides

This Palgrave Macmillan imprint is published by the registered company Springer Nature Switzerland AG
The registered company address is: Gewerbestrasse 11, 6330 Cham, Switzerland

PREFACE

In 1991 I published (with my co-author) *The Democratic Façade*[1], an alternative, critical view of politics in the United States, mostly intended to be used as a companion to the main text for Introduction to American Politics. At the time, I was a regular contributor to the *St. Louis Journalism Review*, and I gave a copy of the new edition to the editor and publisher, Charles Klotzer.

Charles was enthusiastic about the book and said he was going to ask former U.S. Senator Thomas Eagleton to review it. I told Charles that Senator Eagleton, a thoughtful and genuinely liberal person, was going to hate the book. We were challenging the paradigmatic myths of American democracy. We argued, in the spirit of C. Wright Mills,[2] that elites were well-networked and usually able to manage popular discontent and, just as importantly, able to manage their differences among themselves. In a variety of ways, they could use their wealth to influence the media, maintain a consensus about defending capitalism at home and abroad, coopt elected officials through what even then seemed a campaign finance sewer, and in other ways translate their wealth into political power. Both in domestic and foreign policy the record suggested much less respect for democratic norms than the mainstream view in the standard political science literature. In that view, the theory of pluralism, elites are competitive and not in accord with one another on policies. Just as important our book contended that in contrast to the pluralist argument, liberal democratic institutions in the United States do not keep elites responsive to public preferences.

It is important here to specify that we were not arguing that liberal democratic theory and pluralism get American politics all wrong. And this book adopts that view as well. There are substantive differences in perspectives, to name some examples, on taxation, spending, trade policy and, to a less but still significant degree, foreign policy. But elite power circumscribes the policy alternatives put forward, much as Peter Bachrach argued.[3] His remedy for this state of affairs is more participation in democracy. I agree with both of those propositions. However, I think anyone who has examined contemporary populism and especially conspiracism in the years since Donald Trump began his rise to the presidency in 2013 would think that all kinds of participation are equally salutary to democracy.

I hardly imagined that the theme of elite power would lead me to take more seriously the importance of conspiracies and conspiracy theory in politics. My movement in that direction began with Eagleton's review,[4] which was even more damning than we expected. He honed onto a chapter in which we described how the CIA had intervened in Nicaragua and undermined the Sandinista revolutionary experiment, even after the revolutionary government had ratified its democratic legitimacy in an election largely hailed as free and fair by just about all international observers except the U.S. Department of State. Furthermore, U.S. military support of the Contra rebels continued in violation of international law and in violation of an express legislative prohibition by the U.S. Congress. We had cited it as example of the superficiality of the American ruling class's commitment to democracy.

Senator Eagleton took issue, as I thought he would, with our portrayal of weak democracy in America. What I didn't expect was that we would be proclaimed as "conspiracy theorists" for suggesting the CIA and elements of the U.S. national security state shared responsibility for the civil war in Nicaragua and the death squad government then ruling El Salvador. When the second edition of the book came out in 1994 we formulated a response to the "conspiracy theory" allegation: Conspiracies existed, we said, but they do not take us very far toward understanding politics. This is a common reaction among academics who write critically about social justice and American foreign policy. The most widely-read radical theorist of our times, Noam Chomsky, has consistently taken the same position.[5]

It must have been about a year or two later when I was telling this story to a colleague, a professor who had emigrated from Central Asia.[6] Somehow, the conversation turned to the Kennedy assassination, and I casually asserted that alternatives to the "lone gunman" narrative were nothing more than "conspiracy theories."

My colleague offered a response along these lines: "Do you mean to tell me that if the prime minister of Pakistan had been assassinated allegedly by a killer known to the security service, who had sought to work for them, and that the next day the suspect was shot in plain view in a police station by a gunman associated with a shadowy criminal underground; that despite all this you would believe the findings of a government commission that the prime minister's murder was carried out by the alleged assassin acting alone? And would you stand behind that idea even as it became clear that from the start the investigative commission was chosen by the successor of the slain leader to arrive at that opinion before it even began its work?"

Even today I do not discard the theory that Lee Harvey Oswald acted alone; nor on the contrary have I embraced any of the particular JFK conspiracy theory that has been advanced. Having listened to recordings of Lyndon Johnson cajoling politicians and judges to serve on the Warren Commission, as well as having reviewed other materials about his presidency, I believe theories regarding his alleged participation are completely unwarranted. However, I did begin to re-think the anomalies of the assassination and to seek out perspectives critical of the usual views of conspiracy theories. It left me agnostic about the possibility that there was a conspiracy behind the assassination and especially concerned about the way the political class, the mainstream media, and most elites closed ranks around the Warren Commission, despite the evidence that the investigation, if not the assassination itself, was product of a conspiracy to hide something.

Just as importantly, I began to realize that I myself had been panicked into dismissing the plausibility of a conspiracy. I simply rejected the notion that conspiracies could really matter in a politically developed country like the United States. I began to realize that being upset about being labelled a "conspiracy theorist" had to do with worrying about being relegated to the margins of the academy. I began to think that both conspiracies and conspiracy theory needed to be reconsidered within political science.

As a specialist on Latin America politics, I began to think about how military coups, so common in the region's history, require a conspiracy to be carried out. One of the best and most widely read books on coups, a case study of coups in Brazil by the highly respected Alfred Stepan, suggested to me that carrying off the military overthrow of a government requires a conspiracy, and that this element of agency can be combined with attention to larger forces, such as political polarization and the breakdown of consensus among political elites, to understand underlying forces of political instability in a society.[7] To be clear, Stepan does not explicitly address conspiracism in his work; nor, to my knowledge, has any political scientist characterized this aspect of his work as "conspiracy theory." But how can one not see coup making as anything but a project that requires secrecy and collusion to achieve a political goal? These are the elements of a conspiracy, I believe. And they apply to much more than just coup making. What we call today "fake news" is one example.

My desire to explore conspiracies as a form of doing politics has deepened with Donald Trump's ascent to the presidency. I cannot help but take note that political scientists are beginning to doubt American exceptionalism, and that concepts, such as the "Deep State," once regarded by mainstream journalists only for paranoid conspiracy theorists, are beginning to appear in editorial pages and news commentary. Also, another political phenomenon, populism, closely associated with conspiracy theories in mainstream history and political science, has once again made an appearance, this time on a global level, and in the United States in the candidacies of Trump and Bernie Sanders. I began to recognize a form of conspiracy panic in the way that Sanders and left populism have been equated by some pundits to what historian Richard Hofstadter called nearly 60 years ago the "paranoid style in American politics."[8]

Influenced as I have been by Marxist theory and especially by the Italian philosopher Antonio Gramsci,[9] I began to rethink many positivist assumptions about history and explanations of social life. I am still searching for a satisfying synthesis between positivism and post-modern social science that sees history and politics as less patterned and determined. Political life does seem more chaotic and less likely to yield theories and laws comparable to those found in the natural sciences. I certainly cannot agree with Engels, who in his speech at the graveside of Mark said, "Just as Darwin discovered the law of development or organic nature, so Marx discovered the law of development of human history."[10]

This book will not contribute any law-like theories about the root causes of conspiracies and conspiracy theory, but I hope it contributes to some re-thinking about how "conspiracy theory" is used to discredit journal-istic and academic work that raises uncomfortable and unconventional views of liberal democracy. I hope readers will also find some help in its pages as they try to sort out facts from balderdash, progressive populists from political charlatans, and dangerous conspiracy theories from ones that point to needed reforms in our political institutions.

St. Louis, USA   Daniel C. Hellinger

NOTES

1. Daniel Hellinger and Dennis Judd, *The Democratic Façade* (1st ed., Pacific Grove, CA: Brooks Cole, 1991 and 2nd ed., Belmont, CA: Wadsworth 1994).
2. C. Wright Mills, *The Power Elite* (New York: Oxford University Press, 1960, original 1956).
3. See Peter Bachrach, *The Theory of Democratic Elitism* (Boston: Little, Brown Publishers, 1967).
4. Back issues of *The St. Louis Journalism Review*, now called the *Gateway Journalism Review*, unfortunately are not available electronically, and I have not been able to locate the exact issue in which Senator Eagleton's review was published.
5. See Nathan J. Robinson, "Lessons from Chomsky," *Current Affairs* (2017, July 30). Available at https://www.currentaffairs.org/2017/07/lessons-from-chomsky (accessed October 30, 2017).
6. I prefer not to refer to the individual by his real name, as I am reaching far back in my memory banks, and the conversation was private.
7. Alfred C. Stepan, *The Military in Politics: Changing Patterns in Brazil* (Princeton: Princeton University Press, 1971).
8. Richard Hofstadter, *The Paranoid Style in American Politics* (New York: Vintage Reprints, 1968). This is a collection of his essays related to the topic.
9. See Antonio Gramsci, *Prison Notebooks*, ed. and trans. Quentin Hoare and Geoffrey Nowell. Available at http://abahlali.org/files/gramsci.pdf.
10. Retrieved from www.marxists.org/archive/marx/works/1883/death/burial.htm (accessed December 31, 2017).

Acknowledgements

Readers will find that this book leans heavily on investigative journalism. In the face of difficult economic circumstances, in a difficult political environment, and often in dangerous contexts, reporters from a broad range of institutions, some of them mainstream corporate owned newspapers and journals, others working in journalistic refuges from constricting corporate environments, have uncovered troubling, concealed political activities—"conspiracies", whether so-named or not. This book could not have been written without their work, and I hope it shows why this kind of work is essential to the practice of democracy. I want to thank my longtime friend and colleague, James Brasfield, for constant probing and questioning my claims and theories about the role of conspiracies in politics. My late friend and colleague, Arthur Sandler, questioned and encouraged my attempts to theorize conspiracy when I was not sure I wanted to go down this intellectual path toward views that will be seen as apostasy in some quarters of social science. Another colleague, Mike Hulsizer, and my friend, John Sterling, helped me with the survey analyses presented in Chapters 4 and 5.

For more than a decade I have regularly taught Webster University students in an interdisciplinary seminar on conspiracy, and many of their research papers have pointed toward themes I might not otherwise have recognized as fruitful areas of inquiry about the role of conspiracies in history and politics. Teaching them also gave me valuable experience in tempering any tendency to go too far toward extremes in arguing for a more tolerant attitude toward conspiracy theories. Much harm can come from embracing certain kinds of conspiracy theory; much good can come from removing certain taboos about naming secretive political plotting for what it is.

I want to thank Michelle Chen and John Stegner for their encouragement and especially for the patience in granting me more time than I originally estimated to bring this project together. Palgrave-Macmillan's referee, Joseph Uscinski of the University of Miami, provided essential, constructive advice to make this book better. Joann Eng-Hellinger read and marked up drafts of some important chapters and as so often been the case supported me in ways too numerous to recount here. After nearly 50 years together, our journey still feels like it is still beginning. I thank her for her love and everything she has done in the service of peace and justice.

PRAISE FOR *CONSPIRACIES AND CONSPIRACY THEORIES IN THE AGE OF TRUMP*

"Hellinger presents a compelling argument that conspiracies are a way of doing politics, of reclaiming agency and of delegitimizing critics. As such, this book is a masterful exposition of why political science needs to engage with conspiracy theories, better problematize conspiracy and, as Hellinger argues, understand conspiracy as a symptom of political decay."
—Julia Buxton, *Professor, Comparative Politics, Central European University, Budapest, Hungary*

"*Conspiracy and Conspiracy Theory in the Age of Trump* is not just a timely look at the swirling conspiracy and counter conspiracy theories involving the 45th President of the United States of America: it is also a deep dive into the kind of civic and intellectual culture which has produced these theories. Hellinger reframes both the debate on these things called 'conspiracy theories' and the kind of societal discourse which lends itself to conspiracy theorising by looking at the evidence. Focusing on how people use (and sometimes abuse) talk of the Deep State, Dark Money, and the effects of Globalisation when talking about Donald J. Trump's rise to power, Hellinger rightly argues we should take theories which cite conspiracies seriously, rather than just dismiss them because they have been labelled 'conspiracy theories.' His analysis of how people can be reluctant to embrace conspiracy theories despite a wealth of evidence, and also how conspiracy theories are sometimes weaponised in public debate is a refreshing antidote to the tired cliché that we should just ignore these theories and move on. Instead, Hellinger argues that rather than reject conspiracy theories as emblems of a paranoid style, we should treat the phenomena seriously,

ask whether these theories are warranted on the evidence, and look at what their truth or falsity tells us about the kind of society we find ourselves in."
—M. R. X. Dentith, *Fellow, New Europe College, Romania*

"This book offers a unique and unsettling take on the many conspiracy theories that now animate political discourse and influence politics in the United States. Hellinger argues that these theories run the gamut from the plausible and the outlandish, but all of them derive from a fundamental truth that a deep state is a sphere of politics that exists in all states to some degree. A transcendent question is whether populist paranoia about 'how it all works' may threaten democratic governance and institutions."
—Dennis Judd, *Professor Emeritus, University of Missouri-St. Louis and University of Illinois at Chicago, USA*

"Perhaps the first book to address conspiracy theories in the Trump era, and one of the first to attempt to connect the epistemology, philosophy, and politics together, *Conspiracies and Conspiracy Theories in the Age of Trump* makes a valuable contribution."
—Joseph E. Uscinski, *Associate Professor, Political Science, University of Miami, USA*

CONTENTS

LIST OF FIGURES

LIST OF TABLES

CHAPTER 1

Introduction: Conspiracy Theory Versus Theorizing Conspiracy

Like Berthold Brecht's allegorical tale of Arturo Ui, ruthless gangster who takes control over the Cauliflower Trust in 1930's Chicago, Donald Trump's rise should have been "resistible." Trump's behavior was outright preposterous; an outlandish TV personality running for the highest office of the global hegemon. The possibility of a Trump presidency was not taken seriously by the vast majority of political scientists, the media, and campaign professionals until he had cut down his Republican primary opponents, one by one, ridiculing and verbally assaulting them, even to the point of strongly suggesting that Ted Cruz's father had been involved in the assassination of John F. Kennedy. How did a political outsider, a celebrity real estate mogul, almost cartoonish in his reality television program, manage to capture the presidency? How did he manage to get away with such wild conspiracy theories?

One answer lies in the myriad studies that demonstrate the decline of trust in American politics and institutions since the 1960s. With Trump, this mistrust has metastasized into vital organs of the body politic (see Chapters 4 and 5). The conspiracy theories that are Trump's political stock in trade resonated with substantial portions of the citizenry because alienated and resentful sectors in American society were "disposed" to believe them, and for the same reason they seemed after 18 months of his presidency very indisposed toward believing that their avenging angel against the political class deserves impeachment or censure. At the same time, can we say with any certainty that charges of collusion between the Trump campaign and operatives linked to the

© The Author(s) 2019
D. C. Hellinger, *Conspiracies and Conspiracy Theories in the Age of Trump*, https://doi.org/10.1007/978-3-319-98158-1_1

1

Kremlin and President Vladimir Putin are not "conspiracy theories"? Should that term be used only for imagined conspiracies?

Despite the important role that conspiracism seems to be playing in politics today, political scientists have almost entirely eschewed serious study of conspiracies themselves. Within both the academic and journalistic worlds, a consensus has prevailed that the very term "conspiracy theory" should be reserved for populist ideology and is to be regarded as toxic to real understanding of social, economic, and political developments. However, in the last twenty years some new studies, ranging across a wide array of disciplines, feature more nuance about conspiracism and some debate about the singular perspective of conspiracism as a form of social pathology. Still today, however, this work is mostly relegated to the margins of academic discourse and punditry in the mainstream news. No few scholars, reports, columnists, and pundits characterize conspiracy beliefs somewhere on a continuum of misguided, at best, to highly dangerous, at worst. A good many of them reflect the viewpoint of Daniel Pipes, who thinks that the ideologies of fascism and communism are at their heart conspiracist and believes that conspiracist political culture is uniquely and pathologically embedded throughout the Middle East.[1] Indeed, it is not difficult to show that some of the most abhorrent anti-Semitic conspiracy theories circulate widely in the Middle East, including in the region's mainstream mass media. However, both anti-Semitism and belief in conspiracies are widespread in the world. Only recently have social scientists begun to experiment with ways to measure generic conspiracism, as opposed to specific theories, across cultures. Even fewer are attempts to separate pathological conspiracism from conspiracy thinking that might be a rational political response to systematic injustices and inequalities in national and international politics.

Conceiving conspiracism as irrational is not confined to right-wing analysts, like Pipes. Chip Berlet's independent investigative journalism, often done in collaboration with the Southern Poverty Law Center, is focused on right-wing conspiracism, which he sees as especially threatening to democracy.[2] But he also has little use for conspiracism on the left. Berlet regards left-wing conspiracism not so much as threatening but as a cul-de-sac for diagnosing and resisting pathological social and political movements, a position with obvious implications for Trumpism's relationship with alt-right movements and its attraction of support and approval from hate groups. Another example of "at best" can be found in a widely quoted characterization of conspiracy theory as "the poor man's cognitive map," made by Frederik Jameson, a Marxist cultural theorist.[3] Jameson had little more to say about conspiracy theory, but the phrase resonated among radical critics as an affirmation that conspiracy theory should be regarded as a form of "false consciousness" that holds the oppressed class back from seeing the root of their exploitation in capitalism.

Rather than rejecting or embracing conspiracy theory, this book argues the need to problematize it; that is, we should subject conspiracy beliefs to examination on their logic and the weight of evidence, rather than *a priori* to reject all of them as false. Some conspiracy theories are bad theory and many serve to foster intolerance. Worse, in unfortunately not so rare historical cases they contribute to scapegoating, ethnic cleansing, and even genocide. Donald Trump's rhetoric, failure to repudiate hate groups, and policies bear hallmarks of what historian Richard Hofstadter identified in his highly influential articles as a recurring tendency toward "the paranoid style in American politics."[4] I agree with the warning that conspiracy theories, when they pretend to full explain major historical events and political turning points, can distract us from addressing larger social and economic forces that contribute to the conditions that encourage conspiracism. Addressing the threats to democracy posed by Trumpism requires that we grapple with the difficult work of building global and national economies that foster social inclusion, address the anxieties fostered by world migrations, and reform democratic institutions to foster more active and participatory citizenship than typical in liberal democracies. Accomplishing these tasks requires us to recognize that conspiracies are among the tools used by elites who resist these changes.

THE RETURN OF THE PARANOID STYLE TO AMERICAN POLITICS

With reason, many Americans and citizens in other wealthy liberal democracy suspect that the gross inequalities and socioeconomic disruptions in our lives are not just unfortunate side effects of an a-political process of globalization but are actively fostered by wealthy and powerful elites who have little empathy for those who are losing out as a result of the inter-related processes of technological change and globalization. If they think that those who a winning are playing by a different set of political rules than they do, are they wrong?

Hofstadter's foundational writings on the paranoid style emphasized that populism has typically arisen in times in which concentrated
economic power and the exercise of imperial policies threatened popular sovereignty—or at least were perceived to do so.[5] Populism is not an
ideology; it is a "discursive vessel," a particular kind of rhetoric, which
can be leftist, rightist, or even centrist. In the United States, populism
has spawned the Tea Party and the Occupy Movement; Donald Trump
and Bernie Sanders; and businessman Ross Perot. Perot achieved some
political traction in 1992 and 1996 by opposing the North American
Free Trade Association (NAFTA) as well as supporting gun control and
electronic democracy, drawing about a fifth of the vote equally among
liberals, conservatives, and moderates.[6] Nor should we think that political extremism and populism are provinces only of the "poor man."
Sociologist Seymour Martin Lipset famously argued on the basis of analysis of voting in Weimar Germany that the social base for fascism was
mainly the center, that is, the middle class.[7]

One thing this book does not attempt is to catalogue and research the
truth about the dozens of conspiracy theories that have appeared in the
Trumpian era. My goal in this book is to situate them within a national
context that has seen the weakening of liberal democratic institutions
and within a global context that has seen the rise of populist resistance to
globalization in a number of nations across the world. Trumpism shares
certain origins and features with right-populist movements, especially
those in Europe, most notably anti-Muslim prejudice, anti-immigrant
discourse, and hypernationalism.

Rather than reject conspiracy theory altogether, this book sees conspiratorial activity as useful for understanding the evolution of what is
sometimes called late capitalism, i.e., a capitalism characterized by global
and technocratic changes that have undermined the culture and politics
of industrial capitalism. I prefer the term "transnational capitalism" as
more descriptive than "late capitalism." Conspiracy theories—theories
about how conspiracies work, their limits and their potential to shape
political life—can help us bring more of political life from the deep and
dark corners of our world to the surface.

One important roadmap for how to do this can be found in Michael
Gray's study of conspiracism in the Arab world. Most work in this field
conjures up in the Western mind stereotypes of mobs of believers in the
Protocols of the Elders of Zion and in the theory that Israel was behind
the 9/11 attacks, and other anti-Semitic tracts. Gray acknowledges

the prevalence of these views in the region, but his book, in his words, "...seeks to discredit the reductionist, often Orientalist, explanations for conspiracies in the region, especially the view that would argue for pathological explanations of conspiracy theories and their frequency in the Arab world."[8] Gray starts from the supposition that conspiracy theories in the Arab world stem from "political structures and dynamics," i.e., the way social groups of different make-ups interact with one another and with the state; how elites interact with one another and the state and how local, regional, and economic conditions impact the outlook of people in the region toward the outside world and each other. Importantly, he points out that conspiracies and betrayal by elites in the Arab world give rise to conspiracy theories that do have some significant foundation. The ideas and discourses that emerge from this stew of social and economic forces are all influenced by history and the collective memory of Western intervention and people's justified mistrust of political elites in the region. This aspect of his analysis goes beyond merely acknowledging that there are conspiracies; it incorporates the impact of elite conspiracies and collaboration with Western imperialism into a richer analysis than the "Why are those people so crazy?" viewpoint typical of most news coverage.

It is notable that in his Preface Gray comments that he was struck by the "many similarities" between conspiracism in the Arab world and conspiracism in the United States. Indeed, his work is highly suggestive about how we might go about studying conspiracism—and what we might learn about our politics from conspiracism—in this age of Trump. For example, although collective memory of national humiliation is quite different in countries recently emerged from colonial rule than in a country that exercises hegemonic power on a global level, in many respects Arabs and peoples in other post-colonial societies want to make their countries, perhaps their civilizations, "great again." Such a comparative thesis requires much more elaboration and research than this book presents, but what it shares with Gray's approach is an attempt to understand conspiracism in the United States on the basis of historical patterns, a sense of eroding national power, mistrust of elites more attuned to global than national social forces, and the way American elites interact with one another and their counterparts in other parts of the world.

Although he regards conspiracy theories as little more that misguided explanations for social, economic, and political change, Timothy Melley appropriately associated conspiratorial impulses with "agency panic." Agency panic refers, he says, to "intense anxiety about an apparent loss of autonomy, the conviction that one's actions are being controlled by someone else," very often external agents.[9] That Melley feels it necessary to characterize loss of autonomy as merely "apparent" suggests that he believes such anxiety is not justified. Indeed, when anxiety about loss of control encourages conspiracy theories as totalistic explanations[10] that reduce economic globalization to the machinations of the Trilateral Commission, the Illuminati, or the United Nations, they do much more harm than good in identifying and evaluating the tectonic changes at work globally over the past 40 years. They thereby attribute enormous power and unity of intent to elite institutions that lack sufficient quotas of either to control historical forces in the way that the notorious Alex Jones of *InfoWar.com* fame would have it. However, it is just as illusory to think that the only "hidden hand" guiding history is the global market, much less to think that it is benign and under no one's control.

An illustration of the inadequacy of structural analysis, which I will explore in more detail in Chapter 5, is the notion that the economic distress being experienced in many rural counties and smaller cities in America is a product of global and technological changes beyond anyone's control. There seems to be a general consensus that areas of the country once firmly within the grasp of the Democratic Party, including the "blue wall" of states in the Upper Midwest, fell to Donald Trump out of exasperation with the political class. After all, the Republican Party had already offered in 2012 a presidential candidate who, in front of a crowd of wealthy donors at a private dinner, and thinking he was out of earshot of voters he needed to win over, said, "There are 47 percent of the people who will vote for the president no matter what...who are dependent upon government, who believe that they are victims...These are people who pay no income tax. ...and so my job is not to worry about those people. I'll never convince them that they should take personal responsibility and care for their lives."[11] And the winner of that election, President Barack Obama, who had campaigned in 2008 on "Keep hope alive," said in June 2016,

> When somebody says like the person [Trump] you just mentioned, who I'm not going to advertise for, that he's going to bring all these jobs back. Well how exactly are you going to do that? What are you going to do?

There's uh-uh no answer to it. He just says. 'I'm going to negotiate a better deal.' Well how? How exactly are you going to negotiate that? What magic wand do you have? And usually the answer is, he doesn't have an answer.[12]

Demanding that Trump explain how he would keep his promises makes sense, but was there no better answer than what Obama offered? And it is not hard to see that by failing himself to provide an answer to the hemorrhaging of jobs and wages in large swaths of the country, Obama suggested that there is no real political answer. This kind of response raises fundamental questions about the efficacy of representative democracy and citizenship in the nation-state. The right to citizenship in a liberal democratic order has been tightly identified with national identity. Is it possible for the political class to make such claims about the inevitability of globalization without raising questions about whose interest they represent? Should it surprise anyone that for many people the forces of globalization raise existential questions of identity, encouraging nativism and retreats into religious fundamentalism, as Benjamin Barber identified in *Jihad versus McWorld* 25 years ago?[13]

Is it just possible that many key policies, that is, political system outcomes, are made in secret and with minimum regard for transparency or public accountability? That conspiracies, if not capable of directly controlling the world economy, do play some role in shaping it and how the United States deals with it?

Not all conspiracy theories warrant serious investigation; conspiracy theories can spur or reflect scapegoating, and much worse, from pogroms to genocide. There are indeed cases in which psychologically ill people act on fears to commit violence, whether an assault on an individual or a murderous rampage. These concerns were on display than in the fall 2016 campaign when ardent opponents of Hillary Clinton circulated on the Internet a far-fetched, malicious claim that emails of her campaign manager (which had been passed on and released by Wikileaks) contained coded messages implicating the Democratic candidate in human trafficking, run through certain restaurants. Among them was the Comet Ping Pong, a Washington DC pizzeria. On December 4, a North Carolina man fired three shots with a rifle inside the Comet restaurant, fortunately wounding no one. The shooter, Edgar Maddison Welch, later told the *New York Times* that although he found no evidence in his self-authorized "investigation" of child trafficking at Comet, he rejected the idea the reports of trafficking were "fake news."[14]

But most people who hold conspiracy theories, even wild ones or evil ones, are not dangers to themselves or society. If they were, just about all of us need to be under some kind of surveillance or court restraint. Evidence from survey research suggests that just about all of us believe one or more conspiracy theories. Our concern, then, should be directed not toward all conspiracy theories but toward those, whether propagated from above by elites who find them political useful or from below by populist movements suspicious of elite power, are used to instill panic, stir pogroms, and motivate violence, usually against groups historically viewed as different or as outsiders, but sometimes as with Clinton, at a political opponent.

But conspiracy theories are not the sole province of the political right. Conspiracy theories are daily promoted in mainstream media, especially late at night in the living rooms and bedrooms of Americans watching the first twenty minutes of late-night comedians. Regardless of their truth value, and regardless of the fact that late-night political satire also has a salutary effect on our politics, these conspiracy theories too, like those of Trump and his enablers, are signs of political decay, of deterioration in the political institutions upon which we rely to settle conflicts and make policies. The fact that the movements similar to those behind Trump have emerged virulently in a number of other countries, especially in Europe, seems linked to forces of economic exclusion fostered by neoliberal capitalist globalization and technological changes that have rocked the bases of political consensus in the West. These right-wing, nationalist movements show similarity to Hofstadter conception of the "paranoid style in American politics," which includes, according to the historian, a strong proclivity toward conspiracy theories about immigrants, political dissidents, and a range of ethnic and religious groups.[15]

Undoubtedly, many readers will recoil at the notion that PizzaGate and Stephen Colbert's (host of the CBS's popular daily evening program, *The Late Show*) insistence that Vladimir Putin has "*compromat*" to blackmail the president are comparable. They are comparable only to a degree. A key point of this book is that the narratives in both cases share certain defining features of what makes a belief a conspiracy theory. It is not just the highly implausible, unwarranted beliefs that should be considered "conspiracy theories." As may already be evident, this book warns about the use of "conspiracy theory" as an epithet to discredit certain challenges to the myth of American exceptionalism and commitment to democracy.

Also at the core of this book is a concern that "conspiracy theory" is loosely used as a label to discredit populism in general, not just racist and hypernationalist populism associated today with the alt-right and Trumpism. The place where we must begin to rethink how we use the term "conspiracy theory" requires a reassessment of the seminal works on conspiracy theory, populism, and the meaning of "theory" in the social sciences. Hofstadter's work on this subject continues to cast both shadow and light on conspiracism. The shadow is well captured by Rob Brotherton, who has developed an important new social science tool to measure predisposition toward conspiracy theories but who also, like most social scientists, subscribes to the view that, "Pretty much everyone seems to agree that there is a distinction to be made. Conspiracy theories are bogus; a claim of conspiracy that's true isn't really a conspiracy theory at all."[16]

Hofstadter's essays on conspiracism were preceded by the influential works of Lasswell, who virtually created the field of political psychology with his studies of the manipulative effects of propaganda in World War II and in "totalitarian" regimes. Lasswell's psychological approach[17] shaped the post-World War II social scientific consensus in two key ways: (1) He placed the focus of social science research on the question of why some people more than others hold conspiracy theories, what a critic of this approach calls "dispositional" factors[18]; (2) he anticipated, well before Hofstadter, the near-unanimous view among mainstream journalists and academics that engaging in conspiracy theory is pathological. Hofstadter, in reaction to Barry Goldwater's radical conservative campaign in 1964 and what he saw as the erosion of reason in public discourse, applied and popularized Lasswell's work on the subject.

The problem with the dispositional research by Brotherton and others is not that it is bad social science about who tends to adopt conspiracy beliefs; what is problematic is its framing the disposition as necessarily irrational at best, pathological at worst. It also limits research on conspiracism to what Jack Bratich, a media sociologist, calls a "symptomatic approach."[19] Bratich argues that this kind of research seeks to explain conspiracy theories as an "individual mental condition, collective delusional state of mind, a cultural/political slackening." Bratich provides a key here to understanding how the term "conspiracy theory" is often used to discredit *a priori* claims of a conspiracy behind world events, especially when those claims challenge the kinds of myths that reinforce hegemony—or in more mainstream parlance, the legitimacy of the political system. As we will see in Chapters 6 and 7, the recent muck-raking and academic research on "Dark Money" and the "Deep State" have attracted the dreaded label of "conspiracy theory," not only from expected quarters (e.g., wealthy conservative think-tanks) but also from sympathetic critics who charge that the authors, though themselves eschewing conspiracy theory, have veered into the realm of irrationality. This kind of criticism is what Bratich regards a "conspiracy panic."

Conspiracism in America in the Trumpian era is not just about the president himself. Nor should every conspiracy theory circulating on the mainstream media, social media and the Internet to be considered an irrational, much less paranoid response to the disconcerting global changes of the last four decades. Whether undertaken by journalists, sociologists, psychologists, historians, or political scientists, most research on conspiracy theory fails to take seriously or to examine the role of con-spiracy in political life. However, the last twenty years have seen some significant but under-appreciated efforts to revise our understanding of conspiracy theory. A number of recent works have highlighted how "conspiracy theory" is used as a meme to delegitimize discourse, jour-nalism, or academic analysis that challenges prevailing "common sense," that is, hegemony.[20]

At work in maintaining hegemony is what Bratich, borrowing from the French philosopher Michel Foucault, calls the "regime of truth."[21] Bratich argues that "conspiracy theory" is used to discipline what is acceptable or not in our public discourse. "Conspiracy theory" is not a description of certain ideas; it is a term of disqualification. "If the mind," says Bratich, "is that sphere that can distinguish between truth and false-hood, then conspiracy theories are beyond that sphere." The bounda-ries, observes Foucault, are set by the means, techniques, and procedures we use to determine truth. My analysis of conspiracy theory in the age of Trump follows Bratich in asking not simply, "What is conspiracy the-ory?" but also "What counts as conspiracy theory?"[22]

While I share Bratich's critical perspective on how "conspiracy the-ory" is a meme used to sow a kind of panic directed against work dis-ruptive of hegemony, I would contest the implication, never fully made explicit in his work, that the "symptomatic" approach is inappropri-ate or necessarily contributes to panic. My issue with symptomology is that the term itself reinforces the idea that a priori the object of expla-nation, a conspiracy theory, is irrational or pathological. As a result, all social science research tends to narrow the focus of its gaze on bad behavior. For example, a recent collection of research by mostly Eastern European scholars focuses almost exclusively upon targets of scapegoating and suspicion, in particular, Jews and in some countries of the region, Russians. Conspiracy theories, the editors say, consist of "looking for causes of [social and political events] in clandestine plots, suppressed knowledge, and secret actions [that] provide simple and logical answers to people's doubts and uncertainties." The editors assert that people in Eastern Europe need conspiratorial explanations because of the "extremely dynamic" processes of social change unleashed by the fall of Communism. This finding is consistent with the research showing that a sense of lack of control over the course of one's life also increases the disposition toward conspiracism. Those most likely to adopt conspiracy theories in these circumstances are less neurotic and more socially agreeable but also more closed-minded and with lower self-esteem.[23] Though Hofstadter warns against taking the term "paranoid style" too literally, effectively this research is corroborates his interpretative analysis of conspiracism in the United States.

The problem here is that like most research on conspiracism, the symptomology is focused exclusively on right-wing conspiracism in a region with an especially dismal history of anti-Semitism and a recent history of dominance by a military superpower whose official ideology was Communism. No studies that I know of examine predispositions toward holding other conspiracy beliefs that might not fit the stereotype implied by "paranoid style." For example, none of the Eastern European researchers cited or included as contributors seem to be interested in a group that perhaps has the most reason to hold a conspiracy theory, Jews. This is not to say that Jews as a group might be more disposed than others toward conspiracism in general so much as to point out that the particular suspicions of a group of people are influenced by their lived as well as historical memory. For ethnic and religious minorities persecuted or oppressed in the past, to suspect that they are targeted by sinister state-sanctioned conspiracies is hardly irrational. Why, then, Jews in countries with histories of especially virulent anti-semitism not be more disposed to the belief that there are groups in the majority that may be conspiring to repress them?

One significant problem in assessing the importance of conspiracism in the age of Trump is that only recently have political scientists begun to use tools of attitudinal and behavioral research to explore public opinion in this area. To be sure, there exist relevant opinion surveys, but these are mostly carried out by polling agencies for use by journalists, most of whom treat conspiracy beliefs as quirky curiosities. Among social scientists, a growing body of research both inside the United States and abroad has focused on dispositional research, i.e., research searching for individual-level motivations for believing conspiracy theories, mostly of the paranoid variety. Most of these studies search for explanations that are psychologically based, with considerable attention to studies behind anti-Semitic and other scapegoating theories, much like the aforementioned studies in Eastern Europe.[24] This kind of research consciously draws upon the legacy of Lasswell. His most important publications in this area spanned the era of the Great Depression and beginning of the Cold War, so it is not surprising that much of his attention was drawn to the "totalitarian" fascist and communist regimes of that era, both of which greatly impacted historical memory in Eastern Europe.[25]

In the United States a significant amount of research has examined proclivities toward conspiracy theories that seem to be widespread among African–Americans, such as suspicions that HIV and AIDS were deliberately introduced into black communities, theories positing genocidal plots against Blacks, and beliefs that the assassinations of M.L. King and Malcolm X involved more than a lone killer. With a few exceptions,[26] academics and journalists approach the topic with paternalism or dismissiveness. The best one can say is that researchers seem to want to explain away apparent irrational beliefs in the African–American community by citing historical wrongs, most notably the deliberate introduction of syphilis into African–Americans in the 1932 Tuskegee medical study.[27] Memory of this historical wrong has at times impeded important measures to protect public health, a fact frequently cited by critics of conspiracism. However, the influence of Tuskegee on the African–American community has also been used by analysts to dismiss theories that deserve closer examination. For example, Tim Golden, reporter for the *New York Times*, wrote off anger and concern among African–Americans about the CIA's role in the introduction of crack cocaine into Los Angeles to their historical experience of exploitation, oppression, and abuse.[28] In fact, there was a basis for their suspicions.

The Los Angeles community was reacting at the time (1986) to a series of articles in the *San Jose Mercury News* that under the title "Dark Alliance" contended that the CIA's complicity in the drug trade was an offshoot of US support for the Nicaraguan Contras, who were fighting to overthrow the Sandinista Revolution and its elected government in the 1980s. Golden dismissed the path-breaking investigative reporting by the *News'* Gary Webb, the first muckraking to find a mass audience mainly through the

Internet. Golden charged, "The force of the *Mercury News* account appears to have relatively little to do with the quality of the evidence that it marshals to its case."[29] Nine years later, the reporter for the *Los Angeles Times*, which mirrored Golden's criticism, formally apologized for his articles,[30] but the *New York Times* has never acknowledged that regardless of shortcomings, Webb's investigative reporting stood up very well in the long run.[31]

The reaction of Golden and other mainstream journalists reflects the convergence of two factors converged to produce a panicked rations against a conspiracy theory that had some merit and went uncovered by establishment institutions: (1) the challenges posed to establishment journalists by the emergence of social media, exacerbated because this was an early case of its challenge to the mainstream media's gatekeeper role[32]; and (2) a defensive institutional response, first denial and later no follow-up investigation, by national security reporters reluctant to confront their own failure to expose the secret collusion in between the CIA and the paramilitary forces it had armed in Nicaragua.

WHAT WE KNOW FROM SURVEY RESEARCH

Given that Hofstadter baptized populist conspiracism as the "paranoid style," it is not surprising that much of the research about conspiracism is done in the subfield of political psychology and is "dispositional," that is, aimed at identifying underlying psychological traits that dispose an individual toward conspiracy theories, as opposed to the social and economic contextual variables that might impact peoples' thinking. Despite its limitations, this approach has led some researchers examining conspiracy theory on the individual level to rethink just what they are trying to explain. In many cases what we call a "conspiracy theory" is better categorized as "conspiracy belief"—e.g., a belief that Oswald did not act alone in assassinating President John F. Kennedy; a belief that Russians rigged the 2016 election; a belief that governments are covering up knowledge of visit by extra-terrestrials. This makes sense. We don't call expressions of faith in the ability of divinities, such as the Judeo-Christian God, as "theories" but "beliefs."

Most of the social science research on conspiracism focuses on beliefs, but we will use the terms somewhat interchangeably because what interests us here is the role that a particular form of collective political activity—a conspiracies—play in shaping history and resolving conflicts. This question raises the question of political subjectivity, the question of how many degrees of freedom human have in shaping the path of history. To think that conspiracies are singularly capable of determining the outcome of major political struggles is to magnify their importance; to think that they have no role to play at all is to discard entirely the role of power, secrecy, and deceit in human affairs.

Until recently, public opinion research on the prevalence of conspiracism in American society has been confined largely to survey companies whose findings are sporadically reported in the mainstream media. There is little coordination or consistency in questions asked. As one baseline for estimating views about conspiracy theories before the 2016 election, we can consult a survey of 1247 registered voters carried out by Fordham University's Public Policy Polling (PPP), March 27–30, 2013, just about the time that Donald Trump began to publically ponder running for president. We should note that this survey, then, excludes a significant portion of the American population—those who have declined or failed to register to vote. One advantage, however, is that the survey breaks beliefs down by demographics, in including race, party ID, ideology, age, and gender. Technically, the margin of error for this poll is plus or minus 2.8 percentage points, but PPP has a mixed track record for accuracy in predicting elections; it uses a combination of online and automated telephone responses. However, the results of the PPP survey were not radically different from a compendium of public opinion studies published six months later by the American Enterprise Institute (AEI).[33] Used with caution, the PPP survey is reliable enough to draw some broad estimates of how widespread is belief in one or more prominent conspiracy theories.[34]

Table 1.1 provides a breakdown of opinion regarding the 20 conspiracy theories studied in the PPP polls, with results ranging from 4% claiming to believe in the "lizard people rule" theory (Perhaps not everyone took the survey seriously!) to 51% expressing belief that a conspiracy was at work in the Kennedy assassination. The PPP cites an Associated Press/ Roper poll's finding of 56% expressing a similar belief. As many observers have noted, the persistence of rejection of the Warren Commission report's single-gunman theory surpasses any other conspiracy belief both in terms of the high levels of endorsement and persistence over time. What is remarkable about the persistence of the JFK theory is that overwhelmingly academics and journalists resist giving any credence to doubts that Oswald acted alone.

Table 1.1 Twenty conspiracy theories; percent holding and partisanship, March 2013

	Democrat (%)	Republican (%)	Independent/other (%)	All answering (%)
Global warming a hoax	11	58	41	37
Believe Bin Laden alive	2	6	10	6
Believe UFO crashed at Roswell	18	27	19	21
Secretive elite behind New World Order	15	34	35	28
Saddam Hussein involved in 911 attacks	22	33	28	28
Childhood vaccines linked to autism	16	26	18	20
Moon landing was faked	7	4	9	7
President Obama is the anti-Christ	6	20	13	13
Bush Administration deliberately lied about WMDs in Iraq	72	13	48	44
Believe aliens exist	27	28	32	29
CIA was instrumental in introducing crack cocaine into US cities	14	9	21	14
Government introduces fluoride in water for sinister reasons	8	9	9	9
Shape-shifting reptilian people in human form control world	3	5	6	4
Larger conspiracy at work in JFK assassination; Oswald not alone	52	55	44	51
Believe in Bigfoot or Sasquatch	14	15	13	14
Media adds mind-control technology to broadcast signals	15	17	13	15
Government sprays chemicals mixed in plane exhaust trailings	5	6	5	5
Pharmaceutical and medical industries create diseases for profit	12	18	14	15
Beatles' Paul McCartney died in 1966 and replaced by look-alike	7	4	5	5
US government knowingly allow 911 attacks	14	8	12	11

Source "Democrats and Republicans Differ on Conspiracy Beliefs," Public Policy Polling, News Release, April 2, 2013. Sample of 1247 registered voters, questioned March 27–30, 2.8% margin of error

The JFK theory far outpaces the belief that the Bush administration knowingly allowed the 9/11 attacks to happen, which drew only 11% support in 2013. However, a Zogby poll in May 2006 found 48% agreement (v. 42% disagreement) with the belief that the 9/11 Commission "concealed or refused to investigate critical evidence." The AEI compendium found somewhat higher support (14% in one case) for the 9/11 theory in some polls, but still much below the support for the JFK conspiracy theory. However, the Bush/Cheney administration did generate considerable skepticism about its motives for going to war in Iraq, as 44% (57% in a *CNN* poll cited by AEI) of the public believes it deliberately lied about weapons of mass destruction (WMDs) in Iraq.

The PPP study is one of the few to break down opinions about conspiracy by race, and the results (See Table 1.2) are somewhat surprising. For example, most research assumes that African–Americans are more disposed toward conspiracism than other groups in the population. What the survey suggests is that the gaps among African–Americans, whites, and Hispanics vary considerably from theory to theory. The gap between whites and blacks is almost nonexistent on 8 of the theories examined, and blacks are actually significantly less likely to believe hold conspiracist beliefs about global warming (as a hoax), a UFO crash at Roswell, elite origins of the New World Order, existence of aliens, Big Foot, and media mind control. Despite the legacy of the Tuskegee experiments, African–Americans are not more likely to endorse the theories about fluoride in water and connecting autism to vaccines. Surprisingly, while there is a gap between white and black views on the CIA's involvement with crack trafficking in the 1980s, only 22% of African–Americans endorsed the conspiracy theory—despite the strong reaction among African–Americans in Los Angeles at the time of the scandal. Unfortunately, the survey did not include questions about some other conspiracy theories that would likely attract African–Americans' endorsements, such as the assassinations of Martin Luther King, Malcolm X, birther theory, and police misconduct in the OJ Simpson murder case.

Most public opinion studies about "conspiracy theories" do not characterize the beliefs as such in survey questions. The characterization arises in the public reporting of the results. Even when the questions or analysis remains neutral, surveys typically mix a variety of theories that range across two variables—level (i.e., magnitude) and plausibility. The national poll conducted by the PPP in spring of 2013 is typical in this respect.[35] The poll asked questions about 20 different theories, ranging from whether the respondent believed in lizard people (4%, yes) to whether they believed there was a larger conspiracy, beyond Oswald, involved in

Table 1.2 Twenty conspiracy theories; percent holding and race, March 2013

	Hispanic (%)	Whites (%)	African–Americans (%)	All (%)
Global warming a hoax	34	41	19	37
Believe Bin Laden alive	15	4	6	6
Believe UFO crashed at Roswell	27	22	6	21
Secretive elite behind New World Order	10	32	21	28
Saddam Hussein involved in 911 attacks	29	28	21	28
Childhood vaccines linked to autism	16	20	18	20
Moon landing was faked	15	5	8	7
President Obama is the anti-Christ	9	15	9	13
Bush Administration deliberately lied about WMDs in Iraq	42	41	54	44
Believe aliens exist	22	30	22	29
CIA was instrumental in introducing crack cocaine into US cities	15	13	22	14
Government introduces fluoride in water for sinister reasons	11	9	7	9
Shape-shifting reptilian people in human form control world	9	3	–	4
Larger conspiracy at work in JFK assassination; Oswald not alone	51	48	66	51
Believe in Bigfoot or Sasquatch	10	15	8	14
Media adds mind-control technology to broadcast signals	18	14	7	15
Government sprays chemicals mixed in plane exhaust trailings	8	5	–	5
Pharmaceutical and medical industries create diseases for profit	19	14	12	15
Beatles' Paul McCartney died in 1966 and replaced by look-alike	8	4	–	5
US government knowingly allow 911 attacks	14	10	8	11

Source "Democrats and Republicans Differ on Conspiracy Beliefs," Public Policy Polling, News Release, April 2, 2013. Sample of 1247 registered voters, questioned March 27–30, 2.8% margin of error the Kennedy Assassination (51%, yes). While the poll was conducted reasonably scientifically given the cost constraints, it relied upon automated telephone interviews, which makes it more difficult to generate a representative sample. Would people attracted to beliefs often characterized as "conspiracy theories" be more inclined to answer a lengthy automated questionnaire than those who see them as mental stigmata?

In what is still very much a young field of research in political science, the most complete sociological study of American conspiracy theories is a book with that title by Joseph E. Uscinski and Joseph M. Parent.[36] They too tend to characterize a conspiracy theory as a pathological belief, asking (p. 6), "Who is most *prone* [my emphasis] to believing conspiracy theories?" On the other hand, Uscinski and Parent do not limit their quest for understanding to right-wing theories, and they make what to my knowledge is the first and only empirical measure of conspiracism over time. They rely upon a working definition of conspiracism that attempts to measure the concept not by beliefs in particular conspiracy theories but via a broader measure of "underlying conspiratorial predispositions."[37] The latter questions attempt to get at individual's degree of prejudice against particular social groups and the degree to which an individual views events and circumstances as caused by conspiracies. Questions measuring these tendencies are used to create a scale ranging from extremely naïve to extremely critical. In the latter regard they asked respondents about their degree of agreement with three statements:

- Much of our lives are (sic)being controlled by plots hatched in secret places;
- Even though we live in a democracy, a few people will always run things anyway;
- The people who really 'run' the country are not known to the voters.

One virtue of this approach is that unlike specific questions about particular conspiracies these questions are pertinent to identifying conspiracist tendencies regardless of where people fall on a left-right spectrum.

Uscinski and Parent's first cut at measuring the levels of conspiracism in America over time, specifically from 1890 to 2010, is based on a sample of more than 100,000 letters to the editor in the *New York Times* and *Chicago Tribune*. The letters were coded for conspiracism by research assistants trained to maximize inter-coder reliability (i.e., consistency in

1 INTRODUCTION: CONSPIRACY THEORY VERSUS ...   19

the coding). In this way they built what is probably the only archive of "conspiracy talk" over more than a century. To qualify as conspiracy talk, the writer had to cite a group to be acting in secret to cover-up or seek a political objective "at the expense of the public good." The researchers supplemented this data with a file of 3000 articles and posts from Internet blogs and news sources. Among their findings is that over this 120 year period the percentage of letters with "conspiracy talk" has actually been lower in the post-World War II era than it was in the 1890s and the first half of the century.[38] There were only two periods when conspiracism in the letters spiked—in the early 1890s and in the very early 1950s, the only times that the percentage of such letters surpassed 3%, with the latter period the only one to exceed 4%. Contrary to the commonly held belief that the Kennedy Assassination inaugurated a new age of conspiracism (with the *X-Files* TV show often cited as evidence), there is no empirical evidence for this claim from analysis of these letters.

Uscinski and Parent contend without much evidence that letter-writers generally differ little from nonwriters regarding political opinions and that professional norms would deter editors from excluding some number of conspiracy letters are cranks. Furthermore, we might wonder how many letters get excluded because they more or less replicate one another's concerns. For example, if an editor received 50 letters defending Oliver Stones' *JFK*, how many might actually have been published? Unfortunately, a year after the Trump election there still had not appeared (to my knowledge, after a search) any follow-up studies, though this is understandable given the cost and time need to replicate the methodology for studying letters.

An intriguing finding by Uscinski and Parent is that "conspiracy theory is for losers." That is, the authors suggest that the losing side in a presidential election is much more likely to suspect the system was rigged against them than are the losers.[39] This finding has been reinforced by a team of political scientists who have found that conspiracy theories are more likely to be endorsed by less trusting and less knowledgeable respondents, especially among conservatives.[40] In keeping with the "conspiracy theories are for losers" hypothesis, researchers found in a follow-up study[41] done just after the November 2016 election that there was evidence of a reciprocal shift among partisans—of Democrats feeling more like losers and victims of an unfair system than Republicans, who were more likely to hold such sentiments after 2008 and 2012. The breakdown in Table 1.1 of partisan opinion about several conspiracy theories is consistent with the idea that endorsement of conspiracy theories is related to which party's ox is being gored, but not unequivocally. Not surprising, the largest gaps in beliefs are on global warming, the New World Order, the 9/11 attacks, and President Obama's character. The 72/13% gap between Democrats and Republicans on whether the Bush administration deliberately lied to get us into war is the most vivid example; but the finding that in 2013 one out of every five Republican identified Obama and the anti-Christ is striking. Chapters 4 and 5 use some available survey data to see whether the "conspiracy theory is for losers" hypothesis holds up post-2016. But we take a preliminary look here at the state of affairs in the pre-Trump era.

The "conspiracy theory is for losers" thesis may have a short shelf-life. The opinion research supporting it was conducted when, arguably, the nation still was living in "normal times," i.e., pre-Trump presidency. The winners, if one considers Republican control over all three branches of government to be "winning," were also crying conspiracy in 2017. One year subsequent to his victory in the Electoral College, President Trump was repeating Twitter assertions that he had actually won the popular vote (not just the Electoral College). He complained that his policy initiatives were being thwarted by the political establishment of both parties. Even before he was inaugurated, some of his supporters claimed that the "Deep State" was plotting to remove him from office, and by May 2018 the president himself was making the claim. One might hypothesize that initial feelings victory among conservatives and Republicans may be fading. It seems like both sides may be feeling as though they lost, Trumpistas because the legitimacy of his victory (and only in the Electoral College) is under attack; Democrats because they feel the election was rigged by Russian interference. We will return to considering it in Chapters 5 and 6.

Many conspiracy theories seem to have a limited shelf-life; so this makes even more remarkable the persistence and degree of shared views regarding the Kennedy assassination across demographic groups. This is a testimony to the enduring doubts and mistrust about what the government is capable of doing. Still, even as a new trove of government files about the assassination were released in October 2017, with thousands more still kept secret in direct violation of law, the *New York Times* once again dismissed public doubts. "The granddaddy of American conspiracy theories has re-emerged in the American psyche," proclaimed the *Times*' Lori Moore. Moore takes it upon herself to dismiss all doubts, claiming the evidence to be overwhelming. "Yet 25 years after the event, a majority of the American public does not believe the truth. Rather, polls have shown that most Americans believe President Kennedy was assassinated as an outgrowth of a conspiracy."[42]

Although motivated reasoning may inflate endorsements of theories with partisan implications, it is difficult to write off Americans' doubts about what happened in Dallas on November 22, 1963, to partisanship. Chapter 3 takes up the issue in more detail, but readers will be disappointed if they expect a clear-cut endorsement or rejection of conspiracy the JFK theories in this book. My focus is on why so many intellectual and journalistic elites are quick in the face of broad public doubts about the lone-gunman theory to be so dismisive conspiracy theories about the assasination. This type of conspiracy theory I think it is because the theory raises serious implications about American exceptionalism.

By now it should be clear that this book takes the argument, "But that's not a conspiracy theory because it has been proven to be true", to be specious. As philosopher Matthew Dentith puts it, "The underlying question we should always ask when someone proposes a theory is, 'What should I believe, given the evidence?'"[43] On the other hand, we should resist thinking that unmasking a conspiracy fully resolves any question about the root causes of major political events or historical watersheds. For example, even if evidence were to emerge to support the conspiracy belief holding that the Roosevelt Administration deliberately allowed the attack on Pearl Harbor to happen (a theory), this would not fully explain why and how the United States entered into World War II. It would, however, significantly alter the way we understand the path to warfare and eventually US hegemonic power.

The process by which we evaluate the degree to which a belief in a conspiracy or an explanation embodied in a conspiracy theory is valid requires judgments not unlike those that take place in a court of law. How we should go about distinguishing theories that are, respectively, warranted, plausible, or unwarranted (perhaps ridiculous) is taken up in Chapter 2.

Conspiracies and Conspiracy Theories Defined

I define political conspiracies as collective activity in which several actors plan and work together to achieve a political goal in a manner marked by three interrelated characteristics: (1) secrecy; (2) vulnerability to defeat by exposure; and (3) illegal, deceptive, or unethical behavior. A conspiracy involving illegal or deceptive behavior (leaving aside unethical actions) does not necessarily mean a conspiracy or its goals is malevolent. For example, one might see as fully justified by history the "generals' plot" to kill Hitler, involving a conspiracy in 1944 among the German high command to end the Nazi regime via assassination. Whether ill-conceived or not, John Brown's raid on Harper's Ferry to foment a slave revolt in 1859 in the American South is generally framed as a heroic conspiracy, especially in popular culture. On the other hand, within a democratic republic conspiracies by their nature—the need for secrecy, vulnerability to defeat by exposure, and unlawful, deceptive and unethical behavior—are likely to be perceived, and accurately, as directed against the public interest or as Rousseau put it, the "general will."

This latter concern became clearly visible as the very visible and hotly allegation of a secret, illegal political plot by Trump and his campaign gained traction early in the first year of his presidency. Nothing less than treason is implied in the claim that the Trump campaign colluded with Russian officials to tilt the playing field in the president's favor in the 2016 election. Most proponents of this theory deny that they are propagating a conspiracy theory, "Russiagate", especially the version claiming the Russian president Vladimir Putin has *compromat* (blackmail material) on Trump, meets all the criteria of a conspiracy. So too do Trump's counter theories: (1) that accusations of collusion have been fostered by deliberate leaks from the FBI and other security agencies to engineer his removal from office; and (2) that the Obama administration spied upon his campaign office with electronic eavesdropping and placement of FBI informants within the campaign. Trump's conspiracy theories are put in the context of a larger claim that a "Deep State" is behind attempts to secure his removal from office. We examine the "Deep State", which in the United States was largely, before Trump, associated with radical leftist conspiracy theory, in Chapter 7.

This book also chooses to highlight in Chapter 6 another theory that is sometimes characterized as a "conspiracy theory" by its critics, the claim that some of America's wealthiest families have by stealth shifted the political playing field toward a radical libertarian policies and limits on majority rule well beyond those needed to protect minority civil rights. Unlike Russiagate, this conspiracy is not illegal, as Courts have ruled that the alleged cabal's its most important asset, Dark Money—i.e., massive funding of political campaigns and educational/cultural institutions, without disclosure of donors—has been ruled legally in-bounds. This has been achieved, as historian Zephyr Teachout shows, by redefining the meaning of corruption in politics from the early years of the American Republic, when even small gifts offered without a quid-pro-quo were seen as corrupting of civic virtue.[44]

Conspiracy theories may be perpetrated by elites or the state for purposes hiding uncomfortable truths or to further immediate objectives, such as eroding citizens' use of constitutional rights that stand in the way of economic or security goals. This is one reason why transparency is usually counterpoised to conspiracy. Official actions to block release of information naturally give rise to suspicions of conspiracy among the public. Transparency, argue West and Sanders, has become a more conspicuous ideal in the neoliberal conception of the post-Cold War world, evident in the founding of organizations such as Transparency International, George Soros' Open Society, and World Bank's Transparency and Accountability Capacity Development Project. However, Mark Fenster, a sociologist who is relatively more open-minded about legitimacy of conspiracy theories than most academics, argues that positing transparency as the antidote to conspiracism is idealist.[45] There is a range of circumstances in which secrecy, or more properly perhaps, "confidentiality", may be justified.

We elaborate this concern further on in this book, but here it is worth noting that transparency and conspiracy are often linked to each other in concerns about "fake news"and the notion that we may be living in a "post-truth" society. In reaction to Donald Trump's claim that mainstream media outlets have deliberately manufactured untrue "facts' and stories" to undermine his presidency, more "transparency" in journalism has been posited as a remedy to regain public trust.[46] A "fake news" story may occasionally be traced back to a single origin, but even in this case many of them are deliberately circulated throughout social media as part of what amounts to a conspiracy to secretly influence public opinion. Clearly, a major concern in the Trump era is the systematic creation and diffusion of fake stories by groups and organizations, including foreign governments seeking to meddle in election outcomes. Most fake news stories, then, have origins in conspiracies, as we have defined them here. They require collaboration among plotters; secrecy, lest their exposure undermine their credibility; and they can be characterized as illegal, embarrassing, or unethical.

PARANOID STYLE AND POPULISM

Conspiracy theories stand in a complex relationship to the global rise of neoliberal capitalism. Conspiracy theories can be used by ambitious, populist politicians to mobilize populist support, but they can also generate protests against abuses of power. When they are based on outright fabrications by those who seek power or profit, they lend themselves to scapegoating and in the worst case actual pogroms of various types, including the internment of Japanese Americans during World War II and the Jewish Holocaust. Whether false or not, their proliferation and adoption by large proportions of the population are symptoms of political decay.

Trump's appeal owes much to "the paranoid style" in American politics. Trump skillfully used his celebrity to promote "birther theory", racist stereotypes of immigrants, and fear of Muslims, all of which represent a revival of nativism, which Hofstadter identified as a recurrent feature in populist episodes in America. Trump tied these strands of nativism together. His endorsement of birther theory lent credence to right-wing claims that Obama is a Muslim and by implication that he was unwilling to confront terrorism, or perhaps even that he was complicit with terrorism. Trump told right-wing radio host Laura Ingram in 2011, "He doesn't have a birth certificate or, if he does, there's something on that certificate that is very bad for him. Now somebody told me, and I have no idea whether this is bad for him or not but perhaps it would be, that where it says 'religion' it might have 'Muslim,' and if you're a Muslim, you don't change your religion by the way, but somebody said, 'Maybe that's the reason he doesn't want to show it.' I don't think so. I just don't think he has a birth certificate and everybody has a birth certificate."[47] As late as August 2016, Trump said the President Barack Obama was the creator of ISIS. When a conservative radio host tried to soften the candidate's accusation, suggesting he merely meant Obama's policies had created a power vacuum to exploit, Trump doubled-down, claiming, "No, I meant he's the founder of ISIS."[48]

Conor Lynch argued in *Slate* that Trump "single-handily restored the paranoid style to the mainstream (on the right, at least); giving credibility to wacky conspiracy theories from the bowels of the blogosphere and creating an angry and fanatical movement." The president sees behind every criticism and challenge he faces "...a cunning and calculated group of conspirators who want to destroy America and its culture."[49] This book diverges from Lynch's contention that Trump accomplished this feat "single-handedly", though I would agree that his discourse have properly be characterized as the "paranoid style." Furthermore, conspiracist discourse, paranoid or not, has spread across the political spectrum— for example, in the way that Stephen Colbert has persistently promoted through his comedy monologues the claim that Vladimir Putin, president of Russia, has the power to blackmail the president because he is in possession of compromising video of a highly salacious sexual incident ("golden showers") involving Trump and prostitutes in a Moscow hotel room. This constitutes, I propose, itself a form of conspiracism prevalent among Trump critics; as I write, it can neither to be dismissed nor accepted at face value. But we do not need to have certainty about this conspiracy theory to know that discourse around it signifies democratic decay.

My approach brings to bear on conspiracism in the age of Trump relatively recent scholarship that questions the single-minded way that mainstream news media and scholarship dismiss many uncomfortable realities of American politics as "conspiracy theory." I argue that conspiracies are important political phenomena, a form of political behavior that in some (not all) circumstances help us put agency back into explanations of globalization, technological change, and other explanations of widespread discontent about globalization, the quality of democracy, and the power of elites. Conspiracism can be a social pathology, but conspiracies are an important form of political behavior that contradict a major premise for democratic government—transparency.

Fenster has rightly argued that the goal of complete transparency in a democracy is something of a chimera,[50] but regardless of the practical and moral limits on transparency, there can be little doubt that effective democratic government requires an information environment allowing citizens opportunities to deliberate and contribute to decision-making, as well as to hold government accountable for its policies and actions. Despite calls for more transparency, civic culture in America has become more, not less opaque since the era of Vietnam and Watergate, when more transparency and congressional oversight on security agencies was on the agenda. Both the Bush and Obama administrations attempted with success to roll back enforcement of legal protections of "whistle blowers," with Obama actually exceeding his predecessor's zeal to limit transparency.[51] The Trump administration has not hesitated to use obstructionism and obfuscation in dealing with the White House press corps. The circus-like atmosphere of daily news briefings attracted the attention of pointed satire on *Saturday Night Live*. Less noticed was the singularly uncooperative attitude of Trump appointees to the leadership positions in the executive bureaucracy, especially the Pentagon and State Department. All across government access and communication with journalists were significantly reduced from previous administrations.[52]

Conspiracy theories are not always to be regarded as a sign of individual or social pathology. They are not always dangerous, not always phantasms of overactive imaginations, not always wrong. And they are not found exclusively on the right; in the present era, they also tend to characterize much of the opposition discourse about Trump. Their proliferation and content do, I will argue, signal serious problems with liberal democracy. It is time to reconsider what we think we know about conspiracy theory, where it comes from and whether it still can be disregarded as the product of paranoid minds.

TRUMPIAN CONSPIRACY THEORIES

It would not be difficult to organize this book around a compilation of Trumpian conspiracy theories, delving into each in a chapter. This book, however, is not intended as an encyclopedia of such theories. Here, anticipating that (as was the case with Watergate) some major aspects of scandals fade with time, I want to illustrate some prominent conspiracist themes in his campaign and the early (first 18 months) of his presidency, enough to indicate how prevalent conspiracy theories emanating or endorsed by the White House were in this period.[53]

- Trump significantly boosted birther theory, which claims that President Barack Obama was born in Kenya and ineligible to be president, long before he officially became a candidate but also when he began to hint at a political run. He first raised suspicion about Obama's nationality in March 2011 on the popular daytime TV program, *The View*, asking, "Why doesn't [Obama] he show his birth certificate? There's something on that birth certificate that he doesn't like?"[54]
- In December 2013 Trump upped the ante on the birther theory, suggesting in a tweet that a Hawaiian state official had been murdered as part of the alleged conspiracy to hide the president's true place of birth (Fig. 1.1).
- Trump frequently uses misdirection, raising suspicions but attributing conspiratorial ideas to others. After the death of Supreme Court Justice Antonin Scalia, he told right-wing radio host, Michael Savage, "Well I just heard today, just a little while ago actually, I just

Donald J. Trump
@realDonaldTrump

How amazing, the State Health Director who verified copies of Obama's "birth certificate" died in plane crash today. All others lived

4:32 PM - 12 Dec 2013

↩ ♺ 2,804 ♥ 1,803

Fig. 1.1 Trump Birther Tweet

landed and I'm hearing it's a big topic, the question, and it's a horrible topic but they say they found the pillow on his face, which is a pretty unusual place to find a pillow."[55]

- Trump hyped the notion that vaccines have caused autism. "When I was growing up, autism wasn't really a factor," Trump said in 2007, "And now all of a sudden, it's an epidemic. Everybody has their theory. My theory, and I study it because I have young children, my theory is the shots. We've giving these massive injections at one time, and I really think it does something to the children." He repeated the charge in the second presidential debate. Trump accuses doctors of lying about the connection.[56]

- Typical of Trump's view on global warming was a tweet on January 1, 2014. "This very expensive GLOBAL WARMING bullshit has got to stop. Our planet is freezing, record low temps, and our GW scientists are stuck in ice." Another regular theme is that the Chinese government is behind the "hoax" (Fig. 1.2).

- Trump contended numerous times during the campaign that the Democrats would steal the 2016 election; that it was "rigged." His claims can be seen as capitalization of a longer standing claim of fraudulent voting, linked to efforts to pass more restrictive voter registration laws. Trump upped the ante by linking the questionable truth of fraudulent voting with his anti-immigration stance, having started his campaign with a promise to deport 11 million people. His allegation of voter fraud and a "rigged" election grew more persistent in October when polls showed Trump's support tanking

Donald J. Trump ⊘
@realDonaldTrump

The concept of global warming was created by and for the Chinese in order to make U.S. manufacturing non-competitive.

2:15 PM - 6 Nov 2012

↩   ↻ 28,379   ♥ 17,376

Fig. 1.2   Trump Global Warming Denial Tweet

and his chances of winning steadily receding. However, the theme of a conspiracy to rig the election outcome did not disappear, even after the election, as it served as a way for Trump to claim that he had actually won the popular vote, contradicting official results. And it continued to be an argument for his virulent anti-immigration policies.

- Throughout the campaign, Trump and his supportive media hammered away at the notion that Hillary Clinton has engaged in a cover-up of her culpability for the deaths of American diplomats at the hands of Jihadi fighters in Benghazi, Libya. He accused Clinton and her husband, the ex-President, of destroying evidence and exerting influence over the Attorney General to obstruct the investigation of emails improperly stored on her private server. To some observers, such as *538.com*'s Nate Cohen, FBI Director James Comey's letter announcing a reopening of the investigation (due to emails found on computer of disgraced former Democratic Representative Anthony Wiener), a week before the election, was a critical factor behind the decisive shift of undecided voters in the last days before balloting.[57] Trump led raucous crowds at campaign rallies in chants of "Lock Her Up," revealing mass anger and breakdown of elite decorum not seen in American politics at least since the Great Depression (I would say since the Civil War).

The early months of the Trump presidency demonstrated that Trump would continue to trade in conspiracist discourse and attacks on perceived enemies. Among the more astonishing claims were:

- Trump tweeted on November 27, 2016, "In addition to winning the Electoral College in a landslide, I won the popular vote if you deduct the millions of people who voted illegally." He claimed that massive numbers of immigrants cast ballots and also that busloads of voters moved across state lines from Massachusetts accounted for victories by Clinton and the Democratic Senatorial candidate.
- On March 4, 2017, Trump tweeted, "How low has President Obama gone to tapp [sic] my phones during the very sacred election process. This is Nixon/Watergate. Bad (or sick) guy!"
- In response to the news stories suggesting collaboration between his campaign and the Russian government, Trump approvingly cited claims by *Fox News* and *Breitbart News* that members of national security bureaucracy, especially the CIA and FBI, were leaking information to the media—part of a coordinated campaign by the "Deep State" to oust him from office.[58]
- Major media organizations are "not my enemy," they are "the enemy of the American people," Trump tweeted on February 17, 2017. He habitually refers to the mainstream news reports as "fake news," charging not just media bias but deliberate deception by news organizations.
- Trumpian conspiracy theories are not always authored by the president himself, but also by friendly media. In May 2016, Fox News Network carried an "investigative report" alleging that Seth Rich, a young Democratic Party staffer and victim of an unsolved murder, had leaked Clinton emails to Wikileaks. The story was broadcast just as news media were carrying stories that the Wikileaks were orchestrated by Russian saboteurs of the Democratic campaign. *Fox* later retracted the story without apology.[59]
- Trump did not originate theories that his administration faced enemies in the "Deep State," that is, the constellation of national security agencies that are often alleged (e.g., by Oliver Stone in two films, *JFK* and *Nixon*) to have conspired against constitutional authorities. He left it to close advisors, like Steve Bannon, to *Fox News* pundits, and to Internet conspiracy gurus, such as Alex Jones of InfoWars.com, to peddle it.[60] However, the president himself re-tweeted a message (June 17, 2017) from *Fox* host Sean Hannity, who was promoting his speech to be given that evening on "the Deep States allies in the media." Finally in May 2018, as the investigation of collusion between the Trump campaign and Russian

operatives, being carried out by Special Counsel Robert Mueller, a former FBI director and a registered Republican, began to yield indictments against Trump campaign officials and advisors, Trump began to speak openly of a Deep State conspiracy, coining the term "SpyGate" as a counterpart of "Russiagate."

This book treats not only these Trumpian assertions (and others) as conspiracy theories, but also does the same with many of the claims of his opponents. This does not mean that Trumpian theories have equal epistemological status, that is, have equal plausibility or warrant as those of his critics. For example, the Trumpian claim of a politically motivated murder of a Hawaiian official cannot withstand the most cursory outside scrutiny—though it was only reluctantly retracted by its original promotor (freerepublic.com). Many of the reports about Russian collusion with the Trump campaign were based on anonymous leaks, but the Special Counsel's indictments in advance of his final report (not released as of this writing) provided significant substantiation for claims of at least some of the allegations. At the same time, some of Trump's claims of conspiracies in the federal bureaucracy, though highly suspect, should not be casually dismissed. Whether as rogue agencies or under direction of constitutional authorities, military, intelligence, and police agencies have been involved in well-documented violations of citizen's rights at home and in conspiring to manipulate politics and overthrow governments elsewhere in the world. A report issued by Office of the Inspector General, US Department of Justice, in June 2018 documented significant anti-Trump sentiment within the FBI and Department during the 2018 election, including quotations that could be interpreted to show significant prejudice on the part of officials and investigators against Trump.[61]

OUTLINE OF THIS BOOK

This book begins with this chapter's call for a more serious theorizing about conspiracies and political phenomenon and a less dismissive attitude toward conspiracy theory in mainstream social science. Chapter 2 elaborates further on this theme, beginning not with Trump's own conspiratorial discourse, but with an example of how opposition responses to Trump have often also taken on a panicky, conspiratorial overtone. The chapter presents some of the key concepts borrowed from relatively recent new research on conspiracy theory, with stress upon the way "conspiracy theory" is used to define a regime of truth. The chapter presents a two-dimensional framework for evaluating conspiracy theories. One dimension is a five-point scale for judging conspiracy theories across a range from "unwarranted" to "warranted," with middle categories for theories about which we should remain agnostic to some degree. The second dimension concerns the level at which a conspiracy is hypothesized to impact social life. At most grand level are those which are global or "world" conspiracies, and at the opposite end of the three-point scale are petty conspiracies that proliferate throughout our everyday lives and in the political world. These are "petty" in the sense that any one of them alone only marginally impacts the course of politics and history, but their proliferation and collective visibility can have an impact on public trust and erode political legitimacy. Widespread, pervasive corruption, a form of political transaction that requires hidden collusion, comes to mind in this regard. In between petty and grand conspiracies are operational conspiracies, which is where the focus of political science ought to be directly. Here is where most consequential conspiracy theories of the Trump era to be found.

The heart of Chapter 3 looks more closely at conspiracy theories in the Trumpian era, evaluating how closely they fit the "paranoid style" but also making a critical evaluation of how the concept of "operational conspiracies" can be fruitfully applied, with a special focus on "fake news." Chapter 4 examines the role played by conspiracy and conspiracy theory in the 2016 election and the first 20 months of the Trump presidency. Although the focus will be on Trump, our lens is widened to include some examination of discourse used more broadly by three most important candidates, i.e., Clinton, Trump and Sanders. Chapter 5 picks up where Chapter 4 leaves off, examining how populist movements, left and right, have emerged in reaction to neoliberal globalization and arguing that not all populist leaders and movements should be stigmatized as practicing the "paranoid style." However, the global surge of right wing populism merits such a designation. Research on the Brexit referendum in Great Britain, the emergence of the National Front in France, and other right-wing parties bear strong commonalities to the Trump phenomenon. In both Chapters 4 and 5, an analysis of election results in Midwestern counties shows that where social and economic conditions are most "distressed" is where Democrats lost the "Blue Wall" that they expect would win them the Electoral College. Both chapters also dispute the tendency in much mainstream analysis to equate the populism associated with the Sanders campaign to that of Trump.

Chapter 6 examines the theme of Dark Money, arguing that it is a sphere of politics that generates conspiracies. Chapter 7 takes a similar approach to the "Deep State," treating it as a sphere of politics related to most of the epic scandals in post-War America. Both Dark Money and the Deep State are not conspiracy theories in themselves; they are spheres of politics where operational conspiracies are recurrent and injurious to democratic, constitutional government. These chapters also content that too often muckraking journalism and radical academic research into these spheres of politics get labeled as "conspiracy theory," a way of defining themselves outside the boundary of acceptable discourse as defined under the regime of truth.

Chapter 8 reprises the need to rethink how we use "conspiracy theory" as a form of thought discipline and urges political scientists to develop it into a theoretical tool to understand the age of Trump. We can expect to find that conspiracism and conspiracist discourse operates differently in societies that have historical memories of both imperial splendor and of humiliating colonialism than they do in the United State, a core, hegemonic society. However, there are also some striking similarities across cultures and nations that can help us understand both the roots of conspiracism not just as a mode of thought in the population but as a way of "doing politics."

CONCLUSION: THE NEED TO THEORIZE CONSPIRACIES

Instead of dismissing all conspiracy theories as pathology, this book argues for viewing conspiracies themselves (drawing on my earlier work) "as a form of collective, subjective behavior that deserves to be integrated into, not marginalized from explanations of a structural and historical character."[62] In fact, under some circumstances, conspiracy theories can be empowering when they are not elevated by their holders into holistic, comprehensive worldviews.

Most political science research and publishing involves theorizing just about every conceivable form of political behavior—except conspiracies. No one who refers to "voting behavior theory" would say that this body of work refers to "nonexistent voting." No one who refers to "democratic peace theory" would say it refers to a nonexistent problem—war and peace. No one who refers to "game theory" would say that their "games" have no place in explaining political outcomes. Yet, most academics and journalists continue to treat "conspiracy theory" as, in the words of Daniel Pipes, "A *conspiracy theory* [italics in the original] is fear of a non-existent conspiracy."[63]

I contend that conspiracies—like voting, civil disobedience, assassinations, political campaigns, making war, among other forms of doing politics—should be taken seriously as a form of subjective behavior, as a way of doing politics. Even that most seemingly deterministic historical and political theorist, Karl Marx, acknowledged that human beings "make their own history." That he added in the same sentence, "but they do not make it as they please."[64] Can conspiracies change history? Never by themselves, but are rarely absent entirely from historical accounts of watershed events. Are they relevant to politics? Now more than ever in the Trumpian era.

NOTES

1. Daniel Pipes, *Conspiracy: How the Paranoid Style Flourishes and Where It Comes From* (New York: The Free Press, 1997).
2. See for one example Chip Berlet, "Clinton, Conspiracism and Civil Society," Political Research Associates, 2009, available at http://www.uni-muenster.de/PeaCon/conspiracy/networks-01.htm (accessed December 31, 2017).
3. Frederic Jameson. "Cognitive Mapping," in *Marxism and the Interpretation of Culture*, ed. C. Nelson and L. Grossberg, 347–360 (Champaign–Urbana: University of Illinois Press, 1960).
4. Richard Hofstadter, *The Paranoid Style in American Politics* (New York: Vintage Reprints, 1968). The book expands on the original article in *Harpers Magazine*, November 1964, available at https://harpers.org/archive/1964/11/the-paranoid-style-in-american-politics (accessed July 18, 2017).
5. Hofstadter, *The Paranoid Style*.
6. See "How Groups Voted in 1992," Roper Public Opinion Research, available at https://ropercenter.cornell.edu/polls/us-elections/how-groups-voted/how-groups-voted-1992.
7. Seymour Martin Lipset, "Fascism—Let, Right and Center," in *Political Man* (Garden City, NY: Anchor Books, 1960). That finding is contested by other scholars, but Lipset's view is notable because of his standing as a founder of political sociology.
8. Matthew Gray, *Conspiracy Theories in the Arab World: Sources and Politics* (London: Routledge, 2010): 3, 37.
9. Timothy Melley, *Empire of Conspiracy: The Culture of Paranoia in Post-War America* (Ithaca: Cornell University Press, 2000): vii.

10. Gray, *Conspiracy Theories*: 35.
11. See Politfact.com, September 2012, available at http://www.politifact. com/truth-o-meter/statements/2012/sep/18/mitt-romney/romney-says-47-percent-americans-pay-no-income-tax (accessed June 12, 2018).
12. See Reddit, available at https://www.reddit.com/r/The_Donald/comments/8idyvj/obama_how_exactly_are_you_going_to_negotiate_that (accessed June 13, 2018).
13. Benjamin Barber, *Jihad vs. McWorld: Terrorism's Challenge to Democracy* (New York: Ballantine Books, 1996).
14. Adam Goldman, "The Comet Ping Pong Gunman Answers Our Reporter's Questions," *New York Times* (December 7, 2016).
15. Hofstadter, *The Paranoid Style*.
16. Rob Brotherton, *Suspicious Minds: Why We Believe Conspiracy Theories* (New York: Bloomsbury-Signet, 2015): 64.
17. See three works by Lasswell noted above: *Propaganda Technique in the World War; Psychopathology and Politics; Power and Personality*.
18. Bratich, *Conspiracy Panics: Political Rationality and Popular Culture* (Albany: Sate University of New York Press, 2008).
19. Bratich, *Conspiracy Panics*: 14–18.
20. I use term in the sense employed by Antonio Gramsci, *Selections from The Prison Notebooks* (London: ElecBook, 1999), available at http://abahlali. org/files/gramsci.pdf (accessed September 19, 2017).
21. Bratich, *Conspiracy Panics*: 3–4.
22. Bratich, *Conspiracy Panics*: 3–4.
23. Michal Bilewicz, Aleksandra Cichocka, and Wiktor Soral, eds., *The Psychology of Conspiracy* (New York: Routledge, 2015): ix–xv.
24. Bilewicz, et al., eds., *Psychology of Conspiracy*.
25. See Harold Lasswell, *Propaganda Technique in the World War* (New York: Knopf, 1927); *Psychopathology and Politics* (New York: Viking Press, 1930); *Power and Personality* (New York: Viking Press, 1948).
26. See David Nivens Jr., "Why Black People Need Conspiracy Theories," *Complex.com*, October 6, 2016.
27. The Center for Disease Control Describes the Study, available at https://www.cdc.gov/tuskegee/timeline.htm (accessed November 9, 2017).
28. Tim Golden, "Though Evidence Is Thin, Tale of C.I.A. and Drugs Has a Life of Its Own," *New York Times*, October 21, 1996, available at http://www.nytimes.com/books/98/09/27/specials/cia-thin.html (accessed December 7, 2017).
29. Golden, "Though Evidence is Thin."
30. http://www.laweekly.com/news/ex-la-times-writer-apologizes-for-tawdry-attacks-2614004.

31. See Kathryn Olmsted, *Real Enemies: Conspiracy Theories and American Democracy, World War I to 9/11* (New York: Oxford University Press, 2009): 188–193.
32. See Bratich, *Conspiracy Panics: Political Rationality and Popular* Culture (Albany: State University of New York Press, 2008): 79–89.
33. American Enterprise Institute for Public Policy Research (AEI), "Public Opinion on Conspiracy Theories," November 2013.
34. See, for example, Nate Silver, "Here's Some Proof Some Pollsters Are Putting Thumb on the Scale," *Fivethirtyeight.com*, November 14, 2014.
35. http://www.publicpolicypolling.com/main/2013/04/conspiracy-theory-poll-results-.html.
36. Joseph E. Uscinski and Joseph M. Parent, *American Conspiracy Theories* (New York: Oxford University Press, 2014).
37. The scale was developed through collaboration among a number of social psychologists and designed to permit cross culture measurement. See Uscinski and Joseph, *American Conspiracy Theories*: 161, fn. 67.
38. Uscinski and Parent, *American Conspiracy Theories*: 110.
39. Uscinski and Parent, *American Conspiracy Theories*: 130–153.
40. Joanne M. Miller, Kyle L. Saunders, and Christina E. Farhart, "Conspiracy Endorsement as Motivated Reasoning: The Moderating Roles of Political Knowledge and Trust," *American Journal of Political Science* 60, no. 4 (October 2016): 824–844.
41. Joanne M. Miller, Kyle L. Saunders, and Christina E. Farhart, "The Relationship between Perceptions or Lower Status and Conspiracy Theory Endorsement," Paper presented at eh Annual Meeting of the American Political Science Association, San Francisco, CA, August 31–September 3, 2017.
42. Lori Moore, "File: Decades of Doubts and Conspiracy Theories," *New York Times*, October 25, 2017.
43. Matthew Dentith, *The Philosophy of Conspiracy Theories* (London: Palgrave Macmillan, 2014): 6.
44. Zephyr Teachout, *Corruption in America: From Benjamin Franklin's Snuff Box to Citizens United* (Cambridge, MA: Harvard University Press, 2014).
45. See Harry C. West and Todd Sanders. "Power Concealed and Revealed in the New World Order," in West and Sanders, eds., *Transparency and Conspiracy: Ethnographies of Suspicion in the New World Order* (Durham, NC: Duke University Press): 1–37. Mark Fenster, *The Transparency Fix: Secrets, Leaks, and Uncontrollable Government Information* (Palo Alto, CA: Stanford University Press, 2017).

46. American Press Institute. *Americans and the News Media: What They Do— And Don't—Understand About Each Other*, The Media Insight Project, June 2018 (available for download from mediainsight.org, accessed June 15, 2018).

47. Broadcast posted on YouTube by BirtherReportDotCom, March 31, 2011 (accessed December 5, 2016).

48. *CNN*. "Donald Trump: I meant that Obama founded ISIS, literally," August 11, 2016.

49. Conor Lynch. "Paranoid Politics: Donald Trump's Style Perfectly Embodies the Theories of Renowned Historian," *Salon*, July 7, 2016, available at http://www.salon.com (accessed September 18, 2017).

50. Mark Fenster, *The Transparency Fix*: 1–16.

51. Tim Shorrock, "Obama's Crackdown on Whistle Blowers," *The Nation*, April 15, 2013.

52. Jason Schwartz, "Pentagon Reporters Frustrated by Mattis," *Politico*, September 19, 2017, and referring to George Schultz, "Former Secretary of State Weighs in on Rex Tillerson's Aversion to the Press," CBS News, September 19, 2017.

53. Links to sources were found at "58 Donald Trump Conspiracy Theories (and Counting!)," available at http://www.alternet.org/right-wing/58-donald-trump-conspiracy-theories-and-counting-definitive-trump-conspiracy-guide (accessed December 5, 2016).

54. "14 of Trump's most outrageous birther claims," *CNN*, September 16, 2016.

55. Clip available at https://w.soundcloud.com/player/?url=https%3A//api.soundcloud.com/tracks/247250427&color=ff5500&auto_play=↖false&hide_related=false&show_comments=true&show_user=true&show_reposts=false (accessed December 5, 2016).

56. Josh Hafenbrack, "Trump: Autism Linked to Child Vaccinations," *Sun-Sentinel* (West Palm Beach, December 28, 2007).

57. Nate Cohen, "The Comey Letter Probably Cost Clinton the Election," *538*, May 3, 2017, available at https://fivethirtyeight.com/features/the-comey-letter-probably-cost-clinton-the-election (accessed June 28, 2018).

58. Julia Manchester, "Trump promotes Hannity's 'Deep State' Monologue," *The Hill*, June 16, 2017.

59. David Folkenflik "Behind Fox News' Baseless Seth Rich Story," National Public Radio, August 1, 2017.

60. Niall Stanage, "Is Trump a Victim of the Deep State?" *The Hill*, June 5, 2017.

61. Office of the Inspector General, U.S. Department of Justice. A Review of Various Actions by theFederal Bureau of Investigation and Department

of Justice in Advance of the 2016 Election (Washington, DC, June 2018, available at https://int.nyt.com/data/documenthelper/39-justice-de-partment-report-fbi-clinton-comey/5e54a6bfd23e7b94fbad/optimized/full.pdf#page=1 (accessed June 15, 2018).

62. Daniel Hellinger, "Paranoia, Conspiracy, and Hegemony in American Politics," in *Transparency and Conspiracy: Ethnographies of Suspicion in the New World Order*, eds. Harry G. West and Todd Sanders (Durham, NC: Duke University Press, 2003): 205.

63. Pipes, *Conspiracy*. 21.

64. Karl Marx, *The Eighteenth Brumaire of Louis Bonaparte* (1852) sought to explain that most conspiratorial of activities, a coup d'etat, available at www.marxists.org/archive/marx/works/download/pdf/18th-Brumaire.pdf (accessed September 19, 2019).

CHAPTER 2

Paranoia, Conspiracy Panic, and the Regime of Truth

The impact of Richard Hofstadter's essay and book[1] on the "paranoid style" in American politics can be measured by the way the phrase is utilized so freely in popular discourse. Entering the phrase in the popular search engine yields well over 1.7 million results. Of these, 1.3 million results appear when we add "conspiracy" to the search. The power of the phrase is also reflected in over 700,000 results obtained by entering "not a conspiracy theory." The results largely consist of claims that challenge the "official story" about some event, that point toward wrongdoing by government, or toward myriad other types of claims whose proponents fear will cause them to be labelled "conspiracy theorists." Some of the links appearing in the first few pages are to a website, "notaconspiracytheory.com" that seeks to debunk theories, using independent but sophisticated discourse and high production values. The "bedrock theory" of conspiracy theories, the series creator tells us, is based upon "the projection of human intentions on complex events."[2]

The first part of this chapter provides an example of a prominent public intellectual who maintains that Russian operatives and important parts of the national security establishment interfered in the 2016 elections, yet who denies that he is engaged in promoting a conspiracy theory. This serves as a useful case for assessing some of the new work on conspiracy in communication theory, revealing how the meme "conspiracy theory" and "paranoid style" are used to discipline discourse—what Foucault calls a "regime of truth." The French philosopher maintained that each society has a "general politics" of truth: that is, has mechanisms

© The Author(s) 2019
D. C. Hellinger, *Conspiracies and Conspiracy Theories in the Age of Trump*, https://doi.org/10.1007/978-3-319-98158-1_2

to determine what types of discourse it accepts as legitimate, the procedures and norms used to distinguish true and false statements, the means for sanctioning violators, and the status of those who are charged with saying what counts as true.[3] We can think of the regime as the rules and procedures by which a belief is considered beyond doubt, at one end of the scale, and "crackpot" on the other. To label an idea as "crackpot" and its holder as "paranoid" are typical of how conspiracy theories are dismissed—a technique all the more effective because some theories are indeed far-fetched, dangerous, or distracting from the underlying causes of social or economic stress in a society and the misfortune that falls upon a segment of the population, such as those living in once vibrant communities now experiencing economic ruin.

After reviewing the issues raised by relatively recent work on conspiracism (post-1990), I propose a way of categorizing conspiracy theories (1) according to the scale and scope of their propositions and (2) according to whether these theories are warranted or not by the evidence provided, rather than a priori as paranoid or not worthy of serious debate, that is, whether they are a priori judged outside the "regime of truth." Probably any social system has such a "regime" e.g., in the sense of rules of debate and civility. Even the most liberal regime should put certain propositions—such as justifications for genocide or eugenics—beyond the pale of serious deliberation. But a broadly liberal "regime of truth" (I use this term to describe tolerance, not a particular socioeconomic order, e.g., laissez-faire capitalism) can facilitate or limit the search for truth.

We then look more closely at the issues surrounding the assassination of President John F. Kennedy, an event that marked the beginning of precipitous decline of trust in American government. More briefly, we will also consider the level of operation and degree of plausibility of "truther" theories, i.e., conspiracy beliefs about the terrorist attacks of September 11, 2001. Our goal is not to verify or refute the notion that a conspiracy lays behind these two very influential events. The goal is to use these cases to illustrate how "conspiracy theory" functions as a feature of a "regime of truth" to discipline what should be taken seriously by journalists, academics, and political pundits. Much of this book concerns itself with how Trump has disrupted this regime in the United States.

The literature theorizing about the uses and abuses of conspiracy theory has grown more diverse and rich in the last two decades, challenging the stereotypes of who believes, why they believe, and whether they are a danger to democracy. Rather simply allow certain theories to be shunted aside as "conspiracy theories," we need clearer notions of what conspiracy theories warrant our contention and which don't; which further demands for more transparency and accountability from government and ruling elites in general, which are indeed dangerous, make us prone to scapegoating and even worse consequences.

I'm Not a Conspiracy Theorist, But...

Perhaps the clearest example of conspiracism in opposition to Trump can be found in the tweets and columns of Paul Krugman, the Nobel Prize winning economist and star liberal columnist for the *New York Times*. First, a disclaimer: I am not arguing for equivalency between the conspiracist claims of Krugman and most of those of Trump and his acolytes at *Fox News*, *Breitbart*, *Infowars*.com, etc., especially regarding conspiracy theories trade in racist and sexist stereotypes. Krugman's rhetoric eschews know-nothing and anti-immigrant sentiments. Far from dismissing his concerns about Russian interference in the 2016 campaign, my purpose is to show that they are plausible *despite* bearing many of the hallmarks of conspiracy theory. Even so, Krugman is at pains to deny that he is a conspiracy theorist. When it comes to judging the truth value of claims related to "RussiaGate," we start with the acknowledgement that there is a plausible motive for Russian intervention, specifically in the Kremlin's toward American involvement in the Ukraine and displeasure with US funding for non-governmental organizations supporting opposition to its leader, Vladimir Putin. And by summer of 2018, there had accumulated considerable evidence for the claim that there was collusion between Trump campaign officials and Russians. Krugman is not simply fabricating fake news.

A second element that makes the charges against Trump and his campaign more credible is that there are some precedents for collusion between American presidential campaigns and foreign powers—by the Nixon campaign in 1968[4] and the Reagan campaign in 1980.[5] In other words, the collaboration between an American campaign and a foreign power with a stake in the outcome is hardly new. It only seems new because the regime of truth has managed to dim historical memory of these incidents, a theme we will reprise in Chapter 6, on the Deep State.

Krugman denies that he is a conspiracy theorist, lest he be labeled "paranoid." On November 22, 2016, referring to his endorsement of efforts to force recounts in Michigan, Wisconsin, and Ohio, he tweeted, "Truly last word: conspiracies do happen. You're only a 'conspiracy theorist' if—like voting fraud types—you won't take no for an answer." We will return to this point later in the chapter, but for now, let us consider the claim that Krugman wants to argue, a claim made even before ballots were cast. On November 7, he wrote, "Let's be clear: this was in fact a rigged election." Mostly, Krugman's argument focused on claims that Russian hackers and dissemination of propaganda shaped the election, but he did not rule out the possibility of vote tampering. "The election probably wasn't hacked," he tweeted on November 23, "but Clinton should demand recounts just in case."

On November 27, Krugman upped the ante, suggesting that Trump became president by the grace of the FBI and Russian President Vladimir Putin. "So Comey and Putin installed a crazy, vindictive can't-handle-the-truth" person in the White House." Perhaps the *Times* columnist only meant that the combined but uncoordinated actions of the two resulted in Trump's victory, but his column of January 16, 2017, was even more conspiratorial in tone and substance. "Did the Trump campaign actively coordinate with a foreign power? Did a cabal within the F.B.I. deliberately slow-walk investigations into that possibility? Are the lurid tales about adventures in Moscow true? We don't know, although Mr. Trump's creepy obsequiousness to Vladimir Putin makes it hard to dismiss these allegations." Once again he felt compelled to deny that his claims and hypotheses could be considered a conspiracy theory. "Remember, saying that the election was tainted isn't a smear or a wild conspiracy theory; it's simply the truth."

Another clear example can be found in his column of December 15, 2016, on reports that the Central Intelligence Agency holds that groups connected to the Russian government and Vladimir Putin were responsible for hacking into Democratic Party campaign computers with the intention of favoring Trump. Krugman writes,

> Let me explain what I mean by saying that bad guys hacked the election. I'm not talking about some kind of wild conspiracy theory. I'm talking about the obvious effect of two factors on voting: the steady drumbeat of Russia-contrived leaks about Democrats, and only Democrats, and the dramatic, totally unjustified last-minute intervention by the F.B.I., which appears to have become a highly partisan institution, with distinct alt-right sympathies.

It bears reflection for a moment on the last phrase of this quotation. A widely read columnist for the most important "newspaper of record" in the United States thinks that a major national security agency interfered in domestic politics to advance the agenda of the alt-right, a movement that includes fascist and racist tendencies.

In his column the next day (December 16), referring to FBI Director James Comey's announcement just before the election that the agency was reopening its investigation into emails kept by Clinton on her private computer, Krugman commented,

> And then there was the Comey letter. The F.B.I. literally found nothing at all. But the letter dominated front pages and TV coverage, and that coverage — by news organizations that surely knew that they were being used as political weapons — was almost certainly decisive on Election Day.

In effect, Krugman alleges that Comey deliberately allowed the FBI to be used to impact the election.

Krugman's renunciation of the label "conspiracy theory" has everything to do with how the phrase has become associated with pathology rather than with "theory." The phrase, "conspiracy theory" could alternatively be defined to mean (1) a theory about the causes and consequences of conspiracies in political life or, as *Merriam-Webster* does, (2) a theory that explains an event or situation as the result of a secret plan by usually powerful people or groups.[6] Quite clearly, Krugman is concerned that his allegations will be interpreted as Daniel Pipes defines conspiracy theories, as "fears of non-existent conspiracies."[7]

To reiterate, in singling out Krugman my point is not to reject, much less ridicule his warnings. What his tweets and columns show is that in the age of Trump conspiracy beliefs are not limited to unscrupulous politicians and to those "deplorables" who voted for a candidate whose racism, hypocrisy, and erratic behavior exceed just about anyone's standards for decency in personal or political relationships. When it comes to the 2016 presidential election, Krugman is a "Truther." Conspiracism in the age of Trump is not just for ultra-conservatives.

In the current era of Trump, we should not be surprised that the right is trying to turn the tables on the left, accusing Krugman and other liberals of conspiracist tendencies quite similar to ones that Hofstadter outlines.[8] Certainly most readers of the *New York Times*, even if not entirely in agreement with Krugman, would reject labeling his views as conspiracy theory. Yet what Krugman and many Trump opponents expound is a theory suggesting that Russian invention significantly aided right-wing political forces to seize a remarkable degree of institutional power,

power used to dismantle significant parts of the welfare and regulatory state, power over a nuclear arsenal that quite literally could end human life on earth. Perhaps this explains why Krugman and other prominent liberal intellectuals have embraced theories that only 18 months earlier would have earned them the scorn reserved in the past for Chomsky or Marxists.

Hofstadter described the paranoid style in American politics as a recurrent, right-wing populist phenomenon characterized by back-lashes against immigration, which at the time he wrote (1964) he saw re-emerging in the Goldwater movement.[9] Trump's campaign can be viewed as yet another episode in this style. However, I contend that the "paranoid style" framework should not be applied to many claims of conspiracy in political life. I argue that conspiracist discourse is articu-lated not only by the president and his supporters, but also by his oppo-nents. Krugman may be right or wrong, but he is not paranoid. He is by many definitions a conspiracy theorist in the sense that he attributes an important political outcome to a conspiracy involving a foreign power and disloyal Americans. Even if we allow, as we should, that Krugman would acknowledge other factors behind Trump's victory, it is unmis-takable that he thinks the election's outcome would have been different without collusion and foreign interference.

Krugman's disavowal of conspiracy theory is the norm, not the excep-tion, and it is just as widespread in academia as in journalism. Take, for example, the intellectual gymnastics of two political scientists who became perplexed when their research produced a finding that seemed to contradict their predictions about pre-dispositions toward conspiracism. Adam Enders and Steven Smallpage found evidence that a set disposi-tions (a Generic Conspiracist Belief Scale, or GCBS) indicative of a suspi-cious mind, taken to be linked to paranoid conspiracism, were predictive to some degree of the likelihood of believing each of the 9 of 10 theo-ries: Birther Theory, Truther Theory, rejection of lone gunman in the JFK assassination, vaccination links to autism, airplane vapor trails (as CIA chemical experiments), faked moon landing, climate change denial, rejection of official story regarding the death of Princess Diana. But the authors were at a loss at first to explain the finding that the 10th theory tested, Russiagate, was generally negatively correlated with belief in the other conspiracies and with the GCBS. They ruminated,

Indeed, the GCBS scale employed here was designed to capture the general predisposition to see the world through the lens of conspiracy. As such, we are somewhat dismayed that it does not aid in classifying "Russiagate" beliefs. While it could be that the specific operationalization of conspiracy ideation (the GCBS) that we employ here is failing in this instance, we find it more likely that the simply is not much truly "conspiratorial" content to the "Russiagate" conspiracy theory.[10]

Effectively, they "explain" the inconsistency of the GCBS by defining away the problem.

THE SHADOW OF HOFSTADTER

There is no settled definition of what constitutes a "conspiracy", much less a "conspiracy theory." Daniel Pipes, a hawkish academic specialist on Middle Eastern affairs and author of one of the most widely read books on the subject, unhelpfully defines a conspiracy theory is "fear of a non-existent conspiracy."[11] Not that some conspiracy theories shouldn't be considered as little more than fanciful, more suitable for entertainment purposes than social science and history. Examples include that the Illuminati, a secretive group of Free Masons, was the author of major revolutions (including the American and French revolutions) and is currently carrying out plans to establish a New World Order.[12] More alarming, given the persistence devastation wrought by anti-Semitism, is the theory that Jews have a secret plan to rule the world through domination of financial institutions.[13] More humorous is the contention that Lizard people populate the US government, which one survey claims to be believed by 12 million Americans.[14]

It is Richard Hofstadter's conception of conspiracy theories as the "paranoid style" of populist politics that has most informed students of conspiracy theory—though Pipes and many others who have embraced Hofstadter's characterization seem to have forgotten that he allowed that such theories are held by "normal" people. Conspiracy theories, he says, are not an actual pathology but style of discourse. Though his concern was focused on the United States, his work dominates the study of conspiracism elsewhere in the world as well. He associates conspiracy theory with four traits: It is (1) a recurrent phenomenon associated with periodic outbreaks of populism in US history; (2) recognizable by suspicion, exaggeration, and fantasy; (3) starts from facts but then leaps up to broader and higher levels of explanation; and (4) attributes the outcomes of large impersonal forces to acts of will by elites.[15]

The notion of "normal" here is ambiguous, at best. Hofstadter wrote out of a sense that extremist ideas were dangerously on the rise in 1964, abetted by the Goldwater campaign. He could not have realized that by associating conspiracy theory with paranoia, even if only in style, he defined the course of research that would treat conspiracy theory as pathological and subject to investigation by psychologists. Still, there is an ominous tone when he warns, "Although the *paranoid style* (my emphasis) is always with us, it tends to wax and wane in relevance, lapsing into long periods of obscurity on the fringes of the political spectrum (left and right) and coming back when least expected."[16] By definition, being on the fringe is not "normal," certainly not in a statistical sense. By using the term "paranoid" and associating it with populism Hofstadter's approach cannot be entirely divorced from psychologically based explanations for conspiracy beliefs or from the tendency to associate populism with conspiracy theories.

This book is partly about revising Hofstadter's legacy, most notably its role in branding, perhaps indelibly, "conspiracy theory" as "paranoia" and in linking populism to irrationality. However, his identification of the recurrent themes of that era harkening back to earlier eras of populism is highly relevant to the threats posed to democracy in America today by Trumpism. His concern was with right-wing populism, which spawned anti-immigrant prejudice, white supremacy, and what he famously coined the "paranoid style" in public discourse. His essays on the subject were inspired by his alarm at the right-wing discourse encouraged by Barry Goldwater, the Republican nominee for president in 1964. As I review and critique aspects of the book, there should be no mistaking that whatever its flaws, Hofstadter's warnings about the recurrent origins and features of right-wing populism in the United States remain highly relevant to Trumpism.

Without exception, everyone who studies and writes about conspiracy theory makes the disclaimer that "conspiracies exist." They differ regarding the status they accord to conspiracy theories. That is, they differ as to whether "conspiracy theory" should be about understanding the role, influence, and causes of conspiracism, or should be about understanding why some people hold what most academics and journalists consider to be crazy or paranoid ideas. In contrast to those who see conspiracy theories as inherently dangerous, or at least posing obstacle to addressing social and economic issues, some new scholarly work, reviewed below, in communication theory warns that the label "conspiracy theory" is used to induce "conspiracy panic" against those who raise uncomfortable issues and question "prevailing understandings" and "simple facts."

If conspiracies exist, why do so many studies devoted to "conspiracy theory" seek to deny their importance as political activities, or sometimes even their existence? Why are conspiracy theorists often portrayed as pathological, as afflicted with a mental illness? Chip Berlet, a prolific student of conspiracism whose research has exposed many of the most bigoted and violence-prone right-wing purveyors of conspiracy theories, denies any legitimacy to treating conspiracy theories as a method of political analysis. According to Berlet, "Even the most sincere and well-intentioned conspiracy theorists contribute to the dangerous social dynamics of demonization and scapegoating."[17]

Something of this nature been a point of criticism of theories positing Kremlin intervention in the American election. Although they do not specifically refer to Krugman by name, two critics of Krugman who are unsympathetic to Trump warned that fears of Russian meddling and suspicions of malfeasance by the Trump administration are feeding "tyrannophobia" in the United States. They argue, "Americans have… embraced…a new Cold War between totalitarianism and democracy." Echoing a frequent theme in Berlet's work, they charge that focusing on Russian collusion is "distracting from the deeply rooted forces that have been fueling right-wing populist politics, notably economic inequalities and status resentments."[18]

While this depiction of conspiracy theories as worse than useless for people seeking to identify the causes and the political sources of their social and economic distress no longer goes unchallenged, it continues to prevail even among cultural critics who treat conspiracy theories as symptomatic of the "real" causes of popular discontent. For example, Peter Knight opens his insightful 2000 study of conspiracy theories in popular culture by acknowledging that they are "no longer the exclusive house-style of the terminally paranoid" and that they are found not only in popular culture but in elite culture as well. They are, he says, "now less likely to give bent to alarmist fears about an occasional irruption of the normal order of things, than to express a not entirely unfounded suspicion that the normal order of things itself amounts to a conspiracy."[19] As promising as this sounds, however, Knight goes on in much of the book to suggest that using conspiratorial frameworks to address oppression is not fruitful. For example, though he praises Betty Friedan's *Feminine Mystique* as "pioneering" in advancing feminism, Knight goes on to criticize Friedan and other feminists who claim that patriarchy requires conscious agency on the part of males. Knight acknowledges that Friedan herself rejects the "conspiracy theory" label, but he argues that she does in fact advance a conspiracy theory by referring to "brainwashing" and contending that male professionals engage in all sorts of sexist practices and social advice to "manipulate" women back to domesticity after World War II.[20]

Had Frieden reduced the explanation of how patriarchy is created and maintained to the machinations of a conspiracy among men one could indeed criticize her for oversimplifying the construction and maintenance of patriarchy. But were men and, one could argue, women such as Phyllis Schlafly who abetted them, to be regarded as without any agency or responsibility in maintaining patriarchy? Were the men who monopolized, even more than today, positions of power in corporate, cultural and political life completely unconscious of the policies and actions they took, not to speak of the myriad little conspiracies (well-depicted in the popular HBO series *Mad Men*) that maintained glass ceilings and required women to return to domesticity, whether they wanted to or not? Could a movie mogul such as Miramax's Harvey Weinstein have assaulted so many Hollywood actresses and other female employees over 20 years before his comeuppance in 2017 without a conspiracy of silence among the nine men who served on the board of his production company?[21]

Cass Sunstein departs somewhat from the paranoid style approach in arguing that a conspiracy theory need not be a delusional explanation. He defines conspiracy theory as "an effort to explain some event or practice by referring to the secret machinations of powerful people who have also managed to conceal their role." However, he finds conspiracy theories as unlikely to explain much because in "free societies" conspiracies with significant consequences are subject to exposure. Sunstein wants to explain "why rational people sometimes believe crazy conspiracy theories."[22] Like so many others he acknowledges that conspiracies exist, but he has no interest in exploring what consequences this has for policy, history, the exercise of policy. He acknowledges that some conspiracy theories turn out to be true, but explains that his focus is on false theories and, within that set, dangerous ones.

Stressed undergraduates and busy professors will find popular sources for defining "conspiracy theory" tie it causally to the paranoid style. *Wikipedia's* definition does not stray far from the paranoid style. Its definition of conspiracy is "an explanation of an event or situation that invokes a conspiracy without warrant, generally one involving an illegal or harmful act carried out by government or other powerful actors." The online encyclopedia adds, "Conspiracy theories often produce hypotheses that contradict the prevailing understanding of history or simple facts. The term is a derogatory one."[23] It should not escape the notice of a critical reader that Wiki's definition is not far from that of Pipes. Even acknowledging that we can tell a "simple fact" when we see one, should a conspiracy theory be dismissed for contradicting a "prevailing understanding of history"?

Historian Kathryn Olmsted partly breaks from the academic consensus in finding that conspiracy theories can sometimes be empowering for people with little influence over elites. One of her case studies of twentieth-century conspiracy theory involved suspicions that the CIA had been complicit in the trafficking of crack from Central America, where the United States was involved in promoting insurgency against the leftist Sandinista government in Nicaragua, into Los Angeles. Another of her case studies involved a group of New Jersey housewives ("Jersey Girls") who believed the Bush administration was conniving to prevent a full and impartial investigation into the 9/11 attacks on the World Trade Centers. Whether or not either effort ultimately exposed the "truth" behind the most heinous suspicions, in each case ordinary citizens forced a degree of accountability that embarrassed and angered officials. In the first instance, the CIA Director felt it necessary to take the unprecedented step of meeting with community activists, whom he tried (unsuccessfully) to reassure that the Agency would fully investigate their charges. In the latter case, the Jersey girls mobilized public support that forced the Bush administration to form an independent commission to investigate the 9/11 attacks.[24]

In her introductory chapter Olmsted defines conspiracy as "when two or more people collude to abuse power or break the law" and a conspiracy theory as "a proposal about a conspiracy that may more may not be true; it has yet been proven." In her conclusion, however, she admonishes readers that conspiracy theories have little use for correcting abuses of power; their proper use is as case studies that may identify the "sources of the illness." In other words, conspiracy theories may uncover facts the government wants to hide, but at base they remain symptoms of social and political pathologies and are themselves more dangerous than useful.[25] This conclusion needs to be reconciled with her Introduction and also needs to be problematized. It seems more persuasive when applied to theories that with a broad brush taint the federal government with heinous and perfidious acts; it is difficult to square with her accounts of how the Jersey Girls and the African-American community forced a defensive response from the state and achieved some accountability from elites for actions that they preferred to remain in the dark.

THE REGIME OF TRUTH

The potential for conspiracy theories to challenge "prevailing under-standings" is at the heart of two works in communication theory raise important issues about the "paranoid style" meme in work on conspiracy theory. Mark Fenster's 1999 book *Conspiracy Theories Secrecy and Power in American Culture* and Jack Bratich's 2008 book *Conspiracy Panics* have especially influenced my approach.[26] Fenster's work was among the first to question the way that the term "conspiracy theory" is used to delegitimize political discourse that questions the assumptions associ-ated with American exceptionalism and pluralist theories of democracy. Critical of both Hofstadter's and Pipes' treatment of conspiracy theory as pathology, Fenster contends that conspiracy theories should not be regarded as a form of paranoia and can have effects that are "wide rang-ing and salutary." Nonetheless, some of Hofstadter's paranoia seems to creep into Fenster's definition of conspiracy theory as an assertion that "a secret, omnipotent individual or group covertly controls the political and social order, or some part thereof."[27]

"Omnipotent" captures the notion of awe that does characterize some of the most fantastic theories or quasi-religious political theories based on a particular hermeneutic, for example, millennialism. But omnipo-tence is more likely to be found in conspiracy theories depicted in popu-lar fiction (James Bond, Wonder Woman, etc.) whereby a hero struggles to save the world from a villainous super-criminal sometimes working on behalf of a Manichean enemy of humankind. Indeed, this theme pre-dominates in many of the best-known theories, such as those associated with MCCarthyism, with its Manichean view of Communism. But are all conspiracy theories of this ilk?

Bratich's critique focuses on how academics and journalists delegitimate certain social criticism as "conspiracy theory," arguing that instead of assuming that we know what is and is not a conspiracy theory, we "need to examine the very conditions of recognition," i.e., how do we qualify some theories as worthy of serious consideration and dismiss others. Those who do this work and their practices constitute what he calls (drawing on the French philosopher, Michel Foucault) a "regime of truth." Instead of dismissing theories, such as those which swirl around 9/11 and the assassination of JFK, we should recognize that conspiracy theories "are portals to specific issues, but more importantly they collectively function as doorways to a broader *context*" (ital. in original).[28]

Bratich (2008: 9) advises, "I would argue that rather than accept conspiracy theories as a real danger to the health of the body politics, we need to ask how the risky thought encapsulated in conspiracy theory is generated discursively, under what conditions, and to what ends." Not all "conspiracy theory" is worthy of serious consideration; but there can be a chilling result from dismissing journalistic and scholarly work that warns of elite duplicity and networking, thereby questioning democratic nature and legitimacy of the American state. Hence, most analyses of conspiracy theories is, says Bratich, "symptomatic," that is, for most academics the main reason to study conspiracism is to uncover the reasons why people believe the unbelievable, not to test the epistemological value of the theory itself.[29] So, for example, although Olmsted allows that conspiracy theories may sometimes serve the interests of the less powerful in a society, her view is that conspiracy theories are symptomatic; that they are distracting at best, pathological at worst.

Bratich does not offer a definition of "conspiracy theory," mainly because his book is devoted to showing how the term is used to discredit certain forms of knowledge. Rather than argue the truth or falseness of a particular conspiracy theory, Bratich argues that characterizing a particular interaction, analysis, or theory ("narrative") as a conspiracy theory is a way of disciplining deviance. This practice is a form of "social panic" that he calls "conspiracy panic." He continues, "'Conspiracy theory' functions as an intolerable line and an antagonism…The scapegoating of conspiracy theories provides the conditions for social integration and political rationality. Conspiracy panics help to define the normal modes of dissent."[30]

I have made a similar argument in a study of three conspiracy theories related to the exercise of American power to maintain its hegemony. The three theories I explored were (1) that US National Security apparatus were responsible for the assassination of John F. Kennedy; (2) that the CIA was complicit in setting off the crack cocaine epidemic in African-American neighborhoods of Los Angeles; and (3) that power elites are conspiring to undermine sovereign, democratic power in the United States and elsewhere in order to replace with global government, often characterized as a "new world order." While the truth value of these theories varies considerably, what they have in common is that in each case there is alleged to be a conspiracy that stands in contradiction to the democratic requirement for transparency in public affairs.[31]

This connection between transparency and democracy was well articulated by Senator Richard Burr (R-NC), chair of Senate Select Committee on Intelligence, in setting the goals of his committee when it convened to take testimony from James Comey, who had been fired from his FBI directorship by President Trump, fueling suspicions that President Trump was guilty of obstructing justice. Burr said, "We will establish the facts, separate from rampant speculation, and lay them out for the American people to make their own judgment. Only then will we as a nation be able to move forward and to put this episode to rest."[32]

Fenster calls this kind of faith in open government "the transparency fix", that is, a belief that it can lead to knowledge and power for citizens.[33] It is an assumption that stands behind federal and state "sunshine acts" that require open meetings and deliberation of public policy, calls for stricter recording of campaign finance, and the press's recourse to "fact checking" political claims. Transparency on the international level is the goal of financier George Soros' Open Society Institute as well as the anti-corruption NGO, Transparency International. The explosion of interest in decentralized cryptocurrencies, such as Bitcoin, has been fueled by the notion that transactions in these currencies are more transparent because they take place in ledgers, called "blockchains," that are open to examination by all who trade them.[34] However, John Griffin, a highly successful identifier of financial scams, found that about half of the exceptional rise in the value of Bitcoins in 2017 was actually the result of manipulation of the currency by Bitfinex, a large trading service, which took advantage of its servicing a number of different cryptocurrencies to use one of the latter to prop up the value of Bitcoins. Its trades were recorded, but it took months of investigation to understand just how the manipulation occurred.[35]

There is much to recommend in Fenster's warnings about making a fetish of transparency. As the Bitcoin example shows, it is doubtful that in a complex society with rapid flows of information and large bureaucracies, full transparency, even if attainable, would not necessarily bring all conspiracies into the daylight. And there are areas of diplomacy, security, and protection of privacy for which full transparency would be hurtful or counterproductive (see Chapter 1). However, there are strong indications that politics and social life are growing more and more opaque in contemporary America. To take two examples explored in Chapters 6 and 7, respectively, national security agencies have a long history of engaging in counter democratic surveillance and operations that have no justification other than defense of state or elite interests; the flow of money in electoral politics has not only increased but become virtually untraceable, resulting in the pernicious influence of Dark Money.

Bratich sees "symptomology" as a form of "conspiracy panic."[36] Given that "symptom" is so closely associated with disease, this is understandable. Insofar as symptomology is associated with the notion that all conspiracy theories are *a priori* irrational, this approach reinforces the hegemony defined by the regime of truth. I would argue, however, that almost all social science is symptomatic in the sense that social scientists, including political scientists, share with conspiracy theorists an agenda to reveal through our research patterns of power and influence that are not evident on the surface of things. Like conspiracy theorists, we social scientists seek to look below the surface of "reality" to get at patterns of social life that are not fully visible or understood. Perhaps this is why sociologist Fredric Jameson is hardly alone in regarding conspiracy theory as the "poor man's cognitive mapping."[37]

At this point, we should take note that conspiracy theories are not solely the cognitive maps of the masses. They frequently originate in elite circles. A historical example can be taken from the American Revolution. Bernard Bailyn, a distinguished historian of the ideology of the American Revolution, examined conspiratorial ideas among the founders in the era of War for Independence and the writing of the Constitution. Bailyn wrote his most important works contemporaneously with Hofstadter, but he took a quite different approach to conspiracy. He argued that conspiracies theories spun by writers on both sides of the independence cause varied in degree of factual basis but simultaneously provide an important window into the thinking of the colonists. They played an important role in political mobilization and influencing political values.[38]

Rather than blaming mass ignorance for some of the more paranoid conspiracy theories in circulation today, it makes more sense to see conspiracism as a complex phenomenon that requires a synergy between elites that have self-interested motives for dissembling such theories and mass publics that live in times of uncertainty and disruption. From the Salem Witch Trials to McCarthyism, political power or disenfranchisement of certain groups has created conditions that can be exploited by propaganda. What is perhaps different today is that the Internet has made mass communication more accessible to non-elites. But even today the ability to spread false conspiracy theories for political or economic gain is limited without the economic and political clout of elites. While an individual in front of a computer scene can post something viral, one lesson of the 2016 election is that most widely disseminated false news on the Internet is, if not fabricated by political operatives, spread by the use of bot-software deployed by campaigns, interest groups, and foreign governments.

HISTORIANS, SOCIAL SCIENCE AND "PROVING" CONSPIRACY THEORY

Central to the project of this book is the argument that the public, especially academics and journalists, be on-guard against dismissing all social and political criticism with conspiratorial undertones as "paranoid", and to also be on guard against being panicked to abandoning radical criticism by being charged with promoting a conspiracy theory. I will take this up further in chapters dealing with "Dark Money" and with the concept of a "Deep State." To accomplish this, first I want to suggest separating theories and beliefs that have little warrant from those worthy on the basis of evidence to be considered plausible. Second, although I think that grand, world conspiracy theories are worthy of attention for the study mass behavior and psychology, I argue that there exist middle range conspiracy theories, which I will call "operational conspiracies," that deserve a place in explanations of many political events, though they must always be placed within the context of historical context and socioeconomic structures.

Olmsted insists that we evaluate a conspiracy theory on the basis whether it has been "proven."[39] This places a requirement on conspiracy theories that goes beyond what is required of the social and natural sciences. The more salient criticism that Olmsted should level is that many conspiracy theories are not subject to disproof, that is, as Krugman put it, promoted by someone who won't "take no for an answer." It is fair to ask someone who advances a conspiracy theory what it would take to prove them wrong, but it exceeds what we ask of the scientists themselves to ask that a conspiracy theory be proved. Karl Popper, one of the most ardent critics of conspiracy, points out that science demands that hypotheses be put forward for disproof. Academic knowledge depends on a process of consensus, that is, upon acceptance of paradigms. But as Kuhn has shown, paradigms are largely schools of thought, sometimes competing, sometimes uncontested, about the way nature works. Conspiracy theories challenge key paradigms of mainstream political science.[40]

Jodi Dean has alerted us to the consensual nature of knowledge in his work on people who have reported UFO sightings or claimed to have been abducted. "This so-called consensus reality is exclusionary;" he writes, "it is based on the silencing and discrediting of real, everyday people, people who want to be heard…As long as they are dismissed and objectified, as long as they don't count as citizens whose voice and opinions are worth taking seriously, then the truth will only be a play of power."[41] In fact, after years of the media dismissing UFO sightings as paranormal, suddenly the news media on December 2017 was carrying reports that a major Pentagon program to study such phenomenon had existed for years behind the innocuous title, "Advanced Aviation Threat Identification Program", and that its most important patron was Senator Harry Reid (D-Nevada), leader of the Democratic Party in the Senate. A former official who led the program, Luis Elizondo, resigned in protest from the Defense Department over what he regarded as excessive secrecy about the program and said, "There is very compelling evidence that we may not be alone."[42]

Historians, especially those doing narrative history, share the academic reluctance to theorize about conspiracy, but it is sometimes impossible to tell the story without referring to conspiracy, sometimes by name. Conspiracies among Roman senators are relevant to understanding Rome's transition from Republic to Empire. The Gunpowder Plot is relevant to understanding the politics of the English monarchy in Shakespeare's day. The conspiratorial tactics of Lenin's Bolsheviks help us understand how and why the Russian Revolution happened, if not "why." The intervention of the CIA in Iran, Guatemala, and Chile help us understand how brutal dictatorships took hold in those countries. In none of these cases can we be satisfied that conspiracy simply explains the outcome, but can conspiracy be left out of the narrative? It is hard to see how.

In some cases, conspiracies, such as persecution of witches, were important tools for stripping women of wealth and influence. Such malevolent conspiracy theories (anti-Semitic ones are another such case) are suitable not only for symptomatic analysis but also for actual investigation. Conspiracy theories that have accompanied the rise of Trumpism can tell us much about American politics, especially as we uncover parallels in the past. We should expect conspiracies to be associated with efforts to reveal and explain recurrent corruption, dirty wars conducted by national security agencies, the massive and hidden transformation of wealth into political power, and other maladies of a threatened democracy. Conspiracies are not just symptoms of "something rotten in Denmark," but a source of the stench.

We need to develop ways to parse unwarranted, often malevolent conspiracy theories from those that are at least plausible, if not warranted as true. My starting point is not that we must eliminate any "regime of truth" to accomplish this task so much as to develop ways to construct a regime that is more democratic and open to ideas on the margins. I want to begin by suggesting the criteria by which we should judge the plausibility of a conspiracy theory. If the age of Trump is likely see more conspiracy theories arise across the political spectrum (not just on the right), we will need to think about how we identify the ones that should be taken seriously, and how we assess whether they are malevolent or, one the other hand, addressing malevolence.

A good example of misuse of "conspiracy theory" by a researcher can be found in how some important issues are characterized by Joseph Uscinski, even though his research is among the few examinations of conspiracy beliefs that can be credited with testing some common assumptions about conspiracism (e.g., that conspiracism reached unprecedented highs in American culture after the Kennedy assassination) (see Chapter 1). In a YouTube video raising concerns about the theory that we live in a post-truth world, Uscinski rightly points to some examples of conspiracy theories that are commonly associated with the paranoid style. He goes on, however, to suggest (perhaps unintentionally) that questioning the safety of vaccinations falls into the same irrational rejection of scientific fact as questioning the safety of Genetically Modified Foods or nuclear power.[43]

My objection is not to labeling such suspicions as conspiracy theories, assuming what is meant is that there are powerful corporate interests that might manipulate scientific examination of these theories. After all, there is plenty of evidence that this has happened with a range of corporate funding of research on tobacco and various foods. The question is whether it is appropriate to argue that the scientific and social facts about vaccination, nuclear power, and GMO seeds are sufficiently established to place concerns about safety as beyond question, outside the regime of truth. While these theories are not "proven," and while refusals to have children vaccinated do pose risks to public health, should we regard questioning vaccinations as in some way pathological? Do all conspiracy theories share the same epistemological status—that is, all are based on fraudulent facts or very faulty logic and must be "proven" before taken seriously? And is the best way to combat a theory, such as resistance of parents to vaccinations or fears about fluoride in water, to alienate its holders by calling them, in effect, crazy?

A TYPOLOGY OF CONSPIRACY THEORIES

Conspiracy theories range from those about relatively petty affairs, such as office promotions, allocation of small grants, etc. to grand theories attributing to some cabal or secret organization the power to make a revolution or engineer new world order. In the first category are conspiracies that singly have little impact on politics, though they may collectively erode confidence and trust in elites. Such is the case with corruption, as citizens that daily deal with minor bribes or read of suborned public officials are understandably likely to develop a jaundiced view of the rule of law. Grand theories pertain to claims that conspiracies operate on a world or civilizational level. The conspiracy theories that merit the most attention are those that fall into the middle ground—"operational conspiracies" that lie behind coups, rigged elections, lies about motives for war, destabilization of other nation's politics, etc. Conspiracy theories at all three levels may be fanciful or grounded in reality; may give rise to scapegoating or identify wrongdoing; may expose the systematic attempt by elites to exploit ethnic or religious prejudice or be used to the incite violence or, in the worst cases, even genocide.

Thus, I propose that we evaluate the historical and political import of conspiracy theories along two axes: (1) level and (2) plausibility of the hypothesized conspiracy.

Level or Scope of a Conspiracy

Level corresponds to the outcome sought by conspirators—world (sometimes called "grand"), operational, and petty. This categorization is adapted from an approach recommended by Pipes. World conspiracies, he says, seek global power in order to "challenge the existing order or humanity at large." By contrast, petty conspiracies have more limited objectives, says Pipes.[44] Level might also be conceived to refer to the magnitude of the consequences posed by a particular conspiracy theory.

Pipes' application of his categories is biased and inconsistent. In his view the Iran-Contra Affair was "petty," even though it did have an ambitious (my term, not his) agenda: improving relations with one regime (the Iranian Revolution), funding the overthrow of another (the Sandinista Revolution in Nicaragua). Pipes categorizes Stalin and Hitler as authors of an operational conspiracy, but in other places he elevates both Communism and Fascism to the status of "world conspiracies." Because Lenin saw the Russian Revolution as a precursor to a global, social order, Pipes says, "His was truly a world conspiracy." He asserts, "The Russian Revolution was a real conspiracy carried out by Lenin and others; it was also subject to conspiracy theories involving everyone from the eighteenth-century Illuminati to contemporary German socialists and the Elders of Zion."[45] It is quite possible that Pipes means in the second part of this quotation to exclude such theories from the regime of truth, but in reality Pipes reveals himself to be a grand conspiracy theorist. It is one thing to recognize that the business of rebelling against an established state requires conspiracy, but it is another to see conspiracy as the essence of Lenin's political project.

Pipes' ideological bias accounts for his confused categorizations. Conspiracy theories linked to Marxism and Muslim culture are usually seen as grand, comparable to theories attributing world-shaking events to the Illuminati, a tendency that also marks his other major work on conspiracism, *Hidden Hand: Middle East Fears of Conspiracy.* As Matthew Gray remarks in *Conspiracy Theories in the Arab World,* Pipes work is polemical and "flawed by Pipes' pathological explanations for conspiracism, his preoccupation with anti-Semitism, and his oversimplification." Pathological explanations for conspiracism in the Arab world are too often, says Gray, "driven by Orientalist simplification of the region's political culture."[46]

Gray's insights have considerable relevance for understanding conspiracism not only in other post-colonial societies, but in the United States itself (see Chapter 8). Here I mainly want to appropriate the usefulness of Pipes' distinguishing not only between "grand" or "minor" conspiracies but to a third category that he also mentions, but confusingly conflates with grand conspiracy theories. This middle level is an "operational conspiracy theory," referring "to circumstances in which conspiracy theories have an influence of policy decisions of governments or other powerful institutions."[47] Pipes uses this category to classify (in 1999) the states of Iran and Iraq. However inconsistent and biased his application, his differentiation of conspiracy theories (and conspiracies, by extension) by their scope (i.e., "level") is useful. The rows of Table 2.1 differentiate some well-known conspiracy theories by level.

I concede that there is no precise way to categorize theories by scope. Many minor (or "petty') conspiracies often have great consequences for those deceived or victimized—for example, for elderly people defrauded by various consumer scams. Those who placed bets on the Chicago Whites Sox to win the 1919 baseball World Series may have lost a good part of their personal fortunes; owners (like myself) of Volkswagen diesel automobile were deceived by the companies unlawful evasion of environmental protection regulations, and a serious degree of harm was done to the environment. A great number of minor conspiracies can add up to more serious consequences on the same level as that of a single operational conspiracy. By contrast, a simple operational conspiracy can have a devastating consequence for enormous numbers of people, for example, by unleashing weapons of mass destruction, ethnic cleansing, or genocide.

Plausibility

The second variable used here to classify conspiracy theories is even more subjective than level and requires wading into an epistemological minefield. Categorizing a conspiracy theory by its level of plausibility is to make a judgment not only about the truth value but about the degree to which a conspiracy theory should even be entertained. Even carrying out this exercise is in effect to participate in disciplining inquiry; that is, participate in shaping a regime of truth. The judgments I make can and should be contested. My guidelines and their application are intended to broaden rather than narrow the boundaries of the regime of truth.

Table 2.1 Subjective classification of conspiracy theories by scope and plausibility; percent believers in US public, where available

Acceptance	Warranted, beyond reasonable doubt	Highly plausible	Plausible	Highly unlikely	Unwarranted, fictional or fanciful
Level					
World/grand	None—By definition requires total control over historical, social, and economic circumstances	There is an international communist conspiracy to rule the world (52% in 1987)	The US government is covering up knowledge of visits of extra-terrestrial beings at Roswell, New Mexico (21%)	A secretive global elite is conspiring to rule the world and establish a New World Order (28%)	Pope works with the Devil to bring the apocalypse and end times
					Jews control the world economy
Operational	CIA has an operational bureau that has planned overthrows of foreign governments	The Federal Emergency Management Administration has contingency plans to intern pro-testers under martial law	A conspiracy was involved in the assassination of Pres. Kennedy (51%)	Hitler did not die in a Berlin bunker and was spirited from Germany to Argentina (45% in 1947)	Lizard People run the United States (4%)
	Tobacco companies manipulate data and information to hide the impact of tobacco on health (estimated 97%)	Russian operatives used social media in an attempt to further polarize American politics	Deep State operatives seek to remove Trump from the presidency (54%)	The Bush administration allowed or made 911 happen (11%)	The Holocaust is a fictional event propagated by Zionists (1%)
			The Kremlin has *compromat* on Pres. Trump	Global warming is a hoax (37%)	

(continued)

Table 2.1 (continued)

| Petty/minor | Several Chicago White Sox players conspired to throw the 1919 World Series ("Black Sox") | Los Angeles police manipulated some of the evidence that was introduced (8% in 1995, time of trial, indirect measure) | Shakespeare never lived; he was a composite character made up of contemporary playwrights | Paul McCartney died in an auto accident in 1996 and replaced by a look-alike (5%) | The moon is a hologram, not an actual celestial object |

Unless otherwise indicated, percent believers taken from "Democrats and Republicans differ on conspiracy beliefs," Public Policy Polling www.publicpolicypolling.com, April 2, 2013

No opinion data found for Black Sox scandal, Shakespeare, CIA operational branch, FEMA camps (polls generally focus on FEMA, martial law, a bigger claim), moon as hologram; police infiltration, Pope/devil, Jews control world economy (much international survey data, but not on US opinion)

Holocaust denial: Kagay, M. "Poll on Doubt of Holocaust is Corrected." *New York Times*, July 8, 1994

Deep State-Trump: Monthly Harvard-Harris Poll, June 2017

Hitler: 1947 Gallup Poll, cited in http://ropercenter.cornell.edu/nine-historical-polling-results-might-surprise/

OJ Trial: CNN poll http://www.cnn.com/US/OJ/daily/9-15/poll/index.html, says "police not prejudiced"

Tobacco Companies: No direct data on manipulation, but only 3% would "normally believe" a tobacco company statement. Harris Poll, December 12, 2014

Communist conspiracy: Gallup poll, January 27–February 5, 1989. Text of question: "Communists are responsible for a lot of the unrest in the United States today." Completely agree, 18%; mostly agree, 34%

The philosopher Lee Basham urges that we adopt a "studied agnosticism" about conspiracy theory, recognizing epistemological limitations on any kind of knowledge, but especially on social knowledge.[48] We rely extensively for our data and interpretation on mediated sources for our information, that is, on accounts provided in particular by investigative journalists, social scientists, and historians, which are often very suspect themselves. This is not a reason to throw up our hands about every ever approximating certainty, but it is a reason to refrain from "knowing something" simply because it appears in elite media sources, such as the *New York Times, Washington Post*, etc., and also of rejecting a priori something that has been dismissed in those sources as "conspiracy theory."

Following Basham, in assessing plausibility, rather than using "proved" for the most credible theories and "disproved" or "paranoid" for those least credible, I have created a scale with "warranted" and "unwarranted" at the poles, with degrees of plausibility in between. In general, I have followed several criteria in making judgments: (1) parsimony, (2) degree to which a theory is subject to disproof, (3) standards of proof adapted from civil and criminal law in liberal societies, and (4) evaluation of motive. Conspiracy theories typically rely on anomalies in the official story of an event to make a case and often lack positive evidence linking the alleged conspirators to the event. In the weakest cases, they draw a conclusion based solely upon motive. On the other hand, our guardians of the regime of truth tend to disregard motive altogether and to write off anomalies as the result of chaos or chance.

It is not at all clear that the single gunman theory is more parsimonious than the theory that Kennedy was the victim of a murderous conspiracy. One can quite systematically explain all of the myriad anomalies about the case—the zig-zag path of the "magic bullet" that pierced Kennedy's throat, exited through body, and then wounded Governor John Connally alongside the president; the ability of Oswald to get off all the shots he is alleged to have taken; Oswald's various brushes with intelligence and security agencies; the jerk of Kennedy's head to the rear instead of forward upon being shot; the ease with which Oswald's murderer gain access to his victim in a police station; and others. Virtually all the anomalies can be explained hypothetically, and most of them were in Gerald Posner's *Case Closed*, probably the most read book attempting to rebut conspiracy theories about the assassination.[49] The various specific conspiracy theories proposed around the case have their own problems (e.g., how secrecy has been maintained), but considering the number of anomalies that Posner must address, theories that posit multiple gunmen or deliberate negligence by government security agencies are arguably more parsimonious. They remain plausible but are nonetheless not entirely convincing (fully warranted).

A theory that posits supernatural or divine intervention as an explanation of an event is based on faith. My "studied agnosticism" does not extend to theories that posit miracles or other forms of spiritual interventions in human affairs. So I classify as "unwarranted" theories that draw upon imagined cosmologies. To cite an example especially relevant in the Trump era, this criteria brings into play the question of how millenarian and fundamentalist beliefs should be regarded. Supernatural intervention, whether for evil (Satan) or for good (the angels), may be more parsimonious.

If it is unreasonable to demand absolute proof of conspiracy theories, it is reasonable to place the burden of proof on their proponents. Here, legal principles are useful. In the United States, civil cases rely upon preponderance of evidence, a weaker standard than that required in criminal cases, where the burden is proof beyond a reasonable doubt. In assessing the plausibility of various conspiracy theories, demonstrating their occurrence beyond a "reasonable doubt" requires much more evidence and consensus, analogous to the way a jury and/or judge can be said to enforce a "regime of truth" in a court. In similar fashion, we can find theories that marshal a preponderance of evidence less convincing but hard to dismiss.

The columns in Table 2.1 correspond to a variable operationalized as the plausibility of a particular conspiracy theory. I am not in this regard measuring how many people believe a theory but making a judgment about the degree to which a theory should be admitted within the regime of truth as a fitting subject for debate, analysis, and discussion. That is, rather than adopt Bratich's relatively hands off approach, I side more with Fenster in acknowledging the need to make judgments. As an intellectual with a place in the educational academy, I play a role in imposing discipline over what should be admitted or not—though certainly with a relatively small quotient of power within that regime. In other words, I am accepting that we need to distinguish between conspiracy theories that are plausible from those that are completely outlandish, such as the one claiming that lizard-people run America (see Chapter 1), which some claim is apparently believed by 12 million

Americans.[50] Such ideas are best reserved for study by professional psychologists or professional comedians. However, how we parse the realistic from the outlandish demands more attention than typically accorded it in academia and journalism.

Categories of Conspiracy Theories

I propose, then, to classify conspiracies according to level (or scope) and plausibility. The three levels of conspiracy theorizing are:

- World or grand, corresponding to theories that purport to explain events that have an impact on at least a civilizational level, but especially on a global level.
- Operational, corresponding to theories that posit significant shifts in the nature of a political regime or (closely related) a major shift in relative power or distribution of wealth in a society, and also attempts to cover-up embarrassing or illegal abuse of authority and power.
- Petty, or minor, corresponding to typical corruption scandals, evasion of laws (e.g., evasion of environmental regulations), ordinary criminal activity, abuse of bureaucratic sinecures; petty conspiracies individually do not aim or achieve major shifts in regime, power, or wealth distribution, but cumulatively they have a corrosive impact on public confidence in government and major institutions; also, attempts to cover-up such activity. They are, limited in ambition, even if together they may have great consequences.

Plausibility is a variable classifying conspiracy theories along a scale of plausibility with five points, ranging from warranted to unwarranted. Table 2.1 provides an example or two in each of the fifteen possibilities that result when cross-listing conspiracy theories according to level (rows) and plausibility (columns). There is no pretension here to scientific rigor in assigning the theories to different categories. The reader may wish to contest the judgments made. I will offer here a few comments by way of explanation for some of the choices made.

One cell in Table 2.1 concerns revelations by Congress and by Investigative Reporters that during the Reagan administration that the Federal Emergency Management Administration (FEMA) was to be in charge of an internment program that Lt. Col. Oliver North and other

National Security officials envisioned as necessary to deal with protest activities following escalation of American military intervention
in Central America. These plans, explored in more detail in Chapter 7,
were related to a larger project to declare martial law and were fortunately quashed by Attorney General William French Smith, but we
do not know whether they have been subsequently restored by other
administrations.[51]

Undoubtedly there will be readers who find the conspiracy theories about the Kennedy assassination more highly plausible than I do
or, on the other hand, find them totally unwarranted. The latter opinion can be found on the left and on the right. Peter Dale Scott believes
that the widespread rejection of the Warren Commission finding that
Lee Harvey Oswald acted alone in assassinating Kennedy is "the legacy
of the Enlightenment that has left us in this century with the unattractive
choices of academic social science and scientific socialism," also described as
"rationalistic structuralism."[52] That is, a legacy of the Enlightenment's faith
in science and, applied to human affairs, to the discovery of laws that make
history, society, and politics both understandable and subject to change.

The conspiracies regarded as plausible did not necessarily achieve
their perpetrators' objectives. For example, the "highly plausible" theory about the Comintern's objective is based upon the initial revolutionary ambitions of the Bolsheviks than its effectiveness or its functioning
in the Cold War. What is highly plausible is not that the Comintern
achieved the objective but that it developed a secretive network first to
spread, later to defend the Communist regimes that emerged after the
Bolshevik Revolution. That its power and objectives were exaggerated in
anti-Communist conspiracy theories is another matter. Nor do I intend
anything necessarily sinister about its aspirations given the tendency of
revolutionary regimes to see their success as part of wave of history that
they not only seek to ride but to actively encourage.

Once we attribute some measure of causation to conspiracy, we introduce chance, agency, and perhaps chaos into history, unsettling the notion
that social sciences and scientific history can unlock laws of social evolution,
something that sociology in the Marxian and Webster traditions share with
each other. Engels eulogy for Marx praise his friend for having "discovered
the law of development of human history" and "the special law of motion
governing the present-day capitalist mode of production." Marxism as a
school thought today includes quite variegated viewpoints on the viability
of historical materialism to unlock understanding of human affairs.

The very notion of a social science includes a commitment to presumptions of unchanging human nature, something that Peter Winch effectively demolishes with his observation about the "reflective" nature of the subject matter studied. That is, once social science uncovers a pattern of behavior, that same knowledge may lead to changes in those patterns. Conspiracy theories on the grand scale, whether formed by paranoid minds or not, do lack the explanatory power of the best social scientific theories, but operational conspiracy theories, if constructed with the intellectual honesty and openness to criticism of other social scientific and historical understanding of human affairs, can remind us that human beings make history—though not any way they want to.[53]

JFK, 9/11, AND THE REGIME OF TRUTH

Of the operational conspiracies listed in Table 2.1, the two that continue to resonate most persistently in American political discourse are:

1. "Truther" theory about 9/11, i.e., the September 11, 2001 attacks upon the World Trade Center towers in New York City and upon the Pentagon. One variation, "Made It Happen", alleges the attacks were planned by the Bush Administration; the other alleges that the administration "Let It Happen."
2. "JFK", the theory that Lee Harvey Oswald was not the lone assassin of Kennedy in 1963. The staying power of this theory is indicated that the first conspiracy theory mentioned in the popular series of debunking programs on the website "thisisnotaconspiracytheory.com" happened decades before the creation of the web—the assassination of JFK and the killing of Oswald a day later by Jack Ruby.

In Table 2.1, I have classified the Truther theories as "highly unlikely," partly on grounds that it makes little sense to me that the Bush administration would target the most conspicuous symbols of capitalism and US military power. To be sure, there remain anomalies in the official story about the attacks, but most of the anomalies have been to my mind more plausibly explained than in the case of JFK. My conclusion rests mainly on a close reading of the claims made by David Ray Griffin, a highly respected theologian who is the most prominent intellectual to have taken up the Truther cause, and a comparison of his critique with rebuttals offered by those who find more persuasive, despite its flaws, the account given in *The 9/11 Report* of the National Commission on Terrorist Attacks Upon the United States.

My assessment of Truther theories more or less conforms to accounts within the regime of truth, but this is not the case with *JFK*. To justify fully my conclusions would lead us too far astray from the central concern of this book, conspiracism as it has unfolded since Donald Trump began his presidential quest by promoting the Birther theory in 2011. Still, a brief excursion into my reasons for challenging the regime of truth in the Kennedy case seems in order, both to demonstrate the utility of the concept "regime of truth" and because JFK and the notion of a "deep state" challenges the myth of American exceptionalism (see Chapter 7), raising the possibility that coups, usually associated with Third World politics, can happen in the United States. I base my conclusions largely on a close reading and comparison of Scott's most persuasive book, *Deep Politics and the Death of JFK* and Gerald Posner's *Case Closed*, which contends that despite its very serious flaws and pre-conceived conclusion, the Warren Commission essentially got it right in concluding the Oswald acted alone. I have also attempted to fact-check the books, where possible using websites that seem to be willing to take "no" for an answer but remain open to the idea there was a conspiracy.[54]

Scott served as an adviser to Oliver Stone's film, *JFK*, but unlike the case with the movie *Deep Politics* does not so much commit to a specific theory than examine anomalies that strongly suggest that the National Security agencies were complicit in a conspiracy. Scott advances hypotheses and demands public accountability for unexplained lacunae in the record. To some extent, one can say that more credible Truther spokespersons do much the same, but even the most prominent, widely read Truther, Griffin, goes much further in assuming the complicity of the Bush administration in the attack.[55] Much less persuasively, Scott advances the proposition, with which I disagree, that Kennedy's assassination most likely altered the course of American involvement in Vietnam, deepening it—a view promoted as well in Stone's film. What I find more persuasive is Scott's and Stone's contention that historians and social scientists are resistant to the theory that the deep state was involved in the assassination because if there was involvement of the security agencies the only conclusion possible would be that a *coup d' etat* had occurred.

Scott's book was published by a major university press, but it has not received nearly the attention or academic and journalistic approval of Posner's *Case Closed*. While Scott large promoted his book on various media channels with small audiences, Posner was widely featured on talk show circuit, boosting his book to best-seller status. *Case Closed* rose to best-seller status based on a wave of highly favorable reviews endorsing his thesis. The *New York Times Book Review* (Ward 1993) proclaimed in its headline, "The Most Durable Assassination Theory: Oswald Did It Alone."[56] Scott's book is dismissed at the same time as the "opaque" meanderings of a literature professor. Posner, by contrast, is presented as a "former Wall Street lawyer," a credential by which the *Times* seems to validate his research and reasoning skills. In another essay, the *Times*' Christopher Lehmann-Haupt concluded, "The result is more satisfying than any conspiracy theory because at every step its [Posner's] explanation is clearer and more elegant. Posner's use of evidence is often selective and certainly no more convincingly argued than that of Scott." The *Times Literary Supplement, American Heritage* and *Journal of American History* all pronounced themselves convinced by Posner's research. *American Heritage* (February–March 1994: 100) chimed in, "Adult Oswald simply wasn't stable enough to have played a major role in an elaborate far-reaching conspiracy." The *Journal of American History* literally raved that "the range and depth of Posner's research is awesome. Nothing essential escaped him," while simply dismissing Scott as just "a longtime leftist critics" writing "another conspiracy book."[57] A few reviews specializing in library recommendations (*Choice*, v. 31, March 1994, p. 1210; *Booklist*, v. 90, September 15, 1993, p. 107) said kind things about Scott's book, but these have considerably less influence than those gushing about *Case Closed*.[58]

Scott and others who challenge the Warren Commission findings bear the burden of proof for demonstrating a conspiracy; it is not enough to ask merely "what if" or fill in missing evidence with conjecture. On the other hand, in *Case Closed* the burden of proof falls on Posner to vindicate the Warren Commission findings, especially since the Commission's investigation has long been regarded as deeply flawed (as Posner admits). Is Posner's case built more solidly than Scott's? Space does not permit, perhaps mercifully, a full airing over the "who shot Kennedy" debate. Scott's hypothesis of a conspiracy behind the Kennedy assassination certainly remains open to doubt, and Posner's book does provide an explanation for many of the anomalies. What I wish to demonstrate is only that Posner's case is also not air-tight. His approving reviews have more to do with how his thesis conformed to the regime of truth.

Posner builds a portrait of Oswald as a loner, a psychological deviant, and social misfit, absorbed in communism and resentful toward the United States. Scott, by contrast, depicts Oswald as a rational actor. The underlying assumption of both authors is that if Oswald was a misfit, something of a joke among police and national security agencies, the Warren Commission finding that he acted alone is more credible. Why, however, should we assume a rational actor was less likely to have served as a triggerman or fall guy in a conspiracy to kill the president? Posner and Scott provide plenty of evidence that Oswald's ideological positions were highly unstable, that he drifted through a shadowy world, filled with connections to communism and US national security institutions. Consider that Oswald defected to the Soviet Union and lived there for two years but was able upon return to use three different alias to buy firearms. He had contacts with both pro- and anti-Castro groups in New Orleans. None of this is inconsistent with the lone gunman theory, but it does suggest that Oswald moved socially among a dark network of employees and human assets of the national security agencies, American and others.

Like Scott, Posner relies extensively on the testimony of witnesses who have often changed their story (e.g., Oswald's wife, Maria) or have close ties (often unacknowledged) to the CIA or other parts of the national security state. For example, Posner relies extensively on George de Mohrenschildt, described as Oswald's "closest friend in Dallas," to substantiate claims Oswald became interested in Marxism on his own—i.e., was not led to it by co-conspirators seeking to dupe him. But Mohrenschildt was, in fact, a CIA operative with underworld connections going back to cover operations against Mussolini. He also was likely involved with Agency plots to overthrow Duvalier dictatorship in Haiti.[59]

Posner marshals evidence that Oswald's inconsistent tendencies were recorded and were the cause for his rejection by intelligence services on both sides of the Iron Curtain. However, in documenting the attitude of the intelligence services, Poster also reveals the considerable extent that they monitored and used Oswald. Oswald was observed and befriended by figures within the national security apparatus and employed in fairly sensitive military activities. Scott asks how and why Oswald came to have such close associations (e.g., with Mohrenschildt). Oswald's associations do not constitute proof of a conspiracy, but it is reasonable to ask those who defend the Warren Commission why a "loner" had such associations. Much of Posner's own research reinforces the idea that Oswald very much wanted to be employed for work in the security apparatus, and of course Oswald declared on the evening after the shooting that he was just a "patsy" for others.

In attempting to explain the failure of the Warren Commission to take seriously the testimony of a Soviet defector, much of Chapter 3 of *Case Closed* is devoted to defending the credibility of Yuri Nosenko, a KGB defector. Nosenko was charged with overseeing American defectors in the USSR, and his testimony supports Posner's contention that Oswald was not taken seriously by the KGB because he was mentally unstable. But Posner himself provides a chilling account of the brutal treatment and interrogation of Nosenko for several years by James Angleton, the CIA official charged with verifying the credentials of Soviet defectors. Angleton's career included contacts with notorious mafia figures recruited to help the CIA in operations during the first two decades of the Cold War. Posner acknowledges that Angleton and Richard Helms (former Director of the CIA) successfully kept Nosenko from testifying to the Warren Commission, which was interested in him because the FBI found the Soviet defector credible.[60] Again, these facts alone do not prove a conspiracy to kill Kennedy, but the portrait of Angleton demonstrates that those responsible for internal and foreign operations of the CIA at the height of the Cold War were collectively part of a dark, violent part of the state, a world of covert activities and charged with formulating operational conspiracies. It operatives were obsessed with its own grand conspiracy theory in the form of anti-communism, and they within that frame engaged in operations to which we will return when examining the theory of the Deep State in Chapter 7.

Posner's most impressive analysis (Chapter 14) concerns marshalling of scientific support for the Warren Commission contention that it was possible for two bullets (of at least three) fired from the Texas Book Depository (1) to have inflicted all the wounds Kennedy sustained, (2) to have born a relatively light amount of damage sustained as a result of their path, and (3) to have been discharged within the time frame necessary. He also provides a scientific explanation why Kennedy apparently lurched backwards upon being struck by the fatal bullet in the back of his head. Posner's objective is to resolve what appears as a serious problem in the Warren Commission account: the contention of critics Oswald could not have fired all the shots with accuracy, as the Commission contended. This claim has long been made in support of the popular notion that another assassin killed Kennedy with a shot from the infamous "grassy knoll," a term that has entered the American lexicon. As mentioned above, Posner marshals evidence that the "magic" single bullet *could have traveled* the path it took, but he does not entirely convince that a jacketed, tumbling bullet would have changed directions so dramatically. Posner makes much of Oswald's practicing making the bolt action on his rifle, but he fails to mention that Oswald was far from an expert shot. He attained "sharpshooter" status in the military in his first test, barely exceeding the lowest category ("marksman") and far below the next highest category, "expert" (lowest). In his later 1959 test, he barely qualified for marksman.[61]

Posner *does* demonstrate the physical evidence and much testimony *can be interpreted* to be consistent with the Warren Commission's finding, but this evidence is far from closing the case. Posner's lone gunman scenario is possible but also less parsimonious than the hypothesis that bullets were fired from more than one location. Like conspiracy theorists, Posner takes what *could* have happened as proof of what *did* happen, and he substitutes a more complex explanation for a more parsimonious one, but his analysis is widely taken as conclusive and rational.

Ultimately, Posner's book lies somewhere between the lucid, air-tight, logically argued, impeccably researched study seen by his admirers and the deliberately distorted apology posited by his critics. The *Christian Science Monitor* is among the few reviews that provided a more balanced assessment. It praised Posner's forensic research but concluded that the issue of Oswald's motivation leaves the case "far from closed." If I have dwelled on explanations of the book's shortcomings and flawed reasoning, it is only to ask why similar problems in Scott are taken as evidence to dismiss his hypotheses as conspiracy mongering. Posner was made into a celebrity on the television talk show network while Scott was largely relegated to the college and dissident lecture circuits and later the Internet. Scott's research has been marginalized, Posner's largely depicted as decisively having debunked a pathological obsession, i.e., a conspiracy theory.

CONSEQUENCES AND SUMMING UP

The last quarter century—coincidentally or not, since the release of Oliver Stone's influential movie *JFK*—has seen some critical evaluation about thesis that conspiracy theories distract their believers from effectively demanding redress of their grievances. Olmsted finds that most conspiracy theories in twentieth century America, even more fantastical ones, may be rooted in real, past victimization by secretive activities of governments and corporations. Fenster goes further in arguing that conspiracy theory is not necessarily pathological and are a strident, populist call for transparency in government, but even he maintains that conspiracy theories "rarely lead to effective political engagement and are related often are directly or indirectly to virulent forms of scapegoating, skepticism and fascism."[62]

My view is that conspiracy theories can be positive forces for political change, but they can also be used to advance the kind of repressive, authoritarian or even genocidal political events that Posner, Berlin, the Southern Poverty Law Center and other critics see as the only outcome to be expected of a conspiracy theory. The latter type of conspiracism is justly called the "paranoid style," but the proliferation of conspiracy theories in the Trump era, both warranted and unwarranted alike, is a sign of political decay (see Chapter 8). Furthermore, they should give us pause about some conspiracy theories dismissed as paranoid in the past.

Conspiracism in the Trump era tells us much about the political decay of our political institutions, the decline of consensus among elites, the social distance between elites and ordinary people, and the advance of popular mistrust of representative institutions. If we are to face up to the underlying causes of this decay we need to acknowledge that theorizing about conspiracy can have a salutary impact on democracy, identifying whose interests clash with those of the general citizenry and uncovering one of the ways that power operates in a political system. Where plausible or warranted, exposure and correction of what is revealed is crucial not just to preservation but enrichment of democracy.

By showing the conspiratorial discourse in the words of Paul Krugman, a highly influential voice of American liberalism, I am not arguing for dismissing his claims. His allegations about the machinations of American politics in the Trump era cannot be reduced to petty levels. Consider the implication he drew in his December 19 column that focused on the Republican-controlled North Carolina legislature stripping the newly elected Democratic governor of much of his power (later reversed by a court ruling). "Combine

2 PARANOIA, CONSPIRACY PANIC, AND THE REGIME OF TRUTH   73

this sort of thing with continuing efforts to disenfranchise or at least discourage voting by minority groups, and you have the potential making of a de facto one-party state: one that maintains the fiction of democracy, but has rigged the game so that the other side can never win."

No history of Nazism would be complete without acknowledgement of the role that anti-Semitic conspiracy theories played in the Holocaust. Acknowledging this factor is of course not a full explanation of this genocide. Nor can one leave out what was very possibly a "false flag" operation, the arson attack on the Reichstag (parliament building) in an account of Hitler's ascent to power. No account of the Cold War can ignore Senator Joseph McCarthy's allegations that the US government was packed with traitors and spies—i.e., Communists and fellow-travelers, which produced a purge of the Left from the political and cultural influence it had gained in the previous two decades. It is difficult to argue that conspiracies play no role in politics when we review the recurrent political scandals, violations of constitutional rights, and foreign interventions carried out by US national security agencies.

Understanding important shifts in power and wealth in the world to conspiracies cannot be reduced to conspiracy theories. World level conspiracy theories are usually better left to analysis by political psychologists, but conspiracies should not be dismissed as irrelevant to understanding political life and historical events. The most useful approach to reincorporate conspiracy as an object of study by political science is to concentrate our theoretical attention on operational conspiracies, the study of which can help us develop of theories about the limits, potential, dangers of conspiracies in political life. We need to do this today more than at any time since the Civil War—even more than in the populist era or Cold War years. The Trump era is likely to be rife with both conspiracies and conspiracy theories, even after he is no longer President.

Notes

1. Richard Hofstadter, *The Paranoid Style in American Politics* (New York: Vintage Reprints, 1968). The book expands on the original article in Harpers Magazine November 1964, available at https://harpers.org/archive/1964/11/the-paranoid-style-in-american-politics (accessed July 18, 2017).
2. *This Is Not a Conspiracy Theory Episode One: Premise*, available on YouTube, Published January 24, 2015 (accessed September 28, 2017).

3. Michel Foucault, "Truth and Power," in *Michel Foucault: Power/ Knowledge*, ed. Colin Gordon (New York: Vintage Pres, 1980): 131, 109–133.
4. Peter Baker, Nixon Tried to Spoil Johnson's Vietnam Peace Talks in '68, Notes Show, *New York Times*, January 2, 2017.
5. Neil A. Lewis, "New Reports Say 1980 Reagan Campaign Tried to Delay Hostage Release," *New York Times*, April 15, 1991.
6. Available at https://www.merriam-webster.com/dictionary/conspiracy% 20theory.
7. Daniel Pipes, *Conspiracy: How the Paranoid Style Flourishes and Where It Comes from* (New York: The Free Press, 1999): 1.
8. For examples see "Paul Krugman Illustrates the Damaged Pyches of the Left," *Mises Wire*, December 20, 2016, available at https://mises.org/ blog/paul-krugman%E2%80%99s-latest-conspiracy-trump-gold-bug; "The Left Is Pushing Conspiracy Theories to Feel Better about 2016," *The Federalist*, December 23, 2016; http://thefederalist.com/tag/con-spiracy-theories; and "Paul Krugman: Comey, Putin 'installed' the 'Crazy, Vindictive' Trump," *Washington Examiner*, August 1, 2017, available at www.washingtonexaminer.com (all accessed August 22, 2017).
9. Hofstadter, *The Paranoid Style*.
10. Adam Enders and Steven Smallpage, "Who Are Conspiracy Theorists? An Exercise in Predicting Conspiracy Beliefs," Prepared for presentation at the Annual Meetings of the American Political Science Association, San Francisco, CA, August 31–September 3, 2017.
11. Pipes, *Conspiracy: How the Paranoid Style Flourishes*, 21.
12. For a religious based version appearing on YouTube, see https://www. youtube.com/watch?v=ir2yVa0A9q4. For a more secular version, see https://www.youtube.com/watch?v=NXFrmUCK7YI (both accessed August 19, 2017).
13. See https://www.ushmm.org/wlc/en/article.php?ModuleId=10007058 (accessed August 19, 2017).
14. Available at https://www.theatlantic.com/national/archive/2013/04/ 12-million-americans-believe-lizard-people-run-our-country/316706 (accessed August 20, 2017).
15. Hofstadter, *The Paranoid Style in American Politics*. The book expands on the original article in *Harpers Magazine* November 1964, available at https://harpers.org/archive/1964/11/the-paranoid-style-in-ameri-can-politics (accessed July 18, 2017).
16. Hofstadter, "The Paranoid Style," *Harpers Magazine*, 1.
17. Chip Berlet, *Toxic to Democracy: Conspiracy Theories, Demonization, & Scapegoating*. Political Research Associates. 2009 (updated): 3, available at http://www.publiceye.org/conspire/toxic2democracy/Toxic-2D-all-rev-04.pdf (accessed August 17, 2017).

2 PARANOIA, CONSPIRACY PANIC, AND THE REGIME OF TRUTH   75

18. Samuel Moyn and David Priestland. "Trump Isn't a Threat to our Democracy. Hysteria Is." *New York Times*, August 11, 2017.

19. Peter Knight, *Conspiracy Culture: From the Kennedy Assassination to the X-FILES* (London: Routledge, 2000): 3.

20. Knight, *Conspiracy Culture*: 118–124.

21. See Jodi Kantor and Megan Twohey, "Harvey Weinstein Paid Off Sexual Harassment Accusers for Decades," *New York Times*, October 5, 2017.

22. Cass Sunstein, *Conspiracy Theories and Other Dangerous Ideas* (New York: Simon & Schuster, 2004): 3–5.

23. Available at https://en.wikipedia.org/wiki/Conspiracy_theory (accessed September 22, 2017).

24. Kathryn Olmsted, *Real Enemies: Conspiracy Theories and American Democracy* (New York: Oxford University Press, 2009).

25. Kathryn Olmsted, *Real Enemies*: 9, 234.

26. Mark Fenster, *Conspiracy Theories: Secrecy and Power in American Culture* (Minneapolis: University of Minnesota Press, 1st ed., 1999, 2nd ed., 2008). Jack Z. Bratich, *Conspiracy Panics: Political Rationality and Popular Culture* (Albany: State University of New York Press, 2008).

27. Fenster (1999): 1.

28. Jack Bratich: *Conspiracy Panics: Political Rationality and Popular Culture* (Albany: State University of New York Press, 2008): 6.

29. Bratich, *Conspiracy Panics*: 9, 14–18.

30. Bratich, *Conspiracy Panics*: 9, 14–18.

31. Daniel Hellinger, "Paranoia, Conspiracy, and Hegemony in American Politics," in *Transparency and Conspiracy: Ethnographies of Suspicion in the New World Order*, ed. Harry G. West and Todd Sanders (Durham, NC: Duke University Press, 2003).

32. Available at https://www.nytimes.com/2017/06/08/us/politics/senate-hearing-transcript.html?_r=0.

33. Mark Fenster, *The Transparency Fix: Secrets, Leaks, and Uncontrollable Government Information* (Palo Alto, CA: Stanford University Press, 2017).

34. Farhad Manjoo, "Farhad's Week in Tech: Bitcoin and the Scams Under Everything," *New York Times*, June 15, 2018.

35. Majooo, "Fahad's Week in Tech: Bitcoin..."; John. M. Griffin and Amin Shams, "Is Bit-Coin Really Untethered," Social Science Research Network (SSRN), available at https://papers.ssrn.com/sol3/papers.cfm?abstract_id=3195066 (accessed June 16, 2018).

36. Bratich, *Conspiracy Panics*: 14.

37. Frederic Jameson, "Cognitive Mapping," in *Marxism and the Interpretation of Culture*, ed. C. Nelson and L. Grossberg (Champaign–Urbana: University of Illinois Press, 1960): 347–360. Quoted from p. 9 of version available at http://www.rainer-rilling.de/gs-villa07-Dateien/JamesonF86a_CognitiveMapping.pdf (accessed September 26, 2017).

38. Bernard Bailyn, *The Ideological Origins of the American Revolution* (Cambridge, MA: Harvard University Press, 1967). See also Jeffrey Pasley, Jeffrey L. 2000. Conspiracy theory and American Exceptionalism from the Revolution to Roswell. Paper presented at Sometimes an Art: A Symposium Celebration of Bernard Bailyn's Fifty Years of Teaching and Beyond. Harvard University, May 13, 2000, available at http://pasley-brothers.com/conspiracy/CT_and_American_Exceptionalism_web_version.htm (accessed August 25, 2017).

39. Olmstead, *Real Enemies*: 239.

40. Popper, Karl. "The Conspiracy Theory of Society," in *Conspiracy Theories: The Philosophical Debate*, ed. David Coady (Burlington, VT: Ashgate): 17–44. Thomas Kuhn. 1970. *The Structure of Scientific Revolutions* (Chicago: University of Chicago Press, 2nd ed.).

41. Jodi Dean, *Aliens in America: Conspiracy Cultures from Outerspace to Cyberspace* (Ithaca, NY: Cornell University Press, 1998): 45.

42. "Former Pentagon UFO Official: 'We May not be Alone'," *CNN*, December 19, 2017; "Glowing Auras and 'Black Money': The Pentagon's Mysterious U.F.O. Program," *New York Times*, December 18, 2017.

43. The YouTube talk is available at https://www.youtube.com/watch?v=T-N16OBSb_BA (accessed February 21, 2018). On his research, see Joseph Uscinski and Joseph Parent, *American Conspiracy Theories* (New York: Oxford University Press, 2014).

44. Pipes, *Conspiracy*: 21.

45. Pipes, Conspiracy: 102, 147, 217.

46. Matthew Gray, *Conspiracy Theories in the Arab World: Sources and Politics* (New York: Routledge, 2010): 12.

47. Pipes, *Conspiracy*: 26.

48. Lee Basham, "Living with the Conspiracy," in *Conspiracy Theories: The Philosophical Debate*, ed. David Coady (Burlington, VT: Ashgate, 2006): 61–117.

49. Gerald Posner, *Case Closed: Lee Harvey Oswald and the Assassination of JFK* (New York: Random House, 1993).

50. "Conspiracy Theory Poll Results." *Public Policy Polling*. April 2, 2013, available at http://www.publicpolicypolling.com/main/2013/04/conspiracy-theory-poll-results-.html (accessed August 7, 2017).

51. "North Worked on Plan for Martial Law," *Knight-Ridder Newspapers*, July 5, 1987.

52. Peter Dale Scott, *Deep Politics and the Death of JFK* (Berkeley: University of California Press): 10; Posner, *Case Closed*.

53. I formulate this proposition hoping it is consistent with Marx's observation in *Theses on Feuerbach*, "The materialist doctrine that men are products of circumstances and upbringing, and that, therefore, changed men

are products of changed circumstances and changed upbringing, forgets that it is men who change circumstances and that the educator must himself be educated," and also his observation in the *Eighteenth Brumaire of Louis Bonaparte*, "Men make their own history, but they do not make it as they please."

54. Assessing the reliability of evidence and sources cited in both studies is to trod into a political mine field. A good list, clearly biased but carefully compiled, to be suspected more for the triviality of some of its claims than exaggeration, has been compiled by the editors of the *Assassination Web* (1997). An especially useful site that debunks some specific conspiracy theories about JFK, but remains open to possibility that one existed is http://dperry1943.com.
55. See David Ray Griffin, *The New Pearl Harbor Revisited: 9/11, the Cover-Up, and the Exposé* (Northampton, MA: Olive Branch Press, 2008).
56. Geoffrey Ward, Geoffrey. "The Most Durable Assassination Theory: Oswald Did It Alone." *New York Times Book Review* (November 21, 1993).
57. Geoffrey Ward, "The Most Durable Assassination Theory: Oswald Did It Alone," *New York Times Book Review*, November 21, 1993. Christopher Lehmann-Haupt, "The Kennedy Assassination Answers," *New York Times*, September 9, 1993. *American Heritage*, February–March, 1994: 101.
58. *Choice* (v. 31, March 1994): 1210; *Booklist* (v. 90, September 15, 1993): 107.
59. Scott, *Deep Politics*: pp. 59, 79–80 highlights this connection, relying on "George De Mohrenschildt", *Staff Report of the Select Committee on Assassinations*, 1979. U.S. House of Representatives, Ninety-fifth Congress Second Session March 1979.
60. Posner, *Case Closed*: 39.
61. See Warren Commission evidence collected at https://www.maryferrell.org/showDoc.html?docId=1133#relPageId=663 (accessed September 27, 2017).
62. Fenster, *Conspiracy Theories*, 1991: xvi.

CHAPTER 3

Trumpism, Fake News and the "New Normal"

On April 19, 2017, Stephen Colbert, host of CBS's *The Late Show*, greeted comedian Lewis Black, known for his manic commentaries on culture and politics, with a rhetorical "How are you holding up?" Black paused, then responded, "I turn CNN on when I wake up, and, uh, it doesn't help. Because something happens every day; every single day. That I go, What?!! What is this????"

Colbert agrees: "Every hour."

Black: "Yeah. If we can get to noon, it's a whole new landscape."

Of course, Black was referring to the first three months of the presidency of Donald J. Trump, a wealthy (maybe!), New York real-estate tycoon and TV celebrity previously known for bluster and "firing" contestants on his reality TV program, *The Apprentice*. Black probably had to shutter again the day after his appearance on Colbert, as Trump would welcome to the White House Ted Nugent, the right-wing rocker, who had posted on Facebook photos of former mayor of New York City, whom Nugent called "Jew York City mayor Mikey Bloomberg", and New Jersey Senator Frank Lautenberg, with the inscription "Gave Russian Jew immigrants your tax money" (*Washington Post*, February 10, 2017).

It is a good bet that a large part of the world's population feels much like Black does, but with Trump's approval ratings in summer 2017 hovering at their lowest (around 37–39%) for a first-year president,[1] it was clear that a substantial percentage of Americans remained comfortable with Trump as president. His approval ratings dipped even

© The Author(s) 2019

D. C. Hellinger, *Conspiracies and Conspiracy Theories in the Age of Trump*, https://Doi.org/10.1007/978-3-319-98158-1_3

further afterward, but in summer of 2018, despite a highly unpopular, visible, and cruel policy of separating children of immigrant families at the Mexican border and mass detentions in several in-land sites, his approval rating actually increased to over 40%. It is unlikely that these Americans get their late-night diversion from Colbert. Colbert's monologues repeatedly endorsed the conspiracy theory that Vladimir Putin had surveillance tape of Trump engaged in lewd sexual behavior in a Moscow hotel room. In his July 20, 2017 telecast, as part of a week-long visit devoted to promoting the allegation that the Russian government had interfered in the American election, Colbert visited and showed the hotel room and bed where the alleged incident took place.

Colbert's celebrity star took on its brilliance while he was a fake newscaster, taking on the fictional persona of a right-wing pundit in the style of Bill O'Reilly and other bombastic purveyors of conservative populism on the *Fox News Network*. But in that role, Colbert was a satirist. Succeeding David Letterman on *The Late Show*, after initially faltering he hit his stride and ascended in the ratings by skewering first candidate and then President Trump directly. While his monologues and recurring bits retain much of their truth value and bite, by abandoning satire for the bright lights of *Late Night* Colbert seems more intent on instructing his fans on what to think. It may not be fake news, but the humor often seems intended more to polarize and rally than entertain, more randy than satirical.

A question I want to pose here is whether Colbert and his enthusiastic guests and audience should be considered "conspiracy theorists." Are they exhibiting symptoms of paranoia? Are the widespread claims that Russia may have "hacked the election" less conspiratorial than the claims by Trump that the election was "rigged"?

POPULISM, PARANOIA, AND CELEBRITY

Only a handful of academic experts and media commentators anticipated Trump's unconventional campaign could carry him to the presidency itself. I make no claim to having been among them, having also expected to see Hillary Clinton triumphant on election night. Though precedents for vicious smears and character assassinations can be found in the early years of the Republic and in bitter debates over slavery, no candidate since the age of electronic mass media began can match having been caught on tape bragging about molesting women, threatening to jail his opponent, ridiculing a disabled reporter, impugning the patriotism of a war hero killed in action, and refusing to fully disclose his tax and financial dealings.

Trump's political ascent was built in no small measure by capitalizing on partisan polarization and on mistrust of government. As in other episodes of right-wing populism, both in the United States and abroad, the Trump's ascent has been linked to racism, anti-immigrant sentiment, anti-globalization, a cultural backlash against changing social mores, and lingering prejudices about gender roles. These too did not simply spring to life with Trump's iconoclasm.

To illustrate the point, for now, consider the role of male patriarchy. A backlash against feminism, an ideology that Hillary Clinton has openly embraced throughout her career,[2] can be traced back to the successful, last-minute campaign that began in 1977 against the Equal Rights Amendment, a campaign that smacked heavily of conspiracism. In 2014, Phyllis Schlafly, credited with leading the charge against the ERA, freely engaged in paranoid rhetoric in a new book, *Who Killed the American Family?* The back matter for the book warned that the nuclear family was under "concerted assault" by "feminists, judges, lawmakers, psychologists, school districts, college professors, politicians offering incentives and seeking votes...The wreckage of the American family leaves us with the inability to have limited government because government steps into perform tasks formerly done by the nuclear family."[3]

Although Trump is divorced twice and never has disguised his misogynist attitudes, during the campaign and shortly before her death Schlafly endorsed the real estate mogul right. It was right when he needed it most—following the release of a tape in which he bragged about "making a move" on a married woman and about his habit of grabbing women's genitals, that is, assaulting them. Grateful, Trump took time off the campaign trail to attend Schlafly's funeral in the Cathedral of the Archdiocese of St. Louis. He praised her as someone who fought for the "little person" against a "rigged system."[4]

FAKE NEWS

"Fake news" originally came into use to describe false stories, sometimes manufactured by a single individual, that would "go viral" on the Internet. While Trump's hostility toward the media was frequently displayed during his campaign, the meme of "fake news" really became popular after the election.[5] In past eras, we might have referred to such stories as "propaganda" and connected them with the efforts of governments in wartime. The spread of false, malicious information via the Internet about President Obama and notably the Clintons (even tying them to murders) attracted broader public attention, with much of it fostered by or originating from white supremacist groups identified with the "alt-right" and longstanding hucksters, such as Alex Jones (*InfoWars.com*). Trump did not create this media environment, but he knew how to exploit it. Far from erudite or even coherent as a speaker, he understood the power of social media, Tweeting above all else. As Donald Trump began his Shermanesque march to the Republican nomination, Jones, Steven Bannon (head of *Breitbart.com* at this time) and others brought their propaganda apparatus to the service of the real estate mogul's campaign. False stories claiming that the Pope had endorsed Trump, that Clinton sold weapons to ISIS, that an FBI agent investigating Clinton's emails may have been murdered, all outperformed real news stories on Facebook feeds during the campaign, according to a study by BuzzFeed.[6]

After his electoral victory, facing the editorial hostility of the mainstream media, Trump appropriated the "fake news" meme as a weapon in his attempt to undermine the regime of truth maintained by the mainstream media. He was abetted not only by the alt-right networks on the Web but also by popular commentators on *Fox News*, most notably Sean Hannity, who on May 17, 2017 provided an example of how the "fake news" elides with conspiracism. "The deep state in Washington is targeting the president on a daily basis, by leaking information. That's where the *Washington Post* got its latest fake news story," pronounced Hannity.[7]

Much of the attention in the Trump era has been focused on *Breitbart.com*, founded by the right-wing agitator Andrew Breitbart and elevated to greater influence by Bannon; on Alex Jones's *InfoWars.com*; on alt-right Internet sites that promote white nationalist ideas; and on *Fox News'* stable of firebrand conservative pundits. *Fox News* at least separates its newscasts from shows dedicated entirely to spin—though ironically the most influential of the latter, hosted by O'Reilly (no longer with *Fox*), was called the "no-spin" zone. On pundit-shows, it is not hard to detect the right-ward slant, but deliberate propagandizing by Network executives is less easily detected when it spills into its news broadcasts. *Fox's* news anchors have at times clashed with network management and deviated from the "line-of-the-day" technique pioneered for cable news by Roger Ailes, who honed his communication

skills as Richard Nixon's main television advisor in the latter's successful 1968 presidential campaign. Ailes was especially influential in devel-
oping messaging for the "Southern Strategy," which built upon Barry
Goldwater's success (despite his landslide loss) in winning Southern
states by winnowing white voters away from the Democratic Party with a
less than subtle appeal to their resentment over desegregation. In effect,
the right-wing populist media strategy of the Goldwater era, which
inspired Hofstadter's warnings about the paranoid style,[8] effectively
became institutionalized at Fox News. What Hofstadter saw as a periodic
surge of "know-nothingism" has through Fox now become a fixture of
American politics. This is not to say that racism has never been far from
the surface in American political culture; it is only to point out that how
it is exploited and how its level of salience has been raised varied in the
Trump era.

The institutionalization of outright propaganda in the form of "Fake
News" through cable networks and the Internet tends to obscure the
deeper structural relationships among government, the corporate world
and the media. These work to maintain a "regime of truth" (see Chapters 1
and 2) that limits criticism of the liberal democratic consensus (the welfare
state, internationalism, etc.) associated with the international order that
emerged after World War II. That consensus included (with significant conservative dissent) the policy of "containment" of Communis.

Corporate media contributed significantly to the maintaining Cold
War anticommunism.[9] That may seem like a harsh judgment, because the
journalistic establishment did play a significant role in exposing Senator
Joe McCarthy's witch hunts, the lies of the Vietnam War, and the
Watergate Scandal. On the other hand, mainstream newspapers were lax,
if not complicit, in the Red Scare of the early Cold War, and it did not
oppose the Vietnam War until quite late, after public opinion had already
turned against it. While the media did aggressively pursue the Watergate
scandal, afterward it celebrated Nixon's resignation as a triumph of the
political system rather than a signal that deeper causes lay behind the
narrowly averted constitutional crisis. Since Watergate, the evolution of
both media technology and erosion of the news media's autonomy from
corporate capital have weakened journalism's ability to maintain a liberal regime of truth on its right flank. Again, by "liberal" here I use the
term not in the sense of "leftist" but in reference to the international and
domestic consensus that emerged from the defeat of fascist and militarist
regimes in World War II.

The first generation of TV news reporters and network anchors were drawn from the print media; newsrooms, local and national, and were relatively insulated from commercial pressures. News was not expected to be profitable; news operations operated within the post-World War liberal consensus the welfare state, government regulation, free trade, etc. Mainstream republicans largely shared in the consensus, but more radical right dissent never fully disappeared and emerged visibly in the presidential campaign of the party's nominee, Barry Goldwater, in 1964. Twenty years later the *Fox* mantra "fair and balanced" had success appealing to a significant segment (mostly white) of the mass TV audience that had supported Goldwater and resented the cultural revolutions of the 1960s. It is difficult today to recall that in the elections that took place between 1968 and 1980, the most penetrating critiques of the news media were that it was too deferential to authority. In 1983, journalism professor W. Lance Bennett bemoaned that most reports on Presidents adhered to the rules of "normalized news." Even ones that appeared critical, he argued, had "one of more" of three properties: They were rare; they were ritualized, i.e., adversarial but rarely addressing "the merits of policies or substance of issues"; they were superficial, focused on personalism and drama, and fragmented.[10]

In this Trumpian era of fake news, there is a tendency in some quarters to wax nostalgic for the era when three television networks virtually monopolized news transmission to a mass audience, with the most influential reporters having migrated from print journalism, the prototype being Edward R. Morrow. But if one wants to identify when fake news, as deliberate propaganda consciously designed to influence the public mind on a scale not seen since World War II began to appear, that would be in the Reagan era, starting with his 1980 campaign for the presidency, where a team of media revolutionaries devoted to rolling back the welfare state and to reversing the so-called "Vietnam Syndrome" emerged.[11] As Bennett put it in the 1996 edition of his book (13 years after the one quoted above), they "wrote the textbook on how to manage the news."[12] What Reagan did not have yet was a clearly partisan television network, but that would be created by one of the key members of his Communications Office team, Roger Ailes, who got the media Tycoon Rupert Murdoch to finance the *Fox News Cable Network*. While social media would not emerge as a factor for another 25 years, in many ways the *Fox* phenomenon, made possible by cable, has been a long-lasting and most effective purveyor of not just of news influenced by partisanship, but of partisanship itself. The basis by which a sitting president could enjoy a direct line to a highly supportive and partisan base was laid by Ailes and others who recognized that new developments in commuications technology offered them an opportunity to move beyond manipulating the mainstream media to creating their own pipeline to a mass audience.

The first basic cable network (forerunner of *Turner Broadcasting Network*) of any consequence was launched in 1977, doing little more than simply carrying the programming of its parent, Atlanta-based broadcast network. In that same year, the fundamentalist televangelist, Pat Robertson, launched his cable-based Christian Broadcasting Network, bringing conservative religious propaganda into many more living rooms than television could reach before. In 1980, the year Reagan became president, there were 16 million cable subscribers, but few networks had programing that could compete with the established broadcast networks—CBS, NBC, and ABC. Home Box Office (HBO) began its pay service in 1972, but it would not be until the Cable Regulatory Act of 1984 that networks capable of challenging the influence of the established broadcasting companies came into existence. Commercial Internet Service began to gather momentum in the Bush I era (1988–1992), when more narrow but still large audiences could be reached with news feeds. The full potential of the Internet for revolutionizing mass communication, especially the potential uses of social media for advertising and political messages, began to reveal itself after the World Wide Web began to supplant text-based Usenet groups, which had first appeared in 1989. Meanwhile, preceding the full scale revolution of social media, the conservative right weaponized talk radio, with Rush Limbaugh inaugurating his broadcasts in 1992, creating a syndicated network and stimulating dozens of imitators, reaching conservative suburbs, rural areas and small towns, all of which would become redoubts of Trumpism in the latter part of the Obama years.

The Reagan communication team's focus was to influence the mainstream news at the outset, not to create an actual alternative conduit. But the team deployed other innovations that would be felt as the new communication technologies evolved. The campaign and the White House Communications Office implemented new polling techniques, focus groups, and media messaging heretofore used mainly in presidential campaigns and usually to monitor more than shape public opinion between elections. The Reagan team created synergy among these public relations tools.[13] Of the brilliant team that gave Reagan his "Teflon coating", Ailes was one of the key member of the team member that broke the hegemony of broadcast and print news media and brought the communications synergy of the Reagan/Bush administrations era into the cable and Internet era.

In 2006, Glen Beck, a radical right talk show host with a particular penchant for the theory that a global elite was at work implanting a "New World Order," began trading in related conspiracy theories on Headline News Network (HLN), and then took his show to *Fox*, where until June 2011 he continued to broadcast hype-charged nationalist rants and used his show to promote Tea Party rallies and demonstrations. Why Beck left *Fox* has never been entirely clear. It appears to be a mixture of Beck's belief that he could independently build a more lucrative media operation and his chafing at Ailes' discipline over the message to be delivered by *Fox* hosts. Beck had played a significant role in linking the right-wing Tea Party movement to *Fox*, but he overestimated his role. While Beck was still a ratings success for *Fox*, he was a loose cannon who didn't easily accommodate the tightly disciplined and coordinated messaging (such as issuing "line of the day" memos) imposed on the Network's commentators by Ailes, who had developed this propaganda technique during his service to Presidents Richard Nixon, Ronald Reagan, and George Bush (the elder).[14]

Beck's departure from *Fox* in 2011 provided space for Alex Jones to assume a more prominent role, though not on *Fox* but on his website, *InfoWars.com*. Jones attracted widespread notoriety as a "conspiracy theorist" after claiming that the mass murder of 20 elementary school students and six staff members on December 14, 2012, at Sandy Hook School in Newtown, Connecticut, was a hoax—though it was hardly his first excursion into the paranoid style. Jones's radio programs in 2016 were syndicated to 160 radio stations and his *InfoWars* website attracted over 7 million independent visitors per month. In December 2015, Trump appeared with Jones on *InfoWars* for a 20-minute interview and promised the host, "Your reputation is amazing. I will not let you down."[15]

This dramatic shift in the information environment of American politics prepared the way for a celebrity candidate like Trump to trade on his media fame for political purposes. To be clear, Trump's surge should not be entirely attributed to this mass media revolution. Also, while there is an important genealogical thread linking the important campaign and propaganda techniques of, respectively, the Reagan/Bush era, the George W. Bush era, and the Trump era, the conservatism characteristic of each of these presidential administrations also evolved steadily more toward the right. The early news and propaganda innovations of Ailes took place during the "rise of the Vulcans," the neoconservatives who were much less radically libertarian (on domestic policy) that the Koch brothers, who brought a broader strategy to shift the center of American political culture (see Chapter 6). The Reagan coalition in the 1980s was a broader conglomeration of conservative forces, including (like Reagan himself) defectors from the Democratic Party. While they wanted to "roll back" the welfare state, their ambition at the time was not to achieve the radical libertarian agenda of the Bradleys, Kochs, Scaifes, etc.

Communication strategies in the Reagan and the younger Bush administrations were used effectively to promote the neoconservative agenda of rebuilding the capacity of the United States to project its world power. This capacity, both in terms of military capability and public support for deploying forces abroad, had been eroded in the aftermath of defeat in Vietnam and Watergate. The Carter years had seen the rise the OPEC and the Arab oil boycott; the completion of most anti-colonial liberal struggles in Africa, the Middle East, and Asia; revolutions in Iran and Nicaragua; and the emergence of Japan and the European Union as relatively strong economic units, competing with the United States in the global economy. Prematurely, some saw a new era defined by the relative decline of American hegemony. The Reagan and Bush administration rejected that judgment, and their response included reshaping the information environment. Ailes and the rest of Reagan's communications team were a crucial part of this effort. The propaganda techniques' potential reached its height after 9/11 with deliberate deceptions by neoconservatives, especially Donald Rumsfeld and Dick Cheney, Secretary of Defense and Vice President during the presidency (2000–2008) President George W. Bush designed to generate support for the invation of Iraq in 2003.

Leaving aside the highly questionable theory that the Neocons deliberately planned or allowed the 9/11 attacks to happen, there can be little doubt that they engaged in a "fake news" campaign (the term was not then in use), deliberately manufacturing and dissembling the myth that Saddam Hussein had weapons of mass destruction. There many remain questions about the actions that Cheney, Rumsfeld, and others took in the immediate aftermath of the 9/11 attacks themselves and in limiting cooperation with the commission that investigated various facets of the attacks.[16] We look more closely at this issue when considering the Deep State in Chapter 7.

MUELLER'S CONSPIRACY THEORY AND THE MEDIA

"Fake news" is really a modern term for propaganda. What changed with the rise of social media was the ease with which stories could be planted and disseminated. Late in the 2016 election cycle, Trump began using the epithet "fake news" to characterize what he propagated to be deliberate falsification of facts by the mainstream media, intended to derail his campaign. His use of the term became more frequent in response to allegations that his campaign had colluded with Kremlin operatives to influence the election, and they accelerated again when the allegations were given more substance by Robert Mueller, a life-long Republican and former FBI director who was appointed Special Counsel to investigate Russian interference in the 2016 election and possible collusion. *Breitbart.com*, Sean Hannity of *Fox News*, and Alex Jones on *InfoWars* took up the message and repeatedly referred to Robert Mueller's investigation as part of a Deep State plot to bring down Trump. In effect, we have warring conspiracy theories: Right-wing media outlets accusing the National Security apparatus and mainstream media of conspiring against Trump; mainstream media, especially late night celebrity hosts and guests (especially Stephen Colbert on NBC's *Late Show*) promoting the conspiracy theory of collusion being investigated by Mueller.

The alleged collusion should be considered a conspiracy theory, but one that (rightly) is not considered emblematic of the paranoid style. Mueller's indictment[17] of several Trump associates on February 16, 2018, the Special Counsel's investigation bears the hallmarks (laid out in Chapters 1 and 2) of a conspiracy theory: multiple persons working together secretly to bring about a political outcome, in a way that is either illegal, embarrassing and subject to defeat if exposed. Excerpts from the indictment include:

> From in or around 2014 to the present, Defendants knowingly and intentionally conspired with each other (and with persons known and unknown to the Grand Jury) to defraud the United States by impairing, obstructing, and defeating the lawful functions of the government through fraud and deceit for the purpose of interfering with the US political and electoral processes, including the presidential election of 2016.

* * *

Defendants, posing as US persons and creating false US personas, operated social media pages and groups designed to attract US audiences. These
groups and pages, which addressed divisive US political and social issues,
falsely claimed to be controlled by US activists when, in fact, they were controlled by Defendants. Defendants also used the stolen identities of real US
persons to post on ORGANIZATION-controlled social media accounts.

* * *

Defendant ORGANIZATION had a strategic goal to sow discord in the
US political system, including the 2016 US presidential election…Some
Defendants, posing as US persons and without revealing their Russian
association, communicated with unwitting individuals associated with the
Trump Campaign and with other political activists to seek to coordinate
political activities.

* * *

Starting at least in or around 2014, Defendants and their co-conspirators
began to track and study groups on US social media sites dedicated to US
politics and social issues. In order to gauge the performance of various
groups on social media sites, the ORGANIZATION tracked certain metrics like the group's size, the frequency of content placed by the group,
and the level of audience engagement with that content, such as the average number of comments or responses to a post…They engaged in operations primarily intended to communicate derogatory information about
Hillary Clinton, to denigrate other candidates such as Ted Cruz and Marco
Rubio, and to support Bernie Sanders and then-candidate Donald Trump.

I have quoted at length for two purposes. First, Mueller's indictment
meets all the requirements of a conspiracy theory as outlined in the first
two chapters of this book. It is a good example of a conspiracy theory
that certainly does not merit *a priori* rejection. The indictment lays out
detailed information that warrants a high degree of credibility—allowing
for the presumption of innocence to which those indicted are entitled to
by right. Mueller lays out what is neither a petty nor a grand world conspiracy; it best fits the category of a highly plausible operational conspiracy as define in Chapter 2.

My second purpose is to distinguish the conspiracy alleged in
Mueller's indictment from other, related alleged operational conspiracies
that lack sufficient evidence but may prove warranted upon further investigation. These plausible theories include: (1) that Russian interference

determined the outcome of the 2016 election; (2) that Donald Trump himself "colluded" with others in this effort; (3) that Russian operatives have *compromat*, that is, embarrassing information that can be used to influence Trump; and (4) that Russian operatives have operated under tacit or explicit authorization of Russian President Vladimir Putin. As of June 2018, it was unclear what Mueller will conclude regarding Trump's personal involvement in this conspiracy, but it is likely that whatever he reports will be the object of a contentious exchange of warring conspiracy theories in Congress and in the media. This represents a sea change, certainly, from the Watergate era, or even Iran-Contra.

The *Fox Network's* service as a conduit for Trump's conspiracism was not necessarily discernable before the election. In the 2016 primary season, *Fox News* had distanced itself somewhat from Trump, preferring neutrality and fearing divisiveness with conservative circles. But once Trump secured the nomination in June 2016, *Fox* re-established itself as the information silo of the populist right. Following Ailes' forced retirement after a sexual harassment scandal, *Fox* formally abandoned its "Fair and Balanced" motto in favor of "Most Watched, Most Trusted." As the polarization of American politics proceeded apace in 2017, the network became even more unapologetically aligned with the president, taking dead aim at Mueller and the FBI, and embracing the conspiracy theory of a Deep State. Its pundits enthusiasticlly promoted the theory of a conspiracy against Trump on the part of the FBI and Mueller in collaboration with the main stream media, which the president began to label "the fake news networks." *Fox News* anchors maintained some distance from outright endorsement of Trump's conspiracy theory and sometimes put difficult questions to administration spokespersons, but at the same time the network's line-up of evening hosts (Sean Hannity, Tucker Carlson, and Laura Ingram) pummeled Mueller, mainstream news outlets, and the FBI's former director, James Comey. Its daily morning program, *Fox and Friends*, became downright sycophantic, minute by minute broadcasting the president's Tweets, which could come in blizzard fashion at times. Reports based on White House sources reported reliably that Trump's mornings begin with him in bed watching *Fox* and tweeting commentary.[18] Often Trump would call or even visit the hosts, unannounced, for a friendly chat. For example, on June 18, 2018, with controversies raging and even some usually supportive Republicans critical about the administration's separation of illegal immigrant parents from their children, the *Fox* hosts preferred to ask the president how he had enjoyed his birthday.

Breitbart.com just as enthusiastically amplifies Trump's conspiracy theories. Despite its reputation for sensationalism, its front page typically includes a number of straightforward summaries of news drawn elsewhere, especially from the world of entertainment. Contrary to what one might expect, these reports do not selectively quote or distort these reports and commentaries. *Breitbart's* working assumption, not necessarily faulty, seems to be that celebrity condemnations of Trump will land on the eyes and ears of its audience as elitist rants. Of course, a straightforward quotation from rock guitarist Ted Nugent, infamous for his anti-gun control rants, might have the same effect on a liberal audience, but there simply are not enough visible celebrities on the right to be used to this effect.

If in the Cold War and early post-Cold War era we Americans lived in an information environment characteristic by a single "liberal" media silo,[19] in the Trump era we have transitioned, in a trend that can be traced back at least to Reagan years, if not the Goldwater candidacy, to media silos that separate us into camps.

CONSPIRACY THEORY, FUSION, AND THE ALT-RIGHT

Has the Internet played a significant role in the success of Trumpism? The answer seems obviously, "yes," given Trump's use of Tweets, the rapid growth of Alex Jones's *InfoWars*, the widespread use of bots to spread misinformation, cyber technologies permitting micro-targeting of audiences, and the ease with which anyone with a computer and Internet Service Provider can launch just about any kind of claim, including highly racist and patently fabricated ones, into the information environment. Revelations about how hackers and experts using bots (in particular, Cambridge Analytica; see Chapter 7) were able to target key groups in the electorate in swing states in the election have added to the suspicions of manipulation. Add to this stew of political cyber weapons the more generalized commercial practice of tracking Internet use and marketing of personal information, and there is probably more concern about psychological manipulation and brainwashing than in there was in the early era of television, when films like the *Manchurian Candidate* (1962) reflected acute social anxiety about the power of media.

It is logical to hypothesize that the Internet and World Wide Web, as well as developments in rapid transportation, would facilitate conspiracism. The relative anonymity that can be achieved on the Internet also means that disseminators are less likely to be held responsible for disseminating false facts and wild theories. Conspiracy theory investigators, of widely varying opinions and rationality, focusing on the Kennedy Assassination and 9/11 attacks are kept in constant contact with one another and meet often face to face at conferences held to brief one another on the most recent debates and new information.

Despite the general assumption that the ease and speed of disseminating information facilitate conspiracy theories, there simply is no firm evidence that conspiracism is more pronounced today than in the past. As we saw in Chapter 1, a long-term study of letters to the editor provides little evidence that the paranoid style of conspiracism is more common today.[20] Conspiracy theories about the Kennedy assassination flourished before the Internet came into public use. In the highly emotional and conflicted period immediately after the Civil War, unsubstantiated conspiracy theories (including one that accused Johnson—Andrew, not Lyndon—of involvement) around Lincoln's assassination spread rapidly.[21]

Leftist critics like Noam Chomsky have long asserted that the American media has functioned to "manufacture consent" and failed to provide the kind of critical perspective necessary for a democracy. But Chomsky accepts with little qualification the school of thought that sees conspiracy theories as illusory and as threats to democracy, capable only of inspiring hatred and violence. Chomsky, perhaps the most respected radical thinker and widely diffused left thinker, acknowledges that there are conspiracies in political life but argues that they distract activists from "the real, structural causes of injustice." If a group of elites get together to secretly plan initiatives to benefit themselves, this is just "the normal working of political structures."[22]

Closely linked to this idea is the contention, quite common among historians, social scientists, and journalists, that conspiracy theories advanced on the left foster "fusion" of left and right paranoia, thereby empowering right-wing extremism. Chip Berlet, an independent, muckraking journalist, says that scandalous revelations of official wrongdoing pose "the dilemma for the left…that right-wing populist organizers [will] weave these systemic and institutional failures into a conspiracist narrative that blames 'secret elites.'" This leads, he claims, to a kind of sensationalism widely diffused via "infotainment" and talk radio.[23] Michael Barkun uses a similar term, "fusion paranoia," in arguing that arguments highlighting conspiracy, whether on the left or right, now travel through media and foster apocalyptic and millenarian themes.[24] This "seepage" of conspiracism from the left to the right has swelled as a result of the Internet, say critics.

These concerns certainly cannot be dismissed out of hand, but is the solution to rule out from public discourse any talk of conspiracism, even where there may be plausible grounds to charge secretive collusion subversive to democratic culture? Should muckraking journalists, revisionist historians, and critical social scientists simply remove "conspiracy" from their vocabularies? My own position closely resembles that of Fenster, who asserts that conspiracy theories can vary in the degree to which they are democratic and emancipatory or, on the opposite end of the scale, contribute to authoritarianism and violence.[25]

In their infancy, the Internet, the World Wide Web, Cable TV, and social media were each largely welcomed as providing alternative news and information outlets, fostering, it was presumed, a more vibrant democratic culture. Contrary to common understanding, the idea for "alt" Internet did not originate with extreme rightist Richard Spencer's characterization of his white nationalist movement as the "alt-right." Even before the Web, when Internet information was mostly text-based, those with a dial-up modem and internet savvy could find information not widely available in the mainstream print and broadcast media on text-based "alt" networks of varying types.

In Chapter 1 we briefly reviewed the case of Gary Webb, the investigative reporter who in 1996 unearthed the "Dark Alliance" between the CIA and the Nicaraguan contras, whose career was subsequently ruined (possibly contributing to his later suicide) by a conspiracy panic in the journalistic establishment.[26] Subsequent documentation by the National Security Archive (a non-governmental organization housed at George Washington University) demonstrates that several US government officials were fully aware of the Contra organized drug trafficking to the United States.[27]

Something similar had occurred 12 years earlier during the Contra war itself when a Jesuit connected institute, the Christic Institute, charged that Contras trained and equipped by the CIA were responsible for the bombing in 1984 a press conference organized in Costa Rica by a dissident Contra. The bomb killed eight people and injured many more. The Christic Institute played an important role in investigating and organizing support for a suit it brought around charges made by two journalists who were present at the bombing. Fusion critics labeled the Christic campaign a "conspiracy theory" with little foundation.[28] The Institute did not use "conspiracy" prominently in its campaign, but certainly implied a conspiracy was at work by referring to "The Secret Team" and the "Shadow Government." But the major flaw of Christic's campaign was not that it wrongly charged "conspiracy" but that it largely treated the team as a "rogue" operation, rather than a program secretly but clearly authorized by the Reagan administration (see Chapter 7).

After the case was dismissed, colleagues, relatives of the victims, and the plaintiffs themselves did express dissatisfaction with the way Christic politicized the case and went beyond the facts known at the time in its analysis and public relations campaign.[29] On the other hand, many of the key facts in the case were later validated, by among others the respected English language *Tico-Times* in Costa Rica.[30] Later the larger dimensions of what by any reasonable definition was an operational conspiracy were more completely revealed in the congressional Iran-Contra hearings. Unfortunately for Christic, before vindication the Institute lost its tax exempt status when, in 1992, under pressure from conservative groups, the IRS decided that the Institute's actions were "political" rather than educational. (Christic activists later reorganized into the Romero Institute, name for the slain Salvadoran Archbishop Oscar Arnulfo Romero, killed by a right-wing death squad in 1980.) One wonders whether the IRS would make such a determination today in the age of Trump when large foundations funded with "Dark Money" (see Chapter 6) from billionaires are undertaking litigation and "education" around political issues.

The left critique of Christic's tactics anticipates a contemporary concern that the "alternative" moniker ("alt") has opened the door for the entry of white nationalism into the mainstream, under the more benign-sounding "alt-right." Spencer, who prefers the term "white identitarian" or even "white nationalist" to the label "white supremacist", is usually cited as the inventor of the term "alt", however, the "alt" prefix was a common term for a variety of Use-net groups, not all of them political, formed in the early days of the Internet.[31] Whether or not Spencer, formerly a Ph.D. student at Duke, who influenced Steven Miller, the hard-right advisor who was still within Trump's inner White House circle in 2018, actually invented the term, he has used it effectively to promote white race ideology under the more benign-sounding "alt-right" umbrella.

What makes the "alt-right" an "alternative" is not its aversion to leftists and liberals, but its challenge to mainstream conservativism. According to George Hawley, a political scientist at the University of Alabama, the mainstream conservative movement has long served as an important gatekeep, "keeping certain right-wing tendencies out of view and under control."[32] The goal of "less radical voices" in the movement, says Hawley, is to end mass immigration and political correctness and to normalize white identity politics. While white supremacy has been deeply ingrained in American history, it has been maintained below the surface, but Trump's campaign more open and persistent exploitation of fear of mass immigration and Muslims has enhanced the movement.[33]

Trump's reaction to the "Unite the Right" rally in Charlottesville, Virginia in August 2017, staged by white supremacists and white nationalists, which included chants of "Jews will not replace us," was revealing of just how instrumental his rise has been to the alt-right. The marchers boldly headed for a statue of Thomas Jefferson at the University of Virginia, where they encountered approximately 30 students who had locked arms and surrounded it. The mob directed monkey noises toward black students in the cordon. Thereafter a scuffle broke out, with injuries predominately among the students. As the rally continued in town, more violence occurred in encounters between the supremacists and counter-protesters, with the former group chanting, "Our blood, our soil," on at least one occasion. Later in the day, a local citizens' militia arrived, ostensibly to keep the peace, as police seemed to have abandoned any such role. However, before long counter-protesters were under attack from all sides, notably from the "militia."[34]

Rather than condemn the supremacists, who marched in fascist style, Trump said at a news conference, "We condemn in the strongest possible terms this egregious display of hatred, bigotry and violence on many sides, on many sides. It's been going on for a long time in our country." He went on to congratulate the police and Virginia National Guard, "They've really been working smart and working hard. They've been doing a terrific job."[35]

Hawley's study treats the alt-right as dangerous, but he fears that identifying them with right-wing conspiracy theory is both inaccurate and unwise. He argues that most who identify with the alt-right do not pay attention to Alex Jones and *InfoWars*, and he is concerned that Hillary Clinton's campaign speech of August 25, 2016 that linked the alt-right more broadly to leaders of Brexit (the movement to take the United Kingdom out of the European Union) and to Vladimir Putin only served to publicize the supremacist cause. Much like fusion theorists, Hawley sees a risk of legitimating rather than discrediting the movement. Hawley points out that the alt-right reacted favorably to the Clinton speech because of the attention it brought to their cause. Tim Stanley of London's *Daily Telegraph,* commented, "There's a risk of conflating various political projects into some grand movement, and deciding that the whole thing is a coherent conspiracy with a direct line to Trump. The alt-right would love you to think that, as would Hillary Clinton."[36]

NORMALCY AND DISRUPTION

It should be clear by now that I regard most conspiracy theories promoted by Trump and his acolytes as qualifying as fitting the "paranoid style." At the same time, I also have contended that independent of their truth-value, many of the media's stories about collusion with the Russians, administrative cover-ups, financial conflicts of interest, etc., should be considered conspiracy theories. They are neither petty conspiracy theories, nor grand or world in the sense of full explanations of Trump's appeal and electoral success.[37] But they are significant, "operational" conspiracy theories, as defined in Chapter 2. Not all are plausible; some have already achieved some warrant by virtue Mueller's indictments.

Too often the very phrase "conspiracy theory" is utilized by academics and journalists to dismiss, deride, and disqualify claims about conspiracies that are worthy of analysis and investigation, that point toward secretive collaboration kept from public view because they are either illegal, unethical, or politically embarrassing. My approach does not reject entirely the wisdom embodied in Hofstadter's "paranoid style," but this phrase should neither be associated with all conspiracy theories, nor with all forms of populism, as I will try to show in the next two chapters. We need in particular to take note of how frequently the exercise of power elites is conspiratorial. How we parse the realistic from the outlandish demands more attention to conspiratorial behavior than we have typically accorded it in academia and journalism. So too is what ramifications resort to conspiracy has for democratic politics.

I hold no brief for what Daniel Pipes calls "world conspiracy theories," that is, theories that attribute transformational events and

3 TRUMPISM, FAKE NEWS AND THE "NEW NORMAL"   97

tendencies (e.g., revolutions, globalization, rise and fall of civilization, hegemonic rise and decline) exclusively or mainly to conspiracy. But I also want to argue that we need to theorize about conspiratorial behavior as meaning, impactful political activity. I hope to make a start on thinking about how we might theorize and answer questions, such as how and when (if ever) can a conspiracy alter the course of events? How and when (if ever) does exposure of conspiracies alter the course of events?

No suspicion of secretive, illegal conduct by a candidate has gotten more public attention than the allegation the Trump campaign, if not Trump himself colluded with powerful Russian politicians, including Vladimir Putin himself, to undermine the Clinton campaign and swing the election. Yet rarely is this allegation called a "conspiracy theory." The reason why is because we reserve "conspiracy theory" for claims that are outlandish, beyond serious consideration by rational people. It is typically based on evidence that fails the test for being taken seriously, much less for carrying truth value. Yet, in many ways the "golden showers" story and the claim that Putin possesses compromising information with which he can blackmail Trump continued for most of 2017 to rest upon quite shaky ground—on uncorroborated information provided by Christopher Steele, a former British spy, on anonymous leaks from US intelligence agencies, and on speculation about the activities of Russian cybersecurity officials and hackers.

This book was written in summer of 2018, so I am not in a position to judge the degree to which Mueller's investigation may lend credence to conspiracy theories about Russiagate. The dots may yet be connected by the Special Counsel, but many of the key allegations floated nightly in the 24-hour news cycle and late-night comedy monologues are yet to be substantiated. At the time of writing, the situation described by Masha Gessen, a prominent Russian anti-Putin activist, remained valid: "The context, sequence, and timing of the leaks [from the national security sources and the White House] is determined by people unknown to the public, which is expected to accept anonymous stories on faith."[38]

Trumpism has disrupted the power of the regime of truth to discipline political discourse in media, to challenge the "common sense" understandings of what is "normal" about American politics. This has global implications because Trump has dared question American exceptionalism and the key rationales for maintaining a garrison state and projecting American power abroad.

It is remarkable how many story lines being pursued in the mainstream media during the Trump presidency would have appeared outlandish before Trump's Electoral College victory—a phrasing I choose to use because he lost the popular vote by a sizable margin. An explosive example can be seen in Trump's response (February 4, 2016) to *Fox News'* Bill O'Reilly's question about positive comments the new president had made about Russian President Vladimir Putin. After Trump affirming that he "respected" Putin, O'Reilly exclaimed, "But he's a killer."

"There are a lot of killers. You think our country's so innocent?" replied Trump. The interview aired just before America's great undeclared holiday, the football "Super Bowl," the most watched telecast of any year and usually packed with jingoist displays of patriotism and symbolic support for America's military abroad. Yet here was the "leader of the free world" highlighting that the United States too had used tactics of assassination and thuggery. While I doubt that Donald Trump has a clue what "American exceptionalism" means, perhaps no president has given an interview, much less to *Fox News*, that so questions the underlying assumptions about America's role in the world.

My point is not to argue for or against the moral equivalence of the United States to Russia, but to point out that Trumpian discourse shares with conspiracy theory a certain disruptiveness of established order and hegemonic discourse. In some ways, this disruption may open new dialogues and debates. Bernie Sanders also disrupted the regime of truth by challenging the taboo discourse of "socialism." Social movements protesting police violence have challenged both the substance and symbols of racism. The difference is that in contrast to Sanders, Trump's discourse severely undermines something positive, i.e., the way that the regime of truth has upheld civility in political discourse; its disruption can be dangerous to the kind of liberal culture that makes a book like this possible.

This disruptiveness helps explain why our neighbors and relatives, who seem like "good people," engage in or tolerate deplorable words and behaviors, ones which would have mortally wounded campaigns of the past. These disruptions have already changed not only the rules of public discourse, but also the professional standards of the academic and journalistic world. Opposition to Trump, not least on the editorial page the most prestigious newspapers in the country, now includes commentary and investigative reporting stories that would have been dismissed in the past as mere "conspiracy theory." Social science professors try to decide how partisan they should be in the classroom and how tolerant of darker sentiments expressed by students sympathetic to Trump.

CONSPIRACISM AND THREATS TO DEMOCRACY

Too often social scientists and journalists dismiss all theories alleging secretive exertions of power as paranoia. Conspiratorial behavior has been systematically ignored, or worse dismissed as without consequence, in my own discipline, political science. We need to examine conspiracies themselves, as a form of collective, subjective behavior that deserves to be integrated into, not marginalized from explanations of a structural and historical character. Under some circumstances, conspiracy theories can be empowering, even if they are only based on suspicions, when they demand accountability and transparency in political life; they have the opposite effect when elevated by their holders into holistic, comprehensive worldviews.

Trump's success in capturing the GOP nomination and then the presidency itself surprised pundits, politicians, and political scientists alike (and I make no claim to having anticipated his success). However, he has not "single-handedly restored" the paranoid style, nor has it returned when "least expected." Nativism and distrust of not only political authority but also of media, science, universities, etc., draws upon anxieties that have been building in recent decades. The steady erosion of the moral and political certainties, the frayed welfare system, wealth concentration, and celebrity culture are all contributing factors to the growth of conspiracy culture.

There is a good reason to worry, as Conor Lynch claims, that Trumpism "will permeate American politics for years to come."[39] However, is it only only conspiracy theories that are proliferating, but actual conspiracies as well. Conspiracy culture is not just an attitudinal disposition toward belief in conspiracy theories, it is also rooted in actual conspiracies, that is, political practices that are deceptive, secretive, and oriented toward immoral or illegal ends. We err if we continue to dismiss the origins and consequences of conspiracies, not just conspiracy theory, in our political culture. The task is to develop frameworks to assess the truth value of conspiracy beliefs, to analyze what they review about the health of democracy, and the relationship of the state to society in the age of global capitalism.

A good example of how we can accomplish this comes from an unlikely source, a book that examines conspiracism in a part of the world that currently stands at the geographic center of political decay and violence, the Middle East. Matthew Gray asserts "that for the most part conspiracism occurs in the Arab world as a result of political structures, which in turn are the result of historical impacts, the effects of external dynamic, state-society relations, and political culture."[40] He offers three "main explanatory approaches" to understanding conspiracism in the Arab world: marginalization, that is, a sense of being ignored and excluded by global and national elites; the state–society relationship, that is, a sense that the state increasing responds to interests unrepresentative of society; and political dynamics and structures, that is, the institutions that incentivize the way political actors behave.

A few pages later, he argues that the Middle East's...

... search for political and economic development and a place within the globalization process have all helped to create an environment for conspiracism. Conspiracism can often be a discourse by marginalized elements that seeks to popularly deconstruct official or state versions of events, and it is a response to the failures of governments and leaderships to develop effective models of economic development and popular political participation. It is also a sign of diminishing state legitimacy and a breach between state and society."[41]

Middle Eastern states, says Gray, typically respond to economic development challenges and threat to legitimacy with "their own conspiracist rhetoric." Conspiracism becomes "a tool of symbolic manipulation, legitimation and control" (12). Put more simply and by way of example, states may find it useful to distract or rally the people through scapegoating, stereotyping, exaggerating, or actually creating external threats, usually with rhetoric suggesting that the "enemy" is within. In my work on Latin America, I see a similar process at work. Of course, conspiracism in a great, hegemonic state will differ from that of a nation-state that is much less powerful and wealthy. But I contend similar patterns can be identified in the United States (and Europe) in the Trump era.

In my contribution to *Transparency and Conspiracy: Ethnographies of Suspicion in the New World Order*[42] I asked, "Within a political culture that is chauvinistic and militant in its claim to constitute the world's greatest democratic experiment, what explains the widespread conviction that more sinister, conspiratorial forces control of the government (or lurk behind it)?" That essay limited itself largely to the role of intervention abroad in spurring suspicion, but the rise of Trump demands a more comprehensive approach, and it demands we evaluate not just origins but also consequences.

The mainstream media may have "manufactured consent" and played a key role in maintenance of the regime of truth in the era of liberal, international hegemony. Donald Trump's campaign has disrupted that regime by convincing a significant part of the population not only that the *New York Times, Washington Post, CNN*, etc., are not fair and balanced. It may very well be healthy for democracy for the public to be critical, even skeptical about news media. But this is not Trump's project. What he has done, much like right-wing populists in other parts of the world, is promote cynicism about professional journalism. That is not his fault alone, but this particular conspiracy theory moves us further, not closer to an information order encouraging to democracy.

NOTES

1. "How Popular Is Donald Trump," *FiveThirtyEight.com*, September 19, 2017 (accessed September 19, 2017).
2. See transcript of her speech at the United Nations Fourth World Conference for Women 1995, available at http://www.mfa.org/exhibitions/amalia-pica/transcript-womens-rights-are-human-rights (accessed September 15, 2017).
3. I am grateful to Samra Cordic, whose undergraduate paper for my seminar on conspiracy theory alerted me to the instrumental role that conspiracism played in the defeat of the ERA, especially in the rhetoric of Phyllis Schlafly and her Eagle Forum. Among several sources citing the panic created by Schlafly and others, two are Martha Weinman Lear, "You'll Probably Think I'm Stupid," *New York Times* archive (April 11, 1976): 192; Jane J. Mansbridge, *Why We Lost the ERA* (Chicago: University of Chicago Press, 1986). Phyllis Schlafly's *Who Killed the American Family* was published by WND Books, based in Medford, Oregon, issued again in 2014.
4. *New York Daily News*, September 11, 2016.
5. "What Is Fake News? Its Origins and How It Grew in 2016," *The Telegraph* (London, March 16, 2017) with a graph visible at www.telegraph.co.uk/technology/0/fake-news-origins-grew-2016 (accessed September 19, 2017).
6. "This Analysis Shows How Viral Fake News Stories Outperformed Real News on Facebook," *BuzzFeed.com*, November 16, 2016.
7. www.foxnews.com/opinion/2017/05/17/sean-hannity-trump-faces-alliance-haters.html (accessed September 19, 2017).
8. Richard Hofstadter, *The Paranoid Style in American Politics* (New York: Vintage Reprints, 1968).

9. For a wonderfully crafted website with examples of Cold War era propaganda and historical reference works, see https://manspropaganda.wordpress.com/the-cold-war (accessed June 18, 2018).
10. W. Lance Bennett, *News: The Politics of Illusion* (White Plains, NY: Longman Press, 1983): 23.
11. The best of several books on the media's performance during the Reagan presidency are Mark Hertzgaard, *On Bended Knee: The Press and the Reagan Presidency* (New York: Schocken Press, 1989); L. Lance Bennett, *News: The Politics of Illusion*.
12. Bennet, *News ... Illusion*: 96.
13. See Daniel Hellinger and Dennis Judd, *The Democratic Façade* (Belmont, CA: Wadsworth Publishing, 1994): 52–86.
14. Glynnis MacNicol, "Here's the Real Reason Glenn Beck and Fox News Are Parting Ways," *Business Insider*, April 6, 2011.
15. Andy Cush, "How the Donald Trump Campaign Turned America's Greatest Conspiracy Theorist Into a Household Name," *Spin.com*, October 26, 2016, http://www.spin.com/featured/the-invisible-empire-of-alex-jones (accessed February 23, 2017).
16. See Kathryn Olmsted, *Real Enemies: Conspiracy Theories and American Democracy, World War I to 9/11* (New York: Oxford University Press, 2009): Chapter 7.
17. https://www.justice.gov/file/1035477/download (accessed February 20, 2018).
18. Andrew Marantz, "How Fox and Friends Rewrites Trump's Reality," *The New Yorker Magazine*, January 15, 2018.
19. If it is not clear, I am referring to "liberal" in the sense of a broad ideology of individualism and markets, not as "left of center."
20. Joseph E. Uscinski and Joseph M. Parent, *American Conspiracy Theories* (New York: Oxford University Press, 2014).
21. See http://rogerjnorton.com/Lincoln74.html (accessed June 18, 2018). Also, an archive of newspaper articles of the era shows considerable misinformation. See the Fords Theatre archive at http://rememberinglincoln.fords.org (accessed June 18, 2018).
22. Noam Chomsky (Interview). https://www.youtube.com/watch?v=JirrKIQfOmk (accessed July 27, 2017).
23. Michael Kelly, "The Road to Paranoia," *The New Yorker*, June 19, 1995: 60–70. Available at http://www.newyorker.com/magazine/1995/06/19/the-road-to-paranoia (accessed July 27, 2017); Chip Berlet, "Clinton, Conspiracism and Civil Society," Political Research Associates, http://www.uni-muenster.de/PeaCon/conspiracy/networks-01.htm. February 12, 1998 (accessed July 27, 2017).
24. Michael Barkin, *A Culture of Conspiracy: Apocalyptic Visions in Contemporary America* (Berkeley: University of California, 2003).

25. Mark Fenster, *Conspiracy Theories: Secrecy and Power in American Culture* (Minneapolis: University of Minnesota Press, 2nd ed., 2012): 287–288.
26. See Jack Z. Bratich, *Conspiracy Panics: Political Rationality and Popular Culture* (Albany: State University of New York Press, 2008): 79–89.
27. See National Security Archive, *The Contras, Cocaine, and Covert Operations*, National Security Archive Electronic Briefing Book No. 2 (1996), available at https://nsarchive2.gwu.edu/ (accessed December 8, 2017).
28. For example, Chip Berlet, "Big Lies, Spooky Sources," *Columbia Journalism Review* (May/June 1993).
29. Berlet accurately reports on this falling out, attributing the source to conspiracism, though grudgingly acknowledging that the Institute kept the story alive. See "Rightist Influences on the Christic Institute Theories," (n.d., circa 1993), available from http://www.publiceye.org/rightwoo/rwooz9-13.html (accessed December 8, 2017).
30. "La Penca, 30 Years Later," *The Tico Times*, San José, Costa Rica, http://www.ticotimes.net/LaPenca30Years (accessed December 8, 2017).
31. See Molly Osberg, "Not Just Nazis: Alt-Genres Have Always Been 'Safe Spaces' for White People," *Splinternews.com*, December 8, 2016 (accessed June 18, 2018).
32. George Hawley, *Making Sense of the Alt-Right* (New York: Columbia University Press, 2017): 7.
33. Hawley, *Making Sense of the Alt-Right*: 15, 115.
34. This summary is taken from the eyewitness account of reporter Joe Heim, "Charlottesville Timeline," *Washington Post*, August 17, 2018.
35. Transcript at https://www.vox.com/2017/8/12/16138906/president-trump-remarks-condemning-violence-on-many-sides-charlottesville-rally (accessed June 18, 2018).
36. Hawley, *Making Sense of the Alt-Right*: 124–125, including the Stanley quote.
37. Daniel Pipes introduced the distinction between "grand" and "petty" conspiracy theory in *Conspiracy: How the Paranoid Style Flourishes and Where It Comes From* (New York: The Free Press, 1997).
38. Masha Gessen, "Russia: The Conspiracy Trap," *New York Review of Books*, March 6, 2017.
39. Conor Lynch, "Paranoid Politics: Donald Trump's Style Perfectly Embodies the Theories of Renowned Historian," *Salon*, July 7, 2016. http://www.salon.com (accessed September 18, 2017).
40. Matthew Gray, *Conspiracy Theories in the Arab World: Sources and Politics: Sources and Politics* (New York: Routledge, 2010): 2.
41. Gray, *Conspiracy Theories*: 12.
42. Daniel Hellinger, "Paranoia, Conspiracy, and Hegemony in American Politics," in *Transparency and Conspiracy: Ethnographies of Suspicion in the New World Order*, ed. Harry G. West and Todd Sanders (Durham, NC: Duke University Press, 2003).

CHAPTER 4

Suspicious Minds, the 2016 Election and Its Aftermath

"Anger and resentment are not a governing party," said Senator Jeff Flake, the Republican Senator from Arizona as he announced on October 24, 2017, that he would not seek re-election in 2018.[1] Whether Flake was referring to President Donald Trump or broadly to his followers is not entirely clear. Certainly, Trump's tapped into anger and deep-seated resentment among white male voters. These feelings coincide with considerable evidence of more generalized mistrust and suspicion of ruling elites in the electorate.[2] These sentiments lend themselves to the kind of conspiracism that Hofstadter characterized as the "paranoid style,"[3] which we have been critically evaluating in earlier chapters.

Conor Lynch offered a typical but accurate denunciation of Trump's discourse, commenting:

> With Trump, there is always a plot, and every conceivable problem — whether it be social, economic, political — can be traced back to a cunning and calculated group of conspirators who want to destroy America and its culture...Trump has single-handily restored the paranoid style to the mainstream (on the right, at least); giving credibility to wacky conspiracy theories from the bowels of the blogosphere and creating an angry and fanatical movement that will permeate American politics for the years to come.[4]

© The Author(s) 2019
D. C. Hellinger, *Conspiracies and Conspiracy Theories in the Age of Trump*, https://doi.org/10.1007/978-3-319-98158-1_4

We certainly should not think that Trump "single-handedly" brought about this state of affairs. Whether we should put all Trump supporters into an "angry and fanatical" basket is another thing. It might be worth recalling that Barrack Obama won solid victories in several of the Midwestern industrial states that were together considered a "blue wall" for the Democrats. Trump's margin, some polls suggest, was aided by white voters who had cast ballots for Obama in 2008 and 2012.[5] It is worth noting that minority working-class voters remained loyal to the Democratic candidate, but turnout was lower among these groups.

The Trump campaign exploited racist and gender biases as well as anti-elitist sentiment. These attitudes were not created by Trump, but his campaign and his first 18 months in the presidency certainly amplified them. Though more than any other sector my analysis focuses on examining the shift among white working class, I do not pretend to say that the election was won or lost with their votes alone. Hillary Clinton won a sizable majority of votes nationwide; in fact, Democrats have won a plurality or majority of the vote in every presidential election since 1992, excepting George W. Bush's re-election in 2004, the first election after the 9/11 attacks. Institutional bias had a role in inflating the impact of racist and sexist prejudices, because the Electoral College system impacted the weight of votes in smaller states that are more heavily populated by whites. Even so, in the swing states of the upper Midwest, it was not just a shift in votes by poor and rural whites that delivered the crucial electoral votes, it took significant votes by whites in affluent suburbs, as well as money from wealthy donors to deliver victory to Trump.

This chapter focuses on the longstanding, secular decline of confidence in American institutions since the mid-1960s and how many suspicious minds turned not only to Trump but also to Bernie Sanders. Chapter 5 will look more closely at the role socioeconomic distress and globalization may have played and draws some comparisons to other well-noted cases, especially in Europe.

READING VOTERS' ENTRAILS

A great deal of survey evidence, that is, individual-level data gathered by pollsters, suggests that gender and racial prejudices were the most powerful motivating factors explaining crucial swing vote, with economics significant, but less so.[6] However, that finding needs to be put in context; after all, racial and gender prejudice were not new in the 2016 election. Why did they become more salient to enough voters to enable Trump to win the vote in states that were presumed safely in the Clinton column before the election? Here is where the geographical context becomes relevant and can be assessed with aggregate level data, that is, the demographics of areas that swung away from Obama in 2012 and toward Trump in 2016.

Using statistical analysis of the likelihood of an individual voting for Trump, economic dissatisfaction increased the likelihood of voting for Trump by a factor of 0.13; hostile sexism increased the likelihood by 0.35; and economic dissatisfaction by 0.65.[7] Another reason for Clinton's loss, often overlooked in examinations of the voting behavior of residents of small cities and counties, is turnout. National turnout in 2016 was about the same as it was in 2012, but in six states expected to go Democratic where Trump made large inroads (winning five) there were important declines in areas that Clinton needed to win handily. Where Clinton ran strongest (over 70% of the vote), turnout was down 1.7% of the vote; where Trump was strongest, rural areas, voting was up 2.9%.[8] As we will see shortly rural counties and smaller cities tended to be most socioeconomically distressed, and that is where the white working class vote has most shifted away from Democrats.

There is little doubt, then, that on the individual level the factors best predicting a voter's choice are, in order of importance, racist attitudes (by a considerable margin), then sexism, and then economic discontent. However, the statistical evidence does not tell the entire story. Obama, America's first black president ran considerably stronger than did Clinton among white voters, especially in the areas of the country that have been aligned with Democrats but saw a shift toward Republicans. Why did race figure even more prominently in an election featuring a white Democratic candidate four years later? Few would argue that anyone who voted for Obama was thereby clearly not a racist. We could ask the rather impertinent question, why did enough racist voters cast their ballots for Obama to make him president? For that matter, we could ask, why did enough sexist voters cast their ballots for Hillary Clinton to give a national majority? Statistical methods allow us to assess the impact of any one of the three variables (race bias, gender bis, economic status) independently of the others, but they are less useful for examining the interactive, dynamic nature of these social forces as they influenced individual voters. And they are a snapshot at a moment in time, so they do not completely capture cultural and economic shifts that may have reached a tipping point in 2016. I use "tipping" to refer to the

% who trust the govt in Washington always or most of the time

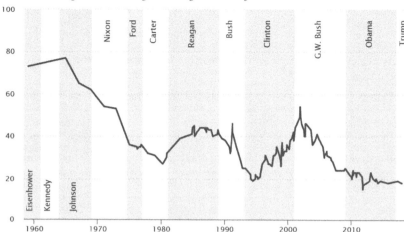

Fig. 4.1 Decline of trust in American government (*Source* Pew Research Center, Public Trust in Government, 1958–2017, available at www.people-press. org/2017/05/03/public-trust-in-government-1958-2017 [accessed March 3, 2018])

unanticipated, hugely consequential shift in political culture toward explicit, intolerant campaign discourse.

Consider political trust as an example. Many students of American politics have documented the precipitous decline in trust of the federal government since the Kennedy assassination. Data compiled by the Pew foundation in Fig. 4.1 shows that it was during the Johnson years, with the unpopularity of the Vietnam War and revelations of government perfidy (e.g., the Pentagon Papers) where distrust began its acceleration, gaining addition velocity in the Watergate years. Essentially, from 4 in 5 Americans trusting the government in Washington always or most of the time to just one in 5 Americans expressing such trust in Obama's second term and the first year of Trump.

One thing the survey data rarely do is to test whether measures of belief in conspiracy theories correlate with the voting tendencies. The exceptions here are a handful of questions drawn from major voting studies on a handful of conspiracies theories dealing with 9/11 and "rigged elections" included in the major nonpartisan, academic surveys.[9]

Ideally these studies and other reputable survey institutions (Pew, Roper, Gallop, etc.) might include questions that examine broader "predispositions" about belief in conspiracy,[10] but this kind of research has only recently begun to appear. Most of what exists continues to focus on explaining conspiracy beliefs as pathological, befitting the paranoid style, an approach critically examined in the first two chapters of this book.

POPULISM AND 2016 ELECTION

Populism and conspiracism are often twinned in analyses of voter rebellions against neoliberal globalization. However, the US election was characterized not only by Trump's rise but also that of Senator Sanders, who openly identified his ideas with socialism, previously anathema to any serious candidacy in the US. Sanders' campaign also drew upon anti-elitism and qualifies as populist, but Sanders' rhetoric and appeal shares little with the "paranoid style." Take, for example, Sanders' response to questions after Wikileaks dumped emails showing that Deborah Wasserman Schultz, Chair of the Democratic National Committee, had urged Hillary Clinton to raise doubts about Sanders' religious background (Jewish) to advance her standing with Southern voters. Sanders expressed dismay but chose to emphasize that the DNC Chair's actions showed the need for a political movement to transform the party and loosen its ties to wealthy donors. His rather temperate statement on Wasserman was, "I don't think she is qualified to be the Chair of the DNC."[11] Some of Sanders' young male followers, the "Bernie Bros", responded with less equanimity. Cenk Uygur, one of a group of young Sanders' supporters dubbed "The Young Turks", was found to have engaged in sexist and racist comments in his blog in the early 2000s. But even Uygur was relatively restrained about DNC influence. There was, he explained in a podcast, no clear plan to deploy DNC operatives to defeat Sanders.[12] One could argue that the DNC had a right to work on behalf of Clinton, a declared Democrat, over Sanders, who has always run as an independent and caucused with Democrats. Still, the secrecy of the operation provides at the least conspiratorial overtones.

Sanders waged an energetic challenge to the well-funded Democratic Party favorite, doing so despite having been written off entirely by the media early in the campaign. Like Trump, Sanders' discourse stressed inequality and the unfairness of globalization and free trade treaties. His candidacy attracted activists from the Occupy movement that had burst on the national scene in September 2011, as well Black Lives Matter—though he was less successful than clinton in mobilizing African-American voters in the primaries and caucuses. While Sanders' longstanding personal identification with socialism may have enhanced his maverick reputation, it is difficult to know much his appeal would have been sapped by a full-bore, red-baiting assault on his character and proposals.[13]

There may be some grounds to chastise Sanders' for failing to curb sexist criticism of Hillary Clinton,[14] but this shortcoming pales in contrast to Trump's repeated reliance on what Hofstadter identified as a central feature of the paranoid style in the United States, nativism and ethnic scapegoating. As a candidate and then as president Trump repeatedly dismissed serious journalism as "fake news," while simultaneously supporting or refusing to disavow unsubstantiated stories circulated on the Internet and right-wing broadcasters. Trump daily smashed taboos associated with civility and moderation, in particular through conspiratorial conjectures that the incumbent president was not a natural-born citizen (birther theory) and hence ineligible to be president—a kind of "Manchurian Candidate," referring to a popular movie (1962) of the Cold War era.

Certainly, there were grounds to criticize Hillary Clinton's record as Secretary of State, as well as a long list of troublesome issues about the Clintons' brushes with unethical if not illegal relations with wealthy benefactors; but nonetheless was extraordinary and unprecedented for a major party candidate to attack an opponent by leading a crowd in a chant to "lock her up." To judge from Trump's discourse, it is no longer the communists or the Catholics that threaten America, as in the days of Know-Nothingism and the Cold War (respectively), but the Muslims, the Mexicans, the Chinese, the "PC" liberal media, and so on. This is not likely to simply disappear should Trump leave the stage. As Lynch contends, Trump's resuscitation of the paranoid style will outlast him because he has brought "wacky conspiracy theories" out of the depth of the dark corners of the Internet, "creating an angry and fanatical movement that will permeate American politics for the years to come."

Trump and Sanders are both populists, but we should not equate the discourse of Sanders with that of Trump. Trumpian conspiracism traded not just on economic discontent but on racism, nativism, sexism, and jingoism in ways that better fits Hofstadter's conception of a style that "evokes the sense of heated exaggeration, suspiciousness, and conspiratorial fantasy." While Sanders may have targeted Wall Street and the Democratic National Committee for undue influence and favoritism, these themes were not central to his campaign. While the Sanders message may provide durable either in his own political future or in the discourse of pre-candidates such as Senator Elizabeth Warren, it is not nearly as dangerous as Trumpism, which, as Lynch warned, will be with us for years to come.

Most of the media and most political scientists (me among them) at first treated Trump's dalliance with running for president as little more than a publicity stunt. Now, in retrospect, we can see that the launch point of his successful run for the presidency was his ability to use his celebrity to trade in unwarranted and toxic ("wacky" seems kind) con-spiracy theories that triggered racist responses in portions of the elector-ate that were ready to hear the message. Long before Trump began to use "fake news" as a defense against what should have in normal times sunk any candidate's political aspirations, he was engaging in creating and spreading fake news, especially through frequent appearances on talk radio programs. He used the platform provided by stations (e.g., on the Howard Stern's syndicated radio program) in big urban markets to reach suburban whites, as well as the platform provided by Alex Jones to reach the most disaffected among white voters to spread unwarranted conspir-acy theories. Trump's celebrity status allowed him to reach America's must marginalized (mostly white) citizens in rural areas and small towns, as well as more affluent conservative white voters in suburbs.

Here it is worth reiterating that one of this book's central arguments is that the term "conspiracy theory" is used to discipline political criti-cism, in particular, to marginalize as "paranoid" radical challenges to the hegemonic consensus about American exceptionalism and the country's role in the world. Chapter 2 argued that conspiracy theories should be treated like other kinds of theories and claims about social reality. But this book does not argue that all conspiracy theories are created equal. Those most deserving of being labeled "paranoid style" are deeply flawed logically or so poorly supported by evidence that they are com-pletely implausible, and clearly some are tainted by the worst forms of scapegoating and prejudice. Some grand conspiracy theories are focused on the "new world order" so happily welcomed by President George Bush in his speech January 1991 after the invasion of Iraq,[15] with the more outrageous ones reducing tectonic shifts in the global economy to one or another cabal (Jewish Banker, the Illuminati, The Rockefellers, etc.). These should be distinguished, however, from claims that elites have engaged in operational conspiracies to shape global outcomes, a claim I will take up in Chapter 5.

What Trump did is to openly bring into a presidential campaign the paranoid style from which candidates in the past (disingenuously) distanced themselves by leaving the most outrageous slanders to outside groups or by playing the race card with implicit rather than explicit political ads and discourse. An example of slander was the campaigning by the "Swift Boat Veterans for Truth" that wrongly impugned in 2004 John Kerry's credentials as a war hero; an example of racism was the Willie Horton ad, which featured a still photo of William R. Horton (He never went by "Willie."), who had committed a murder after being released under a parole program implemented by Michael Dukakis, the former governor of Massachusetts and the Democratic presidential candidate in 1988. The point of the ad was not to criticize the parole program but to highlight Horton's race (African-American) and play to the fear of white voters. The ad was produced by Roger Ailes, the man who would go on to head up *Fox News*. In both examples, the ads were not run by the campaign but by nominally independent groups.

Trump's cozy relationship with Alex Jones and *InfoWars* served the purpose of identifying a most unlikely figure (a New York real estate tycoon) with anti-globalization conspiracy theories and with the paranoid birther theory. Jones rise to national prominence largely coincided with Trump's increased visibility as an Obama critic, exploiting fears that had been generated earlier by Glen Beck was the most infamous purveyor of the paranoid style, with a particular appeal to Tea Party activists. In 2011, *Fox News* and Glen Beck parted ways (see Chapter 2), though *Fox* hardly stopped trading in the paranoid style. But the banishment of Beck from Fox opened the way for Jones to assume more prominence. In 2016, his *InfoWars* site attracted an estimated 4–7.5 million unique visitors per month, and his syndicated radio program was on 160 stations around the country, with more listeners getting the show on the Internet.[16]

Jones' message certainly epitomizes the paranoid style, but contrary to the stereotypical image of those attracted to the paranoid style his popularity is not primarily among the lower social classes. According to Quantcast, a tracker of traffic on the World Wide Web, in February 2018 Jones' demographics were slanted toward white males, and also toward the wealthiest sectors of American society. The most common automobiles owned by visitors to *InfoWars.com* are Lincoln and Mercedes-Benz. Many visitors to *InfoWars* do own entry-level compact vehicles, but even more own large SUVs. Their income skews toward six figures.

Most visitors have college degrees, many graduate degrees. They are closely divided between Democrats and Republicans, with a slight majority tending toward the former. What this data suggests is that those attracted to the paranoid variety of conspiracy theories include white working class and rural voters, but the base is not restricted to them alone.

FAKE NEWS AND RUSSIAN INTERVENTION IN ELECTION 2016

One popular theory among Democrats is that falsified news, tweets, and ads widely circulated through social media tipped the election to Trump. While so-called "fake news" originated domestically, not just from foreign sources, the fake news conspiracy theory posits that it was part of a broader plot on the part of the Russian government aimed, according to US intelligence agencies, at influencing the 2016 election and likely to be replicated for the 2018 midterm elections.

Dan Coats, Director of National Intelligence, told the Senate Intelligence Committee in February 2018, "We expect Russia to continue using propaganda, social media, false-flag personas, sympathetic spokespeople and other means of influence to try to exacerbate social and political fissures in the United States."[17] What neither the Director nor heads of other intelligence agencies have verified, we should note, is that the outcome of the election was much influenced by this operation. Their claim was that the aim of the Russians "to worsen the country's political and social divisions." That is, RussiaGate posits a conspiracy with consequences far beyond the objective of influencing a single election.

Technically, a fake news operation may not be a conspiracy if only one person creates the fiction, but the kinds of fake news that most impact politics, whether hatched by partisan amateurs or skilled propagandists, require cooperation, at least in dissemination if not in fabrication. Manipulation of news media has long been undertaken by CIA and other Intelligence Agencies to influence political overseas. Best known in this respect is propaganda used to destabilize the democratically elected government of Salvador Allende in Chile. This operational conspiracy included using the country's leading newspaper network, *El Mercurio* and its 19 regional editions and 32 radio stations, with the CIA writing articles, as well as paying journalists and editors to write many stories exaggerating economic shortages, mobilizing opposition street protests, and encouraging military plots against the Allende government.[18] Such operations were almost routine for the United States during the Cold War; now they are enhanced by cyber technologies for influencing the messages and ads people receive through social media. Each of the branches of the military has some role in Cyber Defense, but like so much else in the military, the distinction between defensive and offensive capability is slim.

A series of indictments in the first half of 2018, brought by Special Counsel Robert Mueller, alleging illegal Russian operations to undermine Hillary Clinton's campaign and to worsen discord and polarization in American politics stopped short of claiming that these efforts swung the election or affected the vote count. Trump respond to Mueller's actions with his own conspiracy theory alleging it was President Obama's failure to act, not any culpability on the part of himself or his campaign, which merited investigation. And Trump alleged that the real collusion going on was between the FBI (with other Deep State operatives; see Chapter 7) and the "corrupt media," the "failing *New York Times*," and other mainstream media, calling them in one Tweet (November 11, 2017) "the enemy of the people."

Domestic distortion, as opposed to fabrication, of news is hardly new. Since the decline of a partisan press in the nineteenth century, distortions in news largely emanated from biases in the way that journalists and editors choose which stories to cover and selectivity in choices of vocabulary (e.g. "terrorists" vs "guerrillas" vs "freedom fighters") and of sources (official and elite ones having more credibility than protestors or more leftist critics). This may be due simply to commercial pressures or editorial bias, rather than actual fabrication of stories for political purposes, which takes us into the realm of conspiracy. News media may have transmitted many lies, but for the most they part did not manufacture them, even on the editorial page. Before the rise of cable and social media, major newspapers and three national broadcasting networks, for better and for worse, performed a gatekeeping role that ensured that most Americans got their news from organizations operating under very similar professional standards. As discussed in Chapter 2, there is much to criticize about this model, but even harshest critics in this era rarely charged that false stories were fabricated by the very organizations that provided citizens with information. News might be censored or distorted, but not outright faked. One problem today is that fewer citizens are opting to inform themselves from electronic and print sources that operate under the rules of the journalistic profession.[19] This decline has opened the door for propaganda to be diffused and more readily circulated via Facebook, YouTube, Twitter, and other forms of social media. The Obama campaign was the first to use social media to target prospective voters for donations and votes. The Sanders campaign demonstrated that it was possible to build a campaign run on small donors. The Trump campaign adapted micro-advertising techniques based on analytics, especially using Google analytics and Facebook, not only to fund raise but stage spectacular rallies and to circulate paranoid style type conspiracy theories.

"Fake news" entered our vocabulary not with Trump or the Russians but with social media, and sometime in 2016 the meme seemed to take root. Hillary Clinton used the term in a speech in December 2016, taking note of the "epidemic of malicious fake news and false propaganda that flooded social media over the past year."[20] Where Donald Trump enters the history of fake news is not only by his campaign's use of social media analytics to promote dubious stories; this strategy had to be combined with the celebrity mogul's astute sense that there existed a right-populist resentment toward the mainstream media, and that the candidate could exploit this resentment and other disfactisfaction to fuel his run for the presidency. He carried this strategy over into his presidency and his defense against charges of collusion. An example was his tweet of October 5, 2017 asking, "Why Isn't the Senate Intel Committee looking into the Fake News Networks in OUR country to see why so much of our news is just made up-FAKE!."

The ground had already been well tilled, we saw in Chapter 3, for Trump's campaign by *Fox News*. Ailes, its CEO and news director until he fell to a sexual harassment scandal in 2016, originally co-founded the network with media mogul Rupert Murdoch as a partisan vehicle for the neoconservative wing of the Republican Party. The motives were and are not entirely lucrative. For *Fox*, audience loyalty generates high advertising revenues, estimated as $100–$200 million per year, and it is part of a media empire that generates more than $4 billion of revenue.[21] And the network did not early embrace the Trump candidacy. But *Fox*, with Ailes still at the helm, and like other parts of the GOP establishment and the ultra-wealth donor-class, struck a Faustian bargain with the Trump campaign once his victory in the primary season was secured.

Could fake news in the form of bogus stories circulating on social media swing an election? This is a difficult conspiracy theory to test.

Early studies are inconclusive. A *New York Times Upshot* article reviewing some research claimed that most ads, in general, have a very limited effect, with a single TV ad impacting only two of every 10,000 votes cast. Furthermore, looking at the cumulative impact of all kinds of ads, advertising is a wash; so seemed to the consensus arising from studies.[22] Twitter estimates that Russian bots (fake owners of accounts or owners impersonating real people) tweeted 2.1 million times during the campaign, only one percent of all election-related tweets. The *Upshot* author, a political scientist who has researched the area with two colleagues, suggests that whether fake news influences people depends on a number of factors—whether people are disposed to be persuadable in the first place, how many people actually saw the ad, and how much of the total news taken in by recipients is bogus. Trump supporters visited on average 13.1 fake stories on fake news sites, but only 40% of all his supporters visited such sites, and fake news sites were only six percent of all news sites they visited.[23] These metrics reduce the likelihood that the fake news stories much influenced the vote, but given the narrowness of Trump's margin of victory in some key states, and given that fake news is disseminated through social media, not just news organization, we can't rule out its impact. That is, fake news may have been effective it it swung the undecided votes in the key states that tipped the Electoral College to vote. Targeting those voters effectively was the job of analytics.

No shortage of research in political science shows that only a small proportion of the electorate is undecided (and therefore persuadable) before a presidential election. And as the presidential election is decided by Electoral College votes, paid advertising tends to be concentrated in key states, and toward key demographics in those states. Money's influence in the campaign cannot be reduced to a matter of "whosoever has the most money wins." As Table 4.1 shows, Clinton had more money at her disposal, but Trump, not counting his advantage in free media

Table 4.1 Candidate committee and outside support, 2016 presidential election

	Candidate committee money	*Outside money*
Hillary Clinton	$563,756,928	$231,118,680
Donald Trump	$333,127,164	$75,269,043

Source Center for Responsive Politics, https://www.opensecrets.org/pres16 (accessed November 30, 2017)

exposure, had more than sufficient funds as well to run his campaign. Cambridge Analytics, a right-wing contractor whose work for the Trump campaign was paid with dark money from billionaire Robert Mercer provided significant targeting for Trump advertising and mobilization. In fact, the amount of distorted misleading advertising funded openly by candidates and political actions committee, and also in stealth by dark money (see Chapter 6) far outweighs the influence that Russian operatives can bring to bear.

While we cannot say definitively that fake news influenced the electoral outcome, it does constitute one more way in which the 2016 campaign was the most poisonous campaign of the twentieth century. Campaigns in America have long featured villainous personal attacks and severe distortions of the record, but Trump's disparagement of his rivals in the primaries showed a kind of audacious crudeness. His demeaning Carly Fiorina's looks, accusation that Ted Cruz's father may have participated in assassinating Kennedy, belittling of Marco Rubio as "Little Marco" all might have ended other presidential campaigns, but in hindsight his mockery and audacious claims proved to be kind of disruptive discourse that some parts of the electorate embraced—and other parts tolerated to achieve policy objectives favorable to social conservatives, corporations, and the wealthy.

Why would his cultivation of anger and resentment have receded in the general election, or afterward in the presidency? Even in televised debates before the general election, he repeated promises to investigate and prosecute Clinton. At campaign rallies he prompted audiences to chant "lock her up" with every mention of "crooked Hillary." Seemingly unperturbed by a succession of embarrassing revelations of his own abuse and actual assaults on women, Trump responded with frequent allusions to Bill Clinton's affairs and disgraceful sexual behavior in the White House, for which Hillary herself was unfairly held to account for having stood by her husband. At one point a leaked video from 2005 showing Trump graphically degrading women and bragging about groping (i.e., molesting) revealed the depth of his misogyny[24] and seemed to have sunk his bid for the presidency. But in an atmosphere of mistrust, of polarization spurred by highly partisan and truly racist conspiracy theories about President Obama, of gender biases (even before the "Me Too" movement had taken off), and of "normalization" of Trump's personality by late-night talk show hosts (Jimmy Fallon, host of NBC's *Tonight Show* deserves special responsibility in this respect). Trump's boast that he could shoot someone dead on the street and still got elected proved prescient. Whether it would survive damage from Mueller's investigation and a damaging result in 2018's midterm elections was yet to be determined at this writing.

Perhaps had FBI Director James Comey not announced that the FBI was reopening its investigation of Clinton's use of her unsecured private email server for State Department business, Clinton still would have won the election. Even so, Trump's campaign still would have disrupted the regime of truth (however porous it already was) and demonstrated the disjuncture between the way the world had changed and the way national politics was being conducted.

THE YEAR OF VOTING DANGEROUSLY

In the US elections, the presidency is decided not by majority or plurality vote of citizens, but by the Electoral College. Votes in the Electoral College are not distributed proportional to the population of each state, putting more power in the hands of smaller and rural state voters, which in the present-day context skews the College votes more Republican and conservative. We owe this system in part to suspicions of popular democracy among the Founders of the Republic. In fact, there are elements of a conspiracy in the way the Constitution was written. The convention that took place in Philadelphia had been authorized only to reform the Articles of Confederation. Instead, the elites who gathered there met in secret to draft a Constitution that summer of 1787 in Philadelphia, and they did so after closing off the doors and windows in sweltering heat. The course of human events that led to the Constitution cannot be reduced to a conspiracy; and certainly the cabal of planters, financiers, and merchants who met in Philadelphia produced something politically remarkable for the age. Nonetheless, "rules of the game" of politics in America today were negotiated clandestinely, and many of those rules, most notably the Electoral College, continue to shape our politics today.

Many analysts have tried to introduce an element of capriciousness into the election result by noting that a change of only 80,000 votes changed in a few key states could have resulted in a Clinton victory. That explanation is simply cherry picking. As Table 4.2 shows, a shift of fewer than 30,000 votes toward Trump could have offset Clinton had she competed more effectively in the Upper Midwest. The Electoral

Table 4.2 Playing the "what if" Electoral College game

State	Electoral votes	Winner	Winner's margin
New Hampshire	4	Clinton	2326
Nevada	6	Clinton	27,202
Minnesota	10	Clinton	43,175
Total	20		72,703
Michigan	16	Trump	10,604
Wisconsin	10	Trump	22,648
Pennsylvania	20	Trump	44,292
Total	46		77,544

If Clinton had won MI, WI, PA and Trump wins any two of NH, NV, MN, he still wins Electoral College

College not only favors rural, generally more conservative states, it makes the presidential sweepstakes just that—introducing a greater element of chance in the outcome, increasing odds that the president would be elected without a majority, or even a plurality, of votes by citizens. Furthermore, if there were, as Trump charges, an attempt to rig the election through illegal voting, his conspiracy theory takes on large consequences, because only small number of shifts in a key state can determine mathematically the outcome.

Measured directly, racial bias and gender bias seem to have played a more pivotal role than economic bias in influencing white voters to support Trump. A study[25] of trends in white voters' intentions two weeks before the election found that when the influence of typical factors, such as ideology, age, party preference, income, gender were controlled, voters expressing dissatisfaction with their economic condition were significantly more likely to vote for Trump than a typical white voter—60% more so for those most dissatisfied. However, voters who expressed "hostile" sexism and those who tended to deny the existence of racism were even more likely to vote for Trump—70% more likely in the case of voters most hostile toward minorities or most in denial about the existence of racism. Some analysts have apportioned some of the responsibility for Clinton's defeat to defections by Sanders supporters to Trump or to the Green Party candidate, Jill Stein. Mathematically it does appear that the Democrat was hurt by leftist populism as well as the right-wing variety. However, these defections were generally below levels of earlier elections and tended toward older and more conservative supporters of Sanders.[26]

It is not my intention to delve deeply into the voting patterns. Our main concern here is not whether or not voters who hold conspiracy beliefs were more likely to vote for Trump. We have only a few questions from voter surveys that are relevant to testing that hypothesis. We do have more survey data that can measure the influence of mistrust, suspicion of elite power, and sense of powerlessness played a role in the election. As we shall see, there is also some analysis based on contextual data, that is, on analysis examining aggregate voting patterns geographically, suggesting that Democratic attrition between 2012 and 2016, especially among white voters, was greater in geographic areas that were most distressed economically and socially.

Emily Jenkins, director of polling at the Cato Group, using opinion data generated by the Democracy Fund Voter Study group and a methodology (latent class analysis) that sorts cases (in this case, Trump voters) into clusters, persuasively argues that rather one kind of Trump voter, there are five.[27] In the following summaries of Jenkins' description of each group, I am emphasizing what, from her analysis, may indicate a disposition toward conspiracist beliefs.

Staunch Conservatives or "loyalists" (31%): Characteristics: Loyal Republicans, most likely to own guns and belong to NRA, worried about immigration but not as much as those whom Jenkins calls American Preservationists. These loyalists have high levels of social trust and less likely to believe the system is rigged. However, they tend to express concern about "discrimination against white people" and Muslim immigration, and they think that living most of your life in America and being a Christian are important to being a "real American." In other words, these are Trumpistas to whom one can appeal on the basis of identity politics.

Free Marketeers (25%): These voters were more anti-Clinton than pro-Trump. Like Staunch Conservatives, they are fiscally conservative but more liberal on immigration and other identity issues. Jenkins calls them more "cosmopolitan," a word often used by Trump's right-wing supporters and advisers as an epithet, more so than by the more populist right voters, i.e., the American Preservationists.

American Preservationists (20%): Elkin's description provides plenty of clues to think this group would be inclined toward right-wing conspiracism and the "paranoid style." They "lean economically progressive, believe the economic and political systems are rigged, have nativist immigration views, and a nativist and ethnocultural conception of American identity." They think anti-white prejudice is widespread. They smoke and have health issues, yet support repeal of "Obamacare," they seem to best fit the profile of Trump supporters that seem to stick with him on the basis of affect. They are skeptical about free trade, sympathetic to minorities, unhappy about unequal wealth, and see climate change as a real threat. By these traits, they have some commonality with many Democrats. As Jenkins puts it, they feel powerless against big money and the political class, and they have little social trust. Thus, we might conclude, this group would seem to have many of the attitudes that Hofstadter attributes to the "paranoid style."

Anti-Elites (19%): This group shifted their views about Clinton in a negative direction between 2012 and 2016, says Jenkins, and they are most likely of these five groups to see political and economic systems as rigged. On the other hand, they are more moderate on issues such as gun control, and they are less likely to be religious. They express less concern about identity than many other Trump voters, but they do not have favorable views on immigrants and Muslims. Overall, based on Jenkins findings, we seem to have some but not all of the dispositions we would expect in those attracted to the paranoid style of conspiracism.

The Disengaged (5%): Less like to express themselves on most issues, but immigration and Muslims are exceptions. Like Anti-Elites they see the system as rigged against them.

The Trump supporters who raise concerns about the economic and political system being "rigged" are already "conspiracy theorists" by virtue of their belief that the system is "rigged", which implies a "rigger." Many also espouse concerns about Identity issues, a not easily disentangled set of attitudes about values and cultural change involving, among other things, gender (e.g., gay marriage, patriarchy), race (mainly whiteness), language (mainly English), ethnicity (European descent), and religion (mainly Christianity), among other cultural markers. These identity issues also can lead to conspiracism, especially scapegoating. It is not hard to see how Trump's endorse of the birther issue and immigrant bashing appeal to fear about a breakdown in social order.

PARTISAN CONSPIRACY BELIEFS

Unfortunately, we have very limited direct research from the major voting studies on conspiracy beliefs, and despite the visibility of conspiracy theories in the campaign, relatively few surveys enter into the topic in any depth. But we do have some clues about who is most receptive to some of the conspiracy theories floated in the election campaign. As we reviewed in earlier chapters, mistrust of Washington has soared over the past five decades. Empirical evidence, though scarcer than what we need to draw firm conclusions, shows that conspiracy beliefs in the 2000s up until 2010 were not necessarily more widespread than they have been since the 1890s.[28] However, that research was concluded shortly before Trump's quest for the presidency became serious. It is possible that conspiracism has spiked, much like it did in the 1890s and early cold War.

A Pew study in 2012 found already that confidence in the accuracy of the count in presidential elections was already only 48% in 2004, a year in which theories widely circulated that the voting machines had failed to accurate recorded votes in the crucial swing state of Ohio, won narrowly by George W. Bush. Those very confident across the country fell to 43% in 2008 and then to 31% in 2012, with the winners, as predicted by the political scientists, more likely to express confidence than the losers. However, the Pew Center reported that confidence in the vote actually rebounded somewhat in 2016, with 45% expressing themselves as very confident that the vote was counted fairly (and 37% somewhat confident).[29]

One of the most potentially harmful conspiracy theories spread by Trump during the later stages of his campaign, when most polls were giving him little chance of winning, was that the election had been "rigged." When it became clear that despite winning the Electoral College he had lost the popular vote, Trump continued to describe the national vote as "rigged." In polling done late in the campaign, The Voter Study Group (VSG), based at George Washington University, found that overall 28% of voters were either not too confident or not at all confident that ballots were counted fairly across the country outside their own district (see Table 4.3). Using the same data, we break down the responses by presidential vote preference.

Political scientists Uscinski and Parent and others (see Chapters 1 and 2) have demonstrated that conspiracy beliefs are often adopted on the basis of "motivated reasoning"—that is, influenced by partisanship and the tendency for electoral losers to be more susceptible to conspiracism.[30] However, not only was the 2016 election the first in which a major party candidate claimed the election was "rigged," it was the first where the *winning candidate* claimed it, both before and after the

Table 4.3 Presidential voting, party ID, and suspicion

	Clinton voters	Percent	Trump voters	Percent
Did the US government know about 9/11 in advance?				
–Definitely	95	7.6	70	6.2
–Probably	350	28.0	279	24.8
Is Barack Obama a Muslim?				
–Don't know	29	2.3	48	1.9
–Muslim	351	8.5	567	50.3
–Not a Muslim	1251	61.1	488	43.3
Do the rich buy elections?				
–All the time	160	12.8	59	5.2
–Most of the time	334	26.7	233	20.7
–About half of the time	163	13.0	150	13.3
–Some of the time	466	37.3	519	46.0
–Never	115	9.2	158	14.0
Confident votes accurately counted across the country?				
–Very confident	544	16.8	1414	44.5
–Somewhat confident	1255	38.8	1458	45.9
–Not too confident	920	28.4	246	7.7
–Not at all confident	518	16.0	58	1.8

Source Democracy Fund Voter Study Group. *Views of the Electoral Research Survey*, December 2016. [Computer File] Release 1: August 28, 2017. Washington, DC: Democracy Fund Voter Study

election. Still, Table 4.3 provides some support for the motivated reasoning hypothesis, as more Clinton voters expressed doubt about the vote count than did Trump voters, despite the president voicing his own skepticism.

Table 4.3 also looks at three questions related to popular conspiracy beliefs, one of which, that Barack Obama is a Muslim, is predictably and alarmingly higher among Trump voters. I say alarmingly not out of concern that they mistake Obama for a Muslim, but because of the way Trump and many of his prominent supports directly associated being Muslim with terrorism in the campaign. On 9/11 Truther theory, there is little difference between voters in different camps; Trump voters were almost as likely as Clinton voters to say the government knew about the attacks in advance. This is a shift from earlier findings (e.g., see Table 1.1 in Chapter 1) that showed Democrats somewhat more likely to express some faith in 9/11 theories, presumably motivated by partisanship. The VSG survey shows relatively high overall endorsement of this theory compared to more recent surveys, though for a variety of reasons it is risky to directly compare surveys that used somewhat different sampling techniques and questions. Clinton supporters were more likely to see the rich as buying elections, although the margin (39.5–25.9% is not startling). Larger numbers in both camps believe that the rich buy elections "half" or "some of" the time. A "glass half full" analogy is apt here—one can express relief that "only" about 30% of the electorate think the rich rountinely buy elections, or we can feel alarmed that around 70% believe this to be true "only" some, half or all the time.

SOCIAL IMMOBILITY AND UNRESPONSIVE ELITES

Academic research on conspiracy beliefs tends to be judgmental about such beliefs, especially in research on predispositions toward conspiracism, which almost ways focus only on conspiracy theories that indicate social pathologies, such as racial prejudice or anti-Semitism. These investigations usually find that conspiracists tend to feel alienated, powerless; they seek closure on questions that disturb them; they long for more control over their lives; most troubling, they tend toward authoritarianism. Those disposed toward conspiracism are seeking to satisfy a need for order, certainty, and control in their lives. More often than not, the research focuses on the kinds of conspiracy theories that are indeed dangerous, prone to scapegoating and even worse.

However, not all conspiracy theories, I have argued, are of this pathological variety. What if feelings of alienation and powerlessness arise from a real distance between the representative institutions of liberal democracy and the central concerns of their lives? What if they are wondering why the mythical American dream seems to be receding from their grasp as their economic situation deteriorates? What if the explanation for their personal hard times is that their jobs "are just not going to come back"—and no one really seems to care?

One might reasonably ask if unemployed or low-wage workers who have been economically excluded from any share in the expanding economic pie in the post-Cold War era of technological advances and globalization have not been empowered by insisting that someone be held responsible for their plight. The same pertains to other social sectors, such as African-Americans, who are often disposed from personal experience to suspect foul play by the police and other actors in the criminal justice system, or rural residents who think city dwellers sponge off the government and have interest in understanding their problems and lives. A sense that some people are unfairly benefitting from others may reflect the decline in social mobility, some of which had been building even before the end of the Cold War. Already by the 1970s, there were signs that the social contract that accompanied the birth of the liberal international order forged by the United States after World War II was coming undone.

Research by two Stanford University economists shows a steady, precipitous decline in the upper-mobility of children born since 1940–1945, when 90% of more of those born could expect to earn more in their lifetime than their parents.[31] The decline actually began with the baby boom generation and remained acute until the rate flattened out for those born in the late 1960s (those who would have been 46–50 years old in 2016). The last year for which the economists have data is 1985 (i.e., for people who were 31 years old in 2016), when only 50% could expect to earn more than their parents. Not surprisingly, the rate of mobility falls off drastically for everyone in the bottom 30% of income earners, regardless of when they were born. These were years, ironically, in which the United States had assumed the role of global hegemon and there is no doubt that these were overall years of prosperity in macro-economic terms, but it is clear that they were also years in which upward mobility, the defining characteristic of the "American Dream," whether mythical or not, was in decline.

A Pew Center survey taken just before Election Day found that among likely voters, 72% Clinton supporters thought that "the gap between rich and poor" is a "very big problem," compared to only 33% of Trump supporters. However, Trump supporters, by a count of 58–43%, were more likely to see "job opportunities for all Americans" as a very big problem, and the gap was even greater (63–45%) in regard to "job opportunities for working-class Americans." More Clinton supporters (66–38) placed stress on the rising cost of a college education than did Trumpistas. This would seem to support the idea that Clinton and the Democrats appealed to the middle class, eliding this concept with "working class." Data also show Trumpistas putting more emphasis on immigration.[32]

We take up the issue of how globalization and technological change in more detail in Chapter 5, but the tendency toward declining upward mobility certainly provide a plausible reason to think that suspicions about the fairness of American society would grow and eventually register themselves in a populist political response—on the left or the right.

Table 4.4 Doubts about fairness in the electorate

		Clinton general election		Trump general election		Trump primary voters		Sanders primary voters		Clinton primary voters	
America is a fair society where everyone has a chance to get ahead	Strongly disagree	699	21.9%	91	2.9%	35	2.7%	327	29.8%	275	19.1%
	Disagree	1430	44.7%	431	13.7%	222	17.3%	463	42.4%	596	30.1%
	Total	2129	66.6%	522	16.6%	257	20.0%	790	72.2%	871	49.2%
Our economic system is biased in favour of the wealthiest Americans	Strongly agree	2021	63.0%	450	14.3%	168	13.0%	803	73.4%	824	56.7%
	Agree	1009	31.4%	1196	37.9%	511	39.5%	225	20.6%	541	37.3%
	Total	3030	94.4%	1646	52.2%	679	52.5%	1028	94.0%	1365	94.0%
You can't believe much of what you hear from the mainstream media	Strongly agree	424	13.2%	2062	65.8%	868	67.8%	261	23.9%	188	13.7%
	Agree	1187	37.0%	833	26.6%	300	23.4%	354	32.4%	520	35.9%
	Total	1611	50.2%	2895	92.4%	1168	81.2%	615	56.3%	708	49.6%
Elites in this country don't understand the problems I am facing	Strongly agree	1493	46.7%	1262	40.1%	522	40.4%	600	55.0%	582	40.1%
	Agree	1238	38.7%	1321	41.9%	522	40.4%	373	34.2%	651	44.8%
	Total	2731	85.4%	2583	82.0%	1044	80.8%	973	89.2%	1233	84.9%
Confident vote in the 2016 election was accurately counted	Not at all	[a]518	16.0%	[a]58	1.8%	99	7.6%	414	39.1%	560	40.1%
	Not much	929	28.4%	246	7.7%	36	2.9%	450	42.5%	456	32.6%
	Total	1447	44.4%	304	9.5%	66[a]	5.3%	864	81.6%	1016	72.7%

[a]622 (47.8%) Trump primary voters were very confident in vote count; 555 (42.6%) were somewhat confident. General election figures differ somewhat from Table 4.3 because of cases dropped for some of the questions

Source Democracy Fund Voter Study Group. Views of the Electorate Research Survey, December 2016. [Computer File] Release 1: August 28, 2017. Washington, DC: Democracy Fund Voter Study. Group [producer] https://www.voterstudygroup.org/. Consult Voter Study Group for exact questions

Table 4.4 shows results of research by VSG consistent with this hypothesis, but not without nuances. Again, our focus here is on what Clinton, Trump, and Sanders voters believe, not in explaining the choices made in the election; the column percentages reflect that objective.

On the one hand, for both the primary and general elections, those who voted for Clinton, along with those who voted for Sanders in the primary, show high levels of disagreement with the claim that everyone has a chance to "get ahead" in American society, though as one might expect, in the primaries a much higher proportion of Sanders than Clinton voters endorsed this opinion. What is surprising is that even those who voted for Trump in the primaries did not endorse this view in high numbers. Trump voters remained relatively optimistic as a group America is "fair society." A similar distribution of opinion holds regarding the assertion that the economic system is biased toward the rich—though on this question gap is less pronounced between Clinton and Sanders voters in the primary.

One possible explanation for the low percentage of Trump voters who agreed with these two statements is that Trump presented himself, despite the financial help he received early in his real estate career from his father, as a self-made man, whereas Sanders repeatedly hammered hard on the theme of economic fairness, access to higher education, and reform of the tax code in order to increase the contribution of corporations and the wealthy. We should also keep in mind that these questions are cutting close to one of a key cultural assumptions, that America is a land of opportunity, constantly reinforced in popular culture and commercial advertising. As we will see, when we examine aggregate, geographic voting patterns with an eye on social context and events, we see that racism and gender biases most likely interacted with socioeconomic factors to generate Democratic Party losses in areas of the country where people have most suffered economic decline and social exclusion.

Across the board, supporters of Clinton, Trump, and Sanders alike tend to view elites as out of touch with ordinary people. In all cases, at least four out of five voters agreed that elites "don't understand" their problems—reaching nine of every ten voters in the case of Sanders. And as might be expected, trust in the mainstream media takes a beating among all the voters; only among Clinton primary voters do even half of the respondents refrain from harshly judging the media. Trump's bashing of the media seems to have had its effect, as over 90% of his voters in the general election express distrust, with two-thirds "strongly" agreeing that "You can't believe much of what you hear from the mainstream media."

The case for "conspiracy theory is for losers" is strengthened some-what in Table 4.4 when examining the attitudes of primary voters toward the election outcome. This makes sense, as we would expect voters in the primary to be more partisan and more strongly committed to the candidate for whom they voted. Sanders voters may also have felt them-selves double losers, not only it being the case that most of them voted for the losing candidate in the general election, but having seen their preferred choice to the Democratic candidate lose the nomination fight. Their opinions may very well have been reinforced by one of the key revelations of the Wikileaks release of Democratic National Committee email—evidence that the national party took measures to help Clinton and hurt Sanders' chances.

What the declining trust in institutions points toward is what polit-ical scientists who study liberal democracy in the Global South call a "crisis of representation." The last ten years have seen the phrase begin to be used to describe evidence of democratic decline in the European context,[33] but although academic and media commentators have begun to sound an alarm about threats to democratic stability in the United States, neither the Voter Study Group or the American National Election Survey data banks have assessed directly public confidence in what have long been regarded as the key linkages between citizens and parties, the political party system and the parties themselves. In fact, the first two pages resulting from a Google search (February 23, 2018) on "United States crisis of representation" produced only two links to studies focused on the US party system or Congress—one a commentary arti-cle focused on the Republican Party in the conservative *National Review* and the other a *Huffington Post* article focused on under-representation of women in Congress. A slightly different search, using "American crisis of representation," produced seven articles on a crisis of representation in Latin America, but none on the United States.

We have already seen evidence of declining trust in government; this finding is reinforced again in Table 4.5, which displays results from the Voter Study Group survey and one additional question taken from the American National Election Study, with not more than 20% of voters in the general election expressing the view that government can be trusted to do what is right most of the time. Results are even more dismaying among those who voted for Trump or Sanders in the primaries. Most voters showed some agreement with the ideas that politicians cater to the rich and powerful and that public officials "don't care" what people

Table 4.5 Toward a crisis of representation

		Clinton general election		Trump general election		Trump primary voters		Sanders primary voters		Clinton primary voters	
Trust government to do what is right (Data from ANES survey)	About always	33	1.0%	24	0.8%	6	9.5%	6	0.6%	35	2.4%
	Most of time	489	15.3%	200	6.3%	85	6.6%	132	2.3%	293	20.2%
	Some of time	2670	83.6%	2933	92.9%	1196	92.9%	934	87.1%	1122	77.4%
Most politicians do not care about the people (Data from VSG)	Strongly agree	139	11.0%	135	12.0%	43	12.7%	51	15.5%	64	12.6%
	Agree	379	35.2%	460	40.8%	145	42.9%	121	36.8%	157	31.0%
	Total	518	46.2%	595	52.8%	188	55.6%	172	52.3%	221	43.6%
Most politicians only care about interests of rich and powerful (VSG)	Strongly agree	232	18.5%	157	13.9%	56	18.6%	87	26.5%	94	18.7%
	Agree some	602	48.1%	469	41.6%	140	41.5%	156	47.6%	224	44.4%
	Total	834	66.6%	626	55.5%	196	60.1%	243	74.1%	318	63.1%
Most public officials do not care what people think (Data from VSG)	Strongly agree	221	20.8%	255	22.6%	77	22.8%	87	26.5%	89	17.6%
	Agree	355	33.5%	440	39.0%	140	41.5%	125	38.1%	193	38.2%
	Total	576	54.3%	695	61.6%	227	64.3%	212	64.6%	282	55.8%
Strong leader is good for U.S. even if bends rules to get things done (VSG)	Strongly agree	96	7.7%	116	10.3%	44	13.1%	21	6.4%	89	17.6%
	Agree	302	24.1%	355	34.4%	100	29.8%	74	22.6%	193	38.2%
	Total	398	31.8%	471	44.7%	144	42.9%	95	29.0%	282	55.8%
How widespread is corruption among politicians in the U.S.? (VSG)	Very widespread	313	25.0%	310	27.5%	94	27.9%	101	30.8%	114	22.6%
	Quite widespread	572	45.7%	531	47.1%	170	50.4%	133	40.5%	234	46.3%
	Total	885	70.7%	841	74.6%	265	78.3%	234	71.8%	348	68.9%
How satisfied with the way democracy works in the U.S.? (VSG)	Not at all	79	6.3%	49	4.3%	11	3.3%	34	10.3%	30	0.9%
	Not very	351	18.0%	211	18.7%	63	18.6%	128	38.9%	109	1.6%
	Total	430	24.3%	260	23.0%	74	22.9%	162	49.2%	139	2.5%

Sources Democracy Fund Voter Study Group. Views of the Electorate Research Survey, December 2016. [Computer File] Release 1: August 28, 2017. Washington, DC: Democracy Fund Voter Study Group [producer] https://www.voterstudygroup.org/. Consult Voter Study Group for exact questions. The first question (only) on Trust in government is taken from American National Elections Studies (ANES), University of Michigan and Stanford University, data release of May 7, 2017 think. And across the board, seven of ten voters in general election and primaries think there is very or quite widespread corruption among politicians in the United States.

There is not unalloyed alienation from democracy, fortunately. In Table 4.6 we see that fewer than 25% of Trump and Clinton voters in the general election expressed themselves "not at all" or "not very satisfied" with democracy in the United States. Very few of those who voted for Clinton in the primary expressed dissatisfaction, but there is a strikingly high proportion (almost half) of Sanders supporters who do so. However, the relatively positive results for democracy is accompanied by the bad news that such a large percentage of the electorate endorses the idea that a strong leader who sometimes bends the rules would be good for the United States, with a surprisingly high proportion of Clinton primary voters agreeing. This suggests that the Sanders voters are not the kind of populists looking for a messiah figure. This ought to be a caution against the kind of sweeping negative characterizations being made about populism in general.

These survey results do not go fully to the question of representation, but the attitudes toward politicians and public officials confirm the deep chasm that has developed between the electorate and, respectively, their government, public officials, and the information environment. And

Table 4.6 American's confidence in political institutions, January 2018

Do you have a great deal of confidence, quite a lot, not very much confidence or no confidence at all in _____?

	A great deal (%)	Quite a lot (%)	Not very much (%)	No confidence (%)
Military	53	34	8	4
The Supreme Court	22	37	29	7
FBI	24	33	28	11
The Courts	16	35	33	12
The Presidency	19	24	28	26
Democratic Party	13	23	37	25
Media	11	19	38	30
Republican Party	10	19	37	31
Congress	8	17	49	22

Source NPR/PBS NewsHour/Marist poll of 1350 US adults conducted January 8–10. "Overall" results reflect all respondents, and the margin of error is ±2.7 percentage points. Party affiliation results reflect respondents who identified as registered voters (1092 respondents), and the margin of error is ±3.0 percentage points. Figures may not add up to 100% because of rounding. "Unsure" responses not shown while large-scale studies of the electorate do not provide data for evaluation of parties and other institutions, some general polling data led credence to the growth of suspicion of representative institutions. Table 4.6 reveals that the institution in which Americans have the most trust, by a runaway margin over all the others is the military.

On the one hand, the military's high standing can be attributed to the respect that most Americans have for soldiers in the field, for their sacrifice and willingness to put their lives on the line. However, the gap between the public regard for the military and that for other institutions takes on different implications when we consider how the military's relationship to society has changed. Unlike the past, even in periods when there was no draft, the American military was more a citizen-soldier institution than it is today. As we explore in Chapter 7, through advertising, popular culture and effect public relations, soldiers today regarded as warriors—even if, despite growth in their ranks, the special operations forces who best fit the description are still a minority of military personnel.

In the early Trump presidency, two retired high officers occupied key positions in the White House—Chief of Staff John Kelly and Defense Secretary James Mattis. And a third officer, National Security Adviser H. R. McMaster, remained on active duty. By mid-2018, only Kelly remained, amid rumors that he would soon resign. Trump has continued a trend set by his two immediate predecessors of giving the military's high command and even field commanders more autonomy in carrying out combat missions in the "War of Terror" and in advising. Given the dismal rating of Congress, the media, and each of the two political parties, given the unstable nature of the president's personality, and given the high esteem for the military in the public sphere, military influence in the executive should be understood as a danger—regardless of whether military officers are more judicious and rational than the president. This danger, through no fault of the officers themselves, is magnified by the atmosphere of palace intrigue, i.e., conspiracy, within the Trump White House and among the staff.

GLOBALIZATION, ECONOMIC DISTRESS, AND THE VOTE

While survey data tells us something about insecurities and agency panic, ecological (analysis based on votes aggregated geographically) can reveal some tendencies less clear in individual level, opinion data. So next we ask if the geographical distribution of the Trump vote and possibly the Bernie Sanders vote is similar to that in the cases of the Brexit referendum, Le Pen's National Front in France, the AfD (Alternative for Germany) in Germany and other European right-wing populist electoral movements. A recent study of distressed communities in the U.S. can be used in combination with an archive of national primary and presidential results to examine this question. Given that the Electoral College majority achieved by Trump largely resulted from his largely unexpected success in Midwestern states, I focus here on these states where the "Blue Wall" (states thought to be reliably Democratic) was breached or nearly breached. I also include West Virginia, a state that went heavily for Trump that once was rock-ribbed Democratic and a bastion of organized labor because of its heavy dependence on mining.

Relevant data for analysis was taken from the *2017 Distressed Communities Index*, developed and compiled by the Economic Innovation Group and combined with data from Dave Leip's Atlas of US Presidential Elections.[34] The index was developed to measure the vitality of communities in the United States. The report asserts, "Distressed communities are disconnected communities, and the findings…reveal the troubling extent to which the fates of their 52 million inhabitants are diverging from the rest of the country. These are places increasingly alienated from the benefits of the modern economy."[35] Seven indicators are combined into a single index. The indicators are:

- No high school diploma. Percent of the population 25 years and older without a high school diploma or equivalent.
- Housing vacancy rate. Percent of habitable housing that is unoccupied, excluding properties that are for seasonal, recreational, or occasional use.
- Adults not working. Percent of the prime-age population (ages 25–64) not currently in work.
- Poverty rate. Percent of the population whose household income falls below the poverty line.
- Median income ratio. A geography's median income expressed as a percentage of its state's median income.
- Change in employment. Percent change in the number of jobs from 2011 to 2015.

Base data was compiled by zip code and then aggregated and made available to other researchers. As county voting records are the lowest level of consist data provided for all states, it is at this aggregate level that analysis is presented in the figures and the tables presented here in this section.

Clinton registered percentage gains only in some large counties in Illinois, Minnesota, Pennsylvania (and very marginally in Indiana), and a look at the data suggests that this is almost completely a result of strong showings in the large metropolitan areas of Chicago, Philadelphia, Pittsburgh, and Minneapolis (see Table 4.7). It is worth commenting here that even a cursory examination of voting patterns in these areas shows that the Clinton's few gains were somewhat an artifact of combinations of minority voters and more highly educated white voters. Of course, many minorities live in highly distressed urban areas, but they are less likely to have moved to the Trump column than to have turned out in decreased numbers. Census data indicates that black turnout was down 7.1% in 2016 from 2012. The Hispanic vote was down 0.7%.

Table 4.7 Slippage in democratic presidential vote in eight Midwestern states

		WV (%)	IA (%)	OH (%)	WI (%)	MI (%)	MN (%)	PA (%)	IL (%)
2016 vs 2012 percent change democratic votes									
Size Distress level	Large			−6.3	−7.7	−8.5	−0.3	3.8	9.2
	1			0.8		−4.7	1.3	7.0	11.5
	2			−2.8			−3.9	4.2	8.3
	3			−8.5	−13.1				
	4					−12.8			
	5						−0.8		
Size Distress level	Medium	−8.7	−11.8	−18.3	−14.5	−10.5	−11.6	−7.6	−5.0
	1		−9.7	−12.3	−13.6	0.5	−9.8	−0.4	−0.3
	2	−3.8	−19.1	−17.7	−19.1	−14.9	−21.3	−5.0	−3.9
	3	−13.0	−27.3	−37.3		−13.4		−16.8	−5.2
	4			−24.0		−20.3		−24.3	−12.2
	5								
Size Distress level	Small	−24.9	−27.3	−32.2	−22.7	−22.0	−26.3	−20.7	−24.8
	1	−18.9	−21.2	−24.4	−17.6	−11.9	−22.1	−14.4	−16.5
	2	−20.8	−30.6	−31.8	−26.9	−24.0	−28.3	−23.6	−23.9
	3	−23.8	−33.6	−35.9	−27.9	−23.2	−32.2	−20.6	−25.7
	4	−21.9	−36.4	−36.8	−33.2	−28.1	−32.7	−22.1	−26.0
	5								
	Total	−20.8	−20.5	−15.3	−14.7	−11.5	−11.5	−2.1	2.4

Sources Economic Innovation Group. *The 2017 Distressed Communities Distressed Communities Index*, available at eig.org (accessed July 1, 2018); *US Election Atlas*, available at uselectionatlas.org, compiled by Dave Leip

Table 4.7, though complex, illustrates the way that economic distress and social exclusion has played in shaping politics in the Midwest. Within midsized and small counties, in all 8 states considered there is a pattern of nearly consistent total secular decline in the vote between 2012 and 2016 as one moves from least to most distressed counties. The Democratic Party has shown weakness across the board in these state over the last few decades, but it appears the party's fortunes had not bottomed out. There are small digressions in the pattern of decline, but they are slight compared to the overall direction. For example, while the decline in Ohio was more pronounced in the third-most distressed midsized counties than in the fourth-most, the descent in both these categories is much more pronounced for those counties in the first and second categeories (relatively well-off counties). Of course, these counties have many fewer votes to influence in the election, but in close elections in critical states, the ability of Democrats to at least hold their own in these areas is important in statewide elections. While not more pronounced than in the other four states, the shifts in Michigan, Pennsylvania, Wisconsin, and Ohio cost Clinton victory in the Electoral College.

Here we see operating a contradiction between national political structures and their capacity to respond effectively to the challenges being posed by the inter-related processes of technological change and globalization. Mabel Berezin expresses this well in *Illiberal Politics in Neoliberal Times*, which primarily examines European right-wing populism but seems to apply equally to the American context. She writes, "By moving the center of political gravity from the polity to the person, from the state to the market, Europeanization has compromised the bonds of democratic empathy and provided an opportunity for rightwing populists to articulate a discourse of fear and insecurity." The "front story" exploited by this kind of discourse is quite apparent in the individual level data about the relative weight of different factors, such as partisanship, gender, race, social class, occupation, etc. These factors operate in a "contextual space," she reminds us that shapes receptivity to candidates and their messages.[36] That context is shifting economic and social structures on a global scale that are discordant with national identity. We will return to this data in Chapter 5, where we consider globalization's relationship to conspiracy theory and to the 2016 election.

SUSPICION AND THE VOTE

Given the lack of available survey data, little can be done to explore how much conspiracism contributed to the outcome of the 2016 election. Certainly, there are no shortages of incidents, events, and candidate rhetoric to show that conspiracy theories affected the outcome. What we know is that Clinton herself at times traded in conspiracy theories, the most famous incident being her 1995 memo complaining that she and her husband were being victimized by a "vast right-wing conspiracy," a theory not entirely without some foundation. Then there was her reference to the influence of "fake news" after the 2016 election. Regardless of the plausibility of Clinton's conspiracy theories, compared to Donald Trump's claims that Obama had founded ISIS, promotion of birther theory, warnings that the election was fixed, repeated characterizations of credible news stories as deliberated faked, and charge that Clinton had acted criminally in regard to emails and the deaths of diplomats in Benghazi, Cllinton's appeal to conspiracism pales in comparison.

"Trumpism" is more than Donald Trump. It is rooted in factors that point to continuing decay in American politics. Even if and when Trump leaves the political scene, we can expect politicians to "trump-up" fears, and to trump up concerns into fear. The likelihood that Trumpian conspiracism would persist beyond the election was illustrated after a gunman killed 17 students at a Parkland, Florida high school. Almost immediately theories began to fly across social media that students who afterward began to speak and organize for gun control measures were actually actors. A Facebook post to this effect was re-posted 100,000 times. A video on promoting this message was viewed 2 million times before it was removed (only to be re-uploaded). Some of the responsibility was attributed to Russian operatives, but this hypothesis is a conspiracy theory whose warrant is yet to be proved. In any case, Russian interference is insufficient to explain how eagerly a segment of the population felt motivated to pay attention and in some case distributes fabricated conspiracy theories.[37]

While survey data analysis shows that on the individual level the evidence points to racism and sexism as the most important influences over the outcome of the election, I contend that these interacted with economic factors and with the growing disconnect between a liberalized global economy and political world still organized and legitimized by the ideal of a nation-state. In the next chapter will delve into the disjuncture between national identity and sovereign, on the one hand, and on the other a globalized economic order marked in much of the world by inequalities and populist responses.

NOTES

1. "Full Transcript: Senator Jeff Flake Announces He Won't Seek reelection," *The Atlantic*, October 24, 2017, available at https://www.theatlantic.com/politics/archive/2017/10/full-transcript-senator-jeff-flake-announces-he-wont-seek-reelection/543846 (accessed February 15, 2017).
2. Two examples are Mark J. Hetherington, *Why Trust Matters: Declining Political Trust and the Demise of American Liberalism* (Princeton, NJ: Princeton University Press, 2006); Pew Research Center, "Beyond Distrust: How Americans View Their Government," available at www.people-press.org/2015/11/23/beyond-distrust-how-americans-view-their-government (accessed December 27, 2017).
3. Richard Hofstadter, *The Paranoid Style in American Politics* (New York: Vintage Reprints, 1968).
4. Conor Lynch, "Paranoid Politics: Donald Trump's Style Perfectly Embodies the Theories of Renowned Historian," *Salon.com*, July 7, 2016, available at https://www.salon.com/2016/07/07/paranoid_politics_donald_trumps_style_perfectly_embodies_the_theories_of_renowned_historian/.
5. Nate Cohn, "Why the Election Is Close, and What Trump and Obama Have in Common," *New York Times*, November 6, 2016; James W. Ceaser, Andrew Busch, and John Pitney, Jr., *Defying the Odds: The 2016 Elections and American Politics* (Lanham, MA: Roman & Littlefield, 2017): 124–125.
6. For this argument, see James W. Ceaser, et al., *Defying the Odds*; Matthew Fowler, Vladimir E. Medenica, and Cathy J. Cohen, "Why 41 Percent of White Millennials Voted for Trump," The Monkey Cage, *Washington Post*, December 15, 2017; and Brian Schaffner, Matthew McWilliams, and Tatishe Nteta, "Explaining White Polarization in the 2016 Vote for President: The Sobering Role of Racism and Sexism," Paper Prepared for Presentation at the Conference on the U.S. Elections of 2016: Domestic and International Aspects, January 8–9, 2017, IDC Herzliya Campus, available at http://people.umass.edu/schaffne/schaffner_et_al_IDC_conference.pdf (accessed February 21, 2018).
7. For this argument, see Matthew Fowler, Vladimir E. Medenica, and Cathy J. Cohen, "Why 41 Percent of White Millennials Voted for Trump," The Monkey Cage, *Washington Post*, Decembert 15, 2017; Brian Schaffner, Martthew McWilliams, and Tatishe Nteta, "Explaining

White Polarization in the 2016 Vote for President: The Sobering Role of Racism and Sexism," Paper Prepared for Presentation at the Conference on The U.S. Elections of 2016: Domestic and International Aspects, January 8–9, 2017, IDC Herzliya Campus, available at http://people. umass.edu/schaffne/schaffner_et_al_IDC_conference.pdf   (accessed February 21, 2018).

8. Based on YouGov study summarized in David Leonhardt, "The Democrats' Real Turnout Problem," *New York Times*, November 16, 2016.

9. The American National Elections Study done bi-annually by the Stanford University and the University of Michigan, and the newer Voter Study Group survey, sponsored by the Democratic Fund.

10. Rob Brotherton, Christopher French, and Allan Pickering, A. D. (2013), "Measuring Belief in Conspiracy Theories: The Generic Conspiracist Beliefs Scale. Frontiers in Personality Science and Individual Differences," *Frontiers in Psychology* 4, available at https://www.frontiersin.org, 279.

11. E.g., *CNN*, July 25, 2015, interview posted at www.youtube.com/watch?v=gGrVF3WLm1E (accessed June 27, 2017).

12. Podcast of July 23, 2016, available at www.youtube.com/watch?v=fJS5M6irj5g (accessed June 27, 2017).

13. Clinton, to her credit, chose not to redbait Sanders in the primary campaign.

14. For example, see Susan Bordo, "The Destruction of Hillary Clinton: Sexism, Sanders, and the Millennial Feminists," *The Guardian*, April 2, 2017.

15. http://www.presidency.ucsb.edu/ws/?pid=19253 (accessed June 20, 2018).

16. Andy Cush, "How the Donald Trump Campaign Turned America's Greatest Conspiracy Theorist into a Household Name," *Spin.com*, October 26, 2016, available at http://www.spin.com/featured/the-invisible-empire-of-alex-jones, (accessed February 23, 2017). See also Jones' media kit for prospective advertisers at https://static.InfoWars.com/partners/MediaKit2016.pdf (accessed February 24, 2018).

17. Matthew Rosenberg, Charlie Savage, and Michael Wines, "Russia Sees Midterm Elections as Chance to Sow Fresh Discord, Intelligence Chiefs Warn," *New York Times*, February 13, 2018.

18. U.S. Senate Select Committee to Study Governmental Operations with Respect to Intelligence Activities, Staff Report, *Covert Action in Chile (1963–1973)* (Washington, DC: U.S. Government Printing Office, 1975).

19. See Eric Alterman, "No News is Bad News," *The Nation*, May 14, 2018.

20. Quoted in Mike Wendling, "The (Almost) Complete History of 'Fake News'," *BBC.com*, January 22, 2018.

21. Anousha Sakqui, "Fox's Profit Machine Seen Sturdy Enough to Endure O'Reilly Exit," *Bloomberg.com*, April 20, 2017.

22. Brendan Nyhan, "Fake News is Troubling, But Its Effect Is Limited," *New York Times*, February 14, 2018.

23. Andrew Guess, Brendan Nyhan, and Jason Reifler, "Selective Exposure to Misinformation: Evidence from the Consumption of Fake News During the 2016 U.S. Presidential Campaign," January 9, 2018, available at http://www.dartmouth.edu/~nyhan/fake-news-2016.pdf   (accessed February 14, 2018).

24. Of course, this should not have surprised anyone paying attention to his history. See Clare Cohen's rundown of transgressions dating back to 1980 in the *London Telegraph*, November 9, available at http://www.telegraph.co.uk/women/politics/donald-trump-sexism-tracker-every-offensive-comment-in-one-place/.

25. Brian Schaffner and John A. Clark, *Making Sense of the 2016 Elections* (Thousand Oaks, CA: CQ Press, 2018): 26.

26. According to Brian Schaffner of the University of Massachusetts, as reported by Jeff Stein, "The Bernie Voters Who Defected to Trump, Explained by a Political Scientist," *Vox.com*, August 24, 2017.

27. Emily Jenkins, *The Five Types of Trump Voters, Who They Are and What They Believe* (Washington, DC: Democracy Fund, Voter Study Group, June 2016).

28. This is based largely on the work of Joseph Uscinski and Joseph Parent, *American Conspiracy Theories* (New York: Oxford University Press, 2014). Uscincki and Parent compiled a huge archive of litters to the editor since 1890 to analyze and reach this conclusion. This is discussed in Chapter 1.

29. Pew Research Center, "Low Marks for the 2012 Election," November 15, 2012, available at http://www.people-press.org/2012/11/15/section-3-the-voting-process-and-the-accuracy-of-the-vote and "Low Marks for Major Players in the 2016 Election," November 21, 2016, http://www.people-press.org/2016/11/21/the-voting-process/ (both accessed February 21, 2018).

30. Uscinski and Parent, *American Conspiracy Theories*: 130–153. Also, Joanne M. Miller, Kyle L. Saunders, and Christina E. Farhart, "Conspiracy Endorsement as Motivated Reasoning: The Moderating Roles of Political Knowledge and Trust," *American Journal of Political Science* 60, no. 4 (October 2016): 824–844; and Joanne M. Miller, Kyle L. Saunders, and Christina E. Farhart, "The Relationship Between Perceptions or Lower Status and Conspiracy Theory Endorsement," Paper Presented at the Annual Meeting of the American Political Science Association, San Francisco, CA, August 31–September 3, 2017.

31. Ray Chetty, et al., *The Fading American Dream: Trends in Absolute Income Mobility Since 1940* (2016, The Equality of Opportunity Project, available at http://www.equality-of-opportunity.org).
32. Pew Research Center, "A Divided and Very Pessimistic Electorate," November 10, 2016, available at http://www.people-press.org/2016/11/10/a-divided-and-pessimistic-electorate (accessed February 22, 2018).
33. See among many examples, J. G. Shields, "Political Representation in France: A Crisis of Democracy?" *Parliamentary Affairs*, 59, no. 1 (January 2006): 118–137; George Gabriel, "A Crisis of Representation," *OpenDemocracy.net*, May 25, 2009, available at https://cdn.opendemocracy.net/files/u555700/od-uk-x2_8.png (accessed February 23, 2018).
34. Distressed communities data available free for academic use by request from EIG, Economic Innovations Group (eig.org, accessed March 1, 2018). Electoral data purchased from David Leip, *Atlas of American Presidential Elections*, available at uselectionatlas.org (accessed March 1, 2018).
35. EIG (Economic Innovation Group), *The 2017 Distressed Communities Index*, available at http://eig.org/wp-content/uploads/2017/07/ISD-Report.pdf (accessed March 1, 2018).
36. Mabel Berezin, *Illiberal Politics in Neoliberal Times: Culture, Security and Populism in the New Europe* (Cambridge, UK: Cambridge University Press, 2009): 8, 62, 193–200.
37. Matt Pearce, "Conspiracy Theories About Florida School Shooting Survivors Have Gone Mainstream," *Los Angeles Times*, February 21, 2018; Paul Murphy and Gianluca Mezzofiore, "How the Florida School Shooting Conspiracies Sprouted and Spread," *CNN*, February 22, 2018.

CHAPTER 5

Globalization, Populism, Conspiracism

In 2016 globalizing elites gathered for their annual meeting at the Swiss resort at Davos had to take note that resistance to their vision of a transnational order was growing in the form of populist movements. By their 2017 meeting, they felt a little better when President Trump visited Davos for the first time and basked in their welcome. Perhaps the March Brexit vote was not as threatening as they feared. Their concerns about global inequality generating resistance faded. But they had not counted on mercurial personality occupying the White House. A full-scale trade war was looming, and the European Union and NAFTA were in danger of collapse. In anticipation of Davos 2018, they felt compelled to take a full page ad in the *New York Times* (July 1) promoting the upcoming meeting as a gathering of the wisest business and political leaders to grapple with global inequality. No longer could they assume that the world would keep spinning their way. Perhaps this explains why the super-rich were busy buying up old missile silos for conversion into luxury bunkers to be used in the event of nuclear war of natural mega-disasters![1]

For more than seven decades since the end of World War II in 1945, the United States has been the most powerful nation in the world and used that power—economic, cultural, and political—to promote a liberal internationalist world order. Washington promoted international institutions to promote global financial stability (the International Monetary Fund), capitalist development projects in the Global South (the World Bank and foreign aid programs), free trade (the General Agreement on

© The Author(s) 2019
D. C. Hellinger, *Conspiracies and Conspiracy Theories in the Age of Trump*, https://doi.org/10.1007/978-3-319-98158-1_5

Tariffs and Trade, GATT, superseded by the World Trade Organization, the WTO). By the 1990s, with the fall of the Soviet Union and Eastern Bloc countries and with China's embrace of capitalist enterprise, the continued development of global order with a liberal business climate conducive to transnational corporations seemed unstoppable. But signs of popular resistance had already appeared in the Clinton years, especially the 1999 protests that virtually shut down the Seattle WTO Ministerial Conference. A surge of populist electoral strength on both the left and the right in recent years has disrupted the sense of inevitability around globalization.

Matthew Gray outlines three factors linking globalization to conspiracism.[2] They are:

1. Globalization his diminished state sovereignty and in the eyes of citizens diminished the power of state itself. A "deficit of popular legitimacy" simultaneous with a sense of threat (economic and political) from abroad encourages a retreat in some large sectors of society to "substate units of allegiance"—racial, political, linguistic, ethnic, etc.

2. Linked to the first factor is the increased symbolic power of transnational (my adjective, not Gray's) corporations whose brands compete for allegiance. Certainly, this is more of perceived threat in places like the Middle East, but it is not absent even in the United States, as periodic consumer rebellions against foreign products shows, as well as the increased advertising by foreign countries, designed to show just how committed they are to American communities.

3. Technological changes in transportation and communication that has the effect of "disjointing" many people from their transitional moorings. Technological changes have impacted labor and influenced migration flows that have in turn increased tensions subject to exploitation by demagogues. In the Middle East, Gray notes, this has had the effect of creating more rootlessness and contributed to an Islamic revivalism constructed as a reaction against Westernization. One can find parallels in the increased political impact of fundamentalist Christianity in the United States.

Havoc for globalizing elites has arrived in the form of Donald Trump and a host of other right-populist leaders and parties throughout the developed West and post-Communist countries. But the populist surge was not just on the right. For a while, especially in Latin America, left populism seemed to be gathering strength, especially during the years (1999–2013) when Venezuela's populist Hugo Chávez achieved success in rallying most of Latin America and some other parts of the post-colonial world to resist neoliberal globalization. The near collapse of the Bolivarian Revolution after Chavez's death in 2013 coincided with many other setbacks for left populism in the region, but July 2018 saw the specter reappear in Mexico, Latin America's second-largest economy.

More ominous for the global business elite is the emergence of left populism in the form of Bernie Sanders in the United States and Jeremy Corbyn in Great Britain. In addition to Trumpism and Euroskepticism in the form of Brexit, socialism had reappeared on the political in neoliberalism's backyard—the Anglo world. Pro-globalization intellectuals sometimes paint these left populists with the same brush as they apply to populists on the right. Evin McMullen of *NBC News* says, "Populism, whether from Donald Trump or Bernie Sanders, is destabilizing America," and, he claims, they "appeal to bitter sentiments of fear and resentment to rouse and consolidate public support." Early in 2016, Thomas Friedman asked in his influential daily column, "What if our 2016 election ends up being between a socialist and a borderline fascist—ideas that died in 2989 and 1945, respectively."[3] Chapter 4 and other parts of this book dispute this assertion of equivalency between left and right populism.

Sanders and Trump both campaigned by appealing to the electorate's resentment of the political class and more broadly with an anti-elitist appeal. Both campaigns challenged the notion that social and economic hardship is not something that has just passively happened, that it is not just an unfortunate byproduct of inexorable and ultimately beneficial changes in the global economic order. However, unlike Sanders, Trump accompanied his anti-elite message with nativist, racist, and sexist rhetoric, which were largely absent from the Sanders campaign. Trump's populism more closely Hofstadter's notion of the paranoid style.[4] Neither Sanders nor Trump gave a full-throated endorsement to New World Order conspiracy theories that resemble the unwarranted grand theories about Freemasons and the Illuminati (see Chapter 2), but unlike Sanders, Trump pandered to the most notorious purveyor of similar theories, Alex Jones of *InfoWars.com*.

One well-spring of conspiracism in the Western world is the celebratory speech that President George Herbert Walker Bush gave in 1991 when, in the flush of victory after the First Gulf War, he christened the post-Cold War world system as "the new global order."[5] The phrase quickly assumed prominence in resistance to "free trade" and in related conspiracy theories, especially on the right, where it was quickly graphed onto earlier and recurring theories attributing great power to the Order of the Illuminati, Freemasonry, and (often with anti-Semitic intentions) cabals headed by the Rothschild Family. More recently the Rockefellers and the Council and Foreign Relations, the Trilateral Commission, the elites who intend the highly secretive meetings known as "Bilderberg," and the quasi-closed meetings at Davos are portrayed as the conspiratorial forces behind globalization.

While a good deal of the writing about elite meetings and cabals is fanciful, if not paranoid, the "conspiracy theory" label is frequently applied as well to more serious sociological work on the way that elites network with one another on a global scale to advance and shape globalization in the Post-Cold War world. Just as often, on the other hand, globalization is seen has having been generated solely by technological leaps in communications and transportation, with little human agency involved. But these developments have not only restructured and disrupted national economic and social structures, they have also facilitated conscious planning and collaboration among elites—and to some extent among social movements opposed to globalization in the form it has assumed since 1980. These movements are largely made up or represent those most displaced and excluded from its benefits, groups that have not settled for socio-economic, structural explanations that make capitalist globalization seem inevitable. They insist, "Another World is Possible." But it has become clear that the discontent and disruption being wrought by a globalization has also stimulated a reaction that has generated the kind of xenophobic, right-wing populism associated with Trump and similar insurgent parties that bear some disturbing similarities to the fascist movements and parties of the mid-twentieth century.

SUSPICIOUS MINDS IN THE NEW WORLD ORDER

"Globalization" need not mean neoliberal globalization. Generically, globalization should refer in general to the increased interdependency and interaction among the world's peoples—economically, culturally, socially, and politically. However, most of time when both critics and defenders of globalization use the term, they are referring to neoliberal globalization, which has seen the deployment of the aforementioned technologies to facilitate the free movement of financial and other forms of capital across national boundaries, as well as the reorganization of production of goods and services in a way that has largely obeyed the logic of the global market. What makes it "neoliberal," not just capitalist, is that there is relatively little globalized regulation of labor or financial markets or redistribution of accumulated wealth. The impact of this process has produced some winners, it should be acknowledged. On a global scale, a significant decrease in poverty and expansion of the middle class has occurred, especially in East and South Asia. But in the rest of the world, including the United States and other wealthy core countries in the world system, the free movement of capital and reorganization of production has hollowed out the middle class and working class and deepened poverty for many already poor.

For convenience, when I refer to "globalization" in this chapter I am referring to what I have just described as neoliberal globalization. Neoliberal globalization has a political component in so far as it promotes "democratization," emphasizing civil rights and free elections but it eschews social and economic rights as elaborated in, among other places, the United Nations Charter on Human Rights. The real foundation of neoliberal globalization is the elimination of barriers to free movements of financial investment, investment capital, and goods and service across national boundaries. While free movement of people—i.e., labor—might be the preference of some global elites, it is at best secondary to them. The attempts to advance neoliberal economic globalization are the subject of negotiations to extend and deepen treaties and agreements that are said to be about "free trade." These agreements are not, however, mainly about trade but about knocking down barriers further to the movement of capital freely across borders and the reorganization of the production of goods and services—what some critics call a "global assembly line," what in the business world is known as "commodity chains." Advancing this objective means dealing with intellectual property rights (patents, trademarks, copyrights), with reducing the exercise of national sovereignty in disputes about investment (especially in natural resources, such as mining and oil), and economic subsidies that are politically sensitive in national politics (e.g., in agriculture).

The increasingly globalized system of trade, finance, and production has as its counterpart in what William Robinson calls a "transnational capitalist class."[6] Most of the men and (many fewer) women who head the world's largest corporations and financial institutions are sufficiently networked with one another that they form a coherent class that responds to global market forces, not national ones. To even postulate the existence of a transnational capitalist class may give rise to criticism that Robinson and other international political economists who adopt this approach term are "conspiracy theorists," the latest in a line of critics who have seen globalization is driven by the hidden hand of the Illuminati, a TransAtlantic ruling class (often associated with the secretive Bilderberg meetings), or the elites who gather annually at Davos. However, idea of transnational capitalism, whether it is apt or not, is really more of structuralist theory. That is, in the Marxist tradition, it sees capitalism as a constantly evolving economic system, operating something like what Joseph Schumpeter, an admirer of capitalism, called "creative destruction," meaning a "process of industrial mutation that incessantly revolutionizes the economic structure from within, incessantly destroying the old one, incessantly creating a new one."[7] On the one hand, this is a result of the operation of market forces, not a conspiracy of greedy capitalists. On the other hand, structures have to be constructed and maintained by human forces, and in this regard agency enters into any historical account of how globalization has been evolving, and also what kind of globalization is under construction. This should become clearer as we examine how globalization has been promoted, debated, and resisted in the United States and in other countries where populism has challenged the "common sense" idea that free trade and globalization is inevitable and beneficial to everyone.

Until the Trump campaign, resistance to globalization in the United States was mainly identified with leftist social movements, especially after widely visible protests in Seattle achieved the shutdown of an important free trade conference. Most of the political leaders of the major political parties, including the Clintons, were enthusiastic supporters of free trade. Treaties and trade agreements encountered some resistance in Congress, but a coalition of centrists in the two parties could always be cobbled together to achieve passage. NAFTA was negotiated by President George Bush and passed with the support of President Bill Clinton. The Seattle protests slowed the bandwagon; by 2016 major proposals, especially the attempt to revitalize stalled momentum toward a Trans-Pacific Partnership (TPP) were politically dead, even before Trump's march to the White House. Even before the presidential primaries were over, the idea that globalization was inevitable had fallen before the different but equally populist challenges posed by Trump and Senator Bernie Sanders.

Behind this development, which was part of a broader international resistance to the kind of globalization embodied in NAFTA, the TPP and other free trade agreements, was a clash between the way the world has been ordered politically, i.e., around the idea of national sovereignty, and the tectonic changes occurring in economic production fostered by globalization. Consistent with earlier chapters of that book, I hold conspiracy theories that attribute globalization entirely to the machinations of a tightly knit cabal to be unwarranted. However, the opposite of such world theories is the near consensus among mainstream journalists and academics that no one is responsible for globalization, that it has just happened, or that the accompanying technological changes mean that the dislocations and deterioration in the quality of life of the working and middle classes must be accepted as the price for progress.

Benjamin Barber in 1996 was among the first to analyze the contradictions between global technological change, especially in communication and transportation, and the basic principles of political order built on the idea of national sovereignty. In his book, *Jihad versus McWorld*,[8] Barber argued that globalization was spurring a backlash in the form of a turn toward communalism—parochial and fundamentalist, drawing the world apart. Paradoxically the surge in communications technologies, most notably the Internet, responsible for accelerated cultural homogenization (McWorld) were also providing the capability for communal resistance. As Barber put it, one force is "driven by parochial hatreds, the other by universalizing markets, the one re-creating ancient subnational and ethnic borders from within, the other making national borders porous from without. They have one thing in common: neither offers much hope to citizens looking for practical ways to govern themselves democratically."[9]

Barber took inadequate notice of how social movements in different countries were using technology to a global network with one another, though in his defense this was not as evident when he wrote his book. His analysis nonetheless was onto a paradox that persists to this day. "Common markets demand a common language, as well as a common currency," he wrote, "and they produce common behaviors of the kind bred by cosmopolitan city life everywhere." However, unchecked free market globalization has put this assumption into question. On the global scale and the national scale, the New World Order has generated significant improvement in social conditions, concentrated mostly in Asia and South Asia, but elsewhere it has left hundreds of millions of people excluded from the benefits of growth, or in many cases in worse condition. This exclusion is one of the factors that enabled Trump to marshal vital votes in rural and former industrial and mining centers in the northern midsection of the United States. This is where Trump, aided by the parochial, thinly veiled racist propaganda of extreme rightist media, cultivated voters who once were a reliable bastion for Democratic candidates. It is where resentment and exclusion have reinforced nativist elements of populism in America, much as Hofstadter described in the "paranoid style."[10]

I have argued elsewhere[11] that conspiracies and conspiracy theories are nurtured in the United States by tension between the exercise of global hegemony and liberal democratic legitimation. The advance of transnational capital has added a new dimension to this tension because it increasingly demands that the United States act in the interest of the global capitalism, not in defense or advancement of the national economic interests. This tension becomes visible in populist theories of conspiracy, but somewhat differently on the left and the right. For social movements and leftist politicians like Sanders, the rhetoric of resistance tends to revolve around the need to defend universal human rights, the need for international and diplomatic solutions to issues of climate change, redistribution of wealth and income. Contrary to critics who lump the populism of Sanders and Trump together, that of Sanders and "anti-globalization" movements does not seek to do away with internationalist ideals in foreign policy, nor even abandonment of American hegemonic power. Trump, by contrast, appeals to a more raw and dangerous rhetoric. "America First" and "Make America Great Again" directly confronts the idea of the United States as the indispensable nation in world affairs, melding with domestic policies on immigration and trade that smack of nativism and isolationism.

Whether the populist resistance to globalization means that conspiracism has spiked is harder to assess. The creative study by Uscinski and Joseph of conspiracist rhetoric in letters to the editor of the *New York Times* and *The Chicago Tribune* suggests that from 1890 to 2010 suggests levels of conspiracy talk were relatively similar throughout that 20 year period with only two exceptions: the 1890s and the early post World War II era. Otherwise, they find, "conspiracy talk" has been relatively constant and non-pervasive.[12] There was no significant spike even in the era of the *X-Files* television series and in aftermath of Oliver Stone's 1991 film, *JFK*, whose success is often seen as indicative of rising conspiracism in American culture. What is of interest to us is that the two spikes in conspiracism bear some similarity to the present.

The two exceptional periods were, like the present era, ones in which great social and economic shifts seemed to have culminated. The

1890s were such a period, the point at which the United States had begun to emerge as an expansionist power on the world stage, and a period when national politics were being impacted by shift from a rural, agrarian economy to an urban industrial one. And it was a period of great domestic migration and shifts in the origins of immigrants. The trigger for the spike in this populist era seems to have been a severe economic panic. The parallels with the shifts in demographics, technology, and the changes in the US role in world affairs today are striking. The post-World War II era may not share with the present moment the 1890 a context of economic crisis, but like the present post 9/11 moment, it was a time of heightened fear of an international conspiracy. It was also a time when internationalist elites here and abroad depended upon American hegemony to advance construction of a liberal world order.

Historian Kathryn Olmsted argues that in the twentieth-century American conspiracy theories shifted away from fears that alien forces were attempting to capture the American government (characteristic of conspiracy theories in the 1800s), toward the perception that "federal government itself was the conspirator."[13] Based on her case studies, beginning with claims that arms merchants and bankers colluded with government to get the United States into World War I to suspicions about the 9/11 attacks, Olmsted finds that inquiries generated by conspiracy theories rarely confirmed the particular allegations raised, but they did uncover other forms of deception, abuse of powers, and unlawful actions by government officials.

Olmsted characterizes conspiracy theories as irrational and counterproductive, in contrast to the more sympathetic views of theorists like Mark Fenster and Jack Bratich,[14] which we have examined in earlier chapters. Still, she contends there is a need to understand why conspiracy theories have become "endemic to American democracy." Her view is that since World War I government officials have tilled fertile ground for conspiracy theories and provided "fodder" by plotting and concealing "real conspiracies;" they feed "anti-government paranoia by actively suppressing alternative views."[15] Olmsted acknowledges the existence of conspiracy in a valuable historical analysis that shows how ordinary people have sometimes forced elites to respond to their concerns by advancing a conspiracy theory, but in the end (literally, in the last chapter) she warns only of danger, endorsing conspiracy theory in conformity with the paranoid style thesis.

In the twenty-first century, this suspicion of government is entering a new phase in relation to the role of the United States in the world. The first four presidential administrations in the post-Cold War era (two Bushes, Clinton, and Obama) embraced globalization, broadening and deepening the internationalist thrust of American policy in the aftermath of World War II. These administrations put American hegemony into service to build a neoliberal world order in the form of unrestrained flows of capital and trade coupled with promotion of liberal democracy—"polyarchy," as it is christened by political scientists and government officials most closely associated with the democratization project. Not coincidentally, the term "globalization," though not unheard of before, became a "buzzword" very shortly after the fall of the Berlin Wall in 1989, two years before President George Bush (Sr.) coined "new world order."

Technological changes, mainly in cyber sciences applied to communication and transportation, have not only promoted globalization but also contributed to a widening income gap that has stuck hardest at young people, minorities, and the manufacturing working class. These inequalities have created a class cleavage that is less defined by global south versus global north (though certainly that continues to exist) than by an extraordinary gap between the lifestyles and consumption of the world's wealthiest elites, the so-called "one percent", and everyone else in both the core nation-states and those in the poorer periphery.[16] So large is the share of income and wealth of this global elite that a new service, *Wealth X*, with an online daily round-up of news about the wealthy, has come into existence to analyze shifts in its philanthropic, political, and consumption. The service provides free public access to an annual census of the world's billionaires.[17]

At elite levels, Trumpism is based upon an uneasy alliance between sectors of the American economic ruling class that embraces globalization and right-wing populists whose ideology is chauvinistic and nationalistic. There are reasons to think that ultimately the Trump administration will be forced to retreat from its populist anti-globalization policies,[18] but Trump's decisions (as of June 2018) show little sign of that he was disposed to renew negotiation of the TPP, his threat to do the same with NAFTA (he shifted to a posture of renegotiate "or else" later in the summer). Other Trump policies alarmed to globalizing elites were his encouragement of Euroskeptic, right-wing populism, and his imposition of protectionist tariffs without concern for a possible trade war. It may ultimately take an election defeat or impeachment for globalists to prevail, but even in the event of Trump's disposition from the presidency, the social forces that enabled his ascent will not simply go away.

The tensions between globalists and populists are likely to persist because the mass base is cultivated by Trump through an appeal to nativism and conspiracism, consitute the contents of a Pandora's Box. Here is where left critics must take the "fusion" (see Chapter 2) critique of conspiracism seriously. The anti-globalist right shares with left populists who backed Bernie Sanders in 2016 a deep suspicion of elites, but among Trump voters this distrust melds with nativism, thinly disguised racism, and cultural chauvinism. Though there may be times when left and right voting blocs find themselves "strange-bedfellows" in congressional votes on trade agreements, alliances for electoral or other political objectives risk legitimating the latter and conspiracy theories associated with neo-fascist tendencies.

Trump has, of course, eschewed language that blames capitalism as a system from the very real suffering and sense of exclusion felt by those Americans who want to know why they should settle for economic insecurity and who palpably feel loss of control over their personal live. He exploits anger about the country's loss of blood and treasure overseas but simultaneously promotes hyper-nationalism and worship of military prowess. With the closing of the "American Century," in the United States the exercise of global hegemony is increasing at odds with democratic legitimation. This tension becomes visible in populist theories of conspiracy, both on the left and the right. We do not live in an age in which conspiracy theories are more profligate, but we do live in an age in which they offer a more profound challenge to constituted states in the core capitalist states of the world system than in earlier periods.

Economic globalization and technological change explain in part "why now" conpiracy theories are proliferating, but only partly. Trumpism and a more general surge in conspiracism have emerged in a symbiotic relationship to the decay of American political institutions, barely disguised corruption, and increasingly visible intrigue among politicians and wealthy patrons. Conspiracy theories are fed not just by delusions and panics that are nurtured by the economic and social dislocations accompanying technological change and globalization, but also by a widespread sense that impunity and collusion among elites are the hallmarks of contemporary political life in America.

IMMIGRANTS, NATIVISM, AND TRUMP

Immigration was a major theme of Trump's campaign from the moment he announced his candidacy on August 1, 2015. "When Mexico sends its people, they're not sending their best," Trump said. "They're sending people that have lots of problems, and they're bringing those problems with us. They're bringing drugs. They're bringing crime. They're rapists. And some, I assume, are good people."[19] Trump toned down the rhetoric, but only a little in his Phoenix speech. "Countless innocent American lives have been stolen because our politicians have failed in their duty to secure our borders and enforce our laws like they have to be enforced. I have met with many of the great parents who lost their children to sanctuary cities and open borders. So many people, so many, many people. So sad."

After describing several grisly crimes allegedly committed by immigrants and blaming them for costing the jobs of "vulnerable American workers," he accused liberals of a cover-up. "These facts are never reported. Instead, the media and my opponent discuss one thing and only one thing, the needs of people living here illegally. In many cases, by the way, they're treated better than our vets." It was time to throw out the red meat. Quoting from the transcript,

> *Trump*: We will build a great wall along the southern border.
> (APPLAUSE)
> *Audience*: Build the wall! Build the wall! Build the wall!
> *Trump*: And Mexico will pay for the wall.
> (APPLAUSE)
> *Trump*: One hundred percent. They don't know it yet, but they're going to pay for it. And they're great people and great leaders but they're going to pay for the wall.
> *Trump*: On day one, we will begin working on an impenetrable, physical, tall, power [sic], beautiful southern border wall.

Atossa Araxia Abrahamian aptly captures the essence of Trump's nativist rhetoric in her observation that it projects onto the imagination of the crowd the threatening image of a brownish "Glob."

> The Glob, the story goes, is illegally crossing your open border, then sending the factory where you work to Mexico, because of NAFTA. He's fixing your neighbor's roof—illegally, and without paying his taxes, of course—and foreclosing on her home, even though he can't speak English. The Glob is raping your wife, indoctrinating your kids with ISIL propaganda, and donating to Hilary Clinton. The Glob works on Wall Street, but he's definitely, like a communist, or something. Also: Benghazi.

The Glob, says Abrahamiam, is "an ingenious chimera of conspiracy."[20] Steve Bannon was one of the darkest, most powerful conjurers of this chimera. Bannon was, with Andrew Breitbart, a founding board member of *Breitbart News*, the most influential member of what is loosely characterized as the "alt-right" media—though not everyone agrees whether Breitbart and Bannon belong in this movement (see Chapter 3). Bannon became *Breitbart's* CEO after Andrew's sudden death in 2012. In August 2016 he became Trump's campaign manager, at a time when Trump's past dalliances with the Democratic Party and liberal New York elites were raising doubts about his conservatism. Bannon's assumption of a formal role in the campaign did much to qualm right-wing doubts about Trump's *bonafides*. *Breitbart News'* enthusiasm and support of the real estate mogul's political ambitions go back at least to November 2015, but a symbiotic relationship that already existed between Trump's discourse, on the one hand, and on the other hand the kinds of stories that fed Breitbart's audience growth.

Breitbart's earliest breakthrough into public consciousness occurred in 2009 with a kind of conspiracy, a sting operation. A *Breitbart* member channel, *BigGoverment.com*, produced and webcast a video a "sting" against Association of Community Organizers for Reform Now (ACORN), the community activist group. The video, made by James O'Keefe and Hannah Giles, alleged that the organization was engaged in the sex trade of underage girls, with apparently damning audio of ACORN organizers expressing interest in participating in trafficking. However, the video had been edited to make it seem that way. The motive for the sting was that ACORN organizers were deeply involved in minority voter registration efforts. Subsequent mainstream news reports debunked the *Breitbart* report, but not before Congress suspended federal funding for the organization. One detail about O'Keefe, reported but not widely noted at the time, was the O'Keefe's *Project Veritas* was funded, among other sources, by a grant in 2015 from the Trump Foundation.[21] *Project Veritas* had already carried out a similar fake news operation in 2006 and 2007 in which operatives baited Planned Parenthood personnel into statements (recorded secretly) that made it seem that the organization had ignored a statutory rape case and were interested in possible donation to fund abortions of African-American babies. While one can criticize the *Planned Parenthood* personnel for not categorically rejecting the overtures, but considerable editing had to be done to make the story as salacious as O'Keefe presented it.[22]

Having achieved a political success, Breitbart had little reason to improve the accuracy of its reporting and jumped on the birther theory that Trump had already made notorious with his celebrity power. In 2012, when Trump went on CNN with Wolf Blitzer to demand that Obama release his long form birth certificate, it was mostly Breitbart reports that provided his ammunition for casting doubt the America's first African-American president was a native born citizen. Pundits thought Trump had made a fool of himself; obviously, Trump had intuited something they did not—that Obama's name and race offered opportunities to make run for office based on nativism and racism.[23]

Although nativist appeals pandering to social conservatives have been the most notorious of Breitbart's videos, it is not clear that stoking nativist, anti-immigrant sentiments are for Bannon his goal or merely the means to achieve polices more closely aligned with the billionaire libertarianism of the Charles and David Koch (see Chapter 6). Timothy Egan compares Bannon to Thomas Cromwell, the notorious court advisor to King Henry VIII, and apparently the brains behind the lecherous monarch's transformative and brutal reign. Egan compares Bannon's goal of dismantling the administrative state to Cromwell's strategy of first concentrated power by using Henry's desire for a divorce to remove the checks of the clergy on his power and then engineered the sweeping away of Church wealth and power. Bannon, argues Egan, seeks to overturn nothing less than "the existing international order of treaties, trade pacts and alliances that has kept the world relatively safe since World War II. Trump's cabinet is stocked with people whose goal is to neuter the agencies they head."[24] On the other hand, Bannon's populism is not entirely compatible with libertarianism. He has called for raising taxes on the wealthy and backed massive infrastructure spending, neither of which corresponds to the Koch agenda.

Bannon's star continued rising in the transition period and early months of the new administration as he assumed the role of Chief White House Strategist. By April 2017, there were signs that his influence was waning within the White House, as he clashed with other staff members from the mainstream wing of the Republican Party. In August he resigned and returned to *Breitbart*, taking a leading role in extending the outlet's influence in Europe, and personally campaigning for far-right candidates in Republican primaries and in the general election, including Judge Roy Moore, whose notorious admission that he approached and dated teenagers was only the most damaging of several scandals surrounding his

candidacy. Bannon's intemperate (though very possibly accurate) characterization of Trump's ignorance and vulnerability to Special Counsel Robert
Mueller's investigation into his campaign's possible collusion with Russian
operatives finally earned him Trump's explicit ex-communication from the
president's inner circle. On January 9, 2018, he parted ways with Breitbart,
some of whose most important financial backers are aligned with Trump.

Bannon and other alt-right media stars (notably Alex Jones and the
notorious *Infowars.com*) together contributed mightily to creating an
outlandish celebrity presidency by aiding Trump in bringing to the surface polarized, angry politics that the nation has not seen since the Great
Depression, perhaps not since the Civil War era. Breitbart, *Infowars, Fox
News*, and other outlets disrupted the regime of truth maintained by
establishment media outlets, and whether as a means to an end or an
end they have played a key role in constructing a media silo whose walls
are difficult to break down. "When Trump makes wildly over-the-top
claims—he's going to build a wall and make Mexico pay for it—it has
no effect on his supporters to point out that this is hyperbolic nonsense.
Quite the reverse," said the *Washington Post's* Phillip Bump. "Trump's
claim moves them emotionally and persuades them precisely because it is
hyperbolic nonsense. They are angry, and he's showing that he is angry
too—which is vastly more effective communications than the bland
assertions by the professional politicians that they 'understand' there is a
lot of anger out there."[25]

Populism need not be demagogic, need not be built on prejudice and
fear. In fact, though we identify populism with a charismatic leader, neither Trump nor Sanders fits that mold. I would suggest that the appeal
of Bernie Sanders was that of a charisma-challenged outsider whose
mobilization of voters relied upon criticizing globalization and the corruption of elites. Quite unlike Sanders, Trump articulated a vision of
political and media elites in collusion—one could say, "conspiring"—
with one another to expand economic globalization at the expense of
ordinary people. Despite these differences what both did by challenging the inevitability of globalization was to provide their followers with
"agency." They represented the instability and hopelessness of their
social and economic conditions as more than the product of impersonal economic forces and technological change. They identified elites
as agents of globalization, making decisions and planning the future of
the world economy behind closed doors, with little regard for young
people with limited career prospects and for working class and poor

people living in communities left distressed by the force of untamed market forces. Trump and Sanders might be populists in the sense that both were outsiders challenging the consensus and disrupting the "normal" way of things, but they represent different types of populist antiglobalizaton. Trump's celebrity allowed him to tap into discontent from the top; Sanders had to build from the bottom up.

Trump has used anti-immigration rhetoric as a cudgel against elites and the media—the latter an "enemy of the people," he would say in the second month of his presidency. On September 1, 2016, he gave a major speech on immigration in Phoenix, Arizona. On this occasion, he eschewed his widely condemned characterization of Mexicans as rapists and criminals. His audience already had absorbed that message. This time he chose to use immigration as the theme of a broad conspiracy. He told a receptive audience, "The truth is our immigration system is worse than anybody ever realized. But the facts aren't known because the media won't report on them. The politicians won't talk about them and the special interests spend a lot of money trying to cover them up because they are making an absolute fortune. That's the way it is."[26]

A good estimate of the size of Trump's nativist can be gauged from an American Enterprise Institute (AEI) poll taken on the eve of President Trump's retreat from his harshly and widely criticized policy to separate families detained after illegally entering the country. While the poll estimated that nearly half of registered voters agree with prosecuting illegal entrants from Mexico, 18% strongly approved of separating families; another 12% somewhat approved. This would seem to suggest that 20–30% of the electorate (though not necessarily by extension the general population) occupy the nativist political silo. Trump may disappear from the scene, but the silo walls around his constituency will not necessarily fall with him.[27]

WALL STREET AND MONESSEN PA

On June 28, 2016, in the midst of his presidential campaign, Trump addressed an enthusiastic rally of supporters in the Monessen, Pennsylvania, a hard scrapple, economically devastated former steel town with a long history of voting strongly Democratic.[28] The Republican candidate, having just returned from Great Britain where he spoke approving of that country leaving the European Union (Brexit), railed, "Globalization has made the financial elite who donate to politicians very, very wealthy ... but it has left millions of our workers with nothing but poverty and heartache." Whether its globalization or technological change has most impacted employment and wages in the United States is a matter of dispute. However, it is technological change that has made possible the shift to commodity chains, so the two forces would be difficult to disentangle.

Bernie Sanders too made anti-globalization a major theme of his unsuccessful but remarkably resilient campaign to wrest the Democratic nomination from Hillary Clinton. Sanders' rhetoric too was aimed mainly at economic elites and at the influence of concentrated wealth over politicians, but unlike Trump his campaign message revolved around a need to bolster, not weaken public trust in public authority. In an op-ed piece for the *New York Times* (June 29, 2016), Sanders wrote, "Let's be clear. The global economy is not working for the majority of people in our country and the world. This is an economic model developed by the economic elite to benefit the economic elite. We need real change. But we do not need change based on the demagogy, bigotry and anti-immigrant sentiment that punctuated so much of the Leave campaign's rhetoric — and is central to Donald J. Trump's message."

There is little doubt that Hillary Clinton's past association with her husband's support for the North American Free Trade Agreement (NAFTA, upon which the TPP was modeled) and her support as a Senator for other agreements undermined her standing among important sections of the Democratic Party's base of support. The message on the center-left was similar around the world. Liberals, whether the classic variety who believe unfettered market forces function to everyone's benefit or those with social democratic leanings who accept the need for government moderation of market forces, agreed: resistance is futile. Adaptation is the answer.

Political scientist Manfred Steger contends that already by the 1990s elites had begun to portray globalization as something beyond anyone's control. "The public discourse...describing its projected path was saturated with adjectives like 'irresistible', 'inevitable', 'inexorable', and 'irreversible'", he wrote.[29] Frederick W. Smith, founder and CEO of FedEx Corporation, a global delivery service strategically located at the center of the apparent trend, holds that "Globalization is inevitable and inexorable and it is accelerating...It does not matter whether you like it or not, it's happening, it's going to happen."[30]

Like many other transnational executives and corporate directors, Smith's personal story gives him good reason to think that globalization is on automatic pilot. According to the FedEx website, Smith perceived as a college student in 1965 that the time was coming for a service "designed to accommodate time-sensitive shipments such as medicine, computer parts, and electronics." That is, he recognized the coming of the global assembly line. Smith started FedEx with 14 planes in 1973, and after deregulation of the air cargo industry (for which he strongly lobbied), the company's annual revenues had reached $1 billion in 1983. It began to buy-out other companies around the world and its network incorporated 220 nations into its cargo services.

Thomas Friedman, at the time the chief foreign affairs columnist for the *New York Times,* set the tone in many of his writings, including in his best-selling *The Lexus and the Olive Tree,* where he wrote, ""That's why I define globalization this way: it is the inevitable integration of markets, nation-states and technologies to a degree never witnessed before – in a way that is enabling individuals, corporations and nation-states to reach around the world farther, faster, deeper and cheaper than ever before and in a way that is enabling the world to reach into individuals, corporations and nation-states farther, faster, and deeper, cheaper than ever before." Friedman did raise concerns about a backlash, but then too he also called it a "brakeless train wreaking havoc."[31]

By 2016, as Steger had anticipated in his 2005 article, across the world a populist wave of reaction to various forms of globalization had begun to shake the confidence of globalists that the world was spinning their way. Threats to the survival of the European Union, stalled efforts to pass the Trans-Pacific Partnership (TPP) in the United States, the emergence of left social movements challenging the "race to the bottom", and right-wing ethno-nationalist resistance to mass global migrations, were signs that the train had lost momentum. The surge of leftist populism (which also, it must be said, seemed unstoppable in the 2000's) in Latin America had put a halt to creation of a Free Trade Association of the Americas, like the TPP, modeled on NAFTA, in 2005. All of these development, we should note, pre-dated the near collapse of the global economy in late 2008 and 2009, which emasculated the living standards of the middle and working class across the developed world, further eroding mass confidence in political and economic elites.

Hillary Clinton found that the message she was delivering to wealthy audiences on Wall Street behind closed doors resonated poorly among voters she needed to hold onto the nomination of the Democratic Party and, later, to win the general election. It hardly helped her when Wikileaks released transcripts of some of her Wall Street speeches. In one especially revealing speech to a group of housing construction executives, Clinton explained how the political game is played. "If everybody's watching, you know, all of the back room discussions and the deals, you know, then people get a little nervous, to say the least," said Clinton. "So, you need both a public and a private position."[32] Challenged by Sanders, she attempted to put behind her a history of support for trade agreements by finessing the issue of the pending TPP, saying she could not vote for it without revisions. How would we know if that was her "public" or her "private" position?

Nor did it help Clinton when President Obama, fully committed to the TPP, at a rally in Indiana played the "globalization is inevitable" card to answer a question posed by an employee of Carrier Corporation worried about his employer's plans to move production and 1000 jobs to Mexico. Said Obama.

> For those folks who have lost their job right now because a plant went down to Mexico, that isn't going to make you feel better. And so what we have to do is to make sure that folks are trained for the jobs that are coming in now because some of those jobs of the past are just not going to come back, and when somebody says, like the person you just mentioned [Donald Trump] who I'm not going to advertise for, that he's going to bring all these jobs back, well how exactly are you going to do that? What are you going to do?[33]

At a conference in Malaysia in April 2014, Obama complained that critics claiming that the negotiations for the TPP were ignoring popular concerns reflected a lack of knowledge of what is going on in the negotiations. He failed to mention that the negotiations were going on in secret, with corporate interests periodically informed of developments, but no information disseminated to the general public. Then he played the conspiracy panic card, responding to a reporter's question, "My point is you shouldn't be surprised if there are going to be objections, protests, rumors, conspiracy theories, political aggravation around a trade deal. You've been around long enough, Chuck — that's true in Malaysia; it's true in Tokyo; it's true in Seoul; it's true in the United

States of America — and it's true in the Democratic Party"—in all probability an allusion to Sanders.[34]

By contrast, Trump's message and rhetoric emphasized elite agency; he eschewed any claim that globalization was historically or economically inevitable. At his campaign rallies, Trump played the anti-globalization theme in a way that put a human face on the momentum behind globalization. In June 2016 in Monessen, he said, "This is not some natural disaster. It is politician-made disaster. It is the consequence of a leadership class that worships globalism over Americanism." Later, he added, "The TPP creates a new international commission that makes decisions the American people can't veto. These commissions are great for Hillary Clinton's Wall Street funders who can spend vast amounts of money to influence the outcomes." Trump promised the Monessen workers to "make American independent again" from "day one" by renegotiating multilateral trade treaties. He would rebuild its infrastructure with capital investments requiring steel and aluminum made in America. And "it will be American workers who are hired to do the job."[35]

It is not clear that resentment toward imports displacing jobs or lowering wages directly translates to resentment by voters in all parts of the country. One study of voting trends on the country level found that exposure to competition from Chinese imports was significantly correlated with higher wages and a larger share of the vote in both the 2000 and 2016 presidential election.[36] However, this study only examines import competition, not outward investment by employers in the counties. Nor does it consider the logic that imports may have risen because of robust consumption in certain high-income counties, pushing them further into the Republican column on election day. In other words, counties attractive to exporters may very well be the kinds of counties where affluent voters are located. Economically and social distressed counties are most likely unattractive destinations for foreign exporters.

Trump's critics miss the point when they ask why workers, such as the unemployed or threatened workers in Pennsylvania and Indiana would trust a real estate tycoon who bragged openly about his wealth and ability to game the political system. And most seem to have stuck by him throughout his first 18 months in office, despite few signs that they and their families will soon regain prosperity. No one can say that all of these swing voters will stay, but what seems to be operating in generating loyalty in the case of white, working-class men and women in small towns and rural areas of the Midwest is the vulnerability of their communities and families to technological change and globalization, coupled with their loss of status as challenges to patriarchy and white privilege have become more visible culturally. Timothy Melley calls such a reaction "agency panic," a sense that powerful external forces beyond their control are shaping their lives. This agency panic is being exacerbated by the sense the external agents are foreign—that America's political class owes allegiance to these outside actors rather than to the nation of which they are a member. They may not be naïve enough to believe that Trump has no foreign ties—Russian or otherwise, but alleged Russian interference in the election does not pose the same kind of threat to their living conditions and to their social status. And it may very well be helpful to Trump that Vladimir Putin, the Russian president, projects an image fitting the traditional masculine prototype. And as we have already seen, nativism was deeply ingrained in past episodes of populism in America, so it should be no surprise that it too could be summoned again in a world where the nation-state no longer seems to offer security to foreign threats.

If we take into account the inter-relationship of the socioeconomic context with the backlash among parts of what America to the demographic changes (loss of majority status for whites) and cultural change (gay rights, emergence of transgender peoples, Me Too, etc.), we can put the statistical findings suggesting that racism and gender prejudice were more significant factors than economic discontent in determining the outcome of the 2016 election into better. After all, in the last decade, the United States has seen its first African-American president, the first woman to win the presidential nomination of a major party, and the first serious challenge by a self-identified "socialist" in a century. To put the question in too-raw a fashion, we might ask, Why did some racist and sexist white voters shift their vote from Obama to Trump between 2012 and 2016?

Figure 5.1 provides a graphic representation of the analysis linking voting patterns in distress communities, which we examined in Chapter 4. It shows how clearly, especially in the medium and smaller counties of the upper Midwest Iron Belt and the mining country, votes shifted toward the Republicans from 2012 to 2016. What this suggests is that the core Trumpistas, those who inhabit the extreme right media silo, come disproportionately from those areas that have been most distressed by the economic shifts that have been brought about by "inevitable" globalization. We know that minority working-class members did not vote for Trump—though their turnout did drop. The big defections were among white members of the working and middle class in especially distressed areas; it is here that Trump finds the most receptivity to his message of disruption and the

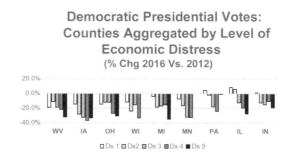

Fig. 5.1 Graphic representation of aggregate vote and distress (*Sources* Economic Innovation Group, *The 2017 Distressed Communities Distressed Communities Index*, available at eig.org [accessed July 1, 2018]; *US Election Atlas*, at uselectionatlas.org, compiled by Dave Leip)

paranoid style has greatest appeal, even as conspiracy theories in America today are not restricted only to the president's supporters.

I do not at all mean to underplay the importance of race-baiting and outright misogyny in Trump's 2016 campaign. The sudden emergence of a "Black Lives Matter" movement against police violence, combined with deliberate ambushes of police officers together brought racial tensions to an all-time high. Certainly, whites in more affluent suburbs have little real reason to fear economic displacement. Race and economic gain mean more to them. I recall after the 2012 election being taken aback by a conservative friend who I never heard utter a racist epithet suddenly blurt out after Barack Obama's re-election, "I don't feel like this is my country anymore." Another friend (I try to get out of my bubble) explained he didn't much like Trump, but he liked the outcome of the 2016 election because "Now we're in control."

Survey research, though persuasive on the role of racism and sexism in shaping the outcome of the 2016 election, is susceptible to underestimating the role of economic forces in understanding the result. Tapping into the seamy underside of Know-Nothingism and white supremacy has historically been linked to period of economic dislocation in America. So it was in 2016. Barely disguised, hardline invectives against immigrants typically accompanied Trump's denunciations of the conditions afflicting poor, working-class, and middle-class families. Trump warned his Monessen audience that if Hillary Clinton were to be elected, "The borders will remain open." In full campaign mode, he promised walls to be built and paid-for by Mexico; political swamps to be drained; and immigrants to be deported en-masse. Prosperity and jobs would return to these hard-pressed areas. "You're gonna' love it." He would lead a robust military buildup and make hard-driving deals with other countries—in sum, "To make America great again."

A lot of ink could be wasted attempting to dissect whether nativist movements originate in the masses or in the elite, both historically and in the present. A better approach may be to recognize that popular discontent with elites offers opportunities to political entrepreneurs to mobilize support for challenges to the prevailing ruling elites. William Kornhauser, an American sociologist specializing in the relationship between discontented citizens and ambitious leaders, contended that these two elements symbiotically work to pose a threat to free societies.[37] As with Hofstadter's "paranoid style" this approach tends to be highly pessimistic about popuism, viewing popular discontent and ambition in leaders as toxic in all its forms, a perspective this book disputes. However, the idea of a "political entrepreneur" is useful for understanding the resistible rise of Donald Trump. Discontent can be mobilized into populism that advances progressive, democratic change or nativist demagoguery. Historically, as was the case of William Jennings Bryan, the populist firebrand of American populism of the last century, populist movements have mixed both types of appeals.

Bryan's most famous quotaton, taken from his "Cross of Gold" speech at the 1896 Democratic Convention, which led to his being nominated for president the next day, was, "You shall not press down upon the borrow of labor this crown of thorns. You shall not crucify mankind upon a cross of gold." "You" in this sentence clearly referred to Eastern bankers and industrialists. The appeal was progressive in its insistence on redressing the inequalities that had accumulated over several decades of industrialization, with Bryan calling for Social Security, a progressive income tax, and other reforms that would eventually follow, especially in the New Deal era. Bryan was also a leading voice in opposition to America's emerging overseas imperialism in Central America and the Caribbean, and as Secretary of State for Woodrow Wilson he advanced, with some initial success, global disarmament. However, 1890s populism was deeply tainted by anti-semitism ("Jewish moneyed-interests") and racism (defense of Jim Crow). Though motivated in part by the attempts to apply Darwin's theories to explain class inequality (social Darwinism), the legacy of Bryan (an Evangelical Christian) was indelibly tarnished by his hostility to science and his prosecution against a teacher of Evolution in the Scopes "monkey trial" of 1925. More recent studies of populism and Bryan paint a more nuanced view of the movement and its most successful political entrepreneur.[38] This is in contrast to Hofstadter, who, seeking to disassociate Bryan from Roosevelt, highlighted the anti-Semitism and anti-modernization features of populism, in a book published eight years before the first "paranoid style" essay.[39]

TRANSNATIONAL CAPITALISM AND THE NATION STATE

The most pernicious conspiracy theory that stimulated Hofstadter's concern about the paranoid style was spawned not by the masses but instead by the ambitious and unscrupulous politicians of the ilk of Senator Joseph McCarthy. Far from repudiating anti-communist hysteria, across the partisan spectrum those favoring the construction of a permanent National Security state found it useful. That usefulness ended after McCarthy, the zealous political entrepreneur, attacked a sector of the security apparatus itself, the Army. Until that overreach, McCarthyism served to contain and roll back leftist influence that had risen during the New Deal and global war against fascism. Though not nearly as violent and tyrannical as the Stalinist variety, McCarthyite conspiracism effectively constituted a purge Leftist influence from key sectors of the state (e.g., the State Department), the labor movement, cultural production (e.g., blacklisted Hollywood artists), and other public redoubts of the activist left in the Roosevelt era.

Alexander Dunst points out that one can easily construct a list of paranoid conspiracy theories emanating from American political leaders, which should force us to ask "…how state and mainstream social actors have been systematically exempted from such diagnoses in a U.S. context."[40] Indeed, in the Cold War period alone Americans were treated not only to McCarthyism, but also to similar episodes of fear mongering. Especially illustrative was Ronald Reagan's "evil empire" rhetoric, used to justify episodes of military interventionism and covert operations against foreign states with a Manichean rhetoric about a global communist conspiracy. The "Great Communicator" once attempted to rally support for intervention in Nicaragua in 1981 by arguing that the Communists (allegedly, the Sandinistas) were only two days away from Brownsville, Texas.

The tension between the exercise of hegemony and democracy in the United States is not entirely new; it was visible in conflicts between "isolationists" and "anti-imperialists", on the one side, and advocates of US expansionism and global leadership, on the other in the period around the Spanish-American War (1898). It manifested itself more fully in the post-World War era, when the consolidation of US hegemony was accompanied by the McCarthyite purge and later abuses of power in response to the anti-war and civil rights movements. But the ability to link together populist challenges to nation and to capitalism is more difficult today. The end of the Cold War ushered-in the new technologies that both drove and were driven by the freer movements of capital across national boundaries. Capital is no longer "multinational," that is firms owned and directed largely by business tycoons from one (and most only one) of the world's wealthy nation states; capital is "transnational" because the owners and directors of global corporations are themselves intertwined. According to an Oxfam study based on research by *Forbes Magazine* and a prominent Swiss Bank, the "one percent" wealthiest people in the world may still be disproportionately from the first world, but in 2009 only 35 of the 80 wealthiest people were (U.S.) Americans; 20 were from other "Trilateral" countries; 25 were from "post-communist" countries or parts of what we once called the "Third World."[41]

The resulting globalized market system is thus "transnational." The term first emerged to describe mass immigration in the nineteenth and early twentieth century, an early indication that the global economic changes were pressing the frontiers of self-contained nation-states. It came into wider use when in reaction to the consequences of what appeared in the 1970s to be deteriorating US power and rising Third World power a "Trilateral Commission," linking intellectual, political, and business elites from North American, European, and Japanese elites. Leslie Sklair and Stephen Gill, respectively, responded to the Commission and other developments with criticism that included labeling this more tightly networked international business elite as a "transnational capitalist class."[42] William Robinson took the idea a step further by distinguishing between an earlier history of corporate expansion abroad and today's era of global capitalism. In the earlier period, "multinational corporations" referred to firms that did business through trade or through investments abroad, with ownership and boards of directors largely from the home nation; case today "transnational corporations" are increasing owned and governed by share- and stake-holders scattered among many nations.[43]

Marx certainly failed in predicting the imminent demise of capitalism, but by now even his most vigorous detractors would have to concede that his characterization of capitalist economic change captures how the processes of globalization driven by the logic of neoliberal capitalism generate anxieties, including the kinds exploited by Alex Jones' *Infowars. com* and by Trump. In the *Communist Manifesto*, a document with a wildly optimistic view of the prospects of humanity, his analysis reads much more darkly today.

> Constant revolutionizing of production, uninterrupted disturbance of all social conditions, everlasting uncertainty and agitation distinguish the bourgeois epoch from all earlier ones. All fixed, fast-frozen relations, with their train of ancient and venerable prejudices and opinions, are swept away, all new-formed ones become antiquated before they can ossify. All that is solid melts into air; all that is holy is profaned, and man is at last compelled to face with sober senses his real conditions of life, and his relations with his kind.[44]

Marx followed this proclamation with myopically optimistic prediction, "National one-sidedness and narrow-mindedness become more and more impossible." He thought that capitalism and "the immensely facilitated means of communication, draws all, even the most barbarian, nations into civilization." Would anyone espouse the faith that the communications revolution of the post-Cold War era has made the world kindlier and gentler? In the *Manifesto*, Marx predicted that the forces of globalization unleashed by capitalism would compel us to face our "real conditions of life." They do seem to have produced anger that in this global capitalist economy "all that is solid melts." His vision of communism seems more distant than ever, but at least in the United States a younger generation that did not live through the Cold War seems more open to making another world possible. And many of this generation are not afraid to call their ideas "socialist."

As has been widely recognized, Trump's rhetoric has "enabled" the alt-right and white supremacy movements, well as other groups that make no effort to hide openly fascist and neo-fascist discourse, using salutes, symbols, and paraphernalia associated with the Axis powers of World War II. Playing on a phrase, "Twenty-first century socialism," popular with leftists seeking to differentiate contemporary socialist experiments from the Communist system of the last century, Robinson argues that Trumpism is a form of "Twenty-first century fascism," which he describes as:

...a response to the grave and increasing crisis of global capitalism, which explains the turn toward the neo-fascist right in Europe, as much in the West and in the East, the resurgence of a neo-fascist right in Latin America, the turn toward neo-fascism in Turkey, Israel, the Philippines, Indian and in many other places. A key difference between fascism of the twentieth century and that of the twenty-first century is that now we are dealing with the fusion of national capital with reactionary political power, but with a fusion of transnational capital with reactionary political power.[45]

But one can question whether Trump himself consciously has the kind of agenda attributed to him by Robinson. On the one hand, Trump's enterprises depend on immigrant labor. Who cleans the floors and makes up the beds in our hotels? Who tends to the fairways and greens on golf courses? Whether it is Trump's intention or not, the result of his scapegoating, nativist rhetoric and Immigration and Customs Enforcement (ICE) sweeps contributes to maintaining an immigrant peonage, due to their vulnerability to exploitation while the work here under an illegal status. But reducing immigrant labor may also impact the labor in businesses that, like Trump's depend on this part of the labor force.

Trump's campaign promises to make the US economy competitive and to "bring back jobs" resonated especially strongly with white workers who have been losing privileges associated with living the "first world." He has lowered taxes on corporations, but he also promised to spend billions on infrastructure. These expenditures, should they ever come about, would be closely linked to privatization of government functions. Trump has buried neoliberal priorities for a Trans-Pacific Partnership trade deal, a top priority of the Obama administration. On March 1, 2018, Trump announced his attention to levy new tariffs on steel and aluminum imports, moves that are threatening to the stability of the global free trade order. None other than *Forbes Magazine*, while eschewing the "neofascist" label, warned of dire consequences of the rise of the global right and the seeming incapacity of neoliberal capitalism and liberal democracy to address mass discontent. Anders Corr, a regular contributor to the *Forbes*, shortly after the US election warned,

Nationalism and racism in international politics lead to a Hobbesian anarchy that in the nuclear age would be nastier, more brutish, and shorter than anything found in the state of nature. The wars of the 20th century were nothing compared to the high-technology wars that are now being prepared in the weapons laboratories of the world's major powers...If major war is unleashed...(t)he main fighting could be over in a matter of hours, and could devastate the planet.[46]

A web search on "neoliberalism and the end of liberal democracy" brings up myriad articles, filling almost all on the first few pages, from both radical and mainstream sources, warning that the spread of global market forces has weakened the kind of politics and states that many expected would broaden and deepen with the end of the Cold War. Robert Reich, who professes himself a progressive liberal who seeks to save capitalism "for the many" called Trump "The American Fascist."[47] As did the early twentieth-century fascists, Trump focused his campaign on the anger of white working people who have been losing economic ground for years, and who are easy prey for demagogues seeking to build their own power by scapegoating others.

Trumpian voters are more likely to link ethnicity to American national identity. The distribution of opinion in Table 5.1, based upon survey data made available by the Voter Study Group, shows that they were significantly more likely than others to think that having been born in America, speaking English, and being a Christian were important to "being an American." These sentiments were even more pronounced among Trump primary voters, who might reasonably be considered his key base for keeping Republican elected official in line. Trump tapped into these sentiments in varying ways, in particular through his characterization of Mexican immigrants as violent criminals, his exploitation of anti-Muslim sentiment, and his profession of evangelical religious convictions. The one area of American identity where Trump voters did not link in great numbers to being American, and only slightly more so than supporters of Clinton and Sanders, is of European heritage.[48]

It is worth noting, however, that while the number Trump voters endorsing English as a requirement to be an American outpaced Trump and Sanders supporters, more than a third of supporters of all three candidates, among both primary and general election voters, endorsed the language requirement, and particularly striking was the high percentage of Clinton primary supporters who tied speaking English to national identity. These results also speak to the false equivalence between the brand of populism advanced by Trump and Sanders, respectively. Sanders

Table 5.1 Nationalism, importance to being an American

How important …		Clinton general election		Trump general election		Trump primary voters		Sanders primary voters		Clinton primary voters	
… to have born in America	Very	690	21.8%	1265	40.3%	633	49.0%	160	15.0%	456	32.1%
	Fairly	618	19.5%	714	22.7%	279	21.6%	180	16.8%	307	21.6%
	Not very	782	24.7%	694	22.1%	239	18.5%	334	31.2%	261	18.4%
	Not at all	917	29.0%	410	13.1%	118	9.1%	371	34.7%	330	23.2%
… to be able to speak English	Very	1227	38.7%	2533	80.6%	1099	85.3%	361	33.7%	692	48.5%
	Fairly	930	29.3%	488	15.6%	154	11.9%	343	32.0%	361	25.3%
	Not very	578	18.2%	63	2.0%	17	1.3%	224	20.9%	215	15.1%
	Not at all	129	4.1%	14	0.4%	2	0.2%	122	11.4%	115	8.1%
… to be Christian	Very	369	12.4%	1033	32.9%	497	38.5%	94	8.8%	309	21.8%
	Fairly	314	10.0%	637	20.3%	282	21.8%	85	8.0%	187	13.2%
	Not very	461	14.7%	724	23.0%	244	18.9%	118	11.1%	202	14.3%
	Not at all	192	6.1%	629	20.0%	214	16.6%	740	69.4%	623	44.0%
… to be of European heritage	Very	166	5.3%	270	8.6%	158	12.5%	53	5.0%	151	10.6%
	Fairly	235	7.4%	385	12.3%	196	15.4%	44	4.1%	143	10.1%
	Not very	647	20.5%	1047	33.5%	454	35.6%	186	17.4%	309	21.8%
	Not at all	1896	50.1%	226	7.2%	371	29.1%	755	70.6%	718	50.6%

Source Democracy Fund Voter Study Group. Views of the Electorate Research Survey, December 2016 [Computer File] Release 1: August 28, 2017. Washington, DC: Democracy Fund Voter Study Group [producer] https://www.voterstudygroup.org/. Conflict Voter Study Group for exact questions

Table 5.2 Attitudes on economic conditions and trade

		Clinton general election		Trump general election		Trump primary voters		Sanders primary voters		Clinton primary voters	
Life in America today for respondent, v. 50 years ago	Better	1286	39.6%	542	17.0%	209	16.0%	376	34.5%	616	41.9%
	Same	773	23.8%	494	15.5%	182	14.0%	222	20.4%	397	27.0%
	Worse	905	27.9%	1956	61.5%	856	65.7%	419	38.5%	350	38.5%
Affect of free trade on amount of products American businesses sell?	Increase	1702	54.6%	1097	35.5%	433	34.4%	505	48.3%	825	57.8%
	Decrease	784	25.1%	1459	47.2%	594	47.2%	363	34.7%	310	21.7%
	No impact	634	20.3%	533	17.3%	232	18.4%	178	17.0%	292	20.5%
Affect free trade will have on the number of jobs for Americans?	Increase	849	27.3%	629	20.2%	289	21.2%	192	18.4%	516	36.2%
	Decrease	1559	50.1%	2122	68.2%	851	67.1%	701	67.1%	572	40.1%
	No Impact	702	22.6%	360	11.6%	149	11.7%	152	14.5%	338	23.7%
Affect free trade will have on the wages of American workers?	Increase	735	23.6%	542	17.5%	219	17.3%	177	16.8%	457	32.2%
	Decrease	1532	49.3%	2023	65.2%	833	65.8%	687	65.2%	584	41.2%
	No impact	842	27.1%	537	17.3%	213	16.8%	189	17.9%	378	26.6%
Affect free trade will have on prices of products available for sale	Increase	887	28.6%	93	22.1%	373	29.4%	270	25.8%	493	34.7%
	Decrease	1615	52.0%	264	62.1%	638	50.3%	621	59.3%	659	46.3%
	No Impact	602	19.4%	64	15.2%	258	20.3%	156	14.9%	270	19.0%
Affect free trade will have on quality of products	Increase	970	31.3%	650	21.0%	285	20.9%	229	22.0%	554	38.9%
	Decrease	1203	38.8%	1836	59.2%	764	60.3%	550	52.7%	453	31.8%
	No Impact	929	29.9%	615	19.8%	238	18.8%	264	25.3%	416	29.2%

Source Democracy Fund Voter Study Group. Views of the Electorate Research Survey, December 2016 [Computer File] Release 1: August 28, 2017. Washington DC: Democracy Fund Voter Study Group [producer] https://www.voterstudygroup.org/. Please consult Voter Study Group for exact wording of questions supporters were by far the least likely, and by a large margin, to endorse any of these ethno-nationalist sentiments, and by far most likely to reject them—although even Sanders voters by a majority tied Americanism to English speaking. Given that Sanders is Jewish, it should not surprise that being Christian is of importance to every view of his primary voters.

The populist appeal of Trump and Sanders coincides and more in attitudes about free trade, displayed in Table 5.2. Considered all together, the distribution of responses of primary voters to the five questions on free trade are remarkably similar and negative on the way that free trade affects three areas that most directly impact ordinary people's well-being: wages, employment, and prices. While a plurality of Clinton primary voters also registers pessimism in this area, the percentages fall considerably short of the strong majorities found among of Trump and Sanders voters. A higher percentage of Sanders voters questioned whether American businesses would sell more products with globalization.

Trump voters are by far more likely than Clinton and even Sanders voters to believe that life in America today is worse than it was 50 years ago, a finding that suggests the appeal of Trump's campaign motto, "Make America Great Again." Combined with Trump's nativist, ethno-nationalist appeal, one sees how the tycoon's campaign for the nomination could be so impactful without the dark money support that went to his Republican rivals (see Chapter 6), none of whom drew so effectively on the clash between national sovereignty and liberal free trade. Journalists and academics are expended considerable effort on the impact of sophisticated analytics, digital advertising, and Russian bots in the election, but the most "innovative" and effective tool to exploit popular discontent in the 2016 campaign may have been the humble baseball cap bearing the "Make American Great Again" slogan—a campaign tactic subject to no little scorn in cosmopolitan circles.

POPULISM VERSUS TRANSNATIONAL CAPITALISM

The most compelling reason to link globalization to populism, especially right-wing populism, is the simultaneous emergence of ethno-nationalist parties and movements in various parts of the developed world, and especially in North America and Europe, since the global financial crisis of 2008–2009. A recent study comparing Tweets of French and American politicians showed remarkable similarity in the themes prevalent in those of Trump and France's National Front leader, Marine Le Pen.[49] The common denominator in this development in the Western core nations is the appeal of radical right parties and movements in areas that have experienced social and economic distress, in urban areas from industrialization and in rural regions from the struggles of smaller scale agriculture.[50] While it may be true that the economic underpinnings of this stress can be traced to technological change, those most impacted by the shift in technology and the relations of production (decline of the factory assembly line and rise of global assembly line production) perceive globalization at the root. Earlier in the chapter, I argued against separating technological change and globalization in favor of recognizing that both processes are related closely to each other and to the shift globally away from nationally based capitalist economies to a transnational one.

The rise of Trump, the Brexit victory in Britain, the emergence of the National Front in France as a political contender, were early indications that the recent wave of right-wing populism is transnational, cropping up in one form or another in wealthy capitalist democracies and European post-communist states. As of this writing, the populist right, made up of leaders and political parties (the latter sometimes personalist organizations built around a charismatic leader) have accumulated enough power to control or strongly influence politics in just about every country in Europe. In some cases, the most important being Germany, these movements have managed to pry away sectors of mainstream conservative parties to undermine leaders more committed to maintaining the welfare systems, acceptance of free movement of people with the European Union, relatively liberal policies toward refugees, and further economic integration ("free trade"). The challenge was vividly demonstrated in June 2018 in Germany, where the Alternative for Germany (AfD) party significantly cut into the appeal of the more moderate, mainstream right. German Chancellor Angela Merkel, a Christian Democrat and the Western leader most identified with maintaining and extending a more globally integrated political and economic order, found herself fighting for her political life as a result of a revolt of the leader of a sister Christian Democratic party in Bavaria, demonstrating the growing unpopularity of her willingness to accept migrants seeking asylum at the border of Bavaria and Austria.

These episodes seem to suggest that the "paranoid style" variety of populism, which Hofstadter lined to recurring nativism in the United States, could now be applied to the European context as well—though certainly the "paranoid" style of politics was visible in the fascist movements of the last century as well.[51] It is legitimate to study the rise of fascism for lessons on resistance to the current wave of xenophobia and resentment toward international economic crisis; at the same time we must keep in mind how much Trumpism and its counterparts in Europe are animated by massive global migrations being spawned by transnational neoliberal economic forces, natural calamities (liked to global warming to some extent), and civil warfare in the Middle East and Africa, all throwing up difficult challenges to a world where barriers (passports, border checks, citizenship linked to ethnicity, etc.) to movements of people remain quite firmly in place—except in Western Europe, where the EU has until now knocked down internal frontiers within its zone. However, the EU accomplishment has been put in jeopardy by the AfD's success in forcing Merkel to roll back her relatively liberal policies on immigration.

Mabel Berezin ties the "rise of illiberal politics" in Europe to forces that clearly manifested themselves as well in the rise of Trump. European integration and globalization, she says, "have altered the social and political landscape of contemporary Europe. Insecurity in both the public and private domain has been one response to these processes. Fear—of immigrants, crime, disease, unemployment–has become a recurrent theme in European public discourse." Surveys only partly capture this phenomenon. Not everyone who indulges in anti-immigrant and racist discourse and racist discourse necessarily has a "thick commitment" to the party or movement expressing these sentiments, she argues. Broader support for Le Pen's National Front and parties of a similar ilk consists of people with only thin commitments, motivated by the erosion of security in their lives and believing their national identity, their ontological status and "collectively defined way of being in the world" to be under attack.[52] Her point is not to defend nativist politics but to point out how deeply ingrained national identity is in our everyday lives, clashing with the cosmopolitan liberal value of "global citizenship." Even the most developed and institutionalized international organization, the European Union, is highly insulated from direct popular influence, and symbols on money and European flags on capitals cannot remedy the democratic deficit.

Although right-populism in Europe has its own roots, the right-wing forces aligned with Trump have begun themselves to take on a transnational character. One good example is the World Congress of Families (WCF), which was founded in Russia to defend the "natural family," that is, the family made up of heterosexual pair of parents couple and their children. In 2016, the group held its international conference in Salt Lake City. Some "pro-family" US conservatives have embraced this Russian initiative, strongly supported by the Kremlin. The network includes social conservatives from European countries as well.[53] These global links reflect an incipient alignment on the right, one that may to some degree be blunting the hostility of traditional conservatives toward Vladimir Putin.

Trumpism simultaneously reflects and fosters tension between democracy and national sovereignty. While catch phrases like "global citizenship" have entered popular culture and curriculums in our schools and universities, the institutions of representative democracy remain based closely tied to what historian Benedict Anderson calls the "imagined community" of a nation. That is, most commonly we think of a "community" as a group of human beings that spend a good deal of time with one another, whether in residential neighborhoods, small towns, workplaces, gathering points (coffee houses, pubs, etc.). Communities in our online era can be virtual, linking individuals into networks on Facebook, for example. But the nation, Anderson points, forms a "community" that is, in reality, a huge conglomeration of individuals that will never lay eyes on one another, never directly communicate.[54] I live in St. Louis, but as an "American" I share an identity with residents on Riverside, California; Brooklyn; New York; Opelika, Alabama; etc.

While most coverage of the radical right, and much of this book, is focused on lower income people who generally fit Berezin's profile, the nativist appeal can cross class boundaries. The media have failed to recognize, for example, that the German AfD's support comes disproportionately from upper income, not lower income and uneducated voters. A University of Leipzig study showed that 81% of its voters were actually middle and upper income, not from those generally seen to be losers from globalization, the same social base of most of the party's activists. However, the same study showed the supporters in general rejected globalization and multiculturalism, and were also attracted to identity politics, the latter clearly related to issues about immigration and asylum.[55] And though the Leipzig study found the party strongly rooted in the upper class, its gains in 2017 were largely concentrated in areas that have most suffered economic decline and experience settling of refugees.[56]

The data reviewed earlier in this chapter do not allow us to directly tie Trump's success in swinging key voters needed for an Electoral College victory to his conspiracist appeal. What they show, consistent with other voting patterns displayed in Fig. 5.1 in this chapter, is that his appeal was strongest where economic distress was greatest, areas that have been excluded from the benefits of economic globalization and technological changes. This distress is not unlike the forces that theorists like Tim Melley have linked to agency panic, not only in the United States but in Europe as well.

It should not be surprising that Trump's political success should call into question the theory that the issues such as environmentalism, quality of life and work, and other "post-materialist" matters are characteristics of capitalist societies that have reached a high stage of development. Supposedly, such societies have left behind the class conflicts typical of industrial capitalism. While, as this theory predicts, higher levels of education are correlated with voting for Clinton and rejection of Trump, the tycoon's ability to attract significant sectors of the white working class and middle class from the Democratic base suggests deeper, more troubling contradictions in the wealthier capitalist world. Political sociologists have acknowledged that "perceived cultural threats" have contributed mightily to rise of authoritarian populism, but the idea that there might be material factors causing or accelerating this process is often downplayed in their analyses.[57]

Developments at both national and global levels that have intensified popular suspicions about the commitment of ruling elites in liberal democracies to pursuit of the national interest. We could spend considerable time considering whether in fact there is such a thing as "national interest." Certainly, Marx and his followers have long maintained that capitalists, i.e., the "bourgeoisie," used nationalism as a false ideology to divide workers of different countries against one another. In the United States, a generation of "revisionist" historians questioned the assumption of the realist school of international relations that the driving force behind diplomacy in the United States was maximization of national power and interests.

Charles Beard's (1934: 3) critique of "national interest" noted, "The thinkers and statesmen who thus present the doctrine of national interest speak in the language of exact science, they apparent conceive of interest as a reality open to human understanding and as a kind of iron necessity which binds governments and governed alike. It binds them so closely that there is no escape, except possibly for an insignificant few minority;

it cuts across the social divisions reflected in political parties and compels a 'united front'" against external enemies and competitors.[58]

Today, "national security" is more often invoked than "national interest," but often to the same effect. Take the official Obama White House communication efforts to achieve ratification of the TPP:

> America's trade policy has an enormous impact on the economic well-being of the American people, and the strategic interests of the United States. Trade can support American jobs, eliminate taxes on American exports, help American businesses reach new markets, protect the environment, promote stronger labor standards, combat human trafficking, defend the intellectual property of American innovators, and shape a better future for our children — those are the types of agreements that President Obama has pursued.[59]

Of course, the same president also said, "Some of those jobs of the past are not gonna come back,"[60] in partial response to a question to Eric Cottonham, an unemployed worker, a member of a Steel Workers union laid off by the Carrier Corporation in Indiana. "What can we look forward to in the future," asked Cottonham, an African-American, who directed himself to the President, not angrily but respectfully. Obama reeled off a series of facts about how many manufacturing jobs had been created by his administration. Obama said he was trying to negotiate trade treaties that would raise wages and working conditions abroad to level conditions. The president said that the real culprit was automation. Without mentioning Trump by name, Obama challenged the hotel mogul to explain how he would bring the jobs back. "There's no answer to it," he claimed.

The president had his economics right. Manufacturing production had been rising with only slight dips around 1998 and 2008 (both years of global financial crisis) for 35 years, resulting in almost 2.5 times the output being produced at the end of the period by almost 50% fewer workers.[61] What the president failed to explain was why the benefits of automation—more production per unit of labor—had not been deployed to benefit the workers. He was fortunate in 2012 to have faced a Republican opponent, Mitt Romney, who was recorded[62] telling a roomful of wealthy supporters behind closed doors that 47% of Americans "believe that they are victims, that the government has responsibility to care for them...I'll never convince them they should take personal responsibility and care for their lives." Certainly, this is a message was even less comforting to Americans like Cottonham, who were asking for a future. But did Obama provide any reason for them to think their distress was of any real importance to the president?

By the end of 2016, Obama's hopes to achieve the TPP had been dashed, though many of the other countries that were to be party to it were working on forming an association without the United States. Two years later, no longer could a "united front" be held together in support of the neoliberal economic doctrines associated with globalization in the TransAtlantic, with or without US participation. Political uncertainties and suspicions have both proliferated and deepened as the nation-state finds itself buffeted by the forces of globalization. Technological developments and untamed market forces that have rent the social and economic fabric of life for the working class and middle class in the core, wealthy countries of the world. This has contributed to a global surge of populism. Trumpism represents the reactionary variant of this surge, but Sanders, Corbyn and a few smaller European parties represent resistance to global neoliberalism rather than globalization per se.

The anti-globalization jeremiads, pronouncements, and proposals of Trump were those of a businessman who profits from retailing clothing made in China and approximately a dozen other countries. He has twice married immigrant women, has either built or brand luxury hotels and golf courses around the world, and in 2013 penned a piece for CNN (January 13) opining, "I think we've all become aware of the fact that our cultures and economics are intertwined. It's a complex mosaic that cannot be approached with a simple formula for the correct pattern to emerge. In many ways, we are in unchartered waters...We will have to leave borders behind and go for global unity when it comes to financial stability." But four years later there was little indication that Trump has fealty to those ideas today.

After the election Trump's transition team got to work installing a coterie of business elites, generals, and ultra-conservative politicians into national security and key economic institutions. A tycoon from the fast-food industry would take over the Labor Department, placing a key opponent of a higher minimum wage and opponent of unionization in the department most responsible for defending workers. The Chief Executive Officer (Tillerson) of the world's largest oil company was tapped for State—he would be replaced in 2018 by a hawkish Mike Pompeo. Three former officials of Goldman Sachs got three top economic posts. A global warming denier was to be put in charge of the Environmental Protection Agency. And the list goes on.

Throughout the transition, Trump's media operations continued to project images of power and nationalism. A deal, in works well before the election, to keep a portion of the Carrier jobs in Indiana was promoted as success of the new administration through Twitter, *Breitbart* news, and other outlets as the first dividend to workers who tipped the scales to Trump in the vital Midwest rust belt states. Although the then president-elect toned down his own rhetoric, the crowd at a Trump "thank-you" rally in Wisconsin made known they had not lost enthusiasm; they cheered rapper Kanye West and booed Paul Ryan, GOP Speaker of the House.

What we have in Trump is a living, breathing contradiction who either radically shifted his worldview as expressed in 2013 or shifted only his rhetoric in order to fulfill his own vocation for power and narcissistic personality needs. Either way, he fits the mold of a certain type of populist, a kind of political entrepreneur who trades on popular angst and prejudices, who exploits mistrust and anger among people who have been marginalized and take refuge in hypernationalism and religious zealotry. The populist appeal is built upon invoking the power of "the people" against corrupt insiders, elites who have only their own interest, not that of the nation at heart. What makes the appeal paranoid is when a politician with a thirst for power, not service, exploits this sentiment.

CONCLUSION: THE GREAT DISRUPTER

It is hard to know if Trump and advisors deliberately planned to meat out embarrassment to well-known politicos of recent vintage, but the videos and photographs of supplicants visiting the triumphant, apprentice president in his gaudy New York tower after the election made for brilliant public theatre. Network news and late night talk show hosts gave exposure to former presidential nominees Al Gore and Mitt Romney meeting awkwardly with Trump, only to be subsequently spurned and scorned publicly for their naiveté. Gore's hopes for moderate policies on global warming and Romney's aspirations to serve as Secretary of State were dashed soon after by the appointment of Scott Pruit, a climate denying Congressman, to head the Environmental Protection Agency and Tillerson, the Chief Executive Officer of Exxon-Mobile, to Secretary of State.

In 1953, Charles Erwin Wilson, the CEO of General Motors Corporation, was asked at Senate Hearings regarding his nomination by President Dwight Eisenhower to serve as Secretary of Defense, how he could reconcile possible conflicts of interest between his company and his country. He responded, "For years I thought that what was good for our country was good for General Motors, and vice versa. The difference did not exist. Our company is too big. It goes with the welfare of the country. Our contribution to the nation is considerable."[63] That philosophy returned with a vengeance in the Trump presidency. Neither Trump nor Tillerson even bothered, as did Wilson, to argue that the corporate interests and national interests were identical. The conservative journal *National Review* lamented, "Sixty years later, where did the "America" in corporate America go? No longer committed to a particular place, people, country, or culture, our largest public companies have turned globalist while abdicating the responsibility they once assumed to America and its workers."[64]

The first 20 months of the Trump presidency left unclear overall just how much neoliberal globalization was being set back. Tillerson did not even last half way through Trump's presidential term. Pruitt would be forced to resign because of a serious of embarrassing revelations of his abuse of EPA funds, but not for his policies. By the middle of 2018, the Koch brothers were ready to commit millions of dollars in spending to fight Trump's tariffs and retreat from free trade agreements. NAFTA talks produced a tentative agreement with Mexico, but not a radical overhaul. Countries that had planned to join the United States in the TPP were forming their own trade block, new tariffs were being announced (but not yet implemented) by the president. Yet Donald Trump made it a point to go to the 2018 Davos summit where he clearly enjoyed basking in the rock-star type of reception that the world's rich had accorded him. Trump had put something of a stamp on his promises of reducing American international leadership, but there was little sign that special operations deployments and drone strikes had abated. Domestically, his minions in Congress had passed a tax "reform" that was heavily weighted toward the wealthy and the transnational corporate sector. All of these matters were subject to the whims of a world leader accustomed to pronouncements via tweeting, engaged in a firefight of words over Russiagate, and presiding over a West Wing revolving door through which high White House Staff came and went. Conspiracy theory? Why wouldn't opponents and supporters not have reason to suspect that conspiracies, petty and grand in design, are a normal feature of doing politics in the toxic political atmosphere of the Trump White House?

NOTES

1. Yarra Elmasry, "Why the Super-Rich Are Buying Luxury Apocalypse-Safe Bunkers for Protection Against Natural Disaters and Nuclear Attack," *The Independent*, July 10, 2017, London.
2. Matthew Gray, *Conspiracy Theories in the Arab World: Sources and Politics: Sources and Politics* (New York: Routledge Conspiracy Theories, 2010): 33–34.
3. Evan McMullin, "Trump's Rise Proves How Dangerous Populism Is to America," *NBCNews.com*, October 11, 2017 (accessed June 22, 2018). See Thomas Friedman, "What If?" *New York Times*, January 20, 2016; John Cassidy, "Bernie Sanders and Donald Trump Ride the Populist Wave," *The New Yorker*, February 10, 2016. A more nuanced perspective is Thomas Edsall, "The Trump-Sanders Fantasy," *New York Times*, February 24, 2016.
4. Richard Hofstadter, *The Paranoid Style in American Politics* (New York: Vintage Reprints, 1968).
5. Available at http://www.presidency.ucsb.edu/ws/?pid=19253.
6. William I. Robinson, *A Theory of Global Capitalism: Production, Class, and State in a Transnational World* (Baltimore, MD: Johns Hopkins University Press, 2004).
7. Joseph Schumpeter, *Capitalism, Socialism and Democracy* (London: Routledge, 1994, original 1942): 82–83.
8. Benjamin Barber, *Jihad vs. McWorld: Terrorism's Challenge to Democracy* (New York: Ballantine Books, 1996).
9. Barber, "Jihad vs. McWorld," *The Atlantic*, March 1992, available at https://www.theatlantic.com/magazine/archive/1992/03/jihad-vs-mcworld/303882 (accessed July 18, 2017).
10. Hofstadter, *The Paranoid Style in American Politics*.
11. Daniel Hellinger, "Paranoia, Conspiracy, and Hegemony in American Politics," in *Transparency and Conspiracy: Ethnographies of Suspicion in the New World Order*, ed. Harry G. West and Todd Sanders (Durham, NC: Duke University Press, 2003): 205.
12. Uscinski and Parent, *American Conspiracy Theories* (New York: Oxford University Press, 2014): 11.
13. Kathryn Olmsted, *Real Enemies: Conspiracy Theories and American Demodracy, World War I to 9/11* (New York: Oxford University Press): 4.

14. Jack Bratich, *Conspiracy Panics: Political Rationality and Poplar Culture* (Albany: State University of New York Press, 2008). Mark Fenster, *Conspiracy Theories: Secrecy and Power in American Culture* (Minneapolis: University of Minnesota Press, 1999).
15. Olmsted, *Real Enemies*: 234.
16. Among myriad reports on inequality, see Paul F. Campos, "White Economic Privilege is Alive and Well," New York Times, July 29, 2017. Also, Ishwar Khatiwada and Andrew M. Sum, "The Widening Socio-Economic Divergence in the U.S. Labor Market," in *The Dynamics of Opportunity in America*, ed. I. Kirsch and H. Braun (Cham: Springer), available at https://link.springer.com/chapter/10.1007/978-3-319-25991-8_7 (accessed June 19, 2018).
17. See https://www.wealthx.com/report/the-wealth-x-billionaire-census-2017 (accessed June 19, 2018).
18. Bill Robinson. "What is Behind the Renegotiation of NAFTA? Trumpism and the New Global Economy." *Truthout*, July 24, 2017, available at http://www.truth-out.org/news/item/41365-what-is-behind-the-renegotiation-of-nafta-trumpism-and-the-new-global-economy (accessed July 27, 2017).
19. Available at http://time.com/3923128/donald-trump-announcement-speech (accessed June 23, 2018).
20. Atossa Araxia Abrahamian, "Donald Trump Hates Globalization, but Globalization is What Made Donald Trump's Life Possible," *Quartz*, November 7, 2016, available at qz.com (accessed June 23, 2018).
21. Leigh Ann Caldwell, "Trump Foundation Paid Activist Filmmaker James O'Keefe," *NBC News*, October 20, 2016, available at nbcnews.com (accessed June 23, 2018).
22. Edited and unedited tapes are still available of YouTube.com as of June 2018.
23. An example of underestimating Trump is *Media Matters* critical review of his performance on Blitzer's program. See "Trump's Birtherism Fueled by Breitbart Reporting," May 29, 2012, available at https://www.mediamatters.org/blog/2012/05/29/trumps-birtherism-fueled-by-breitbart-reporting/186305 (accessed March 2, 2018).
24. Timothy Egan, *New York Times*, March 11, 2017.
25. Phillip Bump, "A Glossary of Trump's Rhetorical Shorthand." *Washington Post*, July 22, 2017.
26. A transcript can be found at http://www.nytimes.com/2016/09/02/us/politics/transcript-trump-immigration-speech.html (accessed December 19, 2016).
27. Poll data available at https://www.aei.org/publication/immigration-issues-public-opinion-on-family-separation-daca-and-a-border-wall (accessed June 23, 2018).

28. The text of speech can be found at https://theconservativetreehouse. com/2016/06/28/donald-trump-policy-speech-monessen-pennsylva- nia-230pm-live-stream/comment-page-1/ (accessed December 19, 2016).
29. Manfred Steger, "Ideologies of Globalization," *Journal of Political Ideologies* 10, no. 1 (February 2005): 18.
30. Quoted in Steger, "Ideologies of Globalization": 18.
31. Thomas Friedman, *The Lexus and the Olive Tree* (London: Picador Books, 2012): 2.
32. Lee Fang, et al. "Excerpts of Hillary Clinton's Paid Speeches to Goldman- Sachs Finally Leaked," *Theintercept.com*, October 7, 2016 (accessed February 23, 2018).
33. Available on YouTube, https://www.youtube.com/watch?v= CKpso3vhZtw (accessed February 24, 2018).
34. From transcript available at https://obamawhitehouse.archives.gov/ the-press-office/2014/04/27/joint-press-conference-president-oba- ma-and-prime-minister-najib-malaysia (accessed June 18, 2018).
35. See note 1. Also available on YouTube, https://www.c-span.org/vid- eo/?c4608283/trump-american-steel (accessed February 24, 2018).
36. David Autor, David Dorny, Gordon Hanson, and Kaveh Majlesi, "A Note on the Effect of Rising Trade Exposure on the 2016 Presidential Election," Revised version of March 2017, available at https://econom- ics.mit.edu/files/12418 (accessed February 24, 2018).
37. William Kornhauser, *The Politics of Mass Society* (Glencoe, IL: The Free Press, 1959).
38. See Michael Kazin, *A Godly Hero: The Life of William Jennings Bryan* (New York: Alfred A. Knopf, 2006).
39. Richard Hofstadter, *The Age of Reform: From Bryan to F.D.R.* (New York: Alfred A. Knopf, 1955).
40. Alexander Dunst, "The Politics of Conspiracy Theories: American Histories and Global Narratives," in *Conspiracy Theories in the United States and the Middle East: A Comparative Approach*, ed. Michael Butter and Maurus Reinkowski (Boston: De Gruyter, 2015): 294–310.
41. Oxfam International, *An Economy of the 99%*, January 2017, available at https://d1tn3vj7xz9fdh.cloudfront.net/s3fs-public/file_attachments/ bp-economy-for-99-percent-160117-en.pdf (accessed March 1, 2018).
42. Leslie Sklair, *The Transnational Capitalist Class* (Hoboken, NJ: Wiley- Blackwell, 2000). Stephen Gill, Stephen, *American Hegemony and the Trilateral Commission* (Cambridge: Cambridge University Press, 1991).
43. Robinson, *A Theory of Global Capitalism*.
44. Karl Marx, *The Communist Manifesto*, available at https://www.marx- ists.org/archive/marx/works/download/pdf/Manifesto.pdf (accessed March 1, 2018).

45. Robinson, William I. (Bill), "Trumpism, 21st-Century Fascism, and the Dictatorship of the Transnational Capitalist Class." *Social Justice Journal* (January 20, 2017), available at http://www.socialjusticejournal.org/trumpism-21st-century-fascism-and-the-dictatorship-of-the-transnational-capitalist-class (accessed March 1, 2018).
46. Anders Corr, "Liberal Democracy Against a World of Nationalist Happenstance," *Forbes Magazine*, November 21, 2016.
47. Robert Reich, "The American Fascist," *Saving Capitalism: For the Many, Not the Few* (New York: Vintage, March 8, 2016), available at robertreich.org (accessed March 1, 2018).
48. It is not entirely clear why this criteria is less often endorsed, especially give the prejudice against Latinos and immigration from Muslim countries. It may be that despite the persistence of racism, the long, strongly rooted presence of African-Americans in the country has impacted national identity in this area.
49. Peter Mauer, "What Kind of Populism, A comparison of Marine Le Pen's and Donald Trump's Tweets in the French and US election campaigns of 2016/2017." Paper Presented at the 113th Meeting of the American Political Science Association, San Francisco, CA, August 2017.
50. On France, see Peter Mauer, "What Kind of Populism." On U.S. see the CNN/Kaiser Foundation collaborative study, "Working Class and Worried," available at https://www.cnn.com/specials/politics/white-working-class-and-worried (accessed March 2, 2018). On Brexit, Katrin Bennhold, "To Understand 'Brexit,' Look to Britain's Tabloids" *New York Times*, May 2, 2017; On Germany's AfD, Amanda Taub, "What the Far Right's Rise May Mean for Germany's Future," *New York Times*, September 26, 2017 and "Germany's Election Results in Charts and Maps," *Financial Times*, September 25, 2017.
51. Richard Hofstadter, *The Paranoid Style in American Politics* (New York: Vintage Reprints, 1968).
52. Mabel Berezin, *Illiberal Politics in Neoliberal Times: Culture, Security and Populism in the New Europe* (Cambridge: Cambridge University Press, 2009): 6, 46.
53. Christopher Stroop, *Russia Social-Conservatism, the U.S.-based WCF and the Global Culture Wars in Historical Perspective*, February 16, 2016. Political Research Associated, available at https://www.politicalresearch.org (accessed June 23, 2018).
54. Benedict Anderson, *Imagined Communities: Reflections on the Origin and Spread of Nationalism* (London: Verso, 1991).
55. The study is summarized in a video embedded in "The AfD is the New CSU'—How the Far-Right Won Big in Germany's Bavaria," *DW Deutsch Welle*, available at http://www.dw.com/en/about-dw/profile/s-30688 (accessed October 4, 2017).

56. See "Germany's Election Results in Charts and Maps," *Financial Times*, September 25, 2017.
57. See Pippa Norris and Ronald Inglehart, "Cultural Backlash: Values and Voting for Populist Authoritarian Parties in Europe." Paper Presented at the Panel, "The Roots of the New Populism," Annual Meeting of the American Political Science Association, San Francisco, August 30–September 2, 2017.
58. Charles Beard and George H. E. Smith, *The Idea of National Interest: Analytical Study in American Foreign Policy* (New York: Greenwood Press, reprint, original 1934): 3.
59. Available at https://www.whitehouse.gov/blog/2016/05/04/why-president-obamas-trade-deal-matters-us-national-security (accessed December 24, 2016).
60. Available at https://www.youtube.com/watch?v=CKpso3vhZtw (accessed July 11, 2017).
61. Mark Muro. "Manufacturing Jobs Aren't Coming Back." *MIT Technology Review* (2017), available at https://www.technologyreview.com/s/602869/manufacturing-jobs-arent-coming-back (accessed June 11, 2017).
62. Available at https://www.youtube.com/watch?v=UrDYd7Agsfw.
63. Available at https://en.wikiquote.org/wiki/Charles_Erwin_Wilson (accessed June 23, 2018).
64. Available at http://www.nationalreview.com/article/352429 (accessed December 24, 2016).

CHAPTER 6

Dark Money and Trumpism

An indication of the conspiracist mentality taking hold in discourse in the United States is the mounting number of news and academic references to "dark" and "deep" forces operating within American politics today. The term "Dark Money," refers to the way some of the country's wealthiest families (notably, the Koch Brothers, Charles and David) have poured hundreds of millions (billions, collectively) not only into electoral campaigns, but also into cultural and intellectual institutions in an attempt to realign the political culture. They have pursued a radical, libertarian agenda, seeking to dramatically reduce welfare programs and state regulation and limit the democratic power of popular majorities. The "Deep State" idea in the past was mostly identified with leftist criticism of the military industrial complex. It was even less accepted in mainstream discourse than "Dark Money," and it was often associated with the paranoid style. That has changed somewhat, we shall see in the next chapter, but conspiratorial overtones remain, especially in the way it has been adopted by Donald Trump and his rightist supporters in the media, and it has found a receptive audience in 20–30% of the electorate.

Chapter 7 will take up the Deep State; this chapter focuses on Dark Money. I conceptualize both theoretical constructs not as referring to one or another overarching conspiracy, but as spheres of politics characterized by a high degree of opaqueness, i.e., where minimum transparency makes them a suitable spawning ground for political conspiracies. Dark Money constitutes a stealth weapon of the super-rich that is deployed in ways that are consistent with our working definition of

© The Author(s) 2019
D. C. Hellinger, *Conspiracies and Conspiracy Theories in the Age of Trump*, https://doi.org/10.1007/978-3-319-98158-1_6

conspiracy, which in Chapter 1 I defined as collective activity in which several actors plan and work together to achieve a political goal in a manner marked by secrecy, vulnerability to defeat by exposure, and involving illegal, embarrassing, or unethical behavior.

This chapter will layout the reasons why it is useful to view Dark Money operations as conspiracies. Consistent with Chapters 1 and 2, I do not propose that the billionaire cabals behind Dark Money are engaged in a "grand" or "world" conspiracy, but that the systematic stealth by which America's wealthiest families have sought to influence American politics has a conspiratorial character and a sinister, corrupting impact on democracy. The Koch brothers and their network of wealthy, like-minded donors provide a good example of an operational conspiracy (see Chapter 2), neither petty nor grand in scale. Two books that have done much to expose the Dark Money operations eschew any association with conspiracy theory, but that has not spared them being accused of endulging in conspiracy theory. Rather than rebut the accusation, the cause of limiting the pernicious influence of torrents of money in our politics would be served, I argue, if we recognized the billionaires' stealth influence over elections and political culture as fostered by conspiracy. Conceiving this activity as an operational conspiracy usefully clarifies that Dark Money politics is not just a form of interest group politics but a subversive influence over democracy.

MONEY, POLITICS, AND TRUMP

Though muckraking reporters and academic researchers have unveiled much of the secretive planning and evasions of accountability by some of America's wealthiest families, the rules of the political game continue to permit this miniscule segment of the citizenry to suborn representative democracy. Laundering their financing through complicated networks of "not-for-profit" organizations has permitted the super-rich to finance a planned a long-term strategy to impact educational and cultural institutions and support the growth of right-wing media. Trump may not have been the first choice of most of America's super-rich; and he remains a less than ideal choice to lead their counterrevolution against the regulatory and welfare institutions constructed post-World War II. Trump's foreign policy, especially his hostility to multilateral trade associations and imposition of tariffs, have met with such disapproval of the Kochs and the powerful libertarian tendency among the rich that some of them have even turned to financing Democrats or more moderate Republicans. Still, domestically their goals have been advanced by Trump's opening the federal bureaucracy to their interests, by his judicial appointments, and by his one significant legislative achievement in his first year—a tax "reform" that significantly prepares the way for downsizing government and checking democratic governance. The Koch network launched an offensive in July 2018, deploying several hundred million dollars of advertising aimed at seven Senators who had voted against President Trump's $15.4 billion spending cuts, which failed by only 2 votes earlier in the year when two Republican Senators defected from their party's congressional leadership. At the same time, the Koch's Americans for Prosperity (AFP) sent a letter to congressional leaders demanding a freeze on discretionary spending for the fiscal year 2019 and further "reforms" to cut spending on Medicaid, Medicare, and Social Security over the next 10 years.[1]

Conspiracies do not have to succeed to influence the course of events. While corporate and individual wealth continued to flow in torrents through the electoral system in 2016, there were two countertrends to the billionaire's success. First, Bernie Sanders mounted a strong campaign against great odds, running openly as a "socialist." Even if Sanders' socialism is more in the European social democratic tradition than radical revolutionary style, his campaign broke a taboo and boosted movements seeking more activist government. Sanders raised over $226 million, of which nearly $135 million came from small contributions. He spent no money of his own and received only $5621 (total) from political action committees.[2] Sanders could hardly be accused of hiding his campaign financing. In this chapter we are more concerned with the candidates—virtually all of the other ones seeking major party nominations—who relied on personal wealth, large corporate contributions, and especially Dark Money.

The other anomaly is that Trump, apparently a very wealthy man himself, was outspent by his Republican opponents in seeking the nomination, defeating several much closer to the libertarian tendencies among the wealthy. That is, the Koch Dark Money was not successful in the phase of their campaign known as the "Money Primary", when prospective candidates demonstrate their viability with large political donors. Trump was able to compete in the early caucuses and primaries that began in January 2016, even though his spending was only $24 million; in contrast, spending by Senators Ted Cruz and Marci Rubio amounted to $60 million and $76 million, respectively. Trump was also outspent by Hillary Clinton in the general election, but this only takes into account officially reported spending by parties and candidates. After he secured the nomination, the great bulk of backdoor (not all of it "dark," as some ads and other support efforts is openly identified) funding went toward Trump. One campaign spending watchdog estimates that when both outside money and candidate funds are summed, Trump outspent Clinton $794 million to $408 million.[3] If one takes into account the ratio of spending in relation to the length of Trump's rivals for the nomination (i.e., when they dropped out, in all but Trump's case), Trump spent less than all of his GOP rivals, except for Ohio Governor John Kasich.[4]

A charlatan, but no fool, Trump's background in real estate speculation and his celebrity fame as a "take-no-prisoners" entrepreneur and star of *The* Apprentice TV reality show were of his own making, not behind-the-scenes handlers. While candidates with the largest campaign treasure chests have not always won nor even proved themselves competitive in seeking major party nominations, rarely has a candidate spent so little to gain a major party nomination. Of course, Trump had staff and volunteers, but he ran his campaign for the nomination, at least until the Republican convention, much like he seemed to prevail over all the contestants on *The Apprentice*. MediaQuant, a tracking firm, estimated Trump's free media time to have been worth the equivalent of $5.2 billion in advertising.

Clinton did not do badly herself, totaling $3.2 billion. Both party nominees had a decided advantage in this regard over their opponents in the race for the nomination.[5] Bernie Sanders could match neither the rating bonanza that Trump's celebrity and crude behavior generated, nor the celebrity status of Clinton, who was not only (like Sanders) a Senator but also a highly visible influence in her husband's presidency and a former Secretary of State in the Obama White House.[6] That changed after the debates began and after Sanders broke through with a win in the New Hampshire primary. And one can argue as well that Clinton's financial advantage was balanced by the baggage she carried into the nomination fight, having to deal with gender stereotypes and with prejudice in reporting on her appearance, clothing, and even her laugh.[7] Even in the political sketches done by *Saturday Night Live*, where female members of the cast virtually endorsed her campaign, she was often depicted in a way that can be compared to Richard Nixon's reputation as "Tricky

Dick." In 2007, in a Halloween sketch, *SNL* depicted Clinton as hostess of a Halloween Party for her rivals for the 2008 nomination. She is clearly dressed as a bride but is repeatedly mistaken for a witch by other candidates—except by then-Senator Barack Obama, the only one who appeared in the sketch as himself.

The need to raise mountains of money and to gain media access are antidemocratic facts of political life in the United States, but not all fundraising from the wealthy is hidden. Before the primaries begin the candidates have incentive to prove their viability by publicizing their success at garnering a large campaign war chest. Many political scientists and liberal/left activists have focused on the pernicious effects of this "money primary," but by and large contributors do not launder their contributions and attempt to hide their identity to citizens. Dark Money operates differently. These super wealthy donors are protected by a series of court decisions that allow them to influence politics through establishing tax exempt organization whose donors are not easily traceable. Incorporated as organizations to promote education and community welfare, these groups often engage in a different kind of partisanship in the form of ideological projects seeking to influence the political culture, not just win an election. This includes systematic funding of institutions and foundations and amplification of the right wing, populist movements, such as the Tea Party.

The last major American political scandal that called the role of money in politics into question was Watergate, a broader set of crimes and corruption that unraveled after a group of operatives with links to the Nixon campaign broke into Democratic Party headquarters in the Watergate office complex in the capital. This was the catalyst for broad campaign finance legislation that among other things sought to limit the size of contributions to campaigns and to ensure more transparency reporting requirements to the newly established Federal Election Commission (FEC). Subsequently, *Buckley v. Valeo* (1976), *Citizens United* (2008), and other court decisions have frustrated public limits on money's influence and allowed anonymity for ultra-wealthy donors under the guise of guaranteeing First Amendment rights of free speech.

Some political scientists believe that party insiders more than money usually decide the outcome of nomination fights, but at least as far as the GOP goes, the theory that "the party decides" did not fare well in 2016.[8] This theory seemed to hold in the 2008 and 2012 election cycles, and certainly the candidate of party insiders prevailed on the Democratic side in

2016, with Hillary Clinton gaining the nomination over Sanders, the populist insurgent. Consistent with the "party decides" Clinton handily won a majority of primary votes, and she locked up the nomination with strong majority support of party appointed "superdelegates" at the convention. While there were tensions at times between the two main Democratic candidates, the primary debates were unusually civil and policy focused. Trump, on the other hand, took no prisoners among his Republican primary challengers and ran a general election campaign drawing on popular anger and mistrust of the entire political class, not just Democrats.

The nonpartisan Center for Responsive Politics, which tracks both candidate committee funds and outside support, found that Hillary Clinton's campaign outspent Trump's campaign by $230 million, but outside groups supporting Trump outspent Clinton's campaign by $256 million (see Table 4.1, Chapter 4). What clearly happened is that despite running the most scorched-earth nomination campaigns in American history, a broad coalition of right-populist forces came together behind the Trump candidacy to snatch victory in an election run under rules originally concocted in the eighteenth century to protect slavery, check political ambition, and protect against "tyranny of the majority." Today the rules of the game not only check majority abuse but enable major policies on taxation, abortion, environmental policy, labor union organizing, etc., to be made by the minority party in the country. The system checks majority rule well short of tyranny. Dark Money is a key resource for elites to check democratic governance.

Trump's campaign did include significant financial help from some of the wealthiest Americans, but not from the Koch brothers, Charles and David. They were disappointed with the GOP presidential choice—a New Yorker, a former Democrat, opponent of immigration, and one who was making promises both to launch a major government-sponsored infrastructure program and to "drain the swamp," America's most stealthy swamp critters had been expected to spend almost $900 million on the 2016 campaign, but, as *Slate's* Reihan Salam put it, "Instead of shaping the outcome of this or that political race, they've sought to amplify the voices of activists and intellectuals who share their suspicion of government power."[9] So they redirected their resources to where they already were proving effective, state and local elections and right-wing foundations. They may have failed to get one of their top choices in presidency, their longer term stealth campaign considerably shaped the first year 18 months of Trump's presidency.

DARK MONEY AND BILLIONAIRE CABALS

The reforms invalidated by *Buckley v. Valeo* and *Citizens United* reopened the funding spigot that was visibly flowing freely in the pre-Watergate era. The 1972 election had seen an unprecedented jump in money raised by both major party presidential candidates, and especially by President Richard Nixon. His fundraising activities included barely disguised collusion with large donors. Campaign spending in 1972 was 4.5 their levels in the 1960 campaign between Nixon and John F. Kennedy, with Nixon's campaign having increased its expenditures from $10.1 exceeded his 1960 to $61.4 million.[10] Worse, funding was increasingly being tied to policy. For example, a dairy farmers' cooperative that had previously supported Democratic candidates delivered $2 million in campaign contributions to Nixon and his campaign staff in exchange for higher subsidies and higher milk prices.[11] If influence peddling were not enough, the money found its way into the conspiratorial activities of the Committee to Reelect the President (aptly named "CREEP") and the activities of the notorious "Plumbers," a covert unit that included former CIA operatives and an FBI investigator. The Plumbers, an early manifestation of what later would be called the "Deep State," was formed to carry out illegal surveillance and activities and stop leaking of classified information, including the Pentagon Papers.

In *Buckley v. Valeo* the Supreme Court severely limited the reach of the campaign finance reform legislation of 1971, largely on grounds that many key provisions limiting expenditures violated the First Amendment. In 2010, the rationale was extended in a new ruling in *Citizens United v. Federal Election Commission*, this time invalidating limits and disclosure requirements for a special category of organizations operating under a provision (501c4) granting tax exempt status to such groups as long as they operate "not-for-profit" and "exclusively to promote social welfare." Unlike the case for 501c3 organizations, contributions to 501c4 the foundations are not tax deductible, but the advantage is that they do not have to disclose donors to the Internal Revenue Service. Dark Money was born.

The Pulitzer Prize winning investigative journalist Jane Mayer of *The New Yorker Magazine* is most responsible for shining a light on the influence of "Dark Money" in several reports for the magazine and in her book by that title, which details the role played by the "billionaires behind the rise of the radical right."[12] Trump was decidedly not the favorite of this elite circle of one-percenters, especially the ones most closely chron-icled by Mayer, i.e., the Koch brothers. That honor goes to Senator Ted Cruz. Nonetheless, Trump attracted crucial support from at least one member of the billionaire's club—Robert Mercer, whose funds signifi-cantly aided the professionalization of the Trump campaign in the general election.

Citizens United, the plaintiff in the ruling that did much to unleash stealth political influence, was founded by a political consultant, Floyd Brown, with significant funding by the Kochs. Brown's legal challenge involved an FEC ruling that said his group's desire to distribute a film, *Hillary, the Movie*, before the 2008 election, was partisan advertising to influence the election, something not permitted for corporations and labor unions; Citizens United would be required to disclose its donors, as required for election advertising. At the time of the film's release, Clinton was widely regarded as the leading candidate for the Democratic nomination for president. The "documentary" not only criticized her public record but featured various public figures on the right claim-ing that she is "steeped in sleaze," is "deceitful" and "will make up any story and will lie about anything as long as it serves her purpose at the moment"; is "venal, sneaky'; etc.

The Kochs seized on the ruling in favor of *Citizens United* to advance the project of a group of right-wing business people already embarked upon a careful and well-funded strategy to move their anti-statist views, according to Mayer, "from the fringe to the center of American political life."[13] The Koch fortune is derived mainly from industries and invest-ments connected to fossil fuels, an industry that is subject to significant regulation, especially environmental protection laws. While this lends a pecuniary interest to this funding strategies, their economic interests are well married to an extreme libertarian ideology; in fact, their initial strat-egy was a failed effort to transform the Libertarian Party into a vehicle for their goals. Although they were not fans of candidate Trump, Koch-funded organizations went into action after the electon to pressure the Senate into confirming Scott Pruitt, Oklahoma attorney general, and a climate change denier, to head the Environmental Protection Agency and Betsy DeVos, whose family's estimated worth is $45 billion, as Secretary of Education. The Devos Foundation makes charter schools and privatization of education their priority goal.[14]

Mayer's book is densely packed with examples of how the Kochs and other billionaires consciously developed a strategy to use the 501c4 provision to create front foundations. Given the source of their fortunes, it should not surprise that among the issues targeted by the brothers is climate change, especially the scientific consensus that human activity and emissions from fossil fuels play an important role. Stealing a page from the tobacco companies, the Kochs indirectly funded research and dissemination of "scholarly" articles challenging the consensus that human activity is contributing to global warming—and the existence of global warming itself. Many of the contributions were channeled through a pair of affiliated organizations, DonorsTrust and Donors Capital Fund, which had been founded by arch-Conservatives. DonorsTrust made no secret that it offered donors anonymity, using its tax status (as a donor-advised, not "donor-run" foundation), providing the anonymity sought by wealthy contributors to prevent their being associated with controversial issues. In 2008, the Kochs' Americans for Prosperity (AFP) launched a successful campaign to have GOP legislators sign a "no climate change" pledge, ensuring synergy between the stealth effort to distort public understanding of the issue with more public lobbying (though donors behind AFP remained anonymous) that successfully erased substantial Republican support for "cap and trade" legislation.[15] The conspiratorial intent was not at that time focused on getting Scott Pruitt appointed to head the EPA but to shift the overall political terrain in a way that made it possible to confirm a climate denier to the agency most responsible for protecting the atmosphere from carbon emissions. This type of operation was more than just normal interest group lobbying; it constituted a stealth propaganda operation.

By Mayer's reckoning, between 1999 and 2015, Donors Trust distributed $750 million to right-wing causes. "What much of the stealth funding bought was dissemination of scientific doubt," writes Mayer. Skeptical scientists were recruited and given public relations training. The purpose was never to carry out research putting the climate change science to the test but mainly to magnify the claims of a small coterie of dissenters and to question the idea that a consensus existed. And hiding the identity of those funding this effort was explicitly recognized as critical to the strategy.[16]

The Kochs were not the only super-rich, nor the wealthiest benefactors that have in stealth bankrolled stealth right-wing foundations. Mayer's book exposes similar activity by the Mercer, Mellon Scaife, Olin, Bradley families, and others who followed a similar playbook. All were instrumental in founding and financing large conservative foundations and political organizations. The history of their movement is now uncovered, but for many years it was effectively cloaked. The stealth not only darkened the money trail behind these "educational" groups, but it also darkened the organizational model, training, and direction provided by these wealthy funders.

Mayer carefully eschews labeling the Koch operation a "conspiracy." But her book provides a vivid description of the stealth planning that occurred after the 2008 Citizens United ruling at the January 2009 edition of a biannual conference of wealthy contributors. According to Mayer, "billionaire businessmen, heirs to some of America's greatest dynastic fortunes, right-wing media moguls, conservative elected officials, and savvy political operatives" were joined at a Palm Springs resort by "eloquent writers and publicists" connected to well-heeled think-tanks and publications.[17] It is at these conferences where key long-range planning to shift the political playing field take place. As at Davos, the conferences include public events where key objectives are openly acknowledged, but as evidenced by a copy of the 2014 agenda obtained by *The Nation*,[18] a good deal of important business is conducted in secret. Unlike Davos, the Koch conclave's agenda includes not just general exchanges of views but hard-nosed planning for coming political battles. The 2014 agenda, besides golf and a panel devoted to rescuing the reputation of President Calvin Coolidge, included breakout sessions on influencing the Senate, "changing the narrative" on Energy, "leverage science and the university," and "Engaging Your Workforce in the Cause of Freedom."

Although in her book Mayer carefully avoids referring to such activity as engaging in a conspiracy, though in an earlier article she refers to the Kochs' activities as "covert operations."[19] Regardless, *Dark Money* describes activity that fits the definition of "conspiracy theory" laid out in this book in Chapter 1. The Kochs and their allies constituted a collusion, planning and working together secretly with one another to achieve a political goal. Not all their activity would be vulnerable to defeat by exposure, and maintaining confidential one's political strategy is not ipso facto engaging in conspiracy. But their stealth operations go well beyond a normal concern not to divulge political tactics to opponents. The purpose of Dark Money operation is to prevent wealthy donors from being identified with promotion of partisan campaigns and controversial issues. Candidates and backers of causes would much rather have political advertising, "educational think-tanks," and financial reports be identifed with "Americans for Prosperity" (who isn't for that?) than "Charles and David Koch" as their source. Thanks to *Citizens United* their political activity is not illegal, but it is deceptive and unethical.

An even more controversial book by historian Nancy MacLean unveiled the deliberate secretive nature of Charles Koch and his super-rich colleagues to reshape American politics via a plan that explicitly anticipated the need for secrecy and deception. The documentary evidence was discovered almost accidentally by MacLean, already a distinguished member of her profession, by virtue of her research and publication on social movements in the American South. She was looking in the archives of economist James Buchanan for material on an early attempt to implement a private school voucher plan in the state of Virginia. In 1954 Brown v. Board of Education had mandated desegregation of schools, and Virginia politicians were looking for a way around it. Buchanan's letters and manuscripts outlined the role that he played in providing intellectual cover for privatization of education, which was one way whites were (and still are) able to evade mandated intervention. His writings eventually attracted the attention of Charles Koch and led to Buchanan founding an institute that was generously funded by the billionaire. Although Buchanan's direct influence over the legislation was limited, his "public choice theory" became a school of thought that provided a more general argument for a radical rollback of the role of government and in privatization of many of its functions, promoted as part of the long-range stealth plan to shift the political culture.

Buchanan, a Nobel Prize winning economist, did not begin this line of thought at the behest of the Kochs, and certainly his scholarly work was not conspiratorial. His academic research and writing was inspired by the ultra-liberal (in the classical sense of *laissez faire*) ideas of the Austrian school of economics. It is difficult today to remember that the idea of the public school to provide universal education was a great American idea, envied elsewhere in the world. But Buchanan regarded it as a state monopoly that lacked the efficiency imposed by market discipline, and in addition infringing on individual freedom of choice. For this reason he was an early advocate privatization of schools.[20] Whether Buchanan advocated racially segregated schools, as MacLean contends, is disputed, but there is little doubt that after *Brown* the idea of privatizing schools had particular appeal in the South, including in Virginia, where Buchanan, who was born and raised in Tennessee, made his academic career.

Buchanan came to the attention of Charles Koch in the 1970s, and the billionaire's interest increased as he became more frustrated with the inability of the Libertarian Party to advance his goals. In 1982, Buchanan took his economic team to George Mason University, where with funding from Koch his public choice theories began to flourish. By MacLean's reckoning, Buchanan may have been less well-known that Milton Friedman, the very visible public intellectual associated with laissez faire economic thought in the Cold War era, but with Koch's backing Buchanan may have exercised even more influence over advancing the laissez faire political cause. His public choice theories provided the intellectual underpinning for academic studies by acolytes in foundations and other universities generously funded by the Kochs. Charles provided key support for Buchanan when he moved his Center for the Study of Public Choice (CSPC) from Virginia Tech to George Mason, which contributed to that institution's ascent to prominence as a first-tier research institution. The institute was renamed the Mercatus Center. Mercatus was among several George Mason institutions that, according to a letter of apology from the University's president in 2018, violated ethical norms in giving conservative donors influence over admissions, appointments, and other academic matters.[21]

Buchanan's papers reveal practical political brilliance in advocating the kind of stealth organizing that the Kochs and their ilk have pursued with great success. They show, according to MacLean, "How and why stealth became so intrinsic to this movement. Buchanan had realized the value of stealth long before encountering Koch, while still trying to influence Virginia politicians. But it was Koch who institutionalized this policy."[22] The problem, in Koch's mind and in Buchanan's public choice theory alike, was that electoral democracy had a built-in bias against the wealthy, who, much as Ayn Rand portrayed in her novels glorifying the individual against the bureaucratic state, were the real guarantors of freedom and prosperity in a society. Buchanan's ideas complemented this libertarian ideology long embraced by the Kochs. His public choice theory argued that in an electoral democracy politicians' careers depend upon votes, so rationally politicians would have an incentive to tax the wealthy to provide benefits for the poor and working class. The theory undermines democracy, MacLean argues, because it views the essence of good government not as virtuous citizens influencing policy through majority rule, but instead inefficiency and nothing less than the theft of the income and property of wealthier citizens. In addition, and something not articulated in his published work, Buchanan explicitly recommended stealth tactics to create momentum for reform and to undermine what he regarded as the self-interested motives of politicians and ordinary citizens.[23] To capture the idea that the central purpose was to strip citizens of their power to exercise majority rule for the public good, MacLean entitled her book *Democracy in Chains.*

The Kochs' main political arm for promoting public choice politically has been AFP. AFP led all outside funders in political advertising in the 2014 election cycle. As mentioned earlier, the Kochs had planned to spend close to $900 million for the 2016 cycle, but it reported spending only $13.6 million on the 2016 presidential election, mostly to its preferred candidate, Texas Senator Ted Cruz. Many other conservative groups followed the Koch example. They outspent liberal ones in 2012 by the count of $235 million to $35 million, Their spending declined in 2016 to $41.9 in that election. The decline can largely be attributed to lack of enthusiasm for Trump and their consequent shifting attention to down-ballot races.[24]

Like other groups funded by billionaires, AFP is registered as a 501c4, technically a foundation to promote social welfare. One might argue that what constitutes promoting social welfare versus partisan political campaigning is in the eye of the beholder, but the large majority of organizations so classified are not engaged in political activity or advocacy.[25] The IRS rules[26] permit qualified organizations to engage in lobbying as their "primary activity," but the regulations make it clear that this is not a pre-dispensation for them to undertake the kind of activity that we associate with partisan political influence or with advancing objectives that mainly benefit the members of the organization. So, for example, an organization of volunteer fire departments can lobby for increased support for fire-fighting. The promotion of social welfare does not include direct or indirect participation or intervention in political campaigns on behalf of or in opposition to any candidate for public office.

It is not very surprising that when, during the Obama administration, the IRS began to investigate the actual purpose and activity of some of the groups, both liberal and conservative, heavily involved in advocacy, especially those that engage in large-scale political advertising, the right-wing media launched a campaign accusing the IRS of political harassment. However, if the leaked agenda[27] from the 2014 Koch brothers' conclave is any guide, there is no question that rather than promoting community welfare the closed door sessions are devoted to prioritizing political work—both long-term strategies for shaping the political culture and planning for the coming electoral cycle, including considerable attention to state and local politics.

While most of the billionaires were not enthusiastic about Trump, often overlooked in analysis of the election outcome is that Trump's Vice President, former Indiana Governor Mike Pence, is a particular favorite of the Kochs. A large contingent of Republicans in Congress, key appointees in Cabinet and executive agencies, and GOP office holders at the state level have been heavily funded by the network of organizations put together and coordinated by the Kochs. If the tax code is further amended to permit churches and other political organizations to undertake political activities, as the GOP's bill before Congress in late 2017 originally provided, an entirely new sector of organizations becomes available to front for conservative billionaires. While this provision did not make it through, the 2017 tax code, the proposal is far from dead.

Dark Money operations are not directed only at the federal government. The Bradley Foundation is headquartered in Milwaukee and like other entities of the billionaires' network has focused on a bottom-up strategy through ALEC, the American Legislative Exchange Council, originally founded by Scaife. One of the more recent campaigns funded by Bradley is an effort to maintain the privacy of donors in the Dark Money network. Many of ALEC's activities involve anti-union initiatives, especially aimed at public employee unions. It is not just money that ALEC funnels to these efforts, but expertise, including ready-to-go, off-the-shelf model legislation for anti-labor and antigay legislation. One reason we know how Bradley's Dark Money is used is that its computers were hacked, and a trove of internal documents was leaked to the Center for Media and Democracy.

Another "not-for-profit" group, the Barber Fund uses generous Bradley money intended for what the latter calls "state infrastructure grant making" to finance projects that go to right-wing organizations that show "quality and promise." The Republican Party is not mentioned as the beneficiary of the projects, but any sensible interpretation suggests that Bradley, operating through Barber, is hardly a nonpartisan organization. States are evaluated by Bradley for effective targeting of grants (through Barber), and it should hardly surprise that many of the upper "blue wall" states in the Midwest have been designated high priority.

Few analysts anticipated that Trump would choose a politician closely aligned with the white Christian right and the Dark Money oligarchs—former Indiana Governor Mike Pence, a longtime favorite of the Bradleys and the Kochs. News reports indicated that Trump was reluctant to choose Pence but was persuaded otherwise by Paul Manafort, the man brought in to assume the campaign chair in order to tame party dissenters, and by Jerod Kushner, the man (Trump's son-in-law) with the analytics. Mainstream news reports were so caught up in "ballgame" reporting and personalities (in particular, the falling fortunes of New Jersey Governor Chris Christie and former Speaker of the House, Newt Gingrich) that they only secondarily did they note Pence's close ties to the Christian right. Also virtually ignored were Pence's close ties to Charles Koch, who tried to induce him to run for president in 2012,[28] and his connections to another powerful, anti-statist billionaire lobby, the Bradley Foundation, which with $835 million in assets is larger than three Koch foundations combined. Outside of the deep South and Kansas, in the Pence years as governor of Indiana the state was the only one rated to achieve the Bradley Foundation's highest ranking for "receptive policy makers."[29]

Pence's history with Bradley includes his participation in a Foundation cosponsored conference on the Tea Party, which, Pence said, is about "going back to the source of our greatness, which is our character, our faith, our belief in limited government."[30] A major benefactor of the Foundation is the "Independent Women's Forum," whose board included Kellyanne Conway, one of Trump's key media spokespersons and whose consulting firm did work for Pence in Indiana. One of Bradley's major projects is promotion of voter fraud theories,[31] and Pence, who championed the cause in Indiana, was been named the cochair of Trump's (now defunct) voter fraud commission, investigating the president's claim that 5 million votes were cast illegally in 2016.[32]

The influence of Dark Money was felt in the campaign by the way it enabled Trump campaign operatives to carefully target audiences on social media with misleading and fabricated stories. Especially active in this area was billionaire Mercer, who over 2011–2016 channeled tens of millions of dollars to several operations closely connected to Bannon, including *Breitbart News* and, especially valuable to the Trump general election campaign, Cambridge Associates, which provided crucial analytics that Trump lacked up to his securing the nomination. Cambridge worked closely with Trump's son-in-law, Jared Kushner. *Forbes Magazine* reported that by the end of the campaign, the data operation determined decisions on "travel, fundraising, advertising, rally locations" as well as the topics and keywords Trump used in speeches. *Business Week* and *Guardian* reports linked Cambridge to voter suppression efforts. There are at least similarities in way analytics were used to the way that Russian sources were able to spread divisive messages on social media.[33]

Dark Money and the Deep State intersected at Cambridge, whose data mining analytics had been involved in "messaging and information services" on behalf of US forces in Pakistan and Afghanistan—that is, the company is experienced in propaganda operations. Mercer, a major stakeholder in the firm, worked on the Brexit campaign (the referendum that endorsed the United Kingdom leaving the European Union). His Mercer Family Foundation funds the Heartland Institute, a key force in the climate change denial movement. In other words, Mercer is not only a key player in the billionaire conspiracy to shrink the democratic state, he is a key enabler of conspiracy theories that have little to no warrant. Steve Bannon credits Mercer with having "laid the ground for the Trump Revolution," more so than the Koch brothers.[34]

Mercer's alliance with Bannon grew out of the billionaire's financial support of *Breitbart News*, where Bannon first made his name and to which he returned after being cut loose by Trump from the White House in 2017. As discussed in Chapter 4, *Breitbart* has played a direct role in promoting the paranoid variety of conspiracy theory in the culture and the alt-right. Mercer, whose fortune was made in hedge funds, remained an ally of Breitbart and Bannon throughout most of 2017, holding an ownership share in Breitbart and providing some of the funds Bannon needed as he tried to expand the influence of the most radical right wing of the Republican Party.[35] This effort, in turn, provoked a backlash from other wealthy elites who backed the party professionals, but Mercer's daughter, Rebekah, remained supportive of Bannon until the latter's vitriolic criticism of Trump became public through quotations in a "tell-all" book released in early 2018 made the relationship untenable. Bannon subsequently resigned as CEO of Breitbart.

Dark Money stealth, both on the part of politicians and donors, is not limited to the federal level (as the aforementioned activities of ALEC showed). In January 2016, seeking the GOP nomination for governor of Missouri, which he eventually became in November, Eric Greitens, tried to separate himself from Republican rivals by promising that the sources of his political funding would always be public knowledge. He told *St. Louis Public Radio*, "The most important thing is that there is transparency around the money," and he accused other candidates of having set up "secretive super PACs." The people are able, he said, to "see every single one of our donors." However, a post-election investigative report found that one single stealth donation to Greitens' campaign alone totaled $1.975 million. The funding originated with a group, the American Political Coalition, but passed first through a super PAC called SEALS for Truth (Greitens was a veteran of the Navy SEALS) before landing in Greitens' campaign fund, thereby evading state disclosure rules and hiding the true donor, who remains unknown. John Messmer of Missourians for Government Reform commented, "When drug dealers do this, it's called money laundering," Greitens also used a list of donors to a veterans support organization he founded to raise $2 million.[36] He was undone and forced to resign in 2018 by a sexual scandal that made him more vulnerable to his political enemies (Republicans as well as Democrats), who pressed for an investigation into his campaign financing.

SHOW US THE DARK MONEY TRAIL

One might reasonably ask if exposure of the Koch strategy by Mayer, MacLean, news organizations and others means that the Koch network and others can no longer act conspiratorially. Dark Money institutions continue to spend prodigiously directly to influence legislative votes (increasingly on the state level) to support or oppose candidates, and to support or oppose state referendums. "Educational" advertising priorities are calculated at secret sessions of the annual conference to influence elections and legislation. And while research by Mayer, MacLean, and others has exposed much about the billionaire "welfare" club, the lack of transparency in their operations and funding makes it extraordinarily difficult for watchdog organizations, much less the supine FEC, to determine the origin of money flowing through the system. By combing 501c3 reports, it is possible to detect some of the money trails. The Center for Responsible Politics and its sister organization, OpenSecrets.org, can trace some of the money, but funds are often laundered through three or four different foundations and committees.

And of course, this task even much more difficult for ordinary citizens. Readers of this book most likely would recognize AFP now as a Koch organization, but what about the general public? In some cases, it is not difficult to identify the source of some of the largest contributors. The National Rifle Association and the NARAL Pro-Choice America are usually not difficult to identify when they take out ads. Both are 501c4 organizations, which means they do not have to identify their donors, but there is little doubt what they stand for and that they have millions of members. They may sometimes move funds to other organizations or to their affiliated PACs, but as associations with a broad base of membership they have an interest in seeing their donors see that they are defending their interests. No matter how you feel about them, a lot (but not all) of their ads and programs are funded openly, not in the dark.

Conservatives have often equated the funding of good governance organizations by George Soros and other wealthy liberals as virtually equally potent and deceptive. The data on campaign contributions, reviewed above, certainly suggests that some liberal groups have benefitted from the largesse of Soros and others. Open Secrets has documented a significant increase in Dark Money flowing to liberal causes and the Democratic Party. A new liberal Dark Money fund was created by Senae democrats for the 2018 midterm elections. As with conservative Dark Money, this allows wealthy donors to hide their political associatons. However, little has surfaced suggesting the kind of coordination (e.g., at the bi-annual Koch conclaves) that conservative billionaires have engaged in. One can also legitimately question (though no definitive proof has emerged) whether the Clinton Foundation,[37] which has attracted seven-figure donations from wealthy interests around the world, was used to enhance donors' access to Hillary Clinton when she was Secretary of State. However, the Clinton Foundation has not sought, like the conservative billionaires' club, to engage in political advertising, to influence policymaking, to reshape the Democratic Party, or shift the overall political climate.

Another favorite target of organizations highlighted by conservative critics are longstanding publications and organizations with a record on nonpartisan criticism of ethics and the influence of money. For example, in 2013 the right-wing Cyber News Network (formerly Conservative News Network) complained that Soros had contributed $6.1 million to organizations, including the Campaign Legal Center (CLC, a 501c3), Democracy 21 (a 501c4), and the Center for Public Integrity (CPI, a 501c3), all of which have urged the IRS to investigate abuse of 501c4's. The CLC's avowed purpose is promoting enforcement of campaign finance laws. Democracy 21 is a similar organization that promotes limitations on money's influence in campaigns and advocates for legal remedies. The CPI carries out nonpartisan investigations of alleged corruption.

On the other hand, consider the 45Committee, which suddenly emerged late in the 2016 campaign but was forced to cease operations after being hacked. The 45Committee says "It was founded in 2015 and has been educating Americans about the challenges facing the 45th president of the United States."[38] That would be Donald Trump, but it didn't do much to educate him apparently. OpenSecrets identifies 45Committee as having spent $21.3 million in its few months of activity, almost all of it against one Democratic candidate—Hillary Clinton. In the final days of the campaign, as it became clear that Clinton's lead in the polls had narrowed, the group spent $10 million dollars on anti-Clinton ads. It turns out that its main benefactor was Todd Ricketts, owner of the Chicago Cubs, who originally stood for "anybody but Trump" but later put his own and money collected from other latecomers into the Trump campaign, anonymously, through 45Committee.[39]

It is logical that the campaign finance reform movement and good governance organizations are likely to shine a brighter spotlight on right-wing Dark Money operations simply because the money flow is larger and because most of the super-rich seek anonymity. Far from ignoring liberal groups, watchdog organizations like OpenSecrets.org and the Committee for Responsible Politics zealously campaign for more transparency in campaign finance, something hard to find as a goal of any of the conservative 501c3 and 501c4 organizations.

The Supreme Court itself has been shaped by Dark Money. When OpenSecrets looked into the financial muscle behind Judicial Crisis Network (JCN), which lobbied heavily and directed much of the conservative effort to block a vote on President Obama's nominee to fill a Supreme Court vacancy nearly a year before the Democrat's term was up, it found not a grassroots network of conservatives but yet another 501c4 organization, the Wellspring Committee. That group provided more than 90% of JCN's funds. Because Wellspring does not have to report its donor base, it is impossible to know exactly who was behind it today, but it was originally created by the Koch network. Among benefactors of Wellspring's funding is a public relations firm, BH Group, which has a mailing address in Arlington, Virginia.[40] When OpenSecrets went to the address, there was only a mailbox. The mailbox apparently spent $7 million on blocking Merrick Garland, Obama's nominee, and then another $10 million to support confirmation of Trump's nominee, Neil Gorsuch. Around the same time, BH Group made a $20 million contribution to George Mason University, whose president later acknowledged in a letter of apology that the donation was one of several gifts from wealthy conservatives that inappropriately gave donors influence over university decisions.[41]

We need to keep in mind that watchdog organizations, such as Center for Responsible Politics and OpenSecrets.org, must spend extensive time and money to track down the true source of money in the political process. The law permits the Kochs and other wealthy donors to create a highly complex labyrinth. Inadequate laws governing campaign finance, interpretations of the tax code that distort the meaning of educational philanthropy, and Court decisions treating spending as speech all provide cover for stealth political funding, making it necessary to make suppositions and carefully guarded conclusions about connections and donor identity. And that is just the point here about the conspiratorial nature of Dark Money in American politics. Yet, the "conspiracy theory" label is frequently used to denigrate or discredit the efforts of those who work to expose Dark Money's origins, a classic case of what Bratich calls "conspiracy panic' (see Chapters 1 and 2).[42]

CONSPIRACY PANIC AND MUCKRAKING

Mayer and MacLean have in common that each in their respective books emphasizes the importance of agency and transparency in political activity. Mayer is less assertive and feels compelled in her introduction to acknowledge that there are internal differences among the super-rich attendees at the Kochs' conclaves. "They were not the predictable cartoon villains of conspiracy theories,"[43] she writes. Mayer mistakenly believes that all participants in a conspiracy must be in full agreement with each other in their goals. What is necessary is that they agree to "breath together" to undertake action in common. And Mayer recognizes conspiratorial elements in the Koch family. She notes that the Koch brothers' father, Fred, was an early member of the far-right John Birch Society. Though Charles Koch saw the Birchers as a handicap to the conservative movement, he and his brother also joined the organization for a while. Appropriately, an overtone of conspiracism can be found in her writing about other billionaire donors as well. Richard Mellon Scaife, a billionaire who created the model that the Kochs would later follow, "had a lifelong infatuation with intrigue, conspiracy theories and international affairs." William Simon, elevated by the billionaire John Olin, claimed that a "'secret system' of academics, media figures, bureaucrats, and public interest advocates ran the country."[44]

Given the right's hostility to organizations promoting campaign finance transparency, it hardly surprises that Mayer and MacLean have attracted the ire of publications and foundations linked to the super-rich. What is more surprising, perhaps, is that friendly reviews of their books sometimes criticize them, especially MacLean, for allegedly veering off into conspiracism. My defense of Mayer and MacLean is not a denial of this charge but a "so what." Keeping the funding targets and strategies of Koch, Bradley, and other wealthy oligarchs hidden allows them to effectively "weaponized philanthropy." Their organizational missions are supposed to be nonpartisan and in the broad public interest. The main reason we know something about their tactics is that investigative reporters, critical academics, and hackers have exposed their strategic planning and funding allocations. In the case of Bradley, a trove of documents were purloined in October 2016 and sent to reporters by hackers that, the FBI believes, also hacked the Democratic National Committee.[45]

Mayer nowhere claims that the Koch network and several other financial fronts of other billionaire donors constitute a conspiracy, but the title of her book refers to "dark" money, a "hidden" history, and the "billionaires behind the rise of the radical right." The text is punctuated with references to legal money laundering to hide the true sources of funding for various political campaigns, strategic planning to fund the Tea Party and other AstroTurf movements, and various educational foundations and think-tanks to promote conservative criticism and sometimes to manufacture criticism without scientific foundation.

At the 2011 Koch gathering, when the brothers were confronted for the first time with protesters and exposure, the Kochs "spoke darkly and inaccurately about the Obama White House conspiring with reporters to smear them," remarks that anticipated the routine response of President Trump to protests and criticism. Koch front organizations are tied to campaigns to spread various conspiracy theories, such as, that voter fraud was a factor in Democratic election victories, that a disinformation campaign that Obama's health care reform would set up "death panels," that global warming was a hoax perpetrated by self-interested scientists.[46]

MacLean, despite a title that refers to a "deep history" and a "stealth plan for America" never outright claims that the collaboration between

Buchanan and the billionaires, especially Charles Koch, constitutes a conspiracy. Intentionally or not, by eschewing that term, which appears in the index of neither her book nor Mayer's, both authors can stake a position within Foucault's notion of the "regime of truth."[47] (See Chapter 2) Though they eschew openly characterizing this "collaboration" as a conspiracy, what they document does point to a conspiracy as conceptually defined in this book. And in this case, we have a conspiracy that matters—keeping in mind, however, that even a conspiracy among such powerful, wealthy actors is only one part of the story, only one factor in an explanation of America's move to the right and the rise of Donald Trump. That is, to propose that Mayer and MacLean are conspiracy theorists is only to judge that what their research has uncovered is an operational conspiracy, not entirely successful but with a significant impact on American politics. To name the activities of the Kochs and other Dark Money billionaires as conspiratorial is only to acknowledge that they are collectively the equivalent of Crassus, whose money played an important role in transforming the Roman Republic into an imperial system, an ancient real estate tycoon who backed Julius Caesar's rise to power.

CORRUPTION IN A REPUBLIC OF MONEY

Zephyr Teachout's history of corruption in America does not deal directly with conspiracy, but it is relevant to the conspiratorial nature of corrupt dealings in a faltering republic. Her book examines how American conceptions of corruption have evolved from the early days of the Republic, when Benjamin Franklin's acceptance of a jeweled snuffbox from the King of France to commemorate his departure from his post of ambassador in Paris generated a scandal in America, to the contemporary era, when even massive donations to political campaigns are regarded as legal and normal methods of influencing politics. Franklin's acceptance of a gift was not in any way tied to an explicit or obvious political objective. It was not a bribe. That it became a scandal in its time, tarnishing Franklin's, is emblematic, according to Teachout, of how the early American concept of civic virtue recoiled against the practice of European politics at the time. Europe was viewed as corrupted by the influence of wealth. This view of what in Europe was non-corrupt, normal behavior as corruption in America led in the young United States enact to laws and rules that were "structural, or antiprophylactic—cover[ing] innocent as well as insidious transactions." Early Americans saw that "temptation and influence work in indirect ways, and that corruption is not merely transactional, or 'quid pro quo.'"[48]

Buckley v. Valeo and the *Citizens United* decision defined money as speech and recognized corporate entities as endowed with First Amendment rights, even though they are not biological human citizens. However, the Constitution, Teachout argues, would not necessarily obstruct campaign finance limits and regulations by the standards of the Founders' era. The key case determining that large gifts and contributions to political figures are not corruption came in 1999 in Supreme Court ruling involving Sun Diamond's gift to Obama's Secretary of Agriculture, Mike Espy, of two tickets and travel expenses for Espy to attend the United States Tennis Open. At the time, Espy's Department was considering new programs to encourage agricultural exports, as well as new regulations governing the use of pesticides in agriculture. Both matters would be of interest to the donor of the tennis trip, Sun-Diamond Growers, a trade organization. After a jury found that the association had sought to curry favor with Espy through the gifts, an Appeals decision upheld by the Supreme Court agreed with the Growers that the government had failed to prove that there was any quid pro quo involved. Though the timing might be suspicious, a trip to a tennis tournament could not be connected to the matters on Espy's plate at the time, "reasoned" the Court.[49]

An irony of the Court rulings that unleashed a torrent of money into the political system is that the majority Justices included several self-described "strict-constructivists." Today that philosophy has been broadened to "originalism", the idea that not only should the Constitution be read strictly to the "letter of the law" but that we should search for the intent of the framers by consulting their writings in the context of their times. Had the Justices chosen to do so, argues Teachout,[50] they could have relied upon Article I, Sect. 9, Clause 8 of the Constitution, which reads,

> No Title of Nobility shall be granted by the United States: And no Person holding any Office of Profit or Trust under them, shall, without the Consent of the Congress, accept of any present, Emolument, Office, or Title, of any kind whatever, from any King, Prince, or foreign State.

This clause is not merely a quaint relic of colonial resentment against the old Aristocratic order but a provision meant to deal with the danger of corruption in a system designed to let "ambition counteract ambition." While it literally pertains only to foreign "gifts", its presence in the Constitution reflects also the Founders' fear of the corrupting influence of those who can afford to be benefactors of public officials. Teachout shows that during eras of heightened concerns about the influence of wealth over politics, such as the Progressive era and post-Watergate decade, many statutes sought not only to limit quid pro quo bribery but also restrict private influence in broader forms, the kind of beneficence that today gives the rich and lobbyists privileged access to the people's representatives, the effluents that steam into public life and feed the "swamp" Trump promised to drain. In early 2018, Trump himself was facing three suits claiming that various of his family's real estate deals and operations are in violation of the Emolument's clause, but thanks to the Sun-Diamond case the plaintiffs will face the difficult hurdle of showing a quid pro quo. Advocates of Trump's impeachment often cite the Emoluments prohibition in Clause 8, which prohibits foreign gifts in the form of compensation for work or services rendered.[51] Trump did not place his international hospitality and entertainment empire into a blind trust but instead entrusted it to his family. The Emoluments clause must appear to his supporters as little more than a technicality that penalizes an entrepreneur for entering public service.

Teachout's argument about the original intent and application of the clause was not developed specifically to deal with Trump's use of office potentially to enrich himself but more broadly with the relationship between great concentrations of wealth and the political class. It is, for example, applicable not only to emoluments from Trump's ongong business activity but also certain activities of the Clintons, in particular to the large donations from foreign princes and heads of state to the charitable Clinton Foundation when Hillary Clinton was Secretary of State. Similarly, this broader notion of corruption lends some credence to Trump's complaints about one member of the team originally assembled by Special Counsel Robert Mueller to investigate possible collusion between Trump's campaign and Russians. As indictments of former members of his campaign and transition team crept ever closer ever to the President's family and perhaps himself, on December 23, 2017, Trump complained in a tweet to his 20 million Twitter followers,

> How can FBI Deputy Director Andrew McCabe, the man in charge, along
> with leakin' James Comey, of the Phony Hillary Clinton investigation

(including her 33,000 illegally deleted emails) be given $700,000 for wife's campaign by Clinton Puppets during investigation?

Trump was referring here to a campaign contribution made before his wife formally entered the race for a state Senate seat from Virginia Governor Terry McAuliffe and the Virginia Democratic Party. One might contend that his is far different from an Emolument from a foreign head of state (such as Russia's Putin), but the larger question raised is whether McCabe's impartiality should be judged on the basis of his record of integrity as a law enforcement officer or by the implications of his spouse having entered a race for a relative minor office and received $700,000 from a highly partisan source.

DARK MONEY AS A SPHERE OF CONSPIRACISM

Does it matter whether or not we use we consider the Dark Money story to be a conspiracy narrative? Although not all conspiracies have illicit goals, the kind of corruption involving bribery, influence peddling, and other forms of illicit relations between public officials (or candidates) and private parties are not carried out in the open. Surely, we need to distinguish corrupt practices from limited contributions to political campaigns, movements, and organizations that seek to influence policy. Increased transparency certainly is one remedy for corruption and undue influence of money on politics, but not every aspect of campaigns, policy deliberations, diplomacy or effort is best conducted under the light provided by "Sunshine Laws."[52]

Not all political activity conducted in secret, then, is conspiratorial. Sports analogies might be useful in this regard. It is part and parcel of the rules of the game that American football teams should huddle before each play; that signals in baseball be designed to not be transparent to the rival team; that practices and scouting reports be kept under wraps. None of these practices would be regarded as conspiratorial because they do not corrupt the game. Often enough, when a team is discovered to have found a way to violate the spirit of the game by gaining knowledge of opponent's strategies, rules are redesigned to protect the integrity of competition. Returning to the broader conception of corruption that informed efforts to promote clean government in the early American Republic may be more effective than more narrowly focused campaign finance rules.

Political parties plan campaign strategies in secret; legislative caucuses do not reveal their planned parliamentary moves before a debate; governments do not reveal what they might settle for during a diplomatic negotiation; and nations do not make their military plans or their preparations to defend against a terrorist attack totally public. However, the civic campaigns and investigative (academic and journalistic) works that have provided raw data and insights for this chapter show that great concentrations of wealth operating mostly in darkness, requiring extraordinary efforts from ordinary citizens to know their origins and true interests, constitute by the criteria offered in this book conspiratorial activities. If we treat such activities in the Dark Money sphere of politics as an operational conspiracies, as one form of political behavior, it can make a significant contribution to rolling back corruption of our democratic republic by putting this form of behavior in disrepute.

"Conspiracy theory" can be what Bratich calls a "portal concept," that is, such theories serve as "doorways into the major social and political issues defining the U.S. (and global) political culture since the end of the Cold War."[53] No wonder that the late Andrew Breitbart, founder of the radical right Internets news site so vital to Trumpism, recognized that "politics is downstream from culture."[54]

Social scientists and mainstream journalists continue to deploy the term "conspiracy theory" to discredit radical critiques of American democracy, only to have the term thrown back in their faces when their research uncovers hidden, intentional plans to circumvent democracy, or worse to dismantle it. Resorting to "fusion theory," liberal critics reinforce conservative complaints that MacLean's work is methodologically and epistemologically unsound, making all the more credible the anti-intellectualism common to the paranoid style. These friendly critics generally maintain that conspiracy theories can only poison mainstream politics and distract us from important organizing and political work to fight back against Trumpism[55] (see Chapter 2 for a fuller elaboration).

The argument is well expressed in a piece on *Vox*, with the panicky headline, "Even the Intellectual Left is Drawn to Conspiracy Theories about the Right."[56] There Henry Ferrel and Steven Teles claim that MacLean's book "has been hailed as a kind of skeleton key to the rightward political turn in American political economy." Joining a chorus of similar criticism is Rick Perlstein, a historian of Southern conservativism, who on *HistoryNews Network* comments, "The foundation of the entire book is a conspiracy theory that suggests that if you understand

THIS ONE SECRET PLAN [sic], you understand the rise of the right in America in its entirety." He goes on to claim that MacLean ignores "any of a score of other important tributaries, some of them not top-down conspiratorial at all but deeply, organically bottom up." He says her book suggests "that you don't need to read anything else. Which is actively dangerous to historical understanding." A favorable National Public Radio review of *Democracy in Chains* drew criticism from a variety of perspectives, and some of it clearly falls into the "nastier" category, according to NPR's ombudsman.[57]

MacLean has attracted pointed criticism (and much worse) for her unflattering narrative about the ideas of Buchanan and his collaboration with the Kochs, in particular with Charles Koch. Some critics have called for her to lose tenure or even be fired. There is room for disagreement about how well MacLean builds her case that Buchanan's ideas and his strategic vision for implementing them have guided the surge of anti-statist, antidemocratic politics on the Right. They same applies to her comparison of Buchanan's ideas to defenders of slavery. Although MacLean builds a strong argument that the ideas and tactics championed by Buchanan bear similarity to those used in defense of slavery by Senator John C. Calhoun in the Jacksonian era, there is no real evidence that Buchanan or Charles Koch were directly influenced by Calhoun's philosophy.

But neither Mayer nor MacLean actually ever make a claim that the Dark Money networks explain everything we need to know about the Right's success. Their books focus on the stealthy collaboration of a relatively small group of people with extraordinary wealth to shape the country's political future. MacLean acknowledges that public choice has some utility for understanding policymaking and bureaucratic behavior. She puts the story of the ascent of Buchanan's school of thought in the context of school desegregation, illuminating how racism and white supremacy has been used by the libertarian right to advance stealthily an agenda—dismantling of majority supported welfare and regulation.

Critics of MacLean have sought to absolve Buchanan of the stain of resistance to school desegregation after Brown v. Board of Education,[58] and indeed MacLean shows no smoking gun in the form of an explicit defense of segregation on his part, but there is compelling documentation to show Buchanan's support of privatization of schools at a time when it was impossible to disassociate that goal from the worst forms of defense of segregation. As MacLean puts it, "Not surprisingly, then, but with devastating consequences all around, attacks on federal power pitched to nonelites have almost always tapped white racial anxiety, whether overtly or with coded language."[59]

Just as alarming to many of her critics is MacLean's recounting of Buchanan's visit to the Chile under the rule of the ruthless General Augusto Pinochet in 1980s, as well as the professor's ongoing association with Pinochet's economic advisors, who implemented a market-oriented economic shock treatment and implantation of a new constitution with exceptionally high barriers to any democratic tampering with neoliberal economic policies afterwards. Dan Mitchell, a founder of the Center for Freedom and Prosperity, defended Buchanan: "There's no evidence, from what I can tell, that Buchanan endorsed or supported Pinochet's bad record on human rights. His defenders say that Buchanan was simply 'guilty' of encouraging a bad government to adopt good policy."[60] But Buchanan never, even upon his return to the United States, expressed criticism of Pinochet. Chile was (and still is) the country in the Global South most closely associated with neoliberal economic thought and limits upon majoritarian rule. And Buchanan was most insistent on the need to implement neoliberal ideas through planning and promotion of its ideas through stealth.

The conservative broadsheet *Reason* goes so far as to claim that MacLean invented Buchanan's 1973 Third Century document, where he advocated for stealth in advancing policies associated with Public Choice theory. In fact, Buchanan delivered "America's Third Century in Perspective" at the first conference of the Atlantic Economic Society, held in Richmond, Virginia, on September 28–29, 1973. The paper was subsequently published in the *Atlantic Economic Journal.*[61] MacLean, though never directly referring to Buchanan's collaboration with Kochs and others as a conspiracy, quotes from the (apparent) earlier draft delivered in an address to his academic associates gathered at his private cabin that to succeed with plans to implement his ideas, "conspiratorial secrecy is at all times essential."

The point here is not to paint Buchanan as a dark lord, master strategist. Indeed, MacLean not only details his personal success in building libertarian institutions that would execute a long-term master plan to change American political culture, but also his personal downfall, as Koch eventually replaced Buchanan with one of the economist's acolytes to lead Mercatur. And Koch himself must be "credited," if that is the right world, with understanding the need for an elite vanguard, which explains how this ultra-conservative tycoon could list Vladimir Lenin as a major influence on his thinking.[62]

It hardly surprises that conservative reaction to the work of Mayer and MacLean should resort to conspiracy panic, that is, seeking to discredit their work by labeling both authors "conspiracy theorists." But both authors have taken some friendly fire from liberal reviewers as well. Theda Skocpol, a leading voice among political scientists warning of threats to democracy in the United States emanating from growing inequality, praises *Dark Money* as "magisterial analysis" but also says that Mayer "fails to put the efforts of the right-wing billionaires into a larger political and social context. By focusing on elite idea production and election messaging, Mayer overlooks divisions within the right and offers no insights that could help us understand the unruly Trump surge." Skocpol acknowledges that the book "alerts us" to "secret, unaccountable machinations," but she devotes little attention to Mayer's account of how this occurs, as though this part of the book is of little importance. Skocpol compares these dark maneuvers with those of foundations that backed movements and progressive social policy in the 1960s to the 1980s—as though these foundations, which were quite open about their goals, can be equated with the hidden torrents of money sent coursing through the body politic by the Dark Money lords.

Skocpol also characterizes the timing of the book's appearance as "awkward" because the Koch's preferred candidate, Ted Cruz, had faltered and because, she judged, Donald Trump is more "statist" that the Koch brothers could possibly tolerate. Skocpol also contends that Mayer portrays the Tea Party movement as exclusively top-down initiated and organized, instead of recognizing that the reality was a more complex, produced by an "interplay of top-down and bottom-up political forces."[63] But Mayer neither denies nor ignores the broader social context in which stealth activities of the billionaires prospered. And though the Kochs continue to contest some issues and candidates favored by Trump in the Republican Party, as noted earlier in this chapter, an important part of the Koch agenda (rolling back regulation, especially environmental legislation; shifting the judiciary further toward a more libertarian philosophy; tax reduction for the wealthy) has in fact advanced under Trump.

Investigative journalists, like Mayer, are muckrakers, and from Ida Tarbell to the present, these reporters have always sought to ferret out a good story, to look for those who should be held accountable for abuses of power and authority. Narrative historians, like MacLean are story-tellers (but not only this) whose accounts shine light on human agents, not just structures. MacLean makes clear that the key to ordinary people prevailing over oligarchs is not to engage in conspiracy but to build social movements, permitting individuals "powerless on their own" to "use their strength in numbers to move government officials to hear their concerns and act upon them."[64] In describing how a group of black high school students managed to force the issue racially segregated Virginia schools onto the national agenda (as part of Brown v. Board of Education) she describes how they first "collaborated" secretly to plan a walk-out, aided by supportive teachers who had to hide their role to protect their jobs. Though MacLean does not refer to their secret planning as a "conspiracy," it qualifies. Not all conspiracies, as argued in Chapter 1, have malevolent ends.

In his thoroughly reasoned response to MacLean's critics, Andrew Seal points out that MacLean's book has evoked such a virulent response from libertarian and conservative critics because they think erroneously that her point is that Buchanan was racist or evil. Quite rightly, Seal points out that MacLean's book is of interest fundamentally because of Buchanan's relationship to Charles Koch and her bold assertion that both of them believed less in gaining majority support of citizens for their ideas than in stealthily building political power to implement them. Her argument about stealth, Seal concludes, is "the one her critics must attack to shake the whole book and I would contend that disproving it would be the most significant way they could demonstrate that she has misunderstood Buchanan's ideas. I do recognize that most of her evidence for the advocacy of stealth is archival, but this is only a problem if we have reason to doubt that MacLean honestly represents her sources."[65]

Skocpol's criticism that Mayer over-simplifies the origins and influence of the Tea Party has some merit, but it is worth noting that the critic herself concedes at the end of her review that "Dark Money oligarchs… have the entire Republican Party in their grasp." The importance of this political fact is magnified, she acknowledges, by the fact that Trump was without his own policy team and would likely come to depend on Republican conservatives to craft and move legislation. Still, Skocpol failed to realize just how firm is the grasp, how large is its embrace, as Dark Money oligarchs or their acolytes came to populate key positions in the executive branch under Trump.

CONSPIRACY OR JUST PLAIN OLD INTEREST GROUP POLITICS?

The working definition of this book (see Chapter 1) is that conspiracy theory ought to be about understanding the role in politics of activity (1) undertaken secretly; (2) is vulnerability to defeat by exposure; and (3) involves illegal, deceptive, or unethical behavior. Together, the research by Mayer, MacLean, and others seeks to demonstrate that there existed a significant stealth alliance between a highly influential intellectual and the powerful, wealthy patrons of a radical right agenda to cripple democracy in order to achieve a radical program of privatization, elimination of welfare, and deregulation, and that this alliance was instrumental, even if not necessarily totally, in shifting the country in this direction.

A *New York Times* editorial[66] just before Congress approved a tax bill the provided massive tax cuts for the wealthy and for corporations, put the process this way: "As a smaller and smaller group of people cornered an ever-larger share of the nation's wealth, so too did they gain an ever-larger share of political power. They became, in effect, kingmakers; the tax bill is a natural consequence of their long effort to bend American politics to serve their interests." The *Times* notes that the Kochs and their network have "methodically" pushing these changes. It should have added that these groups, as Mayer, MacLean, and others have shown, have gone to great lengths to hide this operation, to misrepresent it as philanthropy.

If you want to make an argument that a small group (i.e., the radical right and billionaires) has worked surreptitiously (e.g., in the "dark", "hidden", in "stealth") to subvert democracy, you might as well embrace rather than eschew the "conspiracy theory" label, because you are likely to be the target of a conspiracy panic in any case.

NOTES

1. Brian Schwartz, "Billionaire Koch Network to Unleash Attack Ads Targeting Senators Who Voted against Trump's Tax Cuts," *CNBC*, June 28, 2018.
2. https://www.opensecrets.org/pres16/candidate?id=n00000528.
3. https://www.opensecrets.org/pres16.
4. Michael Caputo, "Trump Was Outspent by His Closest Primary Opponents," *Politifact.com*, July 1, 2016.

5. https://www.mediaquant.net/2016/11/a-media-post-mortem-on-the-2016-presidential-election/.

6. See Thomas Patterson, "Pre-Primary News Coverage of the 2016 Presidential Race," Harvard Kennedy School, Shorenstein Center on Media, Politics and Public Policy, June 13, 2016, available at shorensteincenter.org (accessed December 27, 2017).

7. While focused more on her unsuccessful race for the nomination in 2008, the obstacles she faced are well outlined in Regina D. Lawrence and Melody Rose, *Hillary Clinton's Race for the White House: Gender Politics and Media on the Campaign Trail* (Boulder, CO: Lynne Rienner, 2009).

8. Marty Cohen, David Karol, Hans Noel, and John Zoller, *The Party Decides, Presidential Nominations Before and After Reform* (Chicago: University of Chicago Press, 2008).

9. Reihan Salam, "The Koch Brothers Were Supposed to Buy the 2016 Election. What happened?" *Slate*, May 18, 2016.

10. http://metrocosm.com/the-history-of-campaign-spending.

11. Richard Reeves, *President Nixon: Alone in the White House* (New York: Simon & Schuster, 1981): 309.

12. Jane Mayer, *Dark Money: The Hidden History of the Billionaires Behind the Rise of the Radical Right* (New York: Doubleday, 2016).

13. Mayer, *Dark Money*. 3.

14. Union of Concerned Scientists, "Who's Backing Scott Pruitt to Head the EPA? The Koch Brothers," *Got Science?* February 2017, available at https://www.ucsusa.org/publications/got-science (accessed June 25, 2018).

15. Coral Davenport and Eric Lipton, "How G.O.P. Leaders Came to View Climate Change as Fake Science," *New York Times*, June 3, 2017.

16. Mayer, *Dark Money*: 206–209.

17. Mayer, *Dark Money*: 1–4.

18. https://www.scribd.com/document/230108736/The-Koch-Brothers-Secret-Billionaire-Summit.

19. Jane Mayer, "Covert Operations: The Billionaire Brothers Who are Waging a War Against Obama," *The New Yorker*, August 30, 2010.

20. Nancy MacLean, *Democracy in Chains: The Deep History of the Radical Right's Stealth Plan for America* (New York: Viking, 2016).

21. See letter from George Mason's President at https://ia601504.us.archive.org/19/items/CabreraEmails1and2/CabreraEmails1and2.pdf. Though denying that the contributions impacted academic decisions, see analysis and original emails at http://www.unkochmycampus.org/charles-koch-foundation-george-mason-mercatus-donor-influence-exposed.

22. MacLean, *Democracy in Chains*: xx.

23. MacLean, *Democracy in Chains*: 117.
24. https://www.opensecrets.org/outsidespending/summ.php?cycle= 2016&chrt=V&disp=O&type=U.
25. Jeremy Koulish, "There Are a Lot of 501(c)(4) Nonprofit Organizations. Most are Not Political," The Urban Institute, 2013, available at www. urban.org (accessed December 1, 2017).
26. https://www.irs.gov/charities-non-profits/other-non-profits/ social-welfare-organizations.
27. https://www.scribd.com/document/230108736/The-Koch-Brothers- Secret-Billionaire-Summit.
28. Mayer, *Dark Money*: 306.
29. "Weaponized Philanthropy," Center for Media and Democracy, May 5, 2017, available at www.exposedbycmd.org/2017/05/05/documents- detail-bradley-foundation-efforts-build-right-wing-infrastructure- nationwide (accessed December 6, 2017).
30. http://www.bradleyfdn.org/2010-Symposium.
31. https://www.exposedbycmd.org/2017/06/16/bradley-foundation- bankrolls-art-pope-extreme-agenda-nc.
32. http://www.motherjones.com/politics/2017/05/how-will-trump- turn-voter-fraud-accusations-voter-suppression/.
33. Mary Bottari, "Fake News Machine Ready to Defend Trump White House Against Robert Mueller Center for Media and Democracy," Center for Media and Democracy, November 8, 2017, available at www. exposedbycmd.org/category/news/democracy (accessed December 6, 2017).
34. https://www.sourcewatch.org/index.php/Robert_Mercer.
35. Robert Crilly, "Trump Donor Robert Mercer Denies He Is a White Supremacist as He Sells Stake in Breitbart News," *The Telegraph*, London, November 2, 2017.
36. Quoted in Kevin McDermott, "Greitens' Onetime Vows of Transparency Now Lost Behind a Veil of Dark Money," *St. Louis Post-Dispatch*, December 10, 2017.
37. Steve Eder, "Email About Qatari Offer Shows Thorny Ethical Issues Clinton Foundation Faced," *New York Times*, October 15, 2016.
38. Available at 45.committee.com (accessed January 3, 2018).
39. "Secret Money to Boost Trump," *Politico*, September 28, 2016.
40. Robert Maguire, "Web of Secret Money Hides One Mega-Donor Funding Conservative Court, OpenSecrets.org, November 21, 2017.
41. Anemona Hartocollis, "Revelations Over Koch Gifts Prompt Inquiry at George Mason University," *New York Times*, May 1, 2018.
42. Jack Bratich, *Conspiracy Panics: Political Rationality and Popular Culture* (Albany: State University of New York Press, 2008).

43. Mayer, *Dark Money*: 12.
44. Mayer, *Dark Money*: 63, 101–102
45. "How Did the Bradley Files become Public," *ExposedbyCMD.com*, n.d., (accessed December 14, 2017).
46. Mayer: *Dark Money*: 279, 328–329, 351.
47. As discussed in Jack Bratich, *Conspiracy Panics*.
48. Zephyr Teachout, *Corruption in America: From Benjamin Franklin's Snuff Box to Citizens United* (Cambridge, MA: Harvard University Press, 2014): 4.
49. Teachout, *Corruption in America*: 227.
50. Teachout, *Corruption in America*: 228.
51. Teachout, *Corruption in America*: 227–245.
52. The term refers to law requiring meetings be open and public records be maintained and available to journalists and the public.
53. Jack Bratich, *Conspiracy Panics*: 6.
54. Leif Weatherbe, "Politics is Downstream from Culture, Part 1: Right Turn to Narrative," *The Hedgehog Review*, blog, the *Infernal Machine*, February 22, 2017, available at http://iasc-culture.org/THR/channels/Infernal_Machine (accessed December 5, 2017).
55. Michael Barkin, *A Culture of Conspiracy: Apocalyptic Visions in Contemporary America* (Berkeley: University of California, 2003). Chip Berlet, "Clinton, Conspiracism and Civil Society." Political Research Associates, February 12, 2017, available at http://www.uni-muenster.de/PeaCon/conspiracy/networks-01.htm (accessed July 27, 2017.)
56. Henry Ferrel and Steven Teles, "Even the intellectual left is drawn to conspiracy theories about the right. Resist them," *Vox.com*, Updated Version, October 9, 2017.
57. https://www.npr.org/sections/ombudsman/2017/08/14/542634650/readers-rankled-by-democracy-in-chains-review.
58. Most prominently, Daniel Bernstein, a blogger for the *Washington Post*'s "Volokh Conspiracy." See "Some Dubious Claims in Nancy Maclean's 'Democracy in Chains'" and "yet More Dubious Claims in Nancy Maclean's 'Democracy in Chains'," June 28 and July 26, 2017, available at https://www.washingtonpost.com/news/volokh-conspiracy (accessed December 12, 2017).
59. MacLean, *Democracy in Chains*: 11.
60. Dan Mitchell, "A Taxpayer-Funded Smear Job of Professor James Buchanan," *International Liberty*, June 24, 2017, available at https://danieljmitchell.wordpress.com (accessed December 12, 2017). Not surprisingly, Mitchell's Institute for Freedom and Prosperity, which he founded, has the motto, "Restraining Government in America and Around the World."

61. Brian Doherty, "What Nancy MacLean Gets Wrong about James Buchanan," *Reason*, July 20, 2017, available at https://reason.com/archives/2017/07/20/what-nancy-maclean-gets-wrong-about-jame/print (accessed January 4, 2018). James M. Buchanan, "America's Third Century in Perspective," *Atlantic Economic Journal* 1, no. 1 (1973): 3–12.

62. Charles Koch, *Good Profit* (New York: Crown Press): 13.

63. Theda Skocpol, "Who Owns the GOP," *Dissent Magazine*, February 3, 2016, available at www.dissentmagazine.org/online_articles/jan-mayer-dark-money-review-koch-brothers-gop (accessed December 5, 2017). At a panel on inequality at the Meeting of the American Political Science Association in September, 2017, I began to raise a question to Skocpol about the extent to which Mayer's book demonstrated the kind of secrecy and intentionality that might merit characterizing it as a "conspiracy;" she dismissed any suggestion that conceiving Dark Money as a conspiracy was valid.

64. MacLean, *Democracy in Chains*: xxii.

65. Andrew Seal, "The Controversy Over Democracy in Chains: A Review Essay," Public Seminar.org, July 2017.

66. *New York Times* Editorial Page, December 17, 2017.

CHAPTER 7

The Deep State, Hegemony, and Democracy

As late as 2013, as Donald Trump began to ruminate publically that he might run for president, the concept of an American Deep State was still largely seen as a paranoid conspiracy theory, and certainly not one to be given a serious hearing by conservatives. Few would have guessed that it would be right-wing pundits and White House officials raising charges that an American Deep State was conspiring against a president. As with so many other things, Donald Trump's presidency has disrupted the norm.

Long dismissed by mainstream political scientists and journalists as just another crazy conspiracy theory, the existence of an American Deep State can no longer be discarded cavalierly as paranoia. Many pundits and journalists still do, but the idea has gotten some traction in the mainstream press. In 2013, Mike Lofgren a long-time Capitol Hill staffer and author of the widely read and respected *The Party's Over*, entitled a follow-up book, *The Deep State: The Fall of the Constitution and the Rise of a Shadow Government*.[1] In the same year, two mainstream journalists co-authored *Deep State: Inside the Government Secrecy Industry*.[2] Suspicion about a Deep State has begun also to take root more broadly in American political culture. In response to a question defining the Deep State as the "existence of a group of unelected government and military officials who secretly manipulate or direct national policy," a Monmouth University poll in March 2018 found that about a quarter of respondents thought that a Deep State definitely exists, and a little less than half thought it probably exists.[3] And this was before Donald Trump himself explicitly endorsed the idea of its existence in May 2018.

© The Author(s) 2019
D. C. Hellinger, *Conspiracies and Conspiracy Theories in the Age of Trump*, https://doi.org/10.1007/978-3-319-98158-1_7

President Trump discerned conspiracy afoot in the National Security Agency's surveillance of several of his associates and campaign staffers and in leaks coming from within the intelligence community, the FBI, and possibly Special Counsel Robert Mueller's office about possible collusion between his campaign and Russian operatives. Trump also fumed repeatedly about former director of the FBI, James Comey, whom he accuses of soft peddling an investigation into possible violations of national security laws by Hillary Clinton in her use of a private email server while she was Secretary of State. For a little more than a year Trump refrained from characterizing his alleged enemies within the security establishment as a "Deep State," but even before he began using the term several of his supporters, including his son, Eric, alleged that the "Deep State" was conspiring to bring down his presidency.

The more prominent discussion of a "Deep State" in American public discourse rang alarm bells in some quarters that taking the theory seriously would undermine the country's "soft power," that is, its positive image as an attractive economic and political model for the rest of the world. In March 2018, the *Voice of America*, the official voice of US public diplomacy, tried to maintain a tone of dismissal about "intimations of 'Deep State' conspiracies in the United States [that] have bubbled to the surface from the depths of the far left and right." VOA featured politicians and academic experts warning of the folly of entertaining this idea.[4] But on May 23, 2018, the president himself, referring to a Justice Department report critical of former Director Comey, tweeted, "Look how things have turned around on the Criminal Deep State. They go after Phony Collusion with Russia, a made up Scam, and end up getting caught in a major SPY scandal the likes of which this country may never have seen before! What goes around, comes around!"

Trump had plenty of motivation to raise the specter of a bureaucratic conspiracy against his presidency, one including sectors in the American security establishment. This message deflects attention from the fact that many of the leaks animating him seemed to originated within his own White House staff. But can we say there is no foundation to think that his radical shift in US policy toward European allies and NATO, his undermining of the liberal international trade order, his embrace of Russia, and his mercurial personality would motivate some within the security establishment to seek his downfall? A cloak of secrecy shrouds so much of the activity associated with "national security," and its abuse has repeatedly been a central element of the most notorious American political scandals of the post-World War II era. Yet the dominant view in political science has been that the American state is impervious to the kind of conspiracies carried out by military and intelligence operatives in other countries, even though many of these enjoyed significant encouragement or aid from the United States. Only recently have some political scientists question whether American state is immune to authoritarianism, with democracy now threatened by a president little constrained by constitutional limits on his power.

However much many soldiers, spies, and intelligence analysts may be genuinely motivated by patriotism and personally committed to democracy, they exercise power in ways hidden from the public. Samuel Huntington, a conservative and close advisor to several presidents, including President Jimmy Carter whom he served as Coordinator of Security Planning for the National Security Council, once wrote, "The architects of power in the United States must create a force that can be felt but not seen. Power remains strong when it remains in the dark; exposed to the sunlight it begins to evaporate."[5] What if power in the dark sees a threat in a president that does not share its worldview and openly questions its loyalty? This is at the heart of conspiracy theories about John Kennedy's assassination and to some degree about how effectively the political system responded to Watergate and the issues raised by the Vietnam War. Now the theme of the Deep State is being raised out of the White House itself.

But Trump's relationship with the national security estblishment is more complex and ambiguous than his public attacks suggest. While attacking the "Deep State" rhetorically, and although his 2016 campaign included criticizing the trillions of dollars spent on wars in Iraq and Afghanistan, in the first year of his presidency Trump increased deployment of troops in the Middle East and South Asia, sent new training missions into Africa, continued providing arms and assistance to Saudi Arabia's bombing campaign in Yemen, and extended the same to the Philippines for its fight with Islamist insurgents. Like President Obama, Trump increased the drone strikes and missions by Special Forces under control of both military command and the Central Intelligence Agency (CIA). Though his Twitter criticism still sometimes impetuously targets the CIA or publically exposes sensitive secrets, in 2018 most of his invective was aimed at the criminal justice system and those investigating possible collusion of his campaign with the Russians. Domestically, Trump deployed the Immigration and Customs Enforcement (ICE) agents in mass detentions of undocumented immigrants in operations violating due process. He has unambiguously sided with police and against the Black Lives Matter movement, repeatedly raising the specter of rampant criminal violence in American cities.

These actions have raised the danger that *parapolitics*, dark political activities closely associated with the concept of the Deep State, is becoming more deeply rooted in domestic politics in the United State. Parapolitics can be defined as political activity in violation of constitutional and legal norms and characterized by secrecy and deceit, often carried out by groups in concert with but formally separate from military, polices and other parts of the coercive apparatus of the state. Its normalization is being fostered, the latter part of this chapter will argue, by its increasing presence in pop-culture movies, games, and television programs.

As with "Dark Money," I do not treat the "Deep State" as a conspiracy in itself but as an opaque realm of political power that gives rise to both conspiracies and to conspiracy theories. From the government military and security agencies and from allied forces in the private sector there has emerged a steady parade of scoundrels and profit-seekers masquerading as patriots but engaged in parapolitics. Their activities become somewhat visible in major scandals that have punctuated American politics with regularity since World War II; but the collective historical memory of what happened tends to fade, beginning with assurances that the system worked to bring the threat to a close. When public officials, elected representatives, and investigative journalists threaten the central institutions associated with the national security state, a kind of conspiracy panic has usually been employed to discourage digging too deep. To suggest that a Deep State exists under the surface of constitutional democracy, they are dismissed as paranoid style conspiracy theorists.

This chapter proposes that rather than *a priori* dismissing the Deep State and "parapolitics" as paranoid conspiracism, these themes ought to be serious part of a political science dedicated to democratic values. There are signs of political science turning in this direction (see Chapter 8), and this chapter argues that the concept of operational conspiracies can be useful tool for this purpose.

What Is the Deep State? What Is It Not?

Lofgren, a former senior Republican congressional staffer who worked 16 years on the budget committees of both the House and Senate, broadly defines the Deep State to include almost the entire administrative state and well-heeled lobbyists in the capital.[6] So defined, the Deep State would envelope any bureaucratic agency positioned to obstruct, delay, or mutate the policies put in place by Congress or the White House. For purposes of this chapter, I use the original conception of the Deep State, one well-articulated by Sonam Sheth in a critique of accusations made in several Breitbart articles alleging that Trump faces subversion by a coalition of national security agencies and their allies in financial and the military–industry complex. In an article for *Business Insider* Sheth writes,

> If we understand "real power" to mean not absolute, last word power then it is possible, even allowing for the obvious interest of Trump in portraying himself as a victim of dark force, to acknowledge that possession of license to coerce (much less kill or torture) is, to put it mildly a significant source of power subject to abuse.[7]

Conceptualizing the Deep State and parapolitics as together a sphere of politics prone to conspiratorial activity avoids treating the Deep State as monolithic or unchanging. It makes little sense to treat the Deep State as a unitary, coherent actor in carrying out a conspiracy—be it the alleged assassination of JFK, the transfer of arms sale money from Iran to the Nicaraguan contras, the implementation of warrantless surveillance and "enhanced interrogation" after 9/11, or Trump's claim that the "Deep State" is conspiring to bring down the Trump presidency. Bureaucratic infighting, ideological divisions, contentious or cooperative relations with colleagues in other domestic and foreign services, conflicts between professional and political obligations, all influence and complicate the relationship of the American Deep State to the larger liberal democratic state to which it is supposed to be subordinate.

On the tenth anniversary of the 9/11 attacks on New York and Washington, the *New Yorker Magazine* asked its Pulitzer Prize winning author, Jane Mayer (and other contributors to the magazine) a series of questions, including about how this seminal event—which has led to two major wars, was used to impose a state of emergence that in 2018 entered into its seventeenth year, and unleashed widespread fear of Muslims—had affected her. The Pulitzer Prize winning journalist responsible for bringing Dark Money into the light (see Chapter 6) had earlier authored *The Dark Side: The Inside Story of How the War on Terror Turned into a War on American Ideals,*[8] which gathered together stories revealing the existence of "black site prisons" and warrantless domestic surveillance. Mayer's book joined shelves of studies[9] by other investigators, including many who have served in the military and intelligence sectors. They provide compelling reasons to doubt that clandestine operations, propaganda campaigns, and intervention abroad defend democracy. Indeed, they provide clear evidence of how these kinds of operations in the "dark" threaten it.

Citing her heightened sensitivity to the "importance and frailty of human rights," Mayer prefaced her concern with an acknowledgement that I want to keep in mind constantly as we move on to explore here the Deep State and its corollary, "parapolitics." Mayer wrote,

> I think all that I have seen and learned in this area has profoundly changed me, as it has many others. I developed huge admiration for those who protected the country's laws and values, sometimes at great personal risk, including F.B.I. agents, military and C.I.A. officers, and civil liberties lawyers who refused to degrade the country by engaging in torture.[10]

I share Mayer's judgment and caution. The Deep State, as I conceive it, is not monolithic or all-powerful, and many working within it primarily see their function as defense and promotion of liberal democratic ideals. However, the professionalism and patriotism of many of those who work in military and intelligence and domestic security institutions do not prevent clashes between the national security state and democracy or invalidate President Dwight Eisenhower's warning when in his farewell address he said, "In the councils of government, we must guard against the acquisition of unwarranted influence, whether sought or unsought, by the military–industrial complex. The potential for the disastrous rise of misplaced power exists, and will persist."[11]

There seems to be a consensus, shared by critics and proponents alike, that the "Deep State" is derived from the Turkish *derin devlet*, which refers to an intricate network made up of government officials, often including those from the military and intelligence communities, whose primary goal is to subvert a democratically elected leader's agenda or even conspire to remove that leader from power—by assassination if necessary. David Remnick, a skeptic that the idea applies to the United States, refers to the Deep State as "a network of embedded members of a government's agencies or military…operate against a democratically elected government. It might work to undermine an elected president's authority or legitimacy and has been common in countries such as Egypt and Turkey."[12]

Another way to define the Deep State is to consider what it is to those who reject the idea that such a thing exists in the United States. *Politico* magazine weighed-in accordingly,

> Like the Death Star, the American Deep State does not, of course, exist. An appropriation from countries such as Egypt, Turkey, Pakistan and Algeria, where real networks of intelligence, defense and interior ministry officials exercise real power to drive policy, sideline elected officials and eliminate opponents, the American Deep State is nothing more than an invention of President Donald Trump and his allies.[13]

There are good reasons to suspect Trump's motives, but that does not mean we should dismiss from consideration the possibility of American security institutions wielding power to undermine presidential authority or even depose a president. The persistence of JFK assasination theories suggests that many Americans do not readily dismiss this notion.

The Deep State is often linked to the stubborn persistence of the theory that Lee Harvey Oswald may not have acted alone, especially the variant suspecting involvement of the CIA, as postulated in Oliver Stone's movie *JFK* (1991). The dismissal of Stone's portrayal of a plot to kill Kennedy often combines an admission of its superior cinematic qualities with complete contempt for its message, such as when *The Guardian's* Alex Tunzelmann wrote, "*JFK* is a cleverly constructed, tightly written and sometimes breathtakingly well-acted movie – and one of the most appalling travesties of history you're ever likely to see."[14]

For the most part the notion of an American Deep State remains subject to "conspiracy panic."[15] Conspiracy panic (see Chapter 3) is a way of disqualifying certain modes of thought and discourses that challenge American exceptionalism and ultimately the hegemony of a particular political regime. As Bratich puts it, "The scapegoating of conspiracy theories provides the conditions for social integration and political rationality. Conspiracy panics help to define the normal modes of dissent. Politically it is predicated on a consensus 'us' over against a subversive and threatening 'them'."[16] The "Deep State" has been pushing against the ramparts of the regime of truth, forcing doubters to discuss rather than to ignore it. The need to constantly and repeatedly dismiss the idea that a conspiracy of some kind was behind the assassination of Kennedy, to label it a "conspiracy theory," demonstrates the panic among most intellectuals at the thought that it could be true.

Greg Grandin, a progressive historian, writing in the leftist *The Nation* early in Trump's first year, worries that focusing on Deep State will distract us from abuses of private power.

> The problem with the phrase "Deep State" is that it is used to suggest that dishonorable individuals are subverting the virtuous state for their private ambitions...It's this public virtue/private vice false opposition that makes so much of the "Deep State" writing slide into, if not noxious Bilderberg anti-Semitism, then "we are a republic, not an empire" idiocy.[17]

His critique includes an approving reference to Frederik Jameson's widely cited assertion, "Conspiracy, one is tempted to say, is the poor person's cognitive mapping in the postmodern age."[18] As we have seen (Chapters 4 and 5), there is little evidence that poor and working-class people are more likely attracted to conspiracy theory than the wealthy. Furthermore, the historian Kathryn Olmstead, while endorsing the Hofstadter view of conspiracy theories as the "paranoid style", concedes in her study of twentieth-century conspiracy theories in the United States that sometimes they empower ordinary people to obtain accountability from public officials. Even conspiracy theories that have little warrant, such as the belief that President Franklin Roosevelt knew in advance of Pearl Harbor, produced investigations that brought to light serious malfeasance and abuses of executive authority.[19]

Although he too sees conspiracy theory through the lens of the paranoid style, Tim Melley's work on conspiracism in popular culture actually catches the essence of the concept of the Deep State by characterizing the way movies, games, and TV depict what he calls the "covert sphere."[20] But Melley sees conspiracy theory only as a symptom common people's uneasiness. He attributes their attraction to such entertainment as a symptom of "agency panic," their discomfort with the influence of hidden forces and institutions in their lives. Conspiracies expressed in fiction—elite and popular level cultural products—encourage irrational conspiracy theories to proliferate in a culture infused with "agency panic" (see in Chapter 1).

Melley shows that to a surprising degree the plots of popular fiction mirror how American intelligence operatives play the same spy games that other states do, and they bend the rules because the "the ticking bomb" justifies their actions. Even more surprising, many of these mass entertainment productions are actively created or supported by the institutions of this "covert sphere" (a theme to which we will return later in this chapter). Likewise, Charles Knight, another keen observer of conspiracism in American culture, takes a similar view of conspiracy theories. "It is arguable that a culture *of* conspiracy has become an implicit mode of operation in American politics, with the rise of the national security state over the last half-century," he says.[21] Yet like Melley he regards conspiracy theory as *ipso facto* irrational, reflecting mass distrust of elites but not getting to the roots of people's concerns.

Though skeptical of Deep State conspiracy theories, Melley himself shows in *The Covert Sphere* that fictional conspiracy theories can be a major part of what the most veiled institution of the national security state, the CIA, is charged to produce. The CIA, FBI, and other security agencies all carry out operational institutional conspiracies that are fodder for film television plots.[22] Deep State networks include a more nefarious sector, organized criminals, and even terrorists, providing plenty of villains and ambiguous moral hazzards for plots. Many morally hazardous relationships arise out of covert operations and reliance upon informers, what the CIA calls "assets." They involve the agencies in parapolitics abroad, and these often blowback into the United States. In the next four sections of this chapter discuss some of the ways this happens in reality before returning to how contemporary popular culture helps hide this reality in plain sight.

PARAPOLITICS

As already indicated, closely related to the concept of the "Deep State" is the notion of "parapolitics." Scott describes parapolitics as a level of politics that is "repressed and denied" by mainstream journalists, pundits, and academics. This is a sphere of politics where actors resort "to decision-making and enforcement procedures outside as well as inside those publicly sanctioned by law and society."[23] Elsewhere, he writes, somewhat evocative of Huntington but more ominously, "Power 'in the dark' is the essence of what I...[mean] by a Deep State: a power not derived from the constitution but outside and above it, 'more powerful than the public state.'"[24]

Theorists associated with parapolitics the Deep State, see the exercise of elite power quite differently than envisioned by most political scientists. The latter's orthodoxy is embodied in pluralism, a paradigm that maintains elite politics to be not inherently undemocratic. In a democratic polity, say pluralists, elites are competitive, that is, they have conflicting interests among themselves, and must ultimately appeal to the democratic processes of representative government, especially elections.[25] This school of thought has long been opposed by "elitism", of which C. Wright Mills was and is the foremost exponent.

In his influential *The Power Elite*, Mills wrote, "America is now in considerable part a formal political democracy than a democratic social structure, and even the formal political mechanics are weak." Already in the middle of Eisenhower administration (1953–1960) Mills warned of "the decline of politics as genuine and public debate of alternative positions." Mills avoided romanticizing the character of democracy American past, but he recognized that the erosion of what Deep State theorists would call the "public state" owed much to the changed role of the United States in international affairs and the growth of "military capitalism."[26] Eisenhower expressed a similar sentiment in his famous farewell address warning about the unwarranted influence of the military–industrial complex.

Although Scott's books have received positive reviews in some quarters, his work is often stigmatized with the dreaded "conspiracy theory" label, especially his *Deep Politics and the Death of JFK*. Though not his first book on "deep politics", his questioning of the "lone gunman" theory in this book made what is still the most coherent, plausible case for investigating Kennedy's murder as the result of a conspiracy. Perhaps better than the author himself, the moderator of a radio debate between Scott and Gerald Posner, whose *Case Closed* defended the Warren Commission's finding that Oswald was the lone assassin, defined "deep politics" as "the links of mutual interest between [J. Edgar] Hoover and the FBI, organized crime, big business, and the intelligence community" that he believes led to McCarthyism, Watergate, Iran-Contra, as well as the JFK assassination.[27] The typical reaction to Scott's work, when it is given any attention at all, is summed up in a review by the progressive journalist, Max Holland, who characterized *Deep Politics and the Death of JFK* as "an unreadable compendium of 'may haves' and 'might haves,' non-sequiturs, and McCarthy-style innuendo, with enough documentation to satisfy any paranoid."[28]

Scott's style does bear some of the hallmarks of the paranoid variety of conspiracy theory, with unusually copious notes and a tendency sometimes to back controversial claims with shallow citations, sometimes of his own previous work. Yet, at the same time, Scott relies extensively on public record, scrutinizing primary sources, uncovering contradictions and gaps in the public, asking reasonable questions about why they exist, and asking what might explain the anomalies in the record. Like other kinds of radical scholarship, the very nature of his hypotheses are controversial by nature, but "innuendo", as Holland puts it, is not part of his repertoire. And unlike many other conspiracy theorists, Scott does not hesitate to point out alternative interpretations to his own. He is often criticized for supposition, but supposition is difficult to avoid in researching conspiracies. Exposing what is "hidden" almost inevitably comes with some whiff of conspiracism. Maintenance of official secrets, often long after any threat to security exists, requires a degree of speculation because so much of the record is unavailable, lost, destroyed, or forgotten, and thus unavailable to researchers.

The secretive activities of military and intelligence institutions are not necessarily illegal. However, conspiracies are not solely defined by their being illegal. Some covert activities are legal under national laws but are done in secret mainly because they violate international norms or law. For example, in four of the many notorious interventions carried out by the CIA, such as the 1953 plot to overthrow Mohammad Mossadegh of Iran, the 1954 plot to oust President Jacobo Árbenz of Guatemala, the 1961 invasion Cuba, and the subsequent efforts to assassinate Fidel Castro ("Operatrion Mongoose"), all were authorized by the Executive Branch with its full consent and knowledge. In no way were these operational conspiracies carried out by rogue agents. What made them notorious was their blatant violations of the code of conduct of international relations, specifically, respect of the sovereignty of other governments. That the first two leaders were democratically elected adds to the notoriety of the Agency's operations. Nor were these operations authorized by fully disinterested parties. The Secretary of State, John Foster Dulles and his brother, Allen, Director of the CIA, both had done legal work in private practice for oil companies in Iran and the United Fruit Company in Guatemala.

As Scott puts it, "Covert operations, when they generate or reinforce autonomous political power, almost always outlast the specific purpose for which they were designed...To put it in terms I find more precise, *parapolitics*, the exercise of power by covert means, tends to metastasize into *deep politics*, an interplay of unacknowledged forces over which the original parapolitical agent no longer has control" (italics in original).[29] In this way, the Deep State arises from the covert exercise of coercion and surveillance by the institutions entrusted with those powers in the name of security.

The covert nature of operations can lead to activites that exceed authorized boundaries. Off-the-books money, often generated by the drug trade and other forms of trafficking, create myriad opportunities for corruption. Undercover agents may engage in what otherwise would be criminally sanctioned behavior. This often makes it difficult to ascertain whether illegal actions were corrupt, authorized, or undertaken by rogue actors.

One of the most notorious examples of metastasized corruption was the Bank of Credit and International Commerce (BCCI). The bank's seamy operations were disclosed by investigative reporting and by scrutiny from the New York Federal District Attorney. Their revelations were summarized by the *Washington Post*: "BCCI made phony loans, concealed deposits, hid huge losses, and was the bank for a host of shady customers ranging from terrorists and spies to drug runners and dictators."[30] Another report, by the *New York Times*, was blunt: "The bank maintained secret accounts for a collection of people and institutions that reads like a list of characters and organizations for a spy novel: Saddam Hussein, Abu Nidal, Manuel Noriega, the CIA and an assortment of drug runners and arms merchants."[31] An estimated $5 billion was unaccounted for in bank records. The bank is estimated to have bribed prominent politicians in 71 different countries, prominent among them areas where American forces were involved in counter-insurgency, destabilization, or counter-criminal operations.

A US Senate Foreign Relations Committee investigation documented a long ongoing relationship between the CIA and the bank, but only after overcoming Agency resistance to providing information. The Committee report found that the CIA's use of the bank began with its efforts to investigate narco-dollar laundering, but the Agency discovered its capabilities might be of use for its own purposes. Even the Senate Foreign Relations Committee could not or would not draw a clear conclusion about whether the Agency's use of the bank was authorized or not. "The unofficial story of BCCI's links to U.S. intelligence is complicated by the inability of investigators to determine whether private persons affiliated with U.S. intelligence were undertaking actions such as selling U.S. arms to a foreign government outside ordinary channels on their own behalf, or ostensibly under sanction of a U.S. government agency, policy, or operation," according to the report. The bank's owners and clients were scattered around the globe, but key mony came from Middle Eastern sources and management expertise was provided by Pakistanies.[32]

The BCCI might still be operating today were it not for the Iran-Contra scandal. Space here does not permit a full exploration of the giant reach of the scandal. Suffice it to say that according to the Senate report its tentacles reached not only into the CIA, but also into Hill and Knowlton, a public relations firm that played a key role in creating public support for the First Iraq War; to Kissinger Associates; and to Clark Clifford and Robert Altman, highly connected Washington lawyers. The Senate report said, "The correspondence also highlights BCCI's focus on doing business with, and ability, given its $23 billion in reported assets and 73 countries of operation, to attract interest from some of the most politically well-connected people in the United States."[33]

In the case of Iran-Contra) operations, National Security officials were careful to maintain "plausible deniability" for President Reagan. This tactic itself is a type of conspiracy—a kind of prophylactic cover-up, but with the eyes of officials in the public state half open. Its purpose is to limit damage to the presidency should their activities come to light. Reagan was known to have taken a keen interest in supporting the Nicaraguan Contra insurgency against the Sandinista government in Nicaragua. The operational conspiracy to bring down the democratically elected Sandinista government was, in fact, unlawful under international conventions to which the United States was a signatory, was a violation of an explicit Congressional prohibition on spending to support the Contras, and upon revelatin did subject its perpetrators to a high degree of domestic embarrassment, given that it was funded in part by arms sales to Iran and its revolutionary government. However, the operation was not "rogue." It was carried out under the direction and approval of officials that otherwise were authorized to initiate covert activities. Here, the "Deep State" was not evading the authority of the executive branch but the democratic, constitutional authority of Congress.

If the belief that the CIA and other actors of the national security apparatus were part of a conspiracy to murder President Kennedy were ever to be fully substantiated (an unlikely prospect), this would constitute a rogue operation more akin to the way that similar agencies often operate in Turkey, Pakistan, Egypt, and other politically unstable regimes. But "the Deep State did it" is not much of a hypothesis. Even if a "smoking gun" implicating the CIA or other national security actors in the assassination is ever found, this does not mean that these agencies and their employees acted in one coordinated manner to kill Kennedy or to set him up to be killed. In fact, the history of the US Intelligence Community is rife with bureaucratic rivalries and competition for turf and resources. We should not assume that the 17 national intelligence organizations and their 70,000 employees[34] would all be collectively guilty of such a major crime.

The Manichean logic of the Cold War and the fact that the first generation of CIA officials were employed in dirty operations rationalized by anti-communism lends some credence to the claim that many in the military–industrial complex had motive to assassinate Kennedy. It is often a criticism of conspiracy theories that they rely on motive as proof; that is a fair point, but we should not regard motive as immaterial to a conspiracy belief. Perhaps no career illustrates this phenomenon more than of the CIA's James Angleton. Testifying to the Church Committee, Angleton himself asserted, "It is inconceivable that a secret arm of the government has to comply with all the overt orders of the government."[35] His ruthlessness makes one wonder just what limits, if any there were on his dedication to thwart anything he perceived (real or not) that might lead to retreat from victory over Moscow. His career illustrates how the secrecy and culture of the US intelligence community make it an incubator for conspiracies and conspiracy theories.

Angleton's career began during World War II in Italy in the CIA's predecessor, the Office of Strategic Services (OSS). In his training and service in that theater, he forged relationships with Allen Dulles, William Donavan, Richard Helms, and other major figures of the Cold War era CIA. In line with the priorities of American foreign policy in the post-World War II era (i.e., not acting as a rogue agent), Angleton played an important role in covert efforts to undermine the Communist Party, which had emerged as the single most popular political party in Italy, thanks in part to its leading role in the Resistance. To this end, he worked with the two most powerful institutions in Italian society, the Catholic Church and the Mafia, and he also rehabilitated many officials associated with Mussolini's Fascist party to enlist them in the anti-communist cause. From this milieu, he returned to the United States, and from 1954 to 1974 he headed the CIA's Counter Intelligence Staff. Jefferson Morley, the most recent of several Angleton biographers, describes Angleton as a "dogmatic and conspiratorial operator whose idiosyncratic theories paralyzed the agency's operations...at the height of the Cold War, and whose domestic surveillance operations targeting American dissidents had discredited the CIA in the court of public opinion."[36]

One of the most chilling accounts of Angleton's fanaticism and capacity for cruelty comes from Gerald Posner's *Case Closed*, which is dedicated to arguing that Oswald acted alone to assaasinate Kennedy.[37] Angleton was obsessed with ferreting out Soviet plants inside the spy agency. He was convinced that a defector, Yuri Nosenko, who claimed that Oswald was little regarded by Soviet intelligence and therefore not likely to have acted on their behalf, was a double agent. Besides being convinced that Nosenko was a mole, Angleton thought the defector was hiding information linking Oswald to the KGB during the former's time in Russia. Angleton's suspicions convinced Richard Helms, then a deputy director, to persuade the Warren Commission not to rely on Nosenko as a witness.

According to the Posner, the CIA denied the FBI access to Nosenko. Starting on April 4, 1964, after putting him through a lie detector test administered by a biased technician, Angleton had Nosenko subjected to a strip search and imprisoned in a tiny attic room in the capital, with nothing but a metal bed fastened to the floor for furniture. He was told he would be kept in the room, without heat or air conditioning, for 25 years, fed minimally, and subjected to harsh interrogation. He was moved after 16 months to a CIA training camp and kept in a concrete bunker, with subsistence food only, and monitored by closed-circuit TV. He was finally allowed some exercise. Nosenko never broke, infuriating Angleton and his co-conspirator, Tennant "Pete" Bagley, who at one point urged liquidating the defector. In 1969, Nosenko was finally released and accepted as a real defector.

There have been disputes over the veracity of Nosenko's account of his treatment and about his status, but the main point here is that Angleton's paranoia about Soviet defectors trumped in his mind any need to have Nosenko provide information undermining the notion that the Soviets and Cuba might have been involved in Kennedy's murder. Kennedy was a Cold Warrior, and projections about how the Cold War could have come to a much earlier end and terminated the arms race, a theory mounted in the opening minutes of Oliver Stone's *JFK* (1991) are wildly, speculatively optimistic. Less speculative, however, is the singular paranoia of Angleton, Hoover, and many of their contemporaries in the Cold War era who were convinced that Kennedy was moving toward what later, in the Nixon/Kissinger years, could be called a détente. They had fought communism by cooperating with Mafioso's, funded rebel armies in Southeast Asia and corrupt warlords in Chine, abetted drug running, carried out surveillance of private US citizens, carried out and attempted assassinations of Third World leaders, experimented with brainwashing techniques and mind-altering drugs, among many other operations dedicated to that cause. That they participated in a conspiracy to assassinate Kennedy is far from proven, but neither can it be dismissed. That they participated in one conspiracy—obstruction of an investigation into the murder of the President of the United States— is a fully warranted. Why remains unanswered.

The Conspiratorial Roots
of National Security Ideology and Institutions

The origins of the national security complex are often traced to National Security Act of 1947, which provided the legal basis for coordination of the military services, the creation of the CIA and the National Security Agency, and the National Security Council, among other measures. However, planning for a large permanent military and intelligence establishment began even before the United States entered into World War II, and in quite conspiratorial fashion. In September 1939, more than two years before Pearl Harbor, the New York-based and Rockefeller Foundation funded Council and Foreign Relations approached the State Department about collaborating on a secret study of how various outcomes of the ongoing European war would affect the interests of the United States. The 1947 legislation later linked the results of this study to the concept of "national security," a phrase that was not part of American political language before World War II. The idea was linked in turn to "containment" of Communism, implying the need for a defensive response to a world conspiracy. The Department of War (as it had been called since 1789) was renamed the "Department of Defense."

The foundational legislation for the national security state coincided with the unparalleled power enjoyed by the United States at the time and the determination of internationalist elites to use that power to lay the basis for a liberal international economic and political order. Having emerged from World War II with its economic infrastructure virtually unscathed, and with much of Europe and Japan (the only industrialized economy in Asia) in ruins, a mythology developed around the notion that in building a permanent military establishment and war economy the United States, unselfishly and without pretense to a territorial empire of any size, simply found itself called upon to take up the burden of world hegemony in defense of freedom and the quest for global peace and prosperity. It would thus seem that hegemony was thrust upon Americans, not sought after.

In contrast, the pre-war War-Peace Studies[38] brought together corporate elites, key State Department planners, and intellectuals from the nation's top universities, all of whom constituted the vanguard of an internationalist elite that had been frustrated by the political obstacles posed by isolationists to expansion of American leadership after World War I. Among key conclusions drawn by the group two stand out. One was that the United States could cope with German domination of the European continent but could not permit the markets and natural resources of the European empires, especially the British Empire, to fall into German hands. The elites also rejected acceptance of Japanese competition for influence in Asia and recommended an embargo, which President Roosevelt implemented.

The other conclusion was that the United States would have to break with its tradition of dismantling its war economy and reducing the size and funding of the military after the conclusion of the war. Elites planned in secret, with absolutely no public consultation, to make perhaps the most important decision about the country's future after the war. The Study concluded that the "foremost requirement of the United States in a world in which it proposes to hold unquestioned power is the rapid fulfillment of a program of complete rearmament." Rather bluntly, the elite made clear that the measures should be taken to ensure that war aims (already assuming the United States entry into the war) not be stated in a way that they "seemed to be concerned solely with Anglo-American imperialism." The interests of Africans, Latin Americans, and Asians, not only Europeans, should be stressed because "This would have a better propaganda effect."[39]

The War-Peace project comes as close as we may ever see to fitting criteria for that rare occurrence, a "grand" conspiracy to construct a world order (see Chapter 2). It was conducted in the strictest secrecy, and its results were maintained classified until well after the war. Even after publication, the collusion among some of the country's most powerful economic and political elites as well as influential academics was largely ignored in post-War literature in political science and history; its prescient pre-war consensus on militarization and propaganda remained veiled by the myth of the beneficent hegemon.

One must admire the capacity of the internationalist-minded planners to envision a post-World order that would avoid the calamities that ensued after World War I. But like virtually all conspiracies, their project could not prosper in the absence of historical, social, and economic conditions that suited the moment. Furthermore, not everything unfolded as the elite cabal anticipated or wished. Most importantly, we cannot attribute the emergence of the post-War order to the elite collusion. Their secret planning must be categorized as an operational, not a grand conspiracy, despite scale of their vision for the post-War would. Besides the propitious social and economic forces, the scale of destruction helped make the War/Peace blueprint viable at the end of the war. The elites were not omniscient about the way the war would be conducted. Certainly, they did not anticipate nuclear weapons. There would be significant divisions in elite circles about post-war relations with the Soviet Union, with President Roosevelt anticipating integration of the Soviet bloc into the new world order, and other liberal and conservative elites more bent on isolation or containment.

Absent historical accounts of the secret pre-War planning by internationalist oriented elites, we fail to capture the role of human agency in the process. Viewing the elite planning process as an operational conspiracy brings into question the kind of "manifest destiny" approach to American hegemony and the nation's imagined role as a "beacon" showing the way to a liberal world almost utopian in its conception. Conspiracy theory serves as a gateway to recovering historical memory and our understanding of our place in history. It also highlights how effectively the processes of democracy were insulated from the transition of US political culture from one of suspicion of a military establishment to a permanent war economy and national security state. The pre-war origins of US international policy teach us to raise questions about the neoliberal "new world order" that President George Bush saw emerging in a speech after the First Gulf War in 1991, in particular about its "inevitability" (see Chapter 5).[40]

INSTITUTIONALIZED CONSPIRACY

The most secretive institution of American liberal democracy to come out of elite planning is the CIA. The CIA's authorization to carry out covert operations, that is, conspiracies abroad, was not clearly authorized by its founding legislation, the National Security Act of 1947. That Act charges the CIA only with various advising, evaluation, and coordinating function for the new National Security Council, plus assuming other functions and duties assigned it by the National Security Council. These latter assigned functions were subsequently interpreted to include covert operations; presidential directives and congressional budget authorization provide some further legal grounding for covert operations.[41]

We can classify the CIA's operational section's activities as "institutionalized conspiracy." A recent use of "institutionalized" in another context may clarify its nature and distinctiveness. In December 2016, the World Doping Agency (WDA) produced a report detailing "systematic doping" of 1000 Olympic athletes in 30 different sports from 2011 to 2015, attributing the cheating to a conspiracy among the Russian Sports Ministry, national anti-doping agency, and the Federal Security Service (a domestic intelligence organization). This was a secret ongoing operation that clearly was sanctioned by the Russian state, not a rogue operation by coaches or bureaucrats in these agencies. No Russians laws were broken; the doping was undertaken for reasons of state, and it was secret. For this reason, the WDA has no hesitation in identifying the Russian operation as an institutional conspiracy.[42] So too can we say this about CIA covert activities. The thesis here is the Agency is an institutional incubator of conspiracies; most are authorized, but the environment also spawns rogue operations.

In *The Covert Sphere*, Melley provides a chilling account of several early operations and experiments carried out by the CIA, never really authorized through a deliberative democratic process, nor given significant oversight by the elected Congress. Melley argues that a short-lived brainwashing episode of the early Cold War shaped the "cultural imagery of the covert sphere" in an emblematic way. The CIA's obsession with brainwashing started with an unfounded belief that soldiers who chose to remain in North Korea at the end of the war must have been brainwashed to make such a choice, and that some of those returning could be domestic plants. *The Manchurian Candidate* (1962) film would seize on this conspiracy theory as a plot device. The CIA programs to thwart the imagined Korean operation soon turned into an attempt by the Agency to gain the ability to brainwash and to refine methods of torture used in interrogations. Melley writes, "Brainwashing began as an orientalist propaganda fiction created by the CIA to mobilize domestic support for a massive military build-up. This fiction proved so effective that elements of U.S. intelligence believed it and began a furious search for a real mind-control weapon."[43] That search was futile, but, it provided the model for "enhanced interrogation" that Trump, though he says he defers to the CIA's rejection of its use, would support reinstituting. Maintaining support for institutional conspiracy requires that the public be convinced of its necessity. This can be demonstrated to the public in a number of way, through popular culture, leaked reports, and dramatization in hearings and trials. The trial of Julius and Ethel Rosenberg provided such an opportunity, says Melley. Acknowledging that Julius almost surely did pass secrets to the Soviets, Melley nonetheless shows that the court proceedings against both Rosenbergs were a show trial in which evidence of secrets allegedly passed to the Soviets had the propaganda effect of demonstrating the need for and function of a covert sphere. What was most important about the atomic spying trials of the 1950s, he says, "was not their secret *content* (italics in the original), but their purported revelation of the covert sector itself. They offered the public a window into the shadow world of spies and government agents and government agents operating beneath the rational public sphere."[44] Though Melley eschews the concept, I contend that such a "shadow world" is emblematic of a Deep State.

Even the official histories or informed accounts of historians and analysts without an axe to grind against the CIA and other agencies reveal activities not only subject to moral and legal objections but also replete with plans and secret technological research that border on science fiction. Many of these activities were revealed by the post-Watergate Senate investigations (the Church Committee).[45] For a few years, less than a decade, the Committee's work produced increased restraint and congressional oversight. Temporarily, the Deep State became shallower. That state of affairs did not last long, beginning to disappear during the last years of the Carter administration with the decision in 1978 to support Mujahedeen fighters against the Soviet supported government in Afghanistan, and then it almost vanished in the Reagan years.

The Iran-Contra scandal generated congressional hearings but in retrospect, we can see that compared to the post-Watergate investigations, these had much less impact on the resurgent Deep State. Consider the career of Elliot Abrams, who was one of the key orchestrators of Iran-Contra and was convicted of withholding information from Congress about the affair. What he withheld was important information about one of the most notorious civilian massacres (El Mozote) by a US trained and armed Salvadoran military unit during the War in El Salvador. He also negotiated a $10 million contribution from the Sultan of Brunei to the Contras, who were actively engaged in terrorist activities against the Nicaraguan people.[46] As Assistant Secretary of State for InterAmerican Affairs, Abrams worked under William Casey, one of the veteran Cold Warriors of the CIA, who served as Reagan's campaign treasurer and his CIA director from 1981 until 1987. Despite his key role in one of the most notorious scandals and as a key shaper of US policies in Central America in the 1980s, Abrams went on to serve in the Bush (junior) administration, and today he is a senior fellow at the Council on Foreign Relations and serves on the Committee of Conscience of the US Holocaust Museum.[47] He has never expressed regret for his role.[48]

The attempt by Reagan officials to use the Federal Emergency Management Administration (FEMA), an agency vital to the capacity of the state to respond to catastrophes (natural or human-made), to suppress dissent illustrates the persistence of threats to liberal democratic norms posed by Deep State actors. The most visible human actor in this episode was Lieutenant Colonel Oliver North. North was joined by other administration hawks in a plot that seems more like an updated remake of Sinclair Lewis's 1935 novel *It Can't Happen Here*[49] than the serious, actual covert operation that its authors planned to carry out. But it was hardly fiction.

Reduced to its essentials, in 1984 North, while serving as the National Security Agency liaison to FEMA, drafted a plan to suspend the Constitution, impose martial law throughout the United States, put FEMA in control of the US government, and appoint military commanders to control the state and local governments. North's plan built upon plans that already existed in the blueprint for continuity of government (COG) in case of nuclear attack or a widespread national catastrophe.[50] North at that time was also coordinating the illegal, secret aid and training program for the Nicaraguan Contras. North and his colleagues hatched a plan to use expanded FEMA authority to roundup and detain protesters against American military intervention in Central America in agency camps. Anticipating that a direct American invasion in Central America could generate mass protests like those of the Vietnam War era, North wanted to be prepared. At the time he and his colleagues were also planning to have American troops invade the scarcely populated northeast corner of Nicaragua and place the Contra political leadership in control, then have the US recognize that group the legitimate government of Nicaragua.

Attorney General William French-Smith vetoed the plan, which had already been presented to President Reagan in the form of an Executive Order for him to sign—but not to reveal publicly until an actual emergency would be declared. Whether Reagan ever actually signed it is not clear. The operation was scuttled when Attorney General William French-Smith became alarmed and protested the plan to National Security Advisor Robert McFarland.

Days before North was to appear before the Senate Iran-Contra Committee, Knight-Ridder Newspapers carried an investigative report detailing the plan based on a secret draft report compiled by the Senate Committees chief council, Arthur Liman.[51] When North appeared, Congressman Jack Brooks (D-Texas) began to question the Lieutenant Colonel about the plan, but he was gaveled out of order by the chairman of the joint committee, Senator Daniel Inouye (D-Hawaii), who insisted that testimony on the matter could only be taken in closed session, justifying his action on grounds that "continuity of government" (see below) was a sensitive national security priority.[52] As a result, the Committee's Iran-Contra report, while highly informative and detailed in many respects, never touched upon what its chief counsel regarded as a highly sensitive matter—and the full plot, though reported in a few newspapers, remained deeply submerged.

Institutional checks, specifically, the action of the Attorney General, scuttled the North plan on Nicaragua, but one can question whether they would have worked had Edwin Meese, Smith's predecessor, who was involved in Central American planning and had a close relationship with General Efrain Rios Montt, Guatemala's fierce dictator, been still in office. It is questionable whether any institutional check would have responded effectively once US troops were on the ground in Central America. Protests, which at already involved hundreds of thousands of opponents of US Central America policy, would have mobilized at even greater levels, but the repression would have been exercised more ruthlessly as well.

Liman's report, according to the Knight-Ridder story, depicted North's Central America planning group as a "government within a government," effectively a rogue operation. However, as already noted, North directly reported to the National Security Advisor, and supporting the Contras was one of few policy matters (the other being "Star Wars" missile defense) that Ronald Reagan intensely cared about. His Vice President, former CIA director George H. W. Bush, was charged with special responsibility for Central America policy. In other words, the FEMA plan was an institutional conspiracy, not a rogue operation. Though it ultimately unraveled, this suppressed plan may be considered the most threatening conspiracy lending warrant to the theory presented here that the Deep State is a product of a national security culture and an institutional milieu ("sphere") that spawns conspiracies of this nature.

Given the nature of world nuclear armaments, increased threats of mass violence by non-state actors, and the scale of destruction and casualties that could occur from some plausible natural disasters (e.g., mass epidemics), the notion of planning for COG is rational. This is precisely why involving FEMA in surveillance and social control is not only threatening to democracy but also threatening to one of the very basic functions of government, dealing with calamities that require social and national solidarity. One well-documented confounding of FEMA's legitimate mandate with abuses of privacy and other rights was carried out in 1981, around the same time as the Iran-Contra operation, when FEMA and other government bureaucracies launched the secret Project 908. FEMA, the FBI and other agencies at all levels of government started systematically searching out facilities outside of anticipated blast zones in the event of war. Certainly, in this respect planning is prudent, but the program also, according to the journalist Garret Graff, included identifying possible counterintelligence and spying threats, assessing local immigrant populations, running background checks for possible criminal connections of owners of buildings and businesses, and investigating political affiliations.[53] All of this was done in an era before terrorism replaced Communism as the enemy, and in a period where the American propensity toward "know-nothingism" was in relative abeyance. We cannot know whether similar plans exist in some version today.

We can draw a contrast between how the investigation of Russian collusion has become so partisan with how the Congressional Committee investigating Iran-Contra of 1987 drew firm, bipartisan boundaries designed to wall off public debate about what should have been a very troublesome aspect of the affair, the COG/FEMA plans. This willingness can be attributed to a bipartisan effort to protect the presidency as an institution. In 1992, President Clinton seemed to have ended COG planning altogether, but what his executive order did was only to end planning for a nuclear attack. President Reagan, in two executive orders of November 18, 1988, had already expanding COG and FEMA planning for any emergency and assigned the FEMA director to advise the National Security Council on preparedness.[54] In fact, Donald Rumsfeld and Dick Cheney had continued to practice how COG would be implemented during the Reagan years and later as civilian CEOs of major corporations. On September 11, 2001 they put some of that practice into motion and implemented a number of measures still available to the president and the

Deep State today, including readying Executive Order 13,224, authorizing the president independent of the courts to take measures against "persons who commit, threat to commit, or support terrorism." Subsequent actions long before readied include putting together a legal team to implement more measure concentrating power in the executive branch and (led by John Yoo) a justification for torture ("enhanced interrogation").[55]

Coming little more than a decade after the Vietnam debacle and Watergate, and after seven years under Reagan of restoration of American capacity to intervene with open use of force overseas, (beginning with the invasion of Grenada in 1983 and continuing with deployment of American "trainers" in Central America), American elites were reluctant to fully expose the depth of the conspiracy conceived by North and company. Polarized partisanship is unlikely to spare the Trump presidency in this same way, but this is counterbalanced by the staunch partisan defense of Trump by Congressional Republicans.

The questions about COG should have arisen in another important government investigation, that of the special commission to examine the 9/11 attacks. Scott, who has not endorsed any version of Truther theory, has suggested that "...[Vice President] Dick Cheney responded to 9/11 by using devious means to install a small cabal of lawyers – most notoriously John Yoo – who proceeded conspiratorially in the next weeks to exclude their superiors, while secretly authorizing measures ranging from warrantless surveillance and detention to torture."[56] Cheney and Rumsfeld, Secretary of Defense, were colleagues going back to the Ford administration (1974–1976). Cheney was the ranking Republican Representative on the joint congressional Iran-Contra Committee, where he played an instrumental role in limiting the Committee's investigatory reach. He and Rumsfeld have been ardent exponents of strengthening the executive prerogatives of the presidency. Scott's article relies largely on the work of mainstream, respected investigative reporters and recently (2016) declassified files to make a strong circumstantial case that Cheney and Rumsfeld used 9/11 as a pretext for a declaration of emergency, now in its 18th year, having been extended by both Presidents Obama and (in September 2017) Trump.

We should not assume that the interests and motives of security agencies have remained unchanged since their founding. Specifically, the kind of cutthroat, feverish anti-communism of the first decades of the Cold War, which make plausible (but not fully warranted; see Chapter 2) suspicions about involvement of security agencies in the assassination of John F. Kennedy, does not necessarily define the global perspective of these agencies today. The collapse of the Berlin Wall and then the Soviet Union led to a shift for a decade away from spying to get the upper hand in geopolitical conflicts, as defined by the Cold War ideological rivalry, to intelligence to aid American business to compete in the new neoliberal global order that seemed to be taking root. The attacks on the Twin Towers and Pentagon on September 11, 2001, shifted priorities once again toward fighting an amorphous and war without end, baptized the "War on Terrorism." The work of intelligence agencies has also been impacted by new challenges posed by cyber communications technology and by the debacle of the neoconservative-engineered second-Iraq War.

Trump's use of executive power demonstrates how the failure of Congress to expose the North plan for martial law and abuse of FEMA authority during Iran-Contra may come back to haunt us. In reaction to Black Lives Matter protests and to protests aimed at blocking the controversial North Dakota Access Pipeline, Trump issued an Executive Order calling for a review of laws stiffening criminal penalties, not only for alleged violent incidents at protests but also for illegal action in general. More than 30 states by May 2017 had bills pending stiffening regulation of nonviolent protests. Advanced in the context of mass demonstrations against police killings of blacks and several deadly ambushes of police officers, these bills cast a broad net that in some cases would reverse the burden of proof in some criminal cases, virtually requiring defendants to produce surveillance video to demonstrate their innocence of charges of obstructing not only police, but also in some cases civilian federal employees.[57]

Probably few readers need to be convinced that in many ways the rhetoric and some of the policy positions of Trump, should they come to be fully implemented, represent a dramatic break from the worldview articulated in the War-Peace Studies represents. The inconsistences and vagaries of Trump's appointments and policies since the election portend not so much a break with American hegemonic pretensions so much as a confused and conflicted worldview. What is significant about Trumpism is not a clean break with internationalism so much as a threat to the domestic hegemony of American hegemonic leadership. It certainly represents a severe threat to the optimistic view of the post-Cold War world articulate by George H. W. Bush in 1991 in his speech heralding a New World Order—which subsequently and quickly, we should note, was appropriated as the moniker for revival and dissemination of conspiracy theories about United Nations black helicopter sightings and myths evocative of the Illuminati.

DONALD TRUMP AND THE DEEP STATE

What does all this mean for the claims by Donald Trump that the Deep State has attempted to scuttle his presidency? The Deep State is not, I have argued, a "conspirator," but an opaque sphere of politics where security agencies, the military, police, and (increasingly) actors to whom intelligence, military, and police functions have been privatized. To address the politics of the Deep State we must first ask in what ways Trump might threaten parts of the Deep State by his policies, rhetoric, decisions, and behavior, and how might the relevant Deep State actors respond. The fact that sectors of the Deep State might differ in this respect, as well as the opaque nature of politics in this sector, make the answers somewhat difficult to ascertain. Ultimately, any conspiracy theory must show more than motive; it must address evidence.

The Deep State sphere of politics has acquired more prominence in our politics, but its relationship to Donald Trump is considerably more complicated than it has been with any past president, possibly excepting Kennedy. The theme of a Deep State became a weapon of discourse for an administration that even before Trump inaugurated president. Without using the term directly at that time, the president-elect decided to go on the offensive against several national security institutions, including the FBI, the National Security Agency, and the CIA. Yet, throughout his campaign and presidency, Trump has draped his positions and policies in the mantle of hypernationalism and sought to significantly increase the autonomy of police and military. He has placed high military staff in positions, including Secretary of Defense, usually reserved for civilians. Trump has outsourced to theater commanders approval of both Special Forces operations and drone strikes in the territory of other sovereign countries to theatre commanders around the world. This autonomy may be something that military commanders resist returning in the future. At home, Trump regime encourages with its rhetoric alt-right groups that include some sectors with paramilitary tendencies.

Trump repeatedly called for investigations of leaks from the FBI and of alleged illegal surveillance by the National Security Agency, and on multiple occasions suggested that the Agency's finding of Russian interference in the election was fabricated to bring his legitimacy into question. Clearly, Trump has political motives to cast doubt on these agencies. Throughout 2017 and early into 2018, the headlines, when not generated by the words of the president himself, were dominated by leaks from sources in the White House but also from the security bureau-cracy and possibly investigators that are part of Special Counsel Robert Mueller's team. Trump's claims about leaks are not at all implausible—even acknowledging that many seem to have originated within the White House itself. Cristopher Wray, appointed FBI Director after Trump replaced Comey, reassigned the agency's top lawyer in a move that raised questions about leaks and about NSA surveillance.[58]

There is historical precedent for the security establishment to contrib-ute to the fall of a president. Members of the national security apparatus, most notably within the FBI, contributed to President Richard Nixon's fall by leaking information to the media about Watergate. In fact, Oliver Stone, who is most notorious among those who reject conspiracy theory for *JFK*, made a film, *Nixon* (1995), with a plotline in which Richard Helms, the Director of the CIA at the time, plays an instrumental role. Under threat of a lawsuit, the scene with Helms was withheld from the theatrical release, only to be reinstated in the subsequent video.

In the film, Nixon visits Helms, concerned that the CIA has main-tained files stemming from the politician's vice-presidency that would be politically embarrassing. The records have to do with Nixon's chairing the "special operations" group that oversaw some the Agency's most notorious projects, including efforts to overthrown Fidel Castro. In the film, Nixon wants Helms to gather up and deliver the files. Helms turns the tables, making it clear that Nixon's constitutional authority is no match for the most powerful figure in the Deep State, a man accus-tomed, despite his reputed skepticism about covert and paramilitary operations, to the exercise of authorized (under domestic, not interna-tional law) covert power. Helms had been involved in ruthless and vio-lent covert operations overseas in places like Vietnam, Guatemala, the Congo, Indonesia and myriad other bloody battlefields of the Cold War. Though there was no love lost between Helms and Nixon, this account, much like key scenes in *JFK*, consist mostly of Stone's attempting to fill gaps in the historical record with a Deep State conspiracy theory. In fact, the CIA directorship is a civil service; its director is not subject to removal by the president. Ultimately Helms did resign at the beginning of Nixon's second term, accepting an ambassadorship to Iran.

While Stone is an accomplished filmmaker, he is reviled in many cor-ners, accused of disregard for historical fact and tagged with the dreaded label, "conspiracy theorist." However, as Melley maintains in *The Covert State*, we largely rely upon fiction to depict the reality of the politics of national security. And there is nothing fictional about the questionable constitutionality of the power wielded by Helms and Nixon as the CIA and other agencies carried out covert operations in the Cold War. Besides Helm's involvement in overseas and destabilization operations abroad, it is noteworthy that under Helms directorship, according to reporting by the *New York Times* reporter Seymour Hersh in 1974, "[I]ntelligence files on at least 10,000 American citizens were maintained by a special unit of the C.I.A. that was reporting directly to Richard Helms, then the Director of Central Intelligence."[59]

There are indications that many career military and intelligence officers are deeply concerned about the Trump administration. Josh Campbell, a Special Agent in the FBI for ten years, wrote an op-ed column for the *New York Times* explaining that he was resigning, "So I can join the growing chorus of people who believe that the relentless attacks on the bureau undermine not just America's premier law enforcement agency but also the nation's security. My resignation is painful, but the alternative of remaining quiet while the bureau is tarnished for political gain is impossible."[60]

American security has been associated closely with the exercise of hegemony, and Trumpian populism and policies have shaken the consensus about these principles. Campbell's claim, however, is also that the bureau's reputation is being tarnished for "political gain." This refrain, leaving aside its truth or falsity, is a common complaint of security forces in countries where political corruption is especially rampant. Political corruption may not be as pervasive in the US as in countries where episodes of military rule occur frequently. But the public dissension of some retired American security officials is a sign of divisions and discontent characteristic of countries undergoing decay of civilian control of the military and democratic political institutions.[61]

This chapter neither argue that the Deep State killed John F. Kennedy, nor does it find persuasive Truther theories about Bush administration involvement in the 9/11 attacks. They are certainly not "warranted" in the sense of having the credibility of Watergate conspiracy theories. However, I do agree with Scott, probably the prominent exponent of the claim that the United States has a Deep State, when he argues that recurrent scandals in American politics since World War II point to patterns of "parapolitics" carried out by agencies that operate activities undercover, engaging in institutional conspiracies and abuses of power that commissions investigating them and the representative organs of Congress are unwilling or unable to fully bring to light.[62] What serves us best is to research, as Scott advocated on the eve of the 2016 election, "the politics of 911, Iran-Contra, the assassinations and duplicity of the Vietnam War era, and other large-scale Washington scandals."[63] The polarization of US politics Trump is likely to make that even harder to achieve regarding Russiagate and Spygate alike.

Transparency in all security matters may be an illusory ideal. Confidentiality and secrecy are justifiable in the face of actual threats to security, with respect to individual privacy, and in order to facilitate negotiations and in diplomacy. However, virtually every major scandal in American politics since World War II has had a connection to the institutions associated with the Deep State. McCarthyism was enabled by the uncommon power and political autonomy of FBI Director J. Edgar Hoover. McCarthy's chief counsel, Roy Cohn, served as Federal Prosecutor in New York, and played an instrumental role in Trump's rise to national celebrity. The Watergate burglars were a team called the "White House Plumbers," formed to "plug leaks" from inside the Nixon administration and included CIA veterans E. Howard Hunt and G. Gordon Liddy. The Iran-Contra operation, including the transfer of receipts from arms sales to the Nicaraguan contras, was coordinated out of the National Security Administration as a way of evading Congressional restrictions of funding for the insurgents, who used terrorist tactics in their war against the Sandinistas.

Although Scott's work has attracted considerable notoriety for the questions it has raised about the Kennedy assassination, his questioning of the handling anomalies and suspicions about 9/11, Watergate, and Iran-Contra have contributed to bringing out of the shadows the way that US military and intelligence agencies (and increasingly, privatized security services) have worked closely with counterpart agencies and forces abroad that severely violate human rights, engage in paramilitary activities, and are entangled with various forms of trafficking and the underground economy. Referring to the likely involvement of Pakistan's Inter-Services Intelligence (ISI) with militants connected to the 9/11 attacks, Scott writes,

> [T]mystery of 9/11 must be unraveled at a deeper level, the ongoing groups inside and outside governments, in both Pakistan and America, which have continued to use groups like al Qaeda and individuals like Ahmad [referring to ISI chief, Lieutenant-General Mahmoud Ahmad], for

their own policy purposes...The ongoing collaboration of the ISI and CIA in promoting terrorist violence has created a complex conspiratorial milieu, in which governments now have a huge stake in preventing the emergence of truth.[64]

Going to a "deeper level" requires us to delve more deeply into the origins of the national security state, and also to ask why the serial scandals involving its institutions usually seem to disappear from our collective historical memory. It also is the kind of research that is subject to discipline by the regime of truth, and it will be as long as terming secretive collaboration among elites is treated as taboo.

Many of Trump's most passionate opponents hold the theory that he owes his occupancy of the presidential office to collusion between his campaign and Russian operatives acting under direction of President Vladimir Putin. Trump's ability to avoid removal from office by Congress may ultimately depend upon him and his media allies' attempts to discredit an investigation of his campaign's collusion with Russians seeking to influence the election. To accomplish this goal, Trump supporters responded with their own conspiracy theory, arguing that the collusion story has been hyped by the mainstream "fake" media and fed by leaks from a "Deep State" of Washington bureaucrats and national security agencies.

On March 9, 2017, Sean Hannity, the *Fox News* commentator and staunch Trump supporter, called for Trump to remove Obama era holdovers more rapidly from the federal bureaus. The *Fox* headline for his editorial read, "Opinion: Trump must purge deep-state bureaucrats now." The next day, the administration dismissed 46 federal prosecutors appointed by President Obama. The replacement of federal prosecutors by a new president is not itself unusual, but calling for a "purge" of all holdovers of the previous administration from the federal government certainly is. One would have to go back to the McCarthy era to find right-wing media referring to career civil servants as political "saboteurs," as Hannity does. Perhaps not coincidentally, one of the fired prosecutors, New York's Preet Bharara, had been asked by watchdogs from the federal bureaucracy to investigate Trump for allegedly violating the emoluments clause of the Constitution.

On June 6, 2017, Trump used a tweet to promote Hannity's evening show referring to leaks to the *Washington Post* as the work of the Deep State. Trump's son, Donald Trump Jr., tweeted on July 7, 2017, "If there was ever confirmation that the Deep State is real, & endangers national security, it's this. Their interests above all else [sic]," said Trump Jr., referring to an article in the right-wing Free Beacon claiming that leaks were happening on a daily basis.[65] Throughout Trump's first year in the presidency his supporters used the megaphone of *Breitbart News, Fox News*, and other right-wing outlets, including Alex Jones' notoriously conspiratorial *Infowars*, to accuse the intelligence community of conspiring to remove Donald Trump from the presidency through selective leaks of damaging allegations about his campaign's collusion with the Russian government to influence the 2016 election.

The response campaign was set in motion by *Breitbart News* when it published a warning of trouble four days before the members of the Electoral College were to vote. Entitled "The Deep State vs. Donald Trump" and written by "Virgil," widely believed to be Steve Steve Bannon's pen name, the editorial contended that the Democratic Party, the mainstream media, and "affluent residents of the Washington swamp" were "operating behind the scenes" to block, or at least delegitimize and "cripple" Trump's presidency. The article warned readers that the CIA had twisted and exaggerated evidence to promote the theory that Russia's Vladimir Putin had his "hand of the scale." Virgil alleged that the agency had been coopted by "liberal apparatchiks" implanted during the Obama years; establishment Republicans, said the opinion piece, had joined them in opposition to the President.[66]

As argued in Chapters 2 and 4, an assessment of this conspiracy theory does not require an absolute rejection or acceptance. Given the disruptive nature of the Trump presidency—putting neoliberal globalization into question, breaking alliances, directly attacking the institutions of the national security state, motive exists for the Deep State to want Trump removed. He would, after all, be replaced by a vice president that has a warm relationship with the Dark Money lords (see Chapter 6) and economic elites in general. Motives to undermine Trump exist not only among career civil servants in domestic agencies but also for at least a significant part of those serving in the military and intelligence bureaucracy and the foreign diplomatic corps.

A clue to the levels of concern among foreign policy elites about Trump can be found in the comments of Republican Senator Bob Corker, chair of the Senate Armed Service Committee. Corker said that most Republican senators realized that Trump was a threat to the general world order. Referring to Trump's "volatility," Corker said, "[They] understand the volatility that we're dealing with and the tremendous amount of work that it takes by people around him to keep him in the middle of the road," adding, "As long as there are people like that around him who are able to talk him down when he gets spun up, you know, calm him down and continue to work with him before a decision gets made, I think we'll be fine."[67] *Breitbart News* interpreted Corker's remarks as indicating that "that most Republican senators realized that Trump was a threat to the general world order."[68] The *New York Times* report on Corker's concern did not refer to a "general world order," but did say that Corker, who had announced his retirement from the Senate, felt most of his colleagues agree with his words. According to the *Times,* "Mr. Corker, speaking carefully and purposefully, seemed to almost find cathartic satisfaction by portraying Mr. Trump in terms that most senior Republicans use only in private."[69]

Many liberals and Democrats seem to have accepted, if not welcomed, the advance of military influence into key roles within the White House, especially the role assumed by John Kelly, the White House Chief of Staff who took control of access to Oval Office. The alternative, were Kelly to leave, would be greater influence by the radical, alt-right in Trump's inner circle, especially that of presidential counsel Stephen Miller. Miller along with Bannon once boasted that *Breitbart.com* was a platform of the alt-right. Miller is largely responsible for formulating Trump's anti-immigration policies, including separation of children of detained families from their parents, defending the policies in thinly veiled white nationalist rhetoric.

Polarized politics and decay of constitutional norms generate legitimate moral issues for conscientious military officers. Air Force General John Hyten, commander of the US Strategic Command, has said that he would disobey an illegal presidential order to launch a nuclear strike.[70] Remaining unanswered is, just who determines what is "illegal"? Do we think that military officers, or for that matter thoughtful enlisted soldiers, have not considered these issues? Recall that in during the Watergate scandal, Secretary of Defense James Schlesinger notified key commanders only to obey orders given within the chain of command because he anticipated that President Richard Nixon, constitutionally commander-in-chief, might give a direct order to deploy troops to prevent his removal from the White House. The liberal *Daily Beast* recalled Schlesinger's precautions, calling it "the most patriotic act of treason in American history."[71]

So far, we have concentrated on ways that Trumpism conflicts with the interests of Deep State actors, but there are sectors of the Deep State whose interests are in alignment with the administration. Particularly well-placed vis-vis Trump are corporations that have benefitted from privatization of certain aspects of military operations and the criminal justice system. The "security" functions of the state have increasingly been hived off to the private sector in the era of neoliberalism. This privatization has added an additional reason to heed Eisenhower's warning about in his farewell speech about military–industrial complex, which largely referred to arms manufacturers.[72] Now private capitalism is investing in actually engaging in combat and intelligence activities, using Washington's infamous "revolving door" between the bureaucracy and corporations extends to advance this objective. The latter has close ties with members of Trump's cabinet who are strong advocates of deregulation and privatization in general.

According to investigative journalists Matthew Cole and Jeremy Scahill, Erik Prince, a former Navy Seal who co-founded the Blackwater USA private security corporation, and John Macguire, with assistance from Oliver North (of Iran-Contra fame), in December 2017 proposed to Trump campaign officials setting up a "global, private spy network that would circumvent official U.S. intelligence agencies." These agencies would counter what Prince and Macguire see as "Deep State" enemies engaged in undermining the new administration.[73] Blackwater's mercenary forces and other activities perfectly fit the concepts of paramilitary and parapolitics. Blackwater attained notoriety in September 2007 after a reported 20 Iraqi civilians died in a shootout involving company guards escorting State Department employees.[74] In August 2017, Prince had already proposed that American troops, excepting a few Special Forces personnel, be replaced by a private army of 5500 private contractors, backed by a 90 aircraft.[75]

Prince's sister, Betsy DeVos, is Secretary of Education and a strong proponent of privatizing public education. Prince donated $250,000 to the Trump campaign through a Dark Money conduit headed by Rebekah Mercer. He is an ally of Steve Bannon, who, though banished from the White House, should not be given his political funeral prematurely given the mercurial nature of Trump's personality. Jared Kushner, Trump's son-in-law, has developed an alliance with Prince in promoting contracting out military functions. A *Washington Post* story on the Prince-Trump campaign connection highlights the role played by the United Arab Emirates in attempting to facilitate Prince's access to the

Trump White House, including meetings taking place in New York and in the Seychelles Islands.[76]

Prince's relationship with Jared Kushner, Trump's son-in-law, has attracted critical attention in the mainstream media, but it is not all that new. According to Steven Simon, who was a National Security Council senior director for the Middle East and North Africa in the Obama administration, "The idea of using business cutouts, or individuals perceived to be close to political leaders, as a tool of diplomacy is as old as the hills. These unofficial channels are desirable precisely because they are deniable; ideas can be tested without the risk of failure." Were this meeting simply about the back-channel attempt to foster better relations between two nuclear powers, they could be considered, as Simon indicates, a justifiable, confidential effort at diplomacy. But in this case, the coordination has more to do with the efforts by Prince's Blackwater and other large companies that offer private military forces (PMFs) to expand their role (and profits) in the private security business.

Prince's efforts can be considered as a step toward the transnationalization of Deep State politics. If he can succeed, other PMFs, who already provide significant military and intelligence services (such as Dyncorps, Booz Allen Hamilton, among others), may grow even more rapidly than they have since the 1990s, when they first began to take over support services previously handled within the military. PMFs recruit heavily from Special Forces services around the globe. Their emergence was facilitated by the widespread availability of second generation but nonetheless highly lethal military equipment and ordnance after the collapse of the Soviet Bloc states and the apartheid regime in South Africa.[77]

The departure of Bannon from Trump's favor in early 2018 may have slowed the transfer of military functions to private paramilitary organizations. Also, the generals serving in Trump's inner circle seem intent on resisting the expansion of PMFs in combat roles. But PMF's are likely to become more, not less attractive to American politicians worried about eventually being held accountable by voters for an endless "War on Terrorism", much of it in remote corners of the globe. Consider the powerful rational Prince laid out his proposals in a *New York Times* op-ed piece, one that offers a truly Faustian bargain to politicians keen on avoiding taxation and unpopular casualties in Afghanistan.

> My proposal is for a sustainable footprint of 2000 American Special Operations and support personnel, as well as a contractor force of less than

6000 (far less than the 26,000 in country now). This team would provide a support structure for the Afghans, allowing the United States' conventional forces to return home...

Prince claimed his company would save American taxpayers $40 billion. He concluded,

> Just as no one criticizes Elon Musk because his company SpaceX helps supply American astronauts, no one should criticize a private company—mine or anyone else's—for helping us end this ugly multigenerational war.[78]

Some obvious moral hazards should come to mind. The profitability of PMFs ultimately hinges on the continued prosecution of such a war, not necessarily winning it. As some degree of sovereignty will remain in the hands of nation-states, these companies' continued presence will necessarily engage them in deep diplomacy over their continued presence. And as international alliances shift, will PMFs find themselves at some time fighting one another? Will their clients want to deploy these transnational private armies against US troops in some future conflict? The transnational PMFs ultimately could bring the mercenary warfare of Renaissance Machiavelli's Italy, an era rife with conspiratorial politics, on the global stage that hosts warfare in the twenty-first century.

While many in the military high command may resist privatization of warfare, meeting the personnel and bugetary demands of global warfare may ultimately sway them. General Raymond A. Thomas, commander of the US Special Operations Command, testified in May 2017 at a House Armed Services subcommittee meeting that the pace of deployment of his forces around the globe was "unsustainable." He testified that 8000 Special Ops troops are deployed in 80 different countries.[79] Altogether, the total number of Special Forces troops ranges between 70,000 and 100,000, though there are support personnel and less elite (in terms of combat training) included. These trends threaten to further undermine the constitutional principle of presidential responsibility and accountability for authorization of war-making and rules of engagement.[80]

Military and intelligence functions are being increasingly integrated with one another. Under CIA Director Mike Pompeo, the CIA significantly boosted its involvement in counterterrorist operations, especially in Pakistan, where its clandestine status means that it can undertake missions that would be politically awkward for regular military troops.[81] Pompeo's move to Secretary of Defense puts him in a position to counter the unease of the armed forces with this merging of functions. The tendency to more deeply involve the agency directly in operations rather than only intelligence assistance to military forces is not entirely without precedent. A most notorious prior example was Operation Phoenix, involving the forcible resettlement of Vietnamese peasants into strategic hamlets in order to "drain the water" to kill the fish (National Liberation Front insurgents), in which both the CIA and special operations forces participated. The program included interrogations, torture, and assassinations. Estimates of deaths ranged from 21,000 to 40,000 people, including many civilians caught up in the same net with NLF forces.[82]

In addition to deployments of Special Ops teams and intelligence combat units to Africa, the Middle East, and Central Asia, these elite forces have been deployed in the so-called "anti-drug wars" in various geographical theaters. I say "so-called" because these operations often take place in countries where the United States has geopolitical or economic interests, what Dawn Paley calls "Drug War Capitalism."[83] In Mexico and Central America, the United States has trained thousands of agents and assisted in wiretapping, interrogation, and cultivating informants, without much success in reducing trafficking, and with mounting violence in which government forces are complicit. Drug Enforcement Agents have been implicated in serious human rights violations, including the massacre of civilians in Honduras. In Colombia, forces trained for anti-drug operations were also involved in anti-insurgency operations with forces that operated as death squads. The US Department of Justice has suppressed efforts to bring some of those responsible for mass murders to justice.[84]

Repeatedly, from the earliest days of cooperation with the Italian Mafia and of operations to ease the immigration of tainted German scientists, continuing through the Vietnam War period with cooperation with drug runners in South East Asia, through the Reagan years with funding and arming the Contras and other unsavory allies in Latin America, and today with reliance on warlords in Central Asia, American law enforcement, intelligence, and special operation forces have engaged in relationships with allies complicit in trafficking and gross human rights violations. These alliances are made as part of "low intensity conflicts" that take their toll in lives abroad, but they also reinforce an "ends justify the means" mentality that can blowback into domestic operations and encourage the militarization of domestic law enforcement. Paramilitary and parapolitical operations are often protected by secrecy and subterfuge, but just as often they are hidden in plain sight. Melley's work on the depiction of the covert sphere elucidates how this happens.

CONSPIRACY FICTION, CONSPIRACY REALITY

Given that part of the mandate of the CIA is to carry out covert operations, we should hardly be surprised that the ways its employees and high-level officials operate in a conspiratorial culture are very well depicted in the novels of former spies, such as John le Carre and Ben Macintyre. Referring to le Carre, critic Sarah Lyall recently commented,

> Early in his writing, le Carré introduced the subversive hypothesis that the spies of East and West were two sides of the same tarnished coin, each as bad as the other. It was a stunning idea, espionage painted not in black and white but in shades of gray…His later books are angrier, more polemical, their worldview darker, reflecting the chaotic morality of the post-Soviet era and often presenting the United States — with its exceptionalism, its flouting of international norms, as he sees it — as the villain in the post-Cold War era.[85]

Regarding Trump's dismissal of the dossier put together by former British spy Christopher Steele alleging that Vladimir Putin has blackmail information on Trump (see Chapter 2), Macintyre, a former British operative, commented, "I can tell you what the veterans of the S.I.S. [the British Secret Intelligence Service, or MI6] think, which is yes, *kompromat* was done on him. Of course, *kompromat* is done on everyone. So they end up, the theory goes, with this compromising bit of material and then they begin to release parts of it. They set up an ex-MI6 guy, Chris Steele, who is a patsy, effectively, and they feed him some stuff that's true, and some stuff that isn't true, and some stuff that is demonstrably wrong. Which means that Trump can then stand up and deny it, while knowing that the essence of it is true. And then he has a stone in his shoe for the rest of his administration."[86]

Playing with truth is endemic in the Deep State, especially when it comes to maintaining the fiction that there nothing imperialistic in US covert operations. Melley maintains that "the ideological disavowal of imperialism was dramatically assisted by the segregation of state policy into overt and covert sectors."[87] The institutionalization of deniability for government actors encourages a culture where "I don't know, and don't really want to know" prevails. "Geographical melodrama" in popular fiction helps promote this bifurcation of the overt and the covert. It serves the function of portraying, often with considerable accuracy, the dirty nature of warfare but ultimately justifies this bending of rules or worse, including thuggish threats and torture, as a necessary adaptation to a threatening international environment, rarely examining underlying roots of terrorism. "The dirty work of empire disappears," says Melley, and American exceptionalism persists as a widespread civic belief. Covert war, not so different from the Cold War, defends "freedom", and our warriors abroad are the heroes who risk their lives for our "way of life," the envy of all other nations under the umbrella of the Pax Americana.

Popular fiction does not so much make the "Deep State" invisible as wipe popular memory clean of the stain of scandal, extra-constitutional parapolitics and the seamy side of American foreign intervention. Melley highlights popular films and TV programs as having set the trend for adapting the covert sphere of politics to the post-Cold War era. *Sum of All Fears* (2002), *The Siege* (1998), and *Enemy of the State* (1998) are typical of the genre in which an act of terrorism or threat of such an attack brings a response from the state that is also personally threatening to an American hero who, at least at the start, fights a typically lonely fight against the enemy. Only later does the hero see that corrupt forces in the state bureaucracy or an out-of-control national security official have actually been the ones to provoke the terrorist plot in the first place. In the Jason Bourne series (films starring Matt Damon, based on Robert Ludlum's novels), our hero, an assassin who has had his memory cleansed by the CIA, must battle the bad guys *and* the Agency, defeating both.

In *The Bourne Identity*, the first in the series, Bourne finds he was sent to kill an African dictator, a very bad man to be sure, but he does not complete the act because the man's wife and children would have also been killed—an allegory to the myth that Americans do all possible to avoid collateral damage in warfare. What has to be done is done, but the basic goodness of the American soul prevails. The myth of American exceptionalism—our country retains its liberal values—is reinforced, and at the same time the threats of an evil world are real and justify responses inconsistent with those values.

Zero Dark 30, released in 2012, one year after Navy Seal Team 6 assassinated Osama Bin Laden, features Jessica Chastain as a CIA analyst on the trail of Bin Laden. Her character, Maya, based on an actual female operative who identified Bin Laden's presence at the location where the raid took place, is portrayed as reticent to employ torture. The brutality of the war on terror teaches her the importance of doing what needs to be done, including enhanced interrogation, i.e., torture, to succeed in locating the man who publicly professed to have organized the 9/11 attacks. The film concludes with Navy Seal Team 6 carrying out its operation to kill Bin Laden. The Team kills only in self-defense in the raid, and the film ends with Maya softly crying as she leaves. Is it for the loss of innocence? Her own and America's?

Much of the film is based on fact, including realistic scenes of torture and battles. The main character's actual career is misrepresented, however. Jane Mayer (the author of *Dark Money*) among others found that the real CIA operative involved was not new to her work, as portrayed in film; she participated in intelligence blunders that contributed to failures to anticipate the 9/11 attacks. She "gleefully" participated in torture sessions and misled Congress about the use of torture in interrogations.[88] And is not at all clear that the Seal Team's killing was only done in self-defense. The filmmakers certainly did not sanitize torture, but they certainly reinforced the humanity of the film's protagonists who engaged in torture and extreme violence, especially with the final scene. Both the CIA and Defense Department cooperated with the filmmakers.

The two most influential, long-running television series of this type are *Homeland* and *24*. Homeland began in 2011 and entered its seventh season in 2018; *24*, starred Jack Sutherland as Jack Bauer, leader of a counterterrorism unit. Both programs feature the "ticking bomb" plot device, the race against time to prevent a terrorist attack. Both portray national security agencies in a far less than flattering light, but as with *Zero-Dark 30*, the protagonists' and agencies flaws' are set against a do-what-is necessary background. Amnesty International has harshly criticized both programs for justifying torture.[89] Something similar is portrayed in the screenplay for *Red Sparrow*, a 2018 film starring Jennifer Lawrence, which reprised the early years of the Cold War and was written by a retired CIA agent with more than three decades of service. Brutality is evident on both sides, but that's the point. It's a dirty world and it has to be fought with the dirty means. The Cold War theme that fighting dirty wars to stop the Communist "menace" resonates similarly in fictional depictions of way the "war on terrorism" is conducted.

That terrorism may at least in part have emerged from the kind of world built by Western imperialism and presided over by the United States since World War II is hardly explored at all in these fictional plots. The impact of drone attacks, past interventions abroad, Tomahawk missiles, "enhanced interrogations," rarely appears, and usually only as background, except in a few instances (e.g., *Three Kings*, 1999, set in the Iraq War comes to mind). Films, such as the oeuvre of Costa Gavras (*Z, State of Siege, Missing*, others), that explore more troubling themes usually are relegated to the Art House circuit.

In places where the US footprint has been heavy, we ought not to be surprised that conspiracy theories about the United States tend to proliferate. Examining Pakistani conspiracy theories about Blackwater, Humeira Iqtidar, a lecturer in politics at King's College, London, notes that the US response to these theories usually attributes their rise to ignorance of the locals and their failure to appreciate their own responsibility to deal with terrorist cells on their own territory. American officials, including Hillary Clinton when she was Secretary of State, called on Pakistanis to cease blaming their problems on the United States, for their own good. Coupled with an admission of US lapses in protecting civilian in some cases serves to signal to the audience, says Iqtidar, "a maturity on the part of the U.S. that Pakistan has yet to achieve."[90]

Taking note of two stories that ran on consecutive day in May 2010 in the *New York Times*, the first claiming, "Conspiracy is a national sport in Pakistan," and the second reporting that General Petraeus, military commander at the time, had ordered a "broad expansion" of secret operations throughout the Middle East, Central Asia, and the Horn of Africa against al-Qa'eda, Iqtodar commented, "The sense of humor that allows such reporting on consecutive days is surely one that is developed in a space free of daily threats, actual occurrences of bombings and American-sponsored 'disappearances' of young men."[91] A similar ironic critique might be made of reports highlighting conspiracy theories that circulate in Iran. Many of these beliefs are outright anti-Semitic, but not all of them are. Either way, they are nurtured by the very real history of intervention and unsavory activities of the United States and Israel. For example, the Israeli Mossad has been linked to the murders of five Iranian scientists working on the country's nuclear program, an operation all but confirmed by Israel's own Defense Minister.[92] Similar themes characterize American views of drug trafficking and violence in Mexico. Plot lines in several recent films and TV shows feature violent conflicts in Mexico. While they often include corrupt American's in league with trafficking, they contribute to Trump's stereotyping of Mexicans as rapists and criminals.

In 2017, three new TV programs featuring themes forgiving of moral hazzards facing American warriors debuted with plots and characters drawn from Special Forces. *NBC* touted *The Brave* as a "fresh, heart-pounding journey into the complex world of America's elite undercover military heroes" as each week another "ticking bomb plot" plays out. The casting carefully includes two actresses with South Asian surnames, and plots include operations being aided by "the world's most advanced surveillance technology from headquarters in D.C."[93] *Valor*, produced by *CBS* and Warner Brothers and aired on the *CW Network*, is based on the real-life 160th Special Operations Aviation Regiment (Airborne)—once again an opportunity to elide fiction and reality. Both these shows struggled for renewal, but not so the third program, *Seal Team*, produced by *CBS*.

Seal Team, as *CBS* touts it, "follows the professional and personal lives of the most elite unit of Navy SEALs as they train, plan, and execute the most dangerous, high stakes missions our country can ask of them. Jason Hayes is the respected, intense leader of the Tier One team whose home life has suffered as a result of his extensive warrior's existence."[94] This tension felt by military families is portrayed realistically, though, as Melley would point out, ultimately such plot devices serve to reinforce the domesticity of the home front, stressing the need for Americans to show appreciation for "heroes" and their families, who are protecting us all at enormous costs. *Valor* does this especially well by including a character who has had to overcome opioid addiction because of wounds. As in other films and TV program just discussed, *Seal Team* depicts intelligence operatives working closely with the highly trained combat units. The combat is depicted very realistically, not to horrify but to reassure the audience that it is unavoidable.

Despite the brutality and even cynicism of some programs, none of the TV programs about Special Forces depict other troubling parts of the record of special ops, such as unpunished involvement in unjustified violence and collateral damage to civilians, including the troubling record of *Seal Team 6* itself, i.e., the unit that carried out the Bin Laden raid. The Team's "quiet killings and blurred lines" were revealed in an extensive, in-depth investigation by a team of *New York Times* reporters, who concluded that special operations force "has been converted into a global manhunting machine with limited outside oversight."[95] The *Times* reporters documented lack of civilian oversight; failures to adequately investigate reports of civilian casualties, even when reported by European allies; front companies set up to arm proxy forces. US officials justify the use of Seals and other such operatives because they can be deployed into undeclared war zones, about which a retired admiral admitted, "you certainly don't want that out in public."

A surge in use of Special Forces was ordered by Obama in 2006, and their daily raids resulted in 10 to 25 deaths per night. One Seal Team

6 former officer commented, "These killing fests had become routine." Although team members are supposed to maintain a code of silence, and many closely adhere to it, others have told stories, including providing accounts of the bin Laden raid. "The Team 6 members routinely performed their missions at night, making life-or-death decisions in dark rooms with few witnesses and beyond the view of a camera. Operators would use weapons with suppressors to quietly kill enemies as the slept," according to the *Times* report. Not surprisingly local populations often give different accounts of civilian casualties in such conflicts.

The films and TV programs we have reviewed all began their runs or production before Donald Trump assumed the presidency. But their depiction of Muslims as the enemy, lack of context, and adaption of Cold War memes to the war on terrorism helped prepare the turf of Trump's anti-Muslim policies, his stereotyping of Muslim and other Third World nations, and the militarist attitudes evident at his rallies. And these memes are also now common in movies and television programs that depict domestic crime and police pursuit of criminals, often tied to the "ticking clock" plot device. Television programs are rife with such tropes, especially police procedurals, such as the various *NCIS* (which stands for Naval Crime Investigation Service) shows. They often depict anti-trafficking efforts or involve these specialized anti-crime forces in efforts to protect Third World officials visiting or living in the United States and threatened by nefarious forces from their home government. Sometimes the plots depict bureaucratic or corrupt politicians throwing obstacles in the path of the cops, justifying their bending of rules.

NCIS is one of the few shows that sometimes beats professional football in ratings. The plots are driven by the primal need to attract an audience that can be sold to advertisers, but this comes at the expense of distorting the reality of law and order in America. A summary of research on crime procedurals and reality finds that (among other distortions) these programs magnify the crime rate in urban areas; they exaggerate the percentage of suspects of crimes that are people of color and also the reliability of forensic proof; and they underplay civil rights violations.[96] This distorted image of urban America and the nature of crime, we should note, closely resembles the distorted picture of crime and its threat to white Americans that Trump traded-on in his campaign.

The long-running *NCIS* began as a procedural based in Washington D.C. The show and its various spinoffs rapidly became more violent and more focused on plot lines emphasizing big city corruption. This meme is especially strong in *CSI NCIS New Orleans*. For example, Episode 24 in Season 2 featured a plotline where the "NCIS team uncovers a mole in the ranks while working with the Department of Homeland Security to locate 900 missing pounds of explosives that pose an imminent threat to New Orleans."[97] The teams' work is made more difficult by corruption in the city administration, up to the mayor himself. In the end, the "ticking bomb" plot shows that our heroes are working against bureaucratic obstructionism, in the form of too much concern about the team violating rules.

One way that the nature of the war on terrorism blows back into American civil society is through the employment of returning military officers in police occupations. For the individuals involved, this transition requires a transition from a "warrior culture" to a "guardian" role.[98] At the same time, police forces have become significantly militarized in respect to the kinds of equipment they utilize, including the war-grade vehicles and artillery, and to the common use of paramilitary SWAT teams, especially in difficult urban situations and in confrontations with right-wing paramilitary situations. No fully reliable data on how many veterans hold police jobs exists, but a recent study jointly conducted by the Marshall Project (a nonpartisan, nonprofit collective of news organizations that researches law enforcement issues) and *USA Today* estimated approximately one in five police today are recruited from the ranks of military veterans. That study claims that while many police benefit from military experience and adapt well to their new challenge.

The Marshall study concludes that "...data from two major-city law enforcement agencies, and considerable anecdotal evidence, tentatively concluded (pending more research) that veterans are more likely to get physical, and some police executives agree." The study also raises another caution very salient to the theory of a Deep State and to parapolitics. It warns that "...any large-scale comparison of the use of force by vets and non-vets is hampered by a chronic lack of reliable official record-keeping on issues of police violence." The alarming question here is, why is there so little record-keeping on police violence, whether that of former soldiers or other police?

Despite limitations, the Marshall study felt that three findings more clearly emerged: (1) Veterans in police forces are "more vulnerable to self-destructive behavior — alcohol abuse, drugs and, like William Thomas, attempted suicide." (2) "Little or no mental health screening" or treatment opportunities exist for veterans returning from military employment, something the study attributes, among other factors, to "a culture of machismo and a number of legal restraints." (3) White veterans tend to benefit more from hiring preferences, contributing to forces less likely to reflect the demographic profile of their communities.

As with media depictions of special ops teams, the militarization of police has become a theme in much the same way. Some relatively new TV programs depict America's urban landscape not so differently than Trump did in his campaign, as free fire zones of death and destruction. S.W.A.T is a carnage filled drama in which cops fight crime and race againt the clock in "ticking time bomb" plots, dressed in military gear that might make you think Los Angeles, where it is set, is actually Baghdad. *Training Day* (*CBS*) and *A.P.B.* (*Fox*) feature rogue cops who will resort to torture, teaching younger, more naïve partners that the times and circumstances require breaking rules. Bureaucrats and corrupt officials need to get out of the way of guardians of order.[99] In real life, some urban police forces have engaged in much worse military-style practices that these programs never depict. For example, in 2015 (during the Obama administration, we should note) reporters in Chicago discovered that over 7000 inmates, 6000 of whom were black, were detained, mostly on suspicion of narcotics, and interrogated virtually incommunicado, without access to lawyers in a warehouse complex in Homan Square. The Chicago police justified the center, which drew comparisons to Guantanamo, as a necessary measure to protect the identity of undercover officers.[100]

Reviewing a book that detailed the many bungled operations carried out by the CIA since its inception, Evans Thomas, an editor at *Newsweek*, concluded, "Is an open democracy capable of building and sustaining an effective secret intelligence service? Maybe not. But with Islamic terrorists vowing to set off a nuclear device in an American city, there isn't much choice but to keep on trying." No better quote summarizes how conspiracy fiction serves the interest of a state-sanctioned manufacturer of conspiracies.

PARAPOLITICS AND BLOWBACK

The ascendancy of Trump to the presidency came at a time when surveillance, cybersecurity, use of new technologies (such as drones), reliance on special forces, use of torture under the euphemism "enhanced interrogation", cybersecurity, police violence all were converging together as serious issues. Each of them involves actors and issues that play out as much in the grey parapolitical sphere as in the public sphere of politics. On the one hand, Trump, who had endorsed waterboarding on the campaign trail, chose James Mathis, an opponent of "enhanced interrogation," as his Secretary of Defense. However, Trump also appointed several officials who were connected directly or indirectly to the Bush administration's employment of rendition and "enhanced interrogation." Gina Haspel appointed as deputy director of the CIA, ran a "black site" prison in Thailand where waterboarding was employed destroyed film evidence of the practice.[101] In May 2018 Haspel rose to the position of Director of the Agency. Steven Engel, appointed to lead the Justice Department's Office of Legal Counsel, was among those who reviewed the Bush administration 2007 memo framed to legalize waterboarding.[102]

Edward Snowden's release in 2013 of a massive cache of classified files from the National Security Agency's program of gathering communications between American citizens and foreigners brought into public scrutiny one way that parapolitics is infecting the domestic political game. It is notable that the actual work of surveillance was largely done by Snowden's employer, Booz Allen Hamilton, a large contractor for defense and intelligence.[103] The debate over the propriety of Snowden's actions and the NSA's role in monitoring US citizens has distracted us from the way that this program obscured further the line between public and private government, just as it has been by the deployment of private mercenaries for military purposes. Furthermore, the surveillance program was not a national operation but a transnational one. It was begun with agreements among the United Kingdom, Canada, Australia, and New Zealand to create a global system, code named ECHELON, aimed mainly at the Communist bloc during the Cold War but took on a role of conducting economic espionage in the 1990s, during the period between the collapse of the Soviet bloc and the start of the "war on terrorism" in 2001.[104]

Surveillance issues are prominent in the sprawling Russiagate scandal, centered on allegations of Russian interference into the electoral process, including allegations that the Democratic National Committee was hacked and that Russian operatives passed to Wikileaks emails revealing prejudicial actions favorable to Clinton and harmful to her chief competitor, Bernie Sanders. Wider hacks into corporate and financial institution files have been attributed to a group called the Shadow Brokers, likely Russian. It turns out that Shadow Brokers had somehow obtained the codes used by the National Security Agency to hack and sometimes to sabotage computer information systems in other countries.[105] The United States itself had been carrying out hacks in other countries for industrial espionage and political reasons for years before using the technology stolen by the Shadow Brokers. In 2009 and 2010, security experts believe that the United States with Israel deployed a cyber weapon, Stuxnet, designed to destroy Iranian nuclear centrifuges.[106]

Dueling conspiracy theories about Deep State politics continued to dominate headlines as Donald Trump neared the end of the end of the second year of his presidency. Opponents of Trump, inclusively among political elites, celebrities, and public, subscribe to the conspiracy theory that his campaign colluded with Russian operatives closely connected to the government of Vladimir Putin, to which in response Trump and his supporters allege a conspiracy among mainstream news organization, Deep State institutions, and political opponents to undermine his presidency. Significant corollary conspiracy theories grow out of these principal theories. On the anti-Trump side, conspiracy theorists argue that Russian President Vladimir Putin influenced American elections, seeking to ease economic sanctions by placing the more sympathetic Trump in office and to undermine confidence in American electoral institutions. A second anti-Trump corollary theory argues that the president, even if not directly involved in collusion, engaged in obstruction of justice to cover up collusion involving close associates, including his son and son-in-law.

Trump's "disruptive" rhetoric and the anti-patriotic aura around Russiagate both threaten the narrative of what Melley calls the "geographical melodrama" (discussed above). Trump's excoriating denouncements of the Deep State are disruptive of heroic image of the CIA, the FBI, National Security Agency—contradicting the depiction of the police, soldiers and spies in popular fiction as "heroes" and self-less "first responders." At the same time there are ways that Trump's policies and discourse may be appealing in certain corners of the Deep State. His hypernationalist rhetoric and promotion of increased military spending are two examples. These conflicting aspects of Trumpism is consistent may provoke riffs in the Deep State between elements who find Trump's "Make America Great Again" and "America First" philosophy appealing and those who find his attacks on the FBI, CIA, and National Security Agency personally offensive, institutionally threatening, or simply obstructing fulfillment of their missions. That hypothesis is highly speculative, but leaks and public statements by employees retiring from the security sector suggest that political polarization exists within the security establishment. These evident divisions should caution us about depictions of the Deep State as a monolythic conspiracy and argue for my conception of it as a sphere of politics prone to generating conspiracies.

In January and February 2017 skirmishing broke out between Democrats and Republicans over the release of a memo prepared by the David Nunes (R-CA) Chair of the House Intelligence Committee, which purported to show abuse of FBI surveillance of a Trump campaign official, part of an effort to undermine the credibility of Muller, the Special Counsel. Democrats prepared a memo in response defending the integrity of the FBI. As numerous commentators have suggested, the dispute put on display a remarkable turnout—liberals defending an agency they often have criticized for abuse of power, conservatives said to be undermining the rule of law. Trump in his first year also launched attacks direct attacks on the CIA, prompting Democrats and centrist Republicans to defend the agency.

The Nunes memo focused in part on the FBI's citing a report prepared by the retired British spy, Christopher Steele, which alleged collusion between Trump campaign officials, and was paid for by opponents (first within the GOP, later Clinton supporters) of Trump. In fact, much more was involved in the FBI obtaining the warrant from the Court. But here again, we might note that the entire affair should remind us of the new element of conspiratorial activity that may be routine in our politics. The very fact that the American electoral process now seems to include as routine campaign strategy hiring former intelligence officials to do opposition research is a sign of how transnational the invisible campaign has become, and how dirty. Besides Dark Money, American candidates for office now tap into the sphere of international Deep State politics to advance their cause.

We should take note that Deep State operatives have had roles in other elections as well. Besides using the Plumbers to break into Democratic headquarters at the Watergate, Richard Nixon and H. R. Halderman, his campaign chief of staff, attempted to sabotage Johnson's plans in October 1968 to advance peace talks, using Anna Chennault, a GOP fundraiser who had a back channel to the South Vietnamese government. William Casey, a campaign official for Ronald Reagan, who would become his CIA Director, allegedly supervised an attempted deal with Iran to prevent any release of hostages before the 1980 election, thwarting an "October Surprise."[107] What is of interest here is that in both cases, the political class eventually came together to end to further damage from explosive revelations. In contrast, President Trump publicly accused Democratic members of Congress of "treason" simply for failing to stand and applaud any part of the January 2018 State of the Union Address. Republicans, at least through early March 2018, were not especially keen to work with Democrats to bring an ending where the pundits and politicians could claim, as they did after Watergate, "The system worked."

NOTES

1. Mike Lofgren, *The Party's Over: How Republicans Went Crazy, Democrats Became Useless, and the Middle Class Got Shafted* (New York: Penguin, 2013); Mike Lofgren. *The Deep State: The Fall of the Constitution and the Rise of a Shadow Government* (New York: Penguin, 2016); and Marc Armbinder (Pseudonym) and D. B. Grady, *The Deep State: The Fall of the Constitution and the Rise of the Shadow Government* (New York and Hoboken, NJ: Wiley).
2. Armbinder and Grady (Pseudonym), *Deep State: Inside the Government Secrecy Industry.*
3. "National: Public Troubled by 'Deep State'," *Monmouth University Poll,* March 18, 2018, available at https://www.monmouth.edu/polling-institute/documents/monmouthpoll_us_031918.pdf (accessed June 27, 2018).
4. Steve Herman, "Trump Backers Fear 'Deep State' Aims to Undermine Administration," *VOA News,* March 9, 2017.
5. Samuel Huntington, *American Politics: The Promise of Disharmony* (Harvard University Press): 75. Quoted in Peter Dale Scott, *The American Deep State: Wallstreet, Big Oil, and the Attack on U.S. Democracy* (Lanham, MA: Rowman & Littlefield, 2015): 6 and also by Noam Chomsky, a critic of the idea of the Deep State. See his essay, "Security and State Power," available at https://chomsky.info/20140303 (accessed June 28, 2018).
6. Lofgren, *The Party's Over.*
7. Sonam Sheth," Right-Wing Media Blames Reports That Trump Leaked Classified Information to Russia on the 'Deep State'—Here's Where That Idea Came From," *Business Insider,* available at www.businessinsider.com/trump-deep-state-bannon-cia-fbi-breitbart-fox-news-2017-5 (accessed January 11, 2018).
8. Jane Mayer, *The Dark Side: The Inside Story of How the War on Terror Turned Into a War on American Ideals* (New York: Random House, 2008).
9. To cite only a few, see Chalmers Johnson, *Blowback, The Costs and Consequences of American Empire* (New York: Henry Holt and Company, 2004); *The Sorrows of Empire: Militarism, Secrecy, and the End of the Republic* (New York: Henry Holt and Company, 2004); Christopher Simpson, *Blowback: The First Full Account of Americas*

Recruitment of Nazis, and Its Disastrous Effect on Our Domestic and Foreign Policy (New York: Weidenfeld & Nicholson, 1988); and Andrew Bacevich, *Washington Rules: America's Path to Permanent War* (New York: Henry Holt and Company, 2010).

10. "September 11th: Ten Years, with Jane Mayer," *The New Yorker*, August 31, 2011.

11. Dwight W. Eisenhower, *Farewell Radio and Television Address to the American People*, January 17, 1961, available at www.eisenhower. archives.gov (accessed February 25, 2018).

12. David Remnick, "There Is No Deep State," *The New Yorker*, March 20, 2017.

13. Daniel Benjamin and Steven Simon, "Why Steve Bannon Wants You to Believe in the Deep State: What Better Way to Decimate the Bureaucracy Than to Convince Americans It's Treacherous?" *Politico*, March 21, 2017.

14. Alex Tunzelmann, "Oliver Stone's JFK: A Basket Case for Conspiracy Theory," *The Guardian*, April 11, 2003, drawing substantial on Jack Bratich, *Conspiracy Panics: Political Rationality and Popular Culture*.

15. "Conspiracy panic" refers to dismissal of certain theories as examples of the paranoid style; "regime of truth" is a concept of Foucault referring to social discipline of acceptable thought. Chapter 2 examines both in some depth, drawing substantially upon by Jack Bratich, *Conspiracy Panics: Political Rationality and Popular Culture* (Albany, NY: State University of New York Press, 2008): 5–25.

16. Bratich, *Conspiracy Panics*: 11.

17. Greg Grandin, "What Is the Deep State," *The Nation*, February 17, 2017.

18. Frederic Jameson, "Cognitive Mapping," pp. 347–360, in *Marxism and the Interpretation of Culture*, ed. C. Nelson and L. Grossberg (Champaign–Urbana: University of Illinois Press, 1960): 9.

19. Kathryn S. Olmsted, *Real Enemies: Conspiracy Theories and American Democracy, World War I to 9/11* (New York: Oxford University Press, 2009).

20. Timothy Melley, *The Covert Sphere: Secrecy Fiction and the National Security State* (Ithaca, NY: Cornell University Press, 2012).

21. Peter Knight, *Conspiracy Culture from Kennedy to the X-Files* (New York: Routledge, 2001): 3.

22. See Matthew Dentith, *The Philosophy of Conspiracy Theories* (London: Palgrave Macmillan, 2014): 41.

23. Peter Dale Scott, *The War Conspiracy: JFK, 9/11, and the Politics of War* (New York: Mary Ferrell Foundation Press, 2008): 238.

24. Scott, *The American Deep State*: 3.

25. The most influential pluralist thinker, whose idea of "polyarchy" has become a synonym for democracy in mainstream political science, is Robert Dahl. See *Polyarchy: Participation and Opposition* (New Haven: Yale University Press, 1971).
26. C. Wright Mills, *The Power Elite* (New York: Oxford University Press, 1960): 274, 277.
27. Transcript available at http://www.kenrahn.com/JFK/The_critics/Scott/Debate_Scott_Posner.html (accessed May 10, 2017).
28. Max Holland, "Paranoia Unbound," *The Wilson Quarterly* 18/1 (Winter 1994): 87.
29. Peter Dale Scott, *Drugs, Oil, and War: The United States in Afghanistan, Colombia, and Indochina* (Lanham, PA: Rowman & Littlefield, 2003): vii.
30. Steve Mufson and Jim McGee, "BCCI Scandal: Behind the Bank of Crooks and Criminals," *Washington Post*, July 28, 1991.
31. Steve Lohr, "World-Class Fraud: How B.C.C.I. Pulled It Off—A Special Report: At the End of a Twisted Trail, Piggy Bank for a Favored Few," *New York Times*, August 11, 1991.
32. See *The BCCI Affair. A Report to the Committee on Foreign Relations, United States Senate, by Senator John Kerry and Senator Hank Brown*, December 1992, available at https://fas.org/irp/congress/1992_rpt/bcci (accessed January 31, 2018). This version is the penultimate draft published at by Federation of American Scientists. The final report included redactions request by Henry Kissinger.
33. *The BCCI Affair*, section entitle "BCCI and Kissinger Associates."
34. Agencies and employee figures from Jeffrey T. Richelson, *The US Intelligence Community* (Bolder, CO: Westview Press, 7th ed., 2017): 12–13. Richelson's carefully researched and documented overview is a highly reliable guide to the history and present status of the intelligence community.
35. Tim Weiner, *Legacy of Ashes: The History of the CIA* (New York: Anchor Books, 2008): 390.
36. Quotation from Jefferson Morley, "Wilderness of Mirrors," *The Intercept*, January 1, 2018, available at theintercept.com/2018/01/01/the-complex-legacy-of-cia-counterintelligence-chief-james-angleton (accessed January 22, 2018). Also, Jefferson Morley, *The Ghost: The Secret Life of CIA Spymaster James Jesus Angleton* (New York: St. Martin's Press, 2017).
37. Gerald Posner, *Case Closed. Lee Harvey Oswald and the Assassination of JFK* (New York: Random House, 1993).
38. Council on Foreign Relations. 1940–1943. *Studies of American Interests in the War and the Peace*. Archived at the CFR in New York.

39. Quoted in Laurence Shoup, "Shaping the Post-War World: The Council of Foreign Relations and the United States War Aims During World War II," *The Insurgent Sociologist* 5, no. 3 (Spring 1975): 18–20. For a fuller account see Shoup and William Minter, *Imperial Brain Trust: The Council on Foreign Relations and United States Foreign Policy* (New York: Monthly Review Press, 1977); G. William Domhoff, "The Council on Foreign Relations and the Grand Area: Case Studies on the Origins of the IMF and the Vietnam War," *Class, Race and Power* 2, no. 1 (2014).

40. Available at http://www.presidency.ucsb.edu/ws/?pid=19364 (accessed February 27, 2018).

41. Richelson, *The US Intelligence Community*: 19.

42. "Doping Report Details 'Institutional Conspiracy' in Russia Involving More Than 1000 Athletes," *Associated Press*, December 9, 2016.

43. Melley, *The Covert Sphere*: 61 (Quotation), 68–75.

44. Melley, *The Covert Sphere*: 79.

45. *Senate Select Committee to Study Governmental Operations with Respect to Intelligence Activities* (Washington, DC: US Government Printing House, 1976).

46. Reed Brody, *Contra Terror in Nicaragua: Report of a Fact-Finding Mission: September 1984–January 1985* (Boston: South End Press, 1999).

47. Eric Alterman, "An Actual American War Criminal May Become Our Second-Ranking Diplomat," *The Nation*, February 2, 2017. "Elliot Abrams Appointed to NSC," *Central American and Mexico Report* 3 (2001, No Longer Available). On Casey, see Abrams' Interview with Bill Kristol, available at http://conversationswithbillkristol.org/video/elliott-abrams/?start=1392&end=1890 (accessed January 22, 2018).

48. See his interview of February 2017, Identity, Values and the Conduct of US Foreign Policy with Elliot Abrams-Conversations with History, on YouTube, available at https://www.youtube.com/watch?v=LqSyHhks-JzQ (accessed February 23, 2018).

49. Sinclair Lewis, *It Can't Happen Here* (New York: Signet Classics Edition, 2014).

50. Garrett M. Graff, *Raven Rock: The Story of the U.S. Government's Secret Plan to Save Itself—While the Rest of Us Die* (New York: Simon & Schuster, 2017).

51. "North Worked on Plan for Martial Law," *Knight-Ridder Newspapers*, July 5, 1987.

52. Video of the exchange between Inouye and Brooks can easily be found by searching on "Iran-contra" on YouTube.com.

53. Graff, *Raven Rock*: 304.

54. Both orders can be found at www.presidency.ucsb.edu/executive_orders. php?year=1988&Submit=DISPLAY (accessed February 27, 2018).
55. James Mann, "The Armageddon Plan," *The Atlantic*, March 2004.
56. "Dick Cheney, John Yoo, and COG on 9/11."
57. Adam Gabbat, "Anti-Protest Bills Would 'Attack Right to Speak Out' Under Donald Trump," *The Guardian*, May 8, 2017.
58. Devlin Barrett, Ellen Nakashima, and Carol Leonnig, "FBI's Top Lawyer Said to Be Reassigned," *Washington Post*, December 21, 2017.
59. Seymour Hersh, "Huge CIA Operation Reported in U.S. Against Anti-War Activist, Other Dissidents in the Nixon Era," *New York Times*, December 22, 1974, available at www.nytimes.com/1974/12/22/ archives/huge-cia-operation-reported-in-u-s-against-antiwar-forces-other.html (accessed January 11, 2018).
60. Josh Campbell, "Why I Am Leaving the FBI," *New York Times*, February 2, 2018.
61. Alfred Stepan, *The Military in Politics: Changing Patterns in Brazil* (Princeton, NJ: Princeton University Press, 1971).
62. Scott, *The American Deep State*. His best-known work is *Deep Politics and the Death of JFK* (Berkeley, CA: University of California Press, 1995).
63. Peter Dale Scott, "Dick Cheney, John Yoo, and COG on 9/11" (Letter), *Journal of 9/11 Studies* (September 2016), available at http:// www.journalof911studies.com/dick-cheney-john-yoo-and-cog-on-911 (accessed February 25, 2018).
64. Peter Dale Scott, *The Road to 9/11: Wealth, Empire, and the Future of America* (Berkeley: University of California Press, 2007): 134.
65. Quoted from *The Hill*, available at http://thehill.com/homenews/ news/341074-donald-trump-jr-shares-tweet-he-says-is-confirmation-deep-state-is-real (July 7, 2017).
66. *Breitbart News*, December 12, 2017.
67. Jonathan Martin and Mark Lander, "Bob Corker Says Trump's Recklessness Threatens 'World War III'," *New York Times*, October 8, 2017.
68. *Breitbart News*, October 9, 2017.
69. Jonatan Martin and Mark Lander, "Bob Corker Says...."
70. Marjorie Cohn, "The Duty to Disobey a Nuclear Launch Order," *Truthout.org*, November 25, 2017.
71. Gil Troy, "The Most Patriotic Act of Treason in American History," *The Daily Beast*, February 11, 2017.
72. November 21, 2017, available at https://www.eisenhower.archives.gov/ all_about_ike/speeches/farewell_address.pdf.
73. Matthew Cole and Jeremy Scahill, "Trump White House Weighing Plans for Private Spies to Counter 'Deep State' Enemies," *The Intercept*, December 4, 2017.

74. Peter Singer, "The Dark Truth About Blackwater," October 2, 2007 (accessed February 2, 2018).
75. Chris Lefkow, "Blackwater Founder Resurfaces Selling Plan for Afghanistan," *Military.com*, August 13, 2017 (accessed February 2, 2018).
76. Adam Entous, Greg Miller, Kevin Sieff, and Karen DeYoung, "Blackwater Founder Held Secret Seychelles Meeting to Establish Trump-Putin Back Channel," *Washington Post*, April 3, 2017.
77. Peter W. Singer, *Corporate Warriors: The Rise of the Privatized Military Industry* (Ithaca, NY: Cornell University Press, Updated ed., 2007).
78. Erik Prince, "Mercenaries and Private Military Contractors," *New York Times*, August 30, 2017.
79. Available at https://www.military.com/daily-news/2017/05/05/special-ops-general-rate-of-deployment-unsustainable.html, May 5, 2017 (accessed February 4, 2018).
80. See Jon D. Michaels, *Constitutional Coup: Privatization's Threat to the American Republic* (Cambridge, MA: Harvard University Press, 2017).
81. Thomas Gibbons-Neff, Eric Schmitt, and Adam Goldman, "A Newly Assertive C.I.A. Expands Its Taliban Hunt in Afghanistan," *New York Times*, October 22, 2017.
82. Douglas Valentine, *The Phoenix Program* (Open Road Distribution, 2016) is mostly valuable for the wealthy of primary source material, including interviews. Dale Andrade's less emotional *Ashes to Ashes* (Issues in Low-Intensity Conflict Series; Lanham, MA: Lexington Books, 1990) is more convincingly dispassionate, but is no less disturbing.
83. Dawn Paley, *Drug War Capitalism* (Oakland, CA: AK Press, 2014).
84. Deborah Sontagg, "The Secret History of Colombia's Paramilitaries and the U.S. War on Drugs," *New York Times*, September 10, 2016.
85. Sarah Lyall, "Spies Like Us: A Conversation With John le Carré and Ben Macintyre," *New York Times*, August 25, 2017.
86. Lyall, "Spies Like Us."
87. Melley, *The Covert Sphere*.
88. "Revealed: The True Story of 'Maya', the CIA Analyst Who Hunted Down Osama bin Laden," *The Daily Telegraph*, London, December 20, 2014.
89. "Homeland, Spooks and 24 Have Led More Britons Than Russians To Support Torture, Amnesty International Says," *Huffington Post*, May 13, 2014 (accessed February 6, 2018).
90. Humeira Iqtidar, "Conspiracy Theory as Political Imaginary: Blackwater in Pakistan," *Political Studies* 64, no. 1 (2014): 201.
91. Iqtidar, "Conspiracy Theory": 205–205.

92. Dan Raviv, "U.S. Pushing Israel to Stop Assassinating Iranian Nuclear Scientists," *CBS News*, March 1, 2014; "Isreal Behind Assassinations of Iran Nuclear Scientists," *Jerusalem Post*, August 7, 2015.

93. Available at https://www.nbc.com/the-brave.

94. Available at http://www.cbs.com/shows/seal-team/.

95. Mark Mazzetti, Nicholas Kulish, Christopher Drew, Serge F. Kovaleski, Sean D. Naylor, and John Ismay, "Seal Team 6: A Secret History of Quite Killings and Blurred Lines," *New York Times*, June 6, 2015.

96. Hannah K. Gold, "5 Ways Crimes Shows Mess with Your Head," *Alternet.org*, November 12, 2014 (accessed February 27, 2018).

97. Available at http://www.imdb.com/title/tt5585896/?ref_=tt_eps_rhs_0 (accessed February 7, 2018).

98. See Steve Weichselbaum and Beth Schwartzapfel, *When Warriors Put On the Badge*, The Marshall Project and *USA Today*, March 30, 2017, available at https://www.themarshallproject.org/2017/03/30/when-warriors-put-on-the-badge (accessed February 5, 2018).

99. See James Poniewozik, "'Training Day' and 'A.P.B.,' Where the Rogue Cop Rules," *New York Times*, February 1, 2017.

100. "Homan Square Revealed: How Chicago Police 'Disappeared' 7000 People," *The Guardian*, October 19, 2015.

101. Medea Benjamin, "The Torture-Friendly Trump Administration," *Huffington Post*, July 20, 2017.

102. Seung Min Kim, "McCain Opposes Trump Nominee Over Torture Memos," *Politico*, November 8, 2017.

103. Many sources tell the Snowden saga. Bryan Burrough, Sarah Ellison, and Suzanna Andrews, "The Snowden Saga: A Shadowland of Secrets and Light," *Vanity Fair*, April 23, 2014. See also Wikipedia entry available at https://en.wikipedia.org/wiki/Edward_Snowden (accessed February 2, 2018).

104. Gerhard Schmidt, *Report on the Existence of a Global System for the Interception of Private and Commercial Communications (ECHELON Interception System)* (Brussels: European Parliament: Temporary Committee on the ECHELON Interception System, 2001).

105. Natalie Reneau and Mark Scheffler, "Who Are The Shadow Brokers?" *New York Times*, November 13, 2017; "Security Breach and Spilled Secrets Have Shaken the N.S.A. to Its Core," *New York Times*, November 12, 2017.

106. Ken Dilanian, William M. Arkin and Cynthia McFadden, and Robert Windrem, "U.S. Govt. Hackers Ready to Hit Back If Russia Tries to Disrupt Election," *NBC News*, November 4, 2016.

107. Gary Sick, *October Surprise: America's Hostages in Iran and the Election of Ronald Reagan* (New York: Crown, 1991).

CHAPTER 8

Conclusion: Conspiracy Theories and Political Decay

This book has sought to fulfill two goals simultaneously. One is to contribute to the ongoing process of rethinking the meaning and uses of
"conspiracy theory." The second, to apply some of these insights to
understanding the political shock that Americans and the world received
when Donald Trump, a celebrity real estate tycoon who traded extensively in unwarranted conspiracy theories, rose to the presidency of the
most powerful state in the world system. Is the Trump phenomenon
yet another instance of what Hofstadter[1] called the paranoid style in
American politics? Are conspiratorial beliefs the province only of Trump
and his supporters, or is it more widespread in the political environment?
Are claims of Russian manipulation of the 2016 election and of Trump
campaign collusion with such efforts also "conspiracy theories"?

As I write this conclusion, an independent prosecutor has indicted
former aids and Trump campaign officials for covering up or actually
engaging in collusion with Russian operatives, feeding calls to impeach
the president, Trump protests that the "deep state" is out to destroy
him. Significant numbers of people across the political spectrum see
political processes as rigged. Retired spies are now recruited by political
parties and candidates to dig up dirt on opponents. The most popular
late-night comedian says Russian President Vladimir Putin has material
to blackmail the president. The National Rifle Association portrays every
effort at gun control as an attack on the Constitution and, like climate
change deniers, suspects a socialist plot behind every effort. A Supreme
Court resignation will probably allow Trump to make his second lifetime

© The Author(s) 2019
D. C. Hellinger, *Conspiracies and Conspiracy Theories in the Age
of Trump*, https://doi.org/10.1007/978-3-319-98158-1_8

appointment of a second radical libertarian judge to the bench. And Immigration and Customs Enforcement service is rounding up immigrants and denying due process is a way that resembles what Oliver North, of Iran-Contra fame, in the Reagan presidency hoped to do with protesters of American wars abroad.

The ultra-rich meet in biannual conclaves closed to the public to plan deployment of their wealth, hidden behind the mantle of philanthropy, to weaken democratic regulation of capitalism. Major "trade treaties" that impact global financial flows and systems of production are negotiated in secret with corporate influence but without allowing labor and environmentalist organizations at the same table. Officials in cabinet-level positions and in Congress believe that scientific expertise on climate change is in cahoots with proponents of world government. Social media provocateurs, foreign and domestic, and automated bots that can impersonate real citizens spread conspiracy claims that are often fabricated but so too do partisans post or re-tweet more plausible news.

The financial shock of 2008–2009 shook faith in both the financial system and the government's willingness to hold anyone responsible. In recent years, several major corporations have been caught conspiring to break laws that threaten public safety. Wells Fargo was caught in 2016 and 2017 creating fake insurance and 3.5 million phony savings accounts. Volkswagen was forced to buy back all of its diesel engine automobiles because it rigged its engines to fool emissions tests. Over 143 million consumers had their personal financial information stolen by hackers in Equifax. It has become clear that the tools that hackers are using to steal information from major private and public institutions, as well as from the hard drives of personal computers, were developed first by the National Security Agency not for defense but to unleash viruses and eavesdrop abroad in other sovereign countries.

Is that message on your computer screen warning you that your hard drive has been hacked and demanding that you call the number given the screen a real threat? Did you click on a link in an email before you realized it might be suspicious? Are cryptocurrencies, such a Bitcoin, real alternatives to traditional forms of money, or are they just pyramid schemes? Has that cop pulling me over profiled me racially? Has that fellow in the hoody in this neighborhood got a gun?

Trump may or may not complete his term, but today's social climate of economic uncertainty, mistrust, and polarization ensures that conspiracy theories will be a prominent feature of American politics for many years to come. Conspiracy theories are not just symptomatic of the changing social and political climate; they are in some important ways relevant theories for explaining how politics in America operate. Dark money circulates freely not only through the electoral system but also through culture. Wealthy people and corporations hide their income from tax authorities in offshore havens. Politicians hire detectives and spies to gather dirt on opponents. American forces fight terrorist cells, but not with those with whom the United States has made an alliance of convenience. National and state legislatures are gerrymandered to block progressive adaptation to changing times and political reform. Levels of trust in political institutions, from approximately 80% in the early 1960s to 20% in 2018. Is this because too many people believe conspiracy theories?

Almost in a panic, mainstream academics and media pundits have embraced the perception of populism as a threat to democracy, without any differentiation of the different movements that are challenging elite rule and concentrated wealth. This point of view is nicely summed up on the title of a once popular political science text: The "irony of democracy" is that democracy depends more on elites than the people.[2] This sentiment appears in mainstream views of how democracy succeeds and fails. After a wave of coups ended a period of democracy in Latin America, a series of studies examined the breakdown of elite consensus as the key to why this happened. A similar series, that included some of the same authors, saw restoration of democracy as due to interaction among elites.[3] At best the people appear in these analyses as a kind of Greek chorus or as a kind of mob threatening to obstruct the consensus building process among elites. Yet, without a progressive populist movement to demand accountability of government, how else can democracy become more inclusive, economically as well as politically? Elites collude with one another to deploy stealth funding both to block left populism and majority rule. The danger today is not tyranny of the majority but tyranny of the minority.

Hofstadter's conception of conspiracism as paranoid and his linking it to populism have in recent years tainted populist movements as uniformly antidemocratic. A good example is a recent book by Steven Levitsky and Daniel Ziblatt, *How Democracies Die*,[4] which warns of the dangers of the Trump presidency and argues that the "guardrails" are coming off the American democracy, i.e. constitutional checks and balances are not functioning. There is much to admire in this book, especially in its final chapter's emphasis on the need for progressive social justice to restore democracies health. Beginning in 1992, Republicans have not won the popular vote in a presidential election with one exception, 2004. The House of Representatives has been gerrymandered to reinforce a systematic advantage rural and white suburban conservatism. The Supreme Court, with Trump poised to make his second ultra-conservative appointment thanks to Republican refusal to consider Obama's nominee. But, have the guardrails come off because of excessive populism, or because of the kind of populism we are experiencing? If Trump followers are particularly susceptible to manipulation by "conspiracy theorists" (which cannot be taken for granted), this should motivate political scientists to research not only what "disposes" them toward conspiracism but also what motivates a large sector of American elites with money and power to create, amplify, and disseminate conspiracy theories. For that reason, much of this book argues that conspiratorial manipulation of the rules of the political game is an important way that conservative elites and wealthy oligarchs are imposing minority rule.

NEEDED: A REGIME OF TRUTH OF TRUTHFULNESS

The first few chapters of this book take up the argument of Jack Bratich that the term "conspiracy theory" is used mainly to reinforce a "regime of truth" that attaches a stigma to theories and beliefs that push at the boundaries of acceptable thought.[5] This does not mean that the proper response to this discipline is to treat all theories as equal. In Chapter 2, I argue for differentiating conspiracy theories by their level of impact, if true, and by their plausibility, evaluating them on a scale ranging from unwarranted to warranted. Few if any grand, or world theories will qualify for serious consideration, and petty theories, though cumulatively they many impact politics (e.g., through pervasive corruption), are not singly important enough to be taken seriously as explanations for large-scale socioeconomic and political change. Operational theories are mid-range theories that should be taken more seriously, complementing historical and structural explanations, but also in place of the "things-just-happen" and "no-one's-really responsible" explanations offered by so much of conventional social science.

No longer should the academic approach to the subject be solely and completely defined by Hofstadter's meme, the "paranoid style", i.e., by the idea that all conspiracy theories by their nature violate the principles of social science as defined by Karl Popper and by the notion that mass embrace of a conspiracy necessarily leads to mass pathological behavior. Yet studies of conspiracy theory in political psychology more or less continue to operate with the paradigm established by Hofstadter. The point is not to discard Hofstadter's highlighting of an historical record that reveals populism's serious faults, in particular, its relationship with nativism and racism in past appearances as a force in American politics. There is some very bad conspiracy theorizing going on, and even worse there are conspiracy theories that embrace scapegoating and ethnic hatred. Dangerous or implausible theories deserve our disapproval because of what they propose, because they are circular or not open to reasonable attempts to refute them with evidence, or because they stir hatred toward a class of people.

The rise of Donald Trump to the American presidency has in a number of ways lent new urgency to the re-examination of conspiracy and conspiracy theory. Not all the post-Hofstadter works on conspiracy theory are in agreement. Tim Melley, a cultural theorist, still rejects conspiracy theory but his work on conspiracism in various forms of fiction suggests that conspiracism in popular culture is revealing of how national security and military agencies operate in the real "covert sphere", and how these agencies support popular films, games, and TV programs that cleanse historical memory of the cost to democracy of past abuses.[6] Kathryn Olmsted believes ultimately conspiracy theories are more harmful than helpful, but her research on conspiracy theories in the twentieth shows that contrary to most critics' view, conspiracy theories sometimes empower ordinary people, expose wrongdoing that would otherwise remain covert, and force elites to pay mind to demands they would rather ignore.[7] Bratich, Mark Fenster, and Matthew Dentith go further and advance arguments for treating conspiracy theories, at least in some cases, as worthy of social science theorizing.[8]

This book acknowledges that conspiracy beliefs are fostered by inequality and a sense that the economy is no longer fair, but I argue that the way American politics is influenced by elite conspiracies is just as important as a generator of popular suspicion, contributing to a gathering crisis of representation and mistrust of political institutions. For example, neoliberal globalization agreements are negotiated without impactful input from social global movements that have as much at stake as transnational capitalists, and the latter gather behind closed doors to keep it that way. Not only does money influence politics, it is now deployed systematically by elites who regularly gather to discuss how to deploy their resources covertly. Special Forces and paramilitary organizations fight secret and not-so-secret wars, under cover of national emergency by executive order and bills that have never been actually read by Congress before votes are passed. Most academics and journalists continue to reject that a Deep State exists in the United States, a rejection based more on a state of denial and caricature than on serious consideration of how far some elites in that sphere of politics have advanced preparations to infringe on civil liberties and the Constitution.

WHAT WE CAN LEARN FROM CONSPIRACISM ABROAD

A way that we can assess the significance of conspiracism in America is by looking at the conditions that have given rise to this phenomenon abroad. Given that Trumpism has risen on a wave of right-wing populism occurring in various regions of the world, it seems that this is a propitious moment to see how strong the hypothesized link is, going back to Hofstadter, between populism and conspiracism. The topic has understandably attracted recent attention in Europe, but for various reasons explored in this book, much of the research thus far has uncritically incorporated the idea that conspiracy theory is always a pathological form of discourse. Despite Hofstadter's insistence is that pathological thought is articulated by 'normal' people, some of the research persists in searching for the underlying personality traits that lend themselves to conspiracy thinking (See Chapter 5).

In his fine book, *Conspiracy Theories in the Arab World*, Matthew Gray provides one of the very few studies of conspiracism that has seriously examined this phenomenon in the Middle East (or anywhere in the Global South, for that matter) by a scholar with care to due avoid cultural stereotypes (Orientalism in this case), oversimplification, and a singular focus on anti-Semitism. Gray combines a symptomatic approach (conspiracy theories as signs of deeper social ills and injustices) with the understanding that in the Middle East peoples have in fact been victimized by conspiracies to establish and maintain colonialism and Western hegemony in the post-colonial period. In the Preface, the author, based in Australia, comments that he was surprised about "how many similarities there were in political sources of conspiracism in the US and Arab world."[9]

Gray argues that in the Arab World conspiracism is rooted in "historical impacts, state-society relations, and political culture."[10] Despite the vast cultural and economic chasm between the Global North and South, most of the factors that Gray identifies as symptoms of state weaknesses that apply in both spheres. The principle difference has to do with historical impact, a variable which plays out in much of the Global South as a sense of loss of greatness in the past and resentment toward intervention by colonial powers and more recently by the United States. With the important exception of some Indigenous people, most Latin Americans do not share with the Middle East cultures this same sense of lost civilizational greatness, but their political culture too is characterized by a sense of failures that achieving autonomy in choosing a developmental model, a reason they are attracted to neoliberal dependency theory.

Gray maintains, "A feature that distinguishes Middle Eastern conspiracism from some other countries, such as the US...is the role played by the state in promoting conspiracist explanations and engaging in the narration of conspiracy theories."[11] But I would say that the difference in "role" is just a matter of degree, especially given the degree to which the American state must rely upon the private media to promoted messages. This it does effectively in a variety of ways, not the least in the influence exercise through money and cooperation between producers of popular fiction and the military and intelligence agencies (see Chapter 7). Certainly, no one can underestimate the uses to which anti-communism was put in the Cold War, especially by the enablers of Senator Joseph McCarthy. So too we have seen the ability of the American state to manipulate the press coverage and "wag the dog," most recently in the way that the Bush administration provided pretexts in the form of supposed weapons of mass destruction for the first Gulf War. Fear of terrorism has been manipulated to justify surveillance and to roll back an admirable (despite episodic nativism) heritage of respect and admiration for immigrants. The difference is also rooted, Gray acknowledges, in the historical reality of Western colonialism and intervention, and the quite uncritical support of the West for Zionism.[12] These historical realities feed conspiracy theories that have some warrant because they are rooted in historical fact, but, it must be said, also feeds ones that are extremely anti-Semitic.

Without going into more details about Gray's nuanced analysis of the "sources and politics" of conspiracism, his framework seems to me to applicable in many ways these are highlighted by politics in the Trump era. This leads to hypotheses that ought to be part of theorizing conspiracy.

- Elite interaction—among themselves, with the state, and with society. Conspiracy theories are not necessarily the poor man's social scientific theory, they are fabricated or simply advanced when elite find it difficult to maintain consensus among each other and break into factions. Then too, as polarization and distrust increase, elites may turn more on one another. The history of the United States Congress in the decades leading to the Civil War is illustrative, as political polarization manifested itself not only in social violence but also in incivility and worse in Congress. Today we see extreme polarization in declining congressional decorum, extreme mistrust of executive authority.
- The state–society relationship. Doing politics in a conspiratorial way has become more routine in the United States, which is both a reflection of the widening gap between the political class and society and also between elites and the mass public. Olmsted argues that conspiracy theories in the twentieth century differ from those of the nineteenth century in that with the growth of the federal government's size and reach, the state has replaced foreign enemies as the main source of popular suspicion. Political discourse on the right feeds on this deeply rooted perception, and the political opposition makes little defense of the need for government, certainly nothing in the way that was common in the New Deal.
- History. Here, of course, there are a major ways we must differentiate the U.S. case from the Mideast. As the global hegemon, the idea that the United States is subject to external intervention might seem ludicrous, but during the Cold War the perception was encouraged by what was presented as a Manichean struggle between Communism and the "free world." Today, this Cold War logic is being applied to the War on Terrorism. And certainly Trump's infamous catch-phrase, "Make America Great Again," suggests some comminality between the national sense of lost civilizational greatness in the Arab World and the sense of declining hegemonic power in the U.S.

An Agenda for Research

Once we dispose of the idea that the only use of the term "conspiracy theory" is to warn the public that theories not endorsed by mainstream academics and journalists are irrational and possibly dangerous, we can look to applying the tools of political science and investigative reporting to separating the plausible conspiracy theories from the completely unwarranted, the dangerous from the amusing but not threatening, the ones that point us toward understanding the course of events from the ones likely to distract us from broader social and economic causes, or worse, mobilize pograms against certain sectors in our community.

A few suggestions for a research agenda on conspiracy are:

- Comparative historical studies, perhaps even counterfactual ones, to examine the degree of freedom for conspiracies to shape outcomes at major historical watersheds. For example, we should examine and contextualize the role of conspiratorial behavior in revolutions and subversive movements. Stepan's work on coup-making in Brazil, though not intended as a study in conspiracism, is an exemplary case study of how agency (coup plotting) interacts with larger social and economic forces in a society.[13]
- More cross-cultural and comparative research along the lines recommended by Gray in his study of the conspiracy theories in the Middle East.
- Empirical studies using creative databases to test assumptions about the prevalence of conspiracism. Uscinski and Parent provide an important example of how this can be done with their research on letters to the editor.[14]
- More public opinion and attitudinal research on whether there are indeed "predispositions" toward conspiracism. Studies of this nature should not presume that all belief in conspiracies is pathological. At the same time, it is useful to study predispositions that might lead toward scapegoating, ethnic purification, or genocide, which often involved paranoid conspiracism at it worse.
- The need for continued work in political theory on the ontological status of conspiracy theory. In the United States, we have seen in recent years major studies focused on elites engaged in a "stealth plan,"[15] i.e., their concious and secretive deployment of "dark money" to move promote a libertarian economic agenda.[16]

hidden plans to suspend constitutional rights in a time of national security crisis (See Chapter 7).[17] Studies and investigations of this phenomenon have often to some degree or another been attacked as "conspiracy theories"—even when their authors explicitly reject the notion. This points to the need for normative political theorists, not just empirical researchers, to take up conspiracy theory, much as Dentith, Bratich, Fenster, and others have done.

LAST WORDS: NO TIME TO PANIC

I have laid out suggestions for an agenda for research and development of conspiracy theory as social science theory, not pathology. I suggest that identification and understanding of the role actual conspiracies are playing in our politics might, if not sound alarm bells, at least help us recognize the signs of political decay. A closer examination of political planning and elite collusion in the deep and dark recesses of the Internet gated estates of the wealthy, and in the covert sphere of the National Security state might prevent democracy from falling to more conventional measures of the past.

Trumpism is more than Donald Trump. It is rooted in factors that point to continuing decay in American politics. We can expect politicians to "trump-up" fears, appeal to fear and exploit agency panic, appealing to white privilege and defence of patriarchy as political levers to hold back use of government by democratic majorities to address injustices. Further political decay is not inevitable, but that is the general direction of American politics today. I expect that we not only will see more conspiracism of the paranoid variety, but also more actual conspiratorial behavior by elites threatened by progressive social movements. Neither coups nor revolutions are made without conspiracies. It would be alarmist to predict that either is imminent, but at the same time several mainstream political scientists have analyzed the rise of Trumpism in terms that would have been characterized as paranoia not long ago. Levitsky and Ziblatt point to the gradual deterioration of the constitutional state into an illiberal democracy. They point out that today democracies do not usually disappear through a coup, declaration of martial law; no alarm bells sound when the line is crossed. "Those who denounce government abuse may be dismissed as exaggerating or crying wolf. Democracy's erosion is, for many, almost imperceptible."[18] Conspiracy theory, appropriately developed, can make erosion more perceptible and stop the erosion.

NOTES

1. Richard Hofstadter, *The Paranoid Style in American Politics* (New York: Vintage Reprints, 1968).
2. Thomas Dye, Harmon Ziegler, and Louis Schubert, *The Irony of Democracy* (Boston: Cengage Learning, 15th ed., 2011).
3. Juan Linz and Alfred Stepan, eds. *The Breakdown of Democratic Regimes* (Baltimore, MD: Johns Hopkins University Press, 1978); Guillermo, O'Donnell, Philippe Schmitter, and Laurence Whitehead, ed., *Transitions from Authoritarian Rule: Comparative Perspectives* (Baltimore, MD: Johns Hopkins University Press, 1986).
4. Steven Levitsky and Daniel Ziblatt, *How Democracies Die* (New York: Crown, 2018).
5. Jack Bratich, *Conspiracy Panics: Political Rationality and Popular Culture* (Albany: State University of New York Press, 2008).
6. Timothy Melley, *The Covert Sphere: Secrecy, Fiction, and the National Security State* (Ithaca, NY: Cornell University Press, 2012).
7. Kathryn Olmsted, *Real Enemies: Conspiracy Theory and American Democracy, World War I to 9/11* (New York: Oxford University Press, 2009).
8. Jack Gratich, *Conspiracy Panics*; Matthew Dentith, *Suspicious Minds: Why We Believe in Conspiracy Theories* (London: Palgrave Macmillan, 2014); Mark Fenster. *Conspiracy Theories: Secrecy and Power in American Culture* (Minneapolis: University of Minnesota Press, 1999, second ed. 2012).
9. Matthew Gray, *Conspiracy Theories in the Arab World: Sources and Politics* (London: Routledge, 2010), xii.
10. Gray, *Conspiracy Theories in the Arab World*: 8.
11. Gray, *Conspiracy Theories in the Arab World*: 119.
12. Gray, *Conspiracy Theories in the Arab World*: 49–87.
13. Alfred Stepan, *The Military in Politics: Changing Patterns in Brazil* (Princeton, NJ: Princeton University Press, 1971).
14. Joseph Uscinski and Joseph M. Parent, *American Conspiracy Theories* (New York: Oxford University Press, 2014).
15. Nancy MacClean, *Democracy in Chains: The Deep History of the Radical Right's Stealth Plan for America* (New York: Viking, 2017).
16. Jane Mayer, *Dark Money. The Hidden History of the Billionaires Behind the Rise of the Radical Right* (New York: Doubleday, 2016).
17. Peter Dale Scott, *The American Deep State: Wallstreet, Big Oil, and the Attack on U.S. Democracy* (Lanham, MA: Rowman & Littlefield, 2015); Mike Lofgren. *The Deep State: The Fall of the Constitution and the Rise of a Shadow Government* (New York: Penguin, 2016).
18. Steven Levitsky and Daniel Ziblatt, *How Democracies Die* (New York: Crown Press, 2018): 6.

REFERENCES

American Press Institute. 2018. *Americans and the News Media: What They Do—And Don't—Understand About Each Other.* The Media Insight Project (June), available for download from mediainsight.org, accessed June 15, 2018.

Anderson, Benedict. 1991. *Imagined Communities: Reflections on the Origin and Spread of Nationalism.* London: Verso.

Armbinder, Marc, and D.B. Grady (pseudonym). 2013. *Deep State: Inside the Government Secrecy Industry.* New York and Hoboken, NJ: John Wiley and Sons.

Autor, David, David Dorny, Gordon Hanson, and Kaveh Majlesi. 2017. "A Note on the Effect of Rising Trade Exposure on the 2016 Presidential Election." Revised Version of March 2017, available at https://economics.mit.edu/files/12418, accessed February 24, 2018.

Bacevich, Andrew 2010. *Washington Rules: America's Path to Permanent War.* New York: Henry Holt and Company.

Bachrach, Peter. 1967. *The Theory of Democratic Elitism.* Boston: Little, Brown Publishers.

Bailyn, Bernard. 1967. *The Ideological Origins of the American Revolution.* Cambridge, MA: Harvard University Press.

Baram, Marcus. 2017. "Eavesdropping on Roy Cohn and Donald Trump." *The New Yorker*, April 14.

Barber, Benjamin. 1996. *Jihad vs. McWorld: Terrorism's Challenge to Democracy.* New York: Ballantine Books, 1996.

Barkin, Michael. 2003. *A Culture of Conspiracy: Apocalyptic Visions in Contemporary America.* Berkeley, CA: University of California.

© The Editor(s) (if applicable) and The Author(s) 2019   287
D. C. Hellinger, *Conspiracies and Conspiracy Theories in the Age of Trump*, https://doi.org/10.1007/978-3-319-98158-1

Basham, Lee. 2006. "Living with the Conspiracy." In David Coad (ed.), *Conspiracy Theories: The Philosophical Debate*, 61–117. Burlington, VT: Ashgate.

Beard, Charles, and George H.E. Smith. 1977, original 1934. *The Idea of National Interest: Analytical Study in American Foreign Policy*. New York: Greenwood Press, Reprint.

Benjamin, Daniel and Steven Simon, "Why Steve Bannon Wants You to Believe in the Deep State: What Better Way to Decimate the Bureaucracy than to Convince Americans It's Treacherous?" *Politico*, March 21, 2017.

Bennett, Lance L. 1996 (3rd ed.). *News: The Politics of Illusion*. White Plains, NY: Longman Publishers.

Berezin, Mabel. 2009. *Illiberal Politics in Neoliberal Times: Culture, Security and Populism in the New Europe*. Cambridge, UK: Cambridge University Press.

Berlet, Chip. n.d. circa 1993. "Rightist Influences on the Christic Institute Theories." Available at http://www.publiceye.org/rightwoo/rwooz9-13.html, accessed December 8, 2017.

Berlet, Chip. 1993. "Big Lies, Spooky Sources." *Columbia Journalism Review* (May/June), 67–71.

Berlet, Chip. 2009a. "Clinton, Conspiracism and Civil Society." Political Research Associates, available at http://www.uni-muenster.de/PeaCon/conspiracy/networks-01.htm, accessed December 31, 2017.

Berlet, Chip. 2009b. *Toxic to Democracy: Conspiracy Theories, Demonization, & Scapegoating*. Political Research Associates. 2009 (updated): 3, available at http://www.publiceye.org/conspire/toxic2democracy/Toxic-2D-all-rev-04.pdf. Accessed August 17, 2017.

Bilewicz, Michal, Aleksandra Cichocka, and Wiktor Soral, eds. 2015. *The Psychology of Conspiracy*. New York: Routledge.

Bratich, Jack. 2008. *Conspiracy Panics: Political Rationality and Popular Culture*. Albany: State University of New York Press.

Brecht, Bertolt. 2015. *The Resistible Rise of Arturo Ui*, translated by Alistair Beaton and George Tabori. London: Methuen Drama.

Brody, Reed. 1999. *Contra Terror in Nicaragua: Report of a Fact-Finding Mission: September 1984–January 1985*. Boston: Southend Press, 1999.

Brotherton, Rob. 2018. *Suspicious Minds: Why We Believe Conspiracy Theories*. New York: Bloomsbury-Signet.

Brotherton, Rob, Christopher French, and Allan Pickering. 2013. "Measuring Belief in Conspiracy Theories: The Generic Conspiracist Beliefs Scale. Frontiers in Personality Science and Individual Differences." *Frontiers in Psychology*. Vol. 4, available at https://www.frontiersin.org. Accessed February 23, 2018.

Caute, David. 1978. *The Great Fear*. New York: Simon & Schuster.

Coady, David, ed. 2006. *Conspiracy Theories: The Philosophical Debate*. Burlington, VT: Ashgate.

Cohen, Marty, David Karol, Hans Noel, and John Zoller. 2008. *The Party Decides, Presidential Nominations Before and After Reform.* Chicago: University of Chicago Press.

Corr, Anders. 2016. "Liberal Democracy Against a World of Nationalist Happenstance." *Forbes Magazine,* November 21.

Council on Foreign Relations. 1940–1943. *Studies of American Interests in the War and the Peace.* Archived at CFR in New York.

Dahl, Robert. 1971. *Polyarchy: Participation and Opposition.* New Haven: Yale University Press, 1971.

Dean, Jodi. 1998. *Aliens in America: Conspiracy Cultures from Outerspace to Cyberspace.* Ithaca, NY: Cornell University Press.

Dentith, Matthew. 2014. *The Philosophy of Conspiracy Theories.* London: Palgrave Macmillan.

Domhoff, G. William. 2014. "The Council on Foreign Relations and the Grand Area: Case Studies on the Origins of the IMF and the Vietnam War." *Class, Race and Power* 2, no. 1 (2014):1–41.

Dunst, Alexander. 2015. "The Politics of Conspiracy Theories: American Histories, and Global Narratives." In *Conspiracy Theories in the United States and the Middle East: A Comparative Approach,* eds. Michael Butter and Maurus Reinkowski, 294–310. Boston: De Gruyter.

Dye, Thomas, Harmon Ziegler, and Louis Schubert. 2011. *The Irony of Democracy.* Boston: Cengage Learning, 15th ed.

Fenster, Mark. 1999. 2012 (2nd ed.). *Conspiracy Theories: Secrecy and Power in American Culture.* Minneapolis: University of Minnesota Press.

Fenster, Mark. 2017. *The Transparency Fix: Secrets, Leaks, and Uncontrollable Government Information.* Stanford, CA: Stanford University Press.

Ferrel, Henry, and Steven Teles. 2017. "Even the Intellectual Left Is Drawn to Conspiracy Theories About the Right. Resist them." *Vox.com* (Updated version). Accessed October 9, 2017.

Foucault, Michel. 1980. "Truth and Power." In *Michel Foucault: Power/ Knowledge,* ed. Colin Gordon, 109–133. New York: Vintage Press.

Friedan, Betty. 1964. *The Feminist Mystique.* New York: Dell.

Friedman, Thomas. 2012. *The Lexus and the Olive Tree.* London: Picador Books, 2012.

Gessen, Masha. 2017. "Russia: The Conspiracy Trap." *New York Review of Books,* March 6.

Gill, Stephen. 1991. *American Hegemony and the Trilateral Commission.* Cambridge. Cambridge University Press.

Graff, Garrett M. 2017. *Raven Rock: the Story of the U.S. Government's Secret Plan to Save Itself—While the Rest of Us Die.* New York: Simon & Schuster.

Grandin, Greg. 2017. "What Is the Deep State?" *The Nation,* February 17.

Gray, Matthew. 2010. *Conspiracy Theories in the Arab World: Sources and Politics: Sources and Politics.* New York: Routledge.

Griffin, David Ray. 2008. *The New Pearl Harbor Revisited: 9/11, the Cover-Up, and the Exposé.* Northampton, MA: Olive Branch Press.

Griffin, John, and Amin Shams. 2018. *Is Bit-Coin Really Untethered.* Social Science Research Network (SSRN), available at https://papers.ssrn.com/sol3/papers.cfm?abstract_id=3195066. Accessed June 16, 2018.

Hawley, George. 2017. *Making Sense of the Alt-Right.* New York: Columbia University Press.

Hellinger, Daniel. 2003. "Paranoia, Conspiracy, and Hegemony in American Politics." In *Transparency and Conspiracy: Ethnographies of Suspicion in the New World Order,* ed. Harry G. West and Todd Sanders. Durham, NC: Duke University Press.

Hellinger, Daniel, and Dennis Judd. 1991, 1994. *The Democratic Façade,* 1st ed., Pacific Grove, CA: Brooks Cole and 2nd ed., Belmont, CA: Wadsworth.

Hertzgaard, Mark. 1989. *On Bended Knee: The Press and the Reagan Presidency.* New York: Schocken Press.

Hetherington, Mark J. 2006. *Why Trust Matters: Declining Political Trust and the Demise of American Liberalism.* Princeton, NJ: Princeton University Press.

Hofstadter, Richard. 1955. *The Age of Reform: From Bryan to F.D.R.* New York: Alfred A. Knopf.

Hofstadter Richard. 1968. *The Paranoid Style in American Politics.* New York: Vintage Reprints.

Holland, Max. 1994. "Paranoia Unbound." *The Wilson Quarterly* 18, no. 1 (Winter).

Iqtidar, Humeira. 2014. "Conspiracy Theory as Political Imaginary: Blackwater in Pakistan." *Political Studies* 64, no. 1.

Jameson, Frederic. 1960. "Cognitive Mapping." In *Marxism and the Interpretation of Culture,* ed. C. Nelson and L. Grossberg, 347–360. Champaign–Urbana: University of Illinois Press.

Johnson, Chalmers. 2004a. *Blowback, The Costs and Consequences of American Empire.* New York: Henry Holt and Company.

Johnson, Chalmers. 2004b. *The Sorrows of Empire: Militarism, Secrecy, and the End of the Republic.* New York: Henry Holt and Company.

Kazin, Michael. 2006. *A Godly Hero: The Life of William Jennings Bryan.* New York: Alfred A. Knopf.

Kelly, Michael. 1995. "The Road to Paranoia." *The New Yorker,* June 19, 60–70.

Khatiwada, Ishwar, and Andrew M. Sum. 2018. "The Widening Socio-Economic Divergence in the U.S. Labor Market." In The Dynamics of Opportunity in America, ed. I. Kirsch, H. Braun. Cham: Springer, available at https://link.springer.com/chapter/10.1007/978-3-319-25991-8_7. Accessed June 19, 2018.

Knight, Peter. 2000. *Conspiracy Culture: From the Kennedy Assassination to the X-FILES.* London: Routledge.

Kornhauser, William. 1959. *The Politics of Mass Society.* Glencoe, IL: The Free Press.

Koulish, Jeremy. 2013. "There Are a Lot of 501(c)(4) Nonprofit Organizations. Most Are Not Political." The Urban Institute, www.urban.org. Accessed December 1, 2017.

Kuhn, Thomas. 1970. *The Structure of Scientific Revolutions.* Chicago, IL: University of Chicago Press, 2nd ed.

Lasswell, Harold. 1927. *Propaganda Technique in the World War.* New York: Knopf.

Lasswell, Harold. 1930. *Psychopathology and Politics.* New York: Viking Press.

Lasswell, Harold. 1948. *Power and Personality.* New York: Viking Press.

Lawrence, Regina D., and Melody Rose. 2009. *Hillary Clinton's Race for the White House: Gender Politics and Media on the Campaign Trail.* Boulder, CO: Lynne Rienner Publishers.

Levitsky, Steven, and Daniel Ziblatt. 2018. *How Democracies Die,* 6. New York: Crown Press.

Linz, Juan, and Alfred Stepan, ed. 1978. *The Breakdown of Democratic Regimes.* Baltimore, MD: Johns Hopkins University Press.

Lipset, Seymour Martin. 1960. "Fascism—Let, Right and Center." In *Political Man.* Garden City, NY: Anchor Books.

Lofgren, Mike. 2013. *The Party's Over: How Republicans Went Crazy, Democrats Became Useless, and the Middle Class Got Shafted.* New York: Penguin Books.

Lofgren, Mike. 2016. *The Deep State: The Fall of the Constitution and the Rise of a Shadow Government.* New York: Penguin Books.

Lynch, Conor. 2017. "Paranoid Politics: Donald Trump's Style Perfectly Embodies the Theories of Renowned Historian." *Salon,* July 7, available at http://www.salon.com. Accessed September 18, 2017.

MacLean, Nancy. 2017. *Democracy in Chains: The Deep History of the Radical Right's Stealth Plan for America.* New York: Viking.

Mann, Jame. 2004. "The Armageddon Plan." *The Atlantic,* March.

Mansbridge, Jane J. 1986. *Why We Lost the ERA.* Chicago: University of Chicago Press.

Marx, Karl. 1852. *The Eighteenth Brumaire of Louis Bonaparte,* available at www.marxists.org/archive/marx/works/download/pdf/18th-Brumaire.pdf. Accessed September 19, 2019.

Mauer, Peter. 2017. "What Kind of Populism, A Comparison of Marine Le Pen's and Donald Trump's Tweets in the French and US Election Campaigns of 2016/2017." Paper Presented at the 113th Meeting of the American Political Science Association, San Francisco, CA, August.

Mayer, Jane. 2010. "Covert Operations: The Billionaire Brothers Who Are Waging a War Against Obama." *The New Yorker*, August 30.

Mayer, Jane. 2016. *Dark Money: The Hidden History of the Billionaires Behind the Rise of the Radical Right*. New York: Doubleday.

Melley, Timothy. 2012. *The Covert Sphere: Secrecy, Fiction, and the National Security State*. Ithaca, NY: Cornell University Press.

Michaels, Jon D. 2017. *Constitutional Coup: Privatization's Threat to the American Republic*. Cambridge, MA: Harvard University Press.

Miller, Joanne M., Kyle L. Saunders, and Christina E. Farhart. 2016. "Conspiracy Endorsement as Motivated Reasoning: The Moderating Roles of Political Knowledge and Trust." *American Journal of Political Science* 60, no. 4 (October): 824–844.

Miller, Joanne M., Kyle L. Saunders, and Christina E. Farhart. 2017. "The Relationship Between Perceptions or Lower Status and Conspiracy Theory Endorsement." Paper Presented at the Annual Meeting of the American Political Science Association, San Francisco, CA, August 31–September 3.

Mills, C. Wright. 1960 (original 1956). *The Power Elite*. New York: Oxford University Press.

Morley, Jefferson Morley. 2017. *The Ghost: The Secret Life of CIA Spymaster James Jesus Angleton*. New York: St. Martin's Press.

Moyn, Samuel, and David Priestland. 2017. "Trump Isn't a Threat to Our Democracy. Hysteria Is." *New York Times*, August 11.

Muro, Mark. 2017. "Manufacturing Jobs Aren't Coming Back." *MIT Technology Review*, https://www.technologyreview.com/s/602869/manufacturing-jobs-arent-coming-back. Accessed June 11, 2017.

National Security Archive. 1996. *The Contras, Cocaine, and Covert Operations*, National Security Archive Electronic Briefing Book No. 2, available at nsarchive2.gwu.edu. Accessed December 8, 2017.

Nivens, David, Jr. 2016. "Why Black People Need Conspiracy Theories." *Complex.com*, October 16. Accessed February 23, 2018.

Norris, Pippa, and Ronald Inglehart. 2017. "Cultural Backlash: Values and Voting for Populist Authoritarian Parties in Europe." Paper Presented at the Panel, "The Roots of the New Populism," Annual Meeting of the American Political Science Association, San Francisco, August 30–September 2, 2017.

O'Donnell, Guillermo, Philippe Schmitter, and Laurence Whitehead, ed. 1986. *Transitions from Authoritarian Rule: Comparative Perspectives*. Baltimore, MD: Johns Hopkins University Press.

Office of the Inspector General, U.S. Department of Justice. 2018. *A Review of Various Actions by the Federal Bureau of Investigation and Department of Justice in Advance of the 2016 Election*. Washington, DC. June, available for download at https://int.nyt.com/data/documenthelper/39-justice-department-report-fbi-clinton-comey/5e54a6bfd23e7b94fbad/optimized/ full.pdf#page=1. Accessed June 15, 2018.

Olmsted, Kathryn S. 2009. *Real Enemies: Conspiracy Theory and American Democracy, World War I to 9/11*. New York: Oxford University Press.

Paley, Dawn Paley. 2014. *Drug War Capitalism*. Oakland, CA: AK Press.

Pasley, Jeffrey L. 2000. "Conspiracy Theory and American Exceptionalism from the Revolution to Roswell. Paper Presented at Sometimes and Art: A Symposium Celebration of Bernard Bailyn's Fifty Years of Teaching and Beyond." Harvard University, May 13, available at http://pasleybrothers. com/conspiracy/CT_and_American_Exceptionalism_web_version.htm. Accessed August 25, 2017.

Patterson, Thomas. 2016. "Pre-Primary News Coverage of the 2016 Presidential Race," Harvard Kennedy School, Shorenstein Center on Media, Politics and Public Policy (June 13), available at shorensteincenter.org. Accessed December 27, 2017.

Pew Research Center. 2015. "Beyond Distrust: How Americans View Their Government," available at www.people-press.org/2015/11/23/beyond-distrust-how-americans-view-their-government. Accessed December 27, 2017.

Pipes, Daniel. 1997. *Conspiracy: How the Paranoid Style Flourishes and Where It Comes From*. New York: The Free Press.

Popper, Karl. 2006 (original 1945). "The Conspiracy Theory of Society." In *Conspiracy Theories: The Philosophical Debate*, ed. David Coady, 17–44. Burlington, VT: Ashgate.

Posner, Gerald. 1993. *Case Closed: Lee Harvey Oswald and the Assassination of JFK*. New York: Random House.

Reeves, Richard. 1981. *President Nixon: Alone in the White House*. New York: Simon & Schuster.

Reich, Robert. *Saving Capitalism: For the Many, Not the Few*. New York: Vintage, 2016.

Robinson, Bill. 2017. "What Is Behind the Renegotiation of NAFTA? Trumpism and the New Global Economy." *Truthout.org*, July 24, available at http:// www.truth-out.org/news/item/41365-what-is-behind-the-renegotiation-of-nafta-trumpism-and-the-new-global-economy. Accessed July 27, 2018.

Robinson, Nathan J. 2017. "Lessons from Chomsky." *Current Affairs*, July 30, available at https://www.currentaffairs.org/2017/07/lessons-from-chomsky. Accessed October 30, 2017.

Robinson, William I. (Bill). 2004. *A Theory of Global Capitalism: Production, Class, and State in a Transnational World*. Baltimore, MD: Johns Hopkins University Press.

Robinson, William I. (Bill). 2017. "Trumpism, 21st-Century Fascism, and the Dictatorship of the Transnational Capitalist Class." *Social Justice Journal*, January 20, available at http://www.socialjusticejournal.org/trumpism-21st-century-fascism-and-the-dictatorship-of-the-transnational-capitalist-class. Accessed March 1, 2018.

Schaffner, Brian, and John A. Clark. 2018. *Making Sense of the 2016 Elections.* Thousand Oaks, CA: CQ Press.

Schlafly, Phyllis. 2014 (reissue). *Who Killed the American Family.* Medford, OR: WND Books.

Schmidt, Gerhard. 2001. *Report on the Existence of a Global System for the Interception of Private and Commercial Communications (ECHELON Interception System).* Brussels: European Parliament, Temporary Committee on the ECHELON Interception System.

Schumpeter, Joseph. 1942. *Capitalism, Socialism and Democracy* (London: Routledge, 1994 Reprint).

Scott, Peter Dale. 1996. *Deep Politics and the Death of JFK.* Berkeley: University of California Press.

Scott, Peter Dale. 2003. *Drugs, Oil, and War: The United States in Afghanistan, Colombia, and Indochina.* Lanham, PA: Rowman & Littlefield.

Scott, Peter Dale. 2015. *The American Deep State: Wallstreet, Big Oil, and the Attack on U.S. Democracy.* Lanham, MA: Rowman & Littlefield.

Scott, Peter Dale. 2016. "Dick Cheney, John Yoo, and COG on 9/11" (letter). *Journal of 9/11 Studies* (September), available at http://www.journalof911studies.com/dick-cheney-john-yoo-and-cog-on-911. Accessed February 25, 2018.

Shoup, Laurence. 1975. "Shaping the Post-War World: The Council of Foreign Relations and the United States War Aims During World War II." *The Insurgent Sociologist* 5, no. 3 (Spring): 18–20.

Shoup, Laurence, and William Minter. *Imperial Brain Trust: The Council on Foreign Relations and United States Foreign Policy.* New York: Monthly Review Press, 1977.

Sick, Gary. 1991. *October Surprise: America's Hostages in Iran and the Election of Ronald Reagan.* New York: Crown.

Simpson, Christopher. 1988. *Blowback: The First Full Account of Americas Recruitment of Nazis, and Its Disastrous Effect on our Domestic and Foreign Policy.* New York: Weidenfeld & Nicholson.

Singer, Peter W. 2007. *Corporate Warriors: The Rise of the Privatized Military Industry.* Ithaca, NY: Cornell University Press, Updated Edition.

Sklair, Leslie. 2000. The Transnational Capitalist Class. Hoboken, NJ: Wiley-Blackwell.

Skocpol, Theda. 2016. "Who Owns the GOP." *Dissent Magazine,* February 3, available at www.dissentmagazine.org/online_articles/jan-mayer-dark-money-review-koch-brothers-gop. Accessed December 5, 2017.

Staff Report of the Select Committee on Assassinations. 1979. "George De Mohrenschildt." U.S. House of Representatives, Ninety-fifth Congress Second Session.

Steger, Manfred. 2005. "Ideologies of Globalization," *Journal of Political Ideologies* 10.1 (February): 11–30.

Stepan, Alfred C. 1971. *The Military in Politics: Changing Patterns in Brazil.* Princeton, NJ: Princeton University Press.

Stroop, Christopher. 2018. *Russian Social-Conservatism, the U.S.-Based WCF and the Global Culture Wars in Historical Perspective,* Political Research Associated, available at https://www.politicalresearch.org, February 16. Accessed June 23, 2018.

Sunstein, Cass R. 2014. *Conspiracy Theories and Other Dangerous Ideas.* New York: Simon & Schuster.

Teachout, Zephyr. 2014. *Corruption in America: From Benjamin Franklin's Snuff Box to Citizens United.* Cambridge, MA: Harvard University Press.

Union of Concerned Scientists. 2017. "Who's Backing Scott Pruitt to Head the EPA? The Koch Brothers," *Got Science?* February, available at https://www.ucsusa.org/publications/got-science. Accessed June 25, 2018.

United States House of Representatives. 1979. "George De Mohrenschildt." *Staff Report of the Select Committee on Assassinations,* 1979. U.S. House of Representatives, Ninety-fifth Congress Second Session (March).

United States Senate. 1993. *The BCCI Affair. A Report to the Committee on Foreign Relations, United States Senate, by Senator John Kerry and Senator Hank Brown.* Penultimate Draft, 1992.

Uscinski, Joseph E., and Joseph M. Parent. 2014. *American Conspiracy Theories.* New York: Oxford University Press.

Ward, Geoffrey. 1993. "The Most Durable Assassination Theory: Oswald Did It Alone." *New York Times Book Review,* November 21.

Weatherbe, Leif. 2017. "Politics Is Downstream from Culture, Part 1: Right Turn to Narrative." *The Hedgehog Review,* blog, *The Infernal Machine,* February 22, 2017, available at http://iasc-culture.org/THR/channels/Infernal_Machine. Accessed December 5, 2017.

Weiner, Tim. 2008. *Legacy of Ashes: The History of the CIA.* New York: Anchor Books.

West, Harry G., and Todd Sanders, ed. 2003. *Transparency and Conspiracy: Ethnographies of Suspicion in the New World Order.* Durham, NC: Duke University Press.

INDEX

© The Editor(s) (if applicable) and The Author(s) 2019
D. C. Hellinger, *Conspiracies and Conspiracy Theories in the Age of Trump*, https://doi.org/10.1007/978-3-319-98158-1

CPSIA information can be obtained
at www.ICGtesting.com
Printed in the USA
LVHW072128121118
596823LV00011B/44/P

9 783319 981574